Received on 28th January, 2000

Santosh bistra Beethy

HOW TO DO *just about* ANYTHING ON A COMPUTER

READER'S DIGEST
HOW TO
ANYTHING

DO *just about* ON A COMPUTER

Published by The Reader's Digest Association Limited

LONDON • NEW YORK • SYDNEY • MONTREAL

How to do just about anything on a computer

was edited and designed by The Reader's Digest Association Limited, London.

First edition Copyright © 2000 The Reader's Digest Association Limited,
11 Westferry Circus, Canary Wharf, London E14 4HE.

www.readersdigest.co.uk

3D Landscape CD-ROM: © 1998,1999 Sierra On-Line Inc.
Localisation by FastTrak Software Publishing Ltd. 1999 All rights reserved.

ClipArt images and photographs: © 1999 GraphicCorp
(a division of Corel Corporation). All rights reserved.

Fonts: © 1999 Computer Support Corporation. All rights reserved.

Copyright © 2000 Reader's Digest Association Far East Limited.

Philippines Copyright © 2000 Reader's Digest Association Far East Limited.

Printed in Italy

ISBN 0 276 42435 2

PLANET THREE PUBLISHING NETWORK

Edited, designed and produced by
Planet Three Publishing Network
Northburgh House, 10 Northburgh Street, London EC1V 0AT
Phone +44 (0) 20 7251 3300 **Fax** +44 (0) 20 7251 3399
ISDN +44 (0) 20 7253 0298 **E-mail** postmaster@planet3.co.uk

EDITOR Theresa Brooks • **DEPUTY EDITOR** Jon Asbury
ASSOCIATE EDITORS Gary Irwin Kevin Dunne
ART DIRECTOR Paul Mitchell • **ART EDITOR** Gary Gilbert
DESIGNERS Darren Jordan Harj Ghundale
STILLS ART DIRECTOR Julie Adams
NEW MEDIA DESIGNER Darren Walsh • **INDEXER** Laura Hicks

FOR READER'S DIGEST
Editor Jonathan Bastable • **Art Editor** Neal Martin
Editorial Assistants Caroline Boucher Jenny Rathbone
Proofreader Barry Gage

READER'S DIGEST GENERAL BOOKS
Editor Cortina Butler • **Art Director** Nick Clark
Executive Editor Julian Browne • **Development Editor** Ruth Binney
Publishing Projects Manager Alastair Holmes • **Style Editor** Ron Pankhurst

CONTRIBUTORS
Susannah Hall • Hugh Livingstone • Sandra Vogel • Roger Gann • Steve Malyan
Consultant Barry Plows

CONTENTS

How to use this book

Find out how this book will help you make the most of your PC

With easy step-by-step tuition, expert advice and inspirational ideas, How To Do Just About Anything On A Computer *will help you put your computer to the best use*

Unlike most other computer books, *How To Do Just About Anything On A Computer* assumes that you are more interested in, say, creating a letterhead than you are in becoming an expert on electronics. For this reason, the book is organised into projects – all the things you are likely to want to do with your PC. These projects are designed to be of real, practical benefit to you and your family.

Learning to use your computer is more fun when approached in this way. You'll see why the programs work the way they do, and so you can apply these skills to other tasks.

Each project is set out into easy-to-follow, step-by-step procedures. The steps are accompanied by pictures that show you what you'll see on your screen. This means you'll never be left wondering 'Where's the menu they are telling me to click?' because you'll see a snapshot that shows exactly where the arrow should be when you click it.

Before you explore the full potential of your PC, you need to set it up, learn some housekeeping and get to know Windows, the ringmaster of your PC's programs. All this is covered in the first part of the book called 'You and Your Computer'.

Today's computers are increasingly reliable. But if glitches occur, turn to the Troubleshooting section. In most cases, you'll find what you need to get your PC running smoothly again.

All the rest is down to you: we hope you enjoy the countless tasks you can achieve on your PC.

Getting around the book

How To Do Just About Anything On A Computer contains four sections, taking you from the initial set-up, to connecting to the Internet, applying your skills practically and solving problems. Each follows a similar step-by-step format with snapshots of what should be on your screen at any given stage of a process.

You and Your Computer

This section guides you through setting up your PC, understanding the roles of hardware and software, and learning the basics of key programs. Find out how to care for your computer and how to maximise its efficiency.

The Internet

Learn how to connect to the Internet. Find out how to send and receive electronic mail (e-mail), and access information through the World Wide Web quickly and safely. You can even learn how to create your own Web page for other users to access.

Practical Home Projects

More than 40 practical projects take you through the steps involved in creating a range of documents, including a recipe database, kitchen plan, illustrated stationery, home accounts spreadsheet, greetings cards and posters.

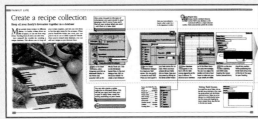

Troubleshooting

Your computer and its related hardware and software can behave unexpectedly at times. If this happens to you, don't panic. This section helps ease your concerns and offers a wide range of easy-to-follow solutions to common problems.

Special features

The book also offers the opportunity to apply your skills to real-life projects.

Make your PC skills work for you

The book contains larger undertakings that require you to draw on the skills you have developed as you try your hand at individual projects. Use your word-processing skills, your spreadsheet know-how and your graphics experience to take the stress and drudgery out of moving house, running a club, or organising a family celebration.

Glossary and Index

Found a word you don't understand? Turn to the back of the book to find clear, concise definitions of the most commonly used terms and phrases. You'll also find a comprehensive index to help guide you around the book.

Which software?

This book assumes that readers are operating PCs that run either Windows 95 or 98. Most of the snapshots of a PC screen are of Windows 98, but all instructions apply to both systems (where Windows 95 differs significantly from Windows 98, additional guidance is given).

With the exception of a few projects that use specialist software, most projects use either Microsoft Office 97 (Standard Edition) or Microsoft Works Suite 99. These suites provide word processing, spreadsheet and database programs. Any instructions regarding, say, Microsoft Word (the word processing program within Office) will also apply to the word processing tool within Works, unless stated otherwise.

Where necessary, the book also refers to other programs that you can buy, and that carry out similar functions.

Finding your way around the page

You are guided through every project in this book by means of a series of illustrated steps and a range of visual features. Here are the key features you should look for on the page.

Before you start

Projects begin with a Before You Start box. This outlines points to consider, documentation to collect, and tasks to do before beginning the project.

Step-by-step

Projects are set out in easy-to-follow steps, from the first mouse click to the last. You get instructions on what keyboard and mouse commands to give, and what programs, folders and menus to access to complete the project.

'Type in quotes'

Words written inside quotation marks are either the exact words you will see on screen, or those that you must type in yourself as part of a step.

Other programs

This tells you which other programs can be used to complete the project, and how to access them. Unless stated otherwise, you should be able to use the program following the steps given.

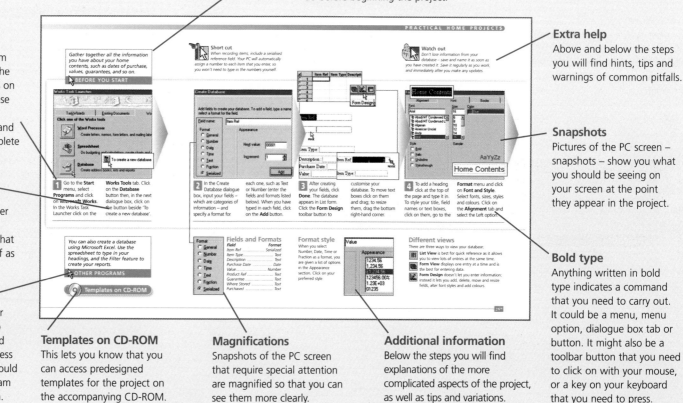

Extra help

Above and below the steps you will find hints, tips and warnings of common pitfalls.

Snapshots

Pictures of the PC screen – snapshots – show you what you should be seeing on your screen at the point they appear in the project.

Bold type

Anything written in bold type indicates a command that you need to carry out. It could be a menu, menu option, dialogue box tab or button. It might also be a toolbar button that you need to click on with your mouse, or a key on your keyboard that you need to press.

Templates on CD-ROM

This lets you know that you can access predesigned templates for the project on the accompanying CD-ROM.

Magnifications

Snapshots of the PC screen that require special attention are magnified so that you can see them more clearly.

Additional information

Below the steps you will find explanations of the more complicated aspects of the project, as well as tips and variations.

Hints and tips

You will find additional information to help you complete the task in hand and to improve your understanding of the workings of your PC.

Short cut

Look for this symbol for guidance on increasing your efficiency by learning quick and easy ways to complete common tasks.

Close-up

These offer an insight into the complicated workings of your computer, allowing you to get an idea of what happens 'behind the scenes'.

Watch out

These warn you about problems that you may encounter, or mistakes you might easily make, as you use your computer.

Key word

Important words or phrases are defined in order to increase your understanding of the process being addressed on the page.

Bright idea

These are suggestions for variations or additions you can make to a project which can help you adapt it to your specific needs.

Talking to your computer

Your PC is always ready to carry out your orders. You can communicate with it in any of the following ways.

Menus

In most programs you will see a menu bar sitting across the top of the program window. On it will be a File menu through which you can select options to save a document and print. There will also be an Edit menu, through which you can cut (remove) text or images and paste (insert) them elsewhere.

To access a menu, click on the menu name. The contents of the menu will appear in a drop-down list. Click on the command you want your PC to perform.

Toolbars

Toolbars feature a series of buttons that can be clicked to access frequently used commands – the command for saving a document, for example. They offer a quick alternative to going through the drop-down menus. The toolbar or toolbars (some programs have several) are located at the top of the program window just below

the menu bar. To find out what a toolbar button does, place your mouse pointer over it – in most programs a description pops up.

Dialogue boxes

If your computer needs you to make a decision or give it additional information (this often happens when you enter a command through a menu or the toolbar), a box will pop up on your screen and ask you to confirm or alter the program's default settings (these are standard settings which you can alter to your own liking).

Do so by clicking in the relevant parts of the box, by selecting choices from lists, or by typing in information. Some dialogue boxes contain identification tabs, much like those used in a filing cabinet, which you click on to access other windows through which you enter related

information. In Excel's Format Cells dialogue box, for example, there are tabs for Number, Alignment, Font, Border, Pattern and Protection. If you click on the Font tab, you can then select a font, font style, size and colour for your text.

Mouse instructions

You will often be asked to use the buttons on your mouse. These are the terms used:

Click Press and release your left mouse button once.
Double-click Press and release your left mouse button twice in quick succession.
Right-click Press and release your right mouse button once (a pop-up menu will often appear).
Drag Press your left mouse button and, keeping it pressed down, move your mouse so that your cursor 'drags' across the screen (this is used to highlight text or reshape an object).

Keyboard help

Use your keyboard to take short cuts to commonly used commands (see page 76 for details). If you are advised to use one of the special 'hot-keys' (shown right), you

will often find a picture of the recommended key, such as the one shown left.

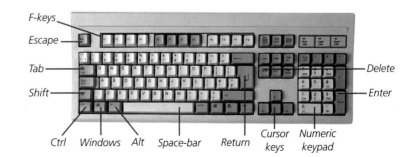

You and your Computer

The better you understand your PC, the more you will get out of it. Knowing what each element of the PC does, and how to set it up properly, will get you up and running. And good housekeeping practices will ensure that your PC functions efficiently. Once you master the basics, you will have laid the foundations for successful computing.

In this section

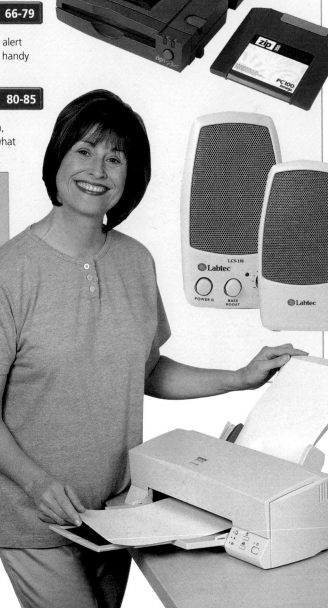

Setting up your computer

Your new PC has arrived. Start off on the right foot by setting up your work area properly

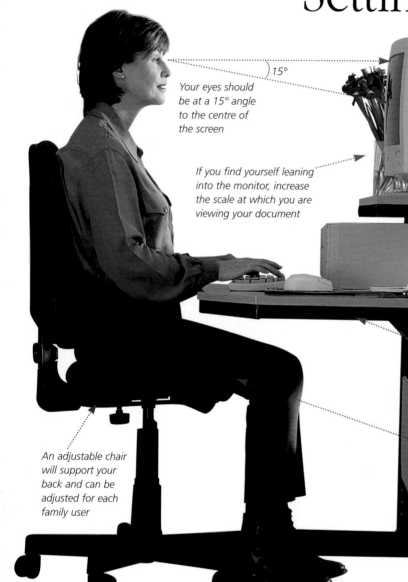

15°

Your eyes should be at a 15° angle to the centre of the screen

If you find yourself leaning into the monitor, increase the scale at which you are viewing your document

Your PC desk should be a comfortable height for typing so that the lower part of your arms are parallel to the floor

An adjustable chair will support your back and can be adjusted for each family user

Legs should remain uncrossed and knees should be lower than hips

Feet should rest flat on the floor

Your computer will be a valuable tool for all the family, so it's worth taking time to plan your computer space and system well, to ensure it is both easy and safe to use.

Ideally, it would be best to convert a small room, or a corner of a larger one, into an office, so all the family can use the computer without being disturbed. When selecting an area, check that there is adequate space and several mains sockets, not just for your equipment but for a desk lamp, too. If you will be sending faxes from your computer, or connecting to the Internet, you also need to be near a telephone point.

Set aside some time – 3 to 4 hours – to set up your computer properly. Think carefully about how to arrange your area, as a poorly laid out system will be irritating and may even prevent you from using your computer to the full.

It's a good idea to spend some time reading those manuals, too. You need to know where to plug in the cables!

- *Invest in a proper computer desk. You can alter the height of the monitor and keyboard, and tuck the keyboard away when not in use.*
- *Buy an adjustable chair, which all the family can adjust for good posture and maximum support.*
- *If your feet don't rest comfortably on the ground, buy a footrest.*

▶ COMPUTER FURNITURE

Naming and placing the parts of your computer

Your PC's hardware comprises all the parts that you can actually see and handle. Knowing exactly where to place each of these elements will ensure a safe and efficient work area.

Monitor
This houses the computer screen. Position your monitor to avoid reflections, but avoid facing a bright window yourself as this may lead to eyestrain.

System unit
This is the part of your computer that connects everything together. Leave space so that you can plug in the cables easily. Don't leave cables trailing.

External speakers
For the best sound quality, speakers should be well spaced apart at desk level or higher, not just pushed under the desk. Ensure that the computer is situated so that others are not disturbed by computer games or alert sounds.

Mouse
Place the mouse to the left or right of your keyboard to minimise arm movement. Use a mouse mat to create the correct amount of friction for the mouse, and be sure there is room to move the mouse back and forth.

Keyboard
Make sure the keyboard is on a stable and level surface within easy reach. Leave enough space in front for hands and wrists. Ensure that the desk is at the correct height.

Printer
Position your printer near the system unit. Make sure there is sufficient space around it for loading the paper trays.

Watch out
Repetitive Strain Injury (RSI) is muscle strain due to repeated actions. Home PC users are unlikely to experience problems but a good posture and typing technique is still essential. When working at your PC, stand up, stretch and move about regularly.

Hardware and software

Understanding how these operate is key to success

Hardware and software work together to allow you to perform the wide variety of functions possible on your PC.

Hardware is the actual 'body' of the computer system, comprising the system unit and all the elements that you can plug into it, such as the keyboard. Your computer's hardware determines which type of operating system you can use. PCs made with Intel processors, for example, cannot run the Apple Macintosh operating system.

Software is the thinking part, or brain, of your computer, putting all the hardware to work. The most important piece of software on your computer is the operating system. By translating your instructions into a language the hardware can understand, the operating system lets you communicate with various computer parts and control how the computer and its accessories work. Windows 98 and 95 are the most popular operating systems for PCs. An operating system is so important to the workings of a computer that, without one, you cannot open any files, use a printer or see anything on the screen.

However, in order to perform specific functions, such as editing a report, playing a computer game or keeping a check on your household spending, your computer also needs to use specialised software, called programs. There are thousands of programs available, each designed to perform different kinds of tasks. Programs enable you to do anything, from writing formal letters and compiling spreadsheets, to editing digital imagery and even making your own films.

Other types of computer

Apple Macintosh computers, or Macs, work in a similar way to PCs in that you access documents through a desktop. Although Macs and PCs often run the same programs, their operating systems are not compatible and you should not assume that software will automatically run on your PC.

This system incompatibility also means that using a Mac's floppy disk to transfer data to a PC is very difficult.

Introducing your software

Understanding what software does will help you to get the most out of your PC. This introduction describes the operating system and the different types of program available.

The operating system

The operating system allows you to interact with the computer's hardware. It manages the saving of files on the hard disk, translates commands given through the keyboard and mouse, and sends data to the screen or printer. It also interacts with other programs you may be running, allowing them to communicate with the hardware.

Any software packages you use rely on the operating system to provide this basic level of communication with the hardware. If your PC was manufactured after 1995 it will almost certainly use Windows 95 or Windows 98 as its operating system.

Which program?

FINANCIAL PROGRAM
For calculating household expenditure, use a financial program. This will enable you to keep a check on your domestic bills, monitor your outgoings and work out your overall balance, enabling you to manage your money effectively.

WORD PROCESSING PROGRAM
To write letters, reports and any other documents that are mainly text-based, use a word processing program or the word processing tool in software suites. Most include a range of fonts and style features and allow you to insert pictures in the text.

GRAPHICS PROGRAM
To work with pictures use a graphics program. This will help you to create greetings cards, invitations, posters and personal stationery. You can use the graphic galleries available on your PC or from CD-ROM galleries. You can even use your own photographs.

DATABASE PROGRAM
To make address lists, or lists of contact details, use a database program. Software suites often have a database tool, or you can use a separate database program for more complex work.

SPREADSHEET PROGRAM
For making complex budget calculations and carrying out financial analysis you can use a spreadsheet program. These programs can also show figures as a chart or graph.

GAMES PROGRAM
Playing with games is an entertaining way of becoming more adept on the computer. You usually have to buy each game program separately, although some systems come with some simple games included.

Key word
Software suite *A software suite incorporates the basic aspects of several programs in one package. While their components may not be as powerful or as versatile as individual programs, low-cost suites such as Microsoft Works offer value for money and let you perform many useful tasks.*

Storing software on your hard disk

All software, whether it be the operating system or programs, uses storage space on your hard disk. This space is measured in terms of 'bits' and 'bytes'.

A bit is the smallest unit of computer storage. A combination of eight bits makes up a byte. A kilobyte (Kb) is 1,024 bytes; a megabyte (Mb) is 1,024 Kb; and a gigabyte (Gb) is 1,024 Mb.

A typical home computer will have as much as 3 Gb of hard disk space. As an example of how much space your programs use, the Microsoft Office suite uses more than 93 Mb of disk space, and the Microsoft Works suite about 26 Mb.

Making the most of hardware

Get the most out of your PC by understanding the purpose of each part

Once you have unpacked your PC and set up the different hardware elements, it's worth taking the time to get to know exactly what each part does.

All personal computers have the same basic elements. Knowing how they fit together and operate as a unit – and understanding where you fit into the picture – will help you and your family to get the most out of home computing.

Your computer is simply a tool that, given the correct instructions and data, will make your day-to-day life easier and more enjoyable. You enter instructions and information into the computer via the mouse and keyboard. The results can be seen on your monitor's screen and printed out on your printer. The most important part of the computer – the system unit – links all these elements together.

Whatever make of computer you have, it will have these same key components that allow you to use it. Although most computers look similar, there are variations between models, so always check instructions in the computer manual to make sure you're using your equipment correctly.

The mouse

A mouse is used to select items on screen and move the text cursor (a flashing line that identifies where new text appears). You move the mouse around with your hand and a mouse pointer moves around on the screen, allowing you to select menus and click on commands.

The keyboard

The keyboard is used for typing in data and commands, and has the familiar typewriter keys plus a number of extra ones. On the right is a separate numeric keypad, plus navigation keys (with arrows) that help you to move around the screen. There is also a series of function keys along the top that allow you to give special commands.

The monitor

Your monitor is home to the computer screen, which shows you what your computer is doing. Monitor screens come in different sizes and, in the interests of preventing eyestrain, the bigger the better. Screens are measured in inches, diagonally. A 15-inch screen or larger is the ideal choice. Monitors have their own power switch.

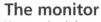

Watch out
Always use the Shut Down command from the Start menu before turning the power switch off. Never turn the power switch off when Windows is running. Some newer PCs automatically switch off power when shutting down.

Bright idea
If environmental issues are a concern for you, look out for 'green' hardware. Some manufacturers have used plastics and packaging in their computer systems that can be recycled.

The system unit
This is where all the cables plug in. Whether your system unit is on its side (a desktop unit), or its end (a tower unit), it acts in the same way. The system unit also contains disk drives (a floppy disk drive and a CD-ROM drive).

Power light
This indicates that power is being supplied to the computer.

Power switch
This is used to turn your PC on and, on older PCs, to turn it off.

CD-ROM drive
This allows you to install new software and play music CDs.

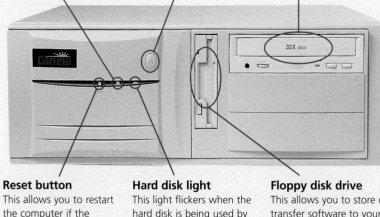

Power to monitor socket
This connects the monitor to the mains.

PC expansion cards
The sockets here let you connect other devices, such as speakers and monitors, to expansion cards fitted inside the PC.

Power-in socket
This is used to connect the PC to the mains supply. Do not turn on the mains supply until you have plugged in all the leads.

Keyboard socket
This is used to connect the keyboard to the PC.

Mouse socket
Used to connect the mouse to the PC.

Printer port
This connects the PC to the printer. Also called the parallel port.

Serial port
Used to connect the PC to a modem. You may be able to plug a mouse in here.

Reset button
This allows you to restart the computer if the system has crashed.

Hard disk light
This light flickers when the hard disk is being used by the computer.

Floppy disk drive
This allows you to store or transfer software to your PC on a floppy disk.

Printers
You need a printer to put your work on paper. The two main types are laser and inkjet. Laser printers produce better quality print-outs and have the fastest printing speeds. However, they tend to be more expensive, especially colour models. Inkjet printers are cheaper and most can print in colour.

Unless you are printing hundreds of pages a week, an inkjet printer will almost certainly meet your needs.

Laptop computers
All the components of a laptop computer are in a single unit. The screen is smaller and not as bright as on a desktop computer. The keyboard is smaller and does not have the extra keys. The mouse is built-in, as a tiny joystick or touchpad.

Laptops can be powered from the mains or by a rechargeable battery, but don't expect more than 3 hours use from a single charge.

Starting up your computer

You've set it all up – now switch on and begin using your PC

Once your computer's been set up properly, you're ready to get going – so remember to make sure it's turned on at the mains.

Turn on the computer via the power switch on the system unit. You also need to turn on the monitor. Screens of data will appear as the computer runs some routine checks on itself. After a few moments you'll see a colour screen that Windows calls the Desktop. Small pictures, or icons, will appear on the Desktop, and you may also see a window called 'Welcome to Windows'. Click on the Close button (the X in the top right-hand corner of the window) to shut down this feature.

Depending on how Windows has been installed, this process may be slightly different on your PC.

The Desktop icons

Through the Desktop icons you can access important utilities and all your work. To open an icon place your mouse pointer over the top of it and double-click with the left mouse button.

 My Computer shows you the different elements of your computer, such as disk drives and printers.

 My Documents leads to a folder that you can use to store any files you create.

Network Neighbourhood allows you to access and view other computers connected to your own.

 Recycle Bin is where files go after deletion. These can either be removed completely or retrieved if you have made a mistake.

 Set Up Microsoft Network helps you join the on-line Internet service that is provided by Microsoft.

 My Briefcase is used to exchange and update files between your computer and a notebook computer (laptop).

 The **Start button** is the point at which you begin most of the tasks you want to do on your computer, such as opening programs.

 Online Services leads to a selection of Internet Service Providers you might want to investigate.

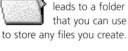

Running along the bottom of your screen is the **Taskbar**. It always contains the Start button and a clock. There may also be other program buttons visible, such as Microsoft Word. As you open new windows, they will appear as buttons on the Taskbar, so you can always see what's open, even when other windows cover them up.

Basic window features

Programs and files are all displayed inside a window, and your computer can display several windows at one time. All windows share these basic features:

Menu bar
This contains drop-down menus through which you issue commands.

Minimise button
This reduces the window to an icon on the Taskbar.

Maximise button
This enlarges the window to fill the screen. Click on it again to return it to its original size.

Title bar
This displays the name of the window. To move the window, click on the Title bar and, with the mouse button pressed down, move the mouse pointer across the computer screen. This is called 'dragging'.

Close button
This closes the window.

Toolbar
Toolbar buttons provide shortcuts to common commands.

Address bar
This shows you where you are, and also allows you access to other files and folders.

Window borders
To resize windows, place the mouse pointer over the window's border. When the pointer changes to a double-headed arrow, hold down the left mouse button and drag the window into the size you want.

Scroll bars
To view any hidden contents of a window, click on the arrows at the ends of the scroll bar.

Status bar
This gives information about the contents of the window.

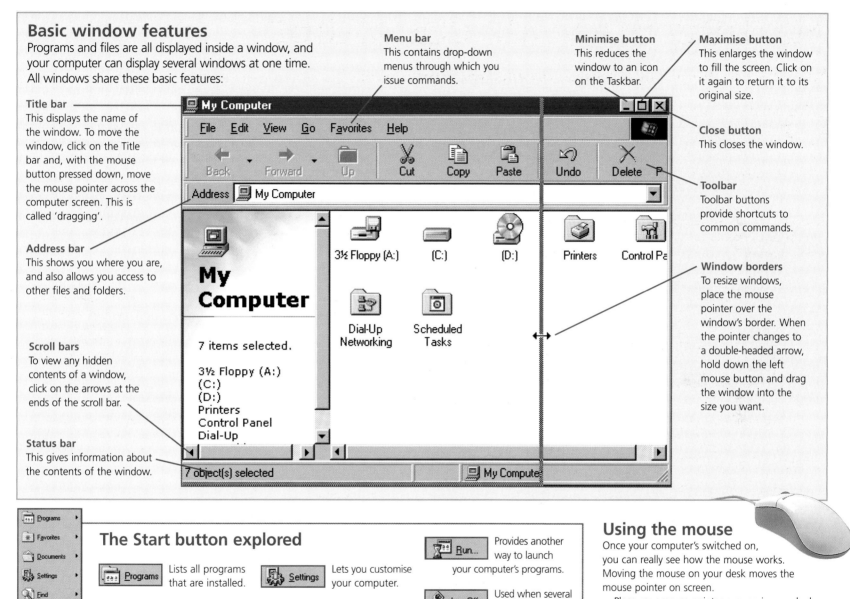

The Start button explored

Programs Lists all programs that are installed.

Favorites Lists most used files and pages.

Documents Lists most recently used documents.

Settings Lets you customise your computer.

Find Searches for files and information.

Help Displays 'help' files about Windows.

Run... Provides another way to launch your computer's programs.

Log Off... Used when several computers are connected on a network.

Shut Down. Turns off the computer.

Using the mouse

Once your computer's switched on, you can really see how the mouse works. Moving the mouse on your desk moves the mouse pointer on screen.

Place your mouse pointer over an icon and a box will appear telling you what the icon does. When you want to look 'inside' an icon, press the left mouse button twice quickly. This is known as 'double-clicking'. The double-click principle applies to the opening of programs or files.

An introduction to programs

Improve your skills more quickly by getting to know your PC's programs

Windows, the operating system, helps connect each element of your PC together but it can't perform practical tasks such as letter writing and calculating your bills. For these jobs you need to use additional software, called applications, or programs, which is designed to carry out specific tasks.

Most personal computers come with a varied package of programs (known as bundled software or software suites) already installed. Two of the most popular packages are Microsoft Works and Microsoft Office.

Your package explained

Works, a package of 'mini-programs' grouped together, offers you tools to perform most of the tasks you might want to carry out on a home computer, and it also includes many pre-set documents, called TaskWizards, that you can customise for your own purposes (you are given step-by-step guidance on how to do this).

Office comprises several individual programs (Word, Excel, PowerPoint and Outlook). The more sophisticated capabilities of each of these programs, compared to their equivalent in Works, means that they can be used to produce a wider range of documents. Because they are more advanced, together they use up more of your hard disk space than Works. You will find Wizards in both Office and Works.

Understanding your bundled software

Knowing what each program in your bundled software can do will help you decide which will be the most appropriate for the tasks you want to perform.

Microsoft Office

Word is an extremely powerful word processor which is able to produce 'written' documents of all kinds, including letters, memos, newsletters and posters. You have the option to create documents from scratch or, for many types of document, to use one of the program's Wizards or templates. The Wizards let you choose the content and how the document looks, while the templates have a preset layout.

Excel is a spreadsheet program, used for organising and calculating numerical data. It is ideal for keeping track of all types of budgets and accounts. Like all spreadsheets, it takes the form of a grid containing 'cells' into which you input figures and formulas to calculate the figures. Excel allows you to have several spreadsheets, or 'worksheets', within the same document, and enter calculations using figures from each of the worksheets. This is particularly useful when organising, say, a major event that comprises mini-projects. Once data is entered, you can then select, or 'filter', specific information to analyse.

Excel can also produce a range of charts and graphs that can be used to illustrate trends in your spreadsheet figures. These are particularly useful as they simplify complicated numerical information, presenting it in a clear, easily understandable manner.

Outlook is a Desktop 'information management' program. It contains an address book into which you can enter contact details for friends, family and business associates. It also has a diary and calendar that will help you to keep track of your current schedule and forthcoming appointments. Outlook can also be used to send and receive e-mails through the Internet or through an internal company network.

PowerPoint is most often used in business. It enables you to create presentations for conferences, company meetings and marketing projects. It gives you the means to structure information efficiently and incorporate graphics within your text. It even offers animation effects to maximise the impact of your presentation. You can create notes for your own use in addition to handouts for your audience.

PowerPoint can also be used at home to make a computerised 'slide' show for your friends and family (see page 220).

Microsoft Works

Word Processor. This program allows you to create a range of word-based documents, or customise one of the TaskWizards. This program is not as sophisticated as Word – you cannot, for example, accurately measure the text boxes needed to create business cards.

Communications. This is an advanced feature that allows you to communicate with other computers through a network. This tool does not connect you to the Internet – you will need to use other Windows features to do this.

Spreadsheet. This program allows you to monitor and analyse numerical data. It also offers a number of TaskWizards for common documents such as household bills, invoices and accounts, which you can customise and use.

Database. This program is ideal for recording details about related items. For example, you can record details of your household contents. Using its ReportCreator function you can sort and group selected information (say, to update your household insurance), perform calculations and add some explanatory notes.

Accessory programs

Accessories are small programs within Windows that perform specific tasks. Your computer will almost certainly contain a calculator, a painting program (Paint), simple games and a basic word processing program (WordPad).

To open an accessory program, go to the **Start** menu and select **Programs** then **Accessories**. Click on the program you want to use.

Getting around a document

Learn how to open a program and navigate around the screen

Opening a program and creating a new document will be among the first things you do on your computer. The process is similar in most programs. The steps are the same whether you are using a spreadsheet, database or word-processing program.

All programs can be accessed by clicking on the **Start** button on the Taskbar that runs along the bottom of the screen, then clicking on **Programs** in the menu that pops up. Another menu appears listing all the programs on your system. Click on the program you wish to open. The program opens and a blank document appears. You can now start typing in your information.

Before you do this, it's useful to understand the different parts of the window. The window shown is from the Microsoft Word word-processing program (Microsoft Works is very similar).

Inputting commands

Whichever program you are using, you input commands using your mouse and keyboard. These commands might relate to the look of the document or to the material it contains.

The mouse
The mouse is the best way to access the command options available through your document's menus and toolbars (see opposite). To activate items on screen (menus, shortcut icons, and so on), use the mouse to move the cursor over them and press your left mouse button down then release it (this process is known as 'clicking').

If you are asked to 'click', press and release the left mouse button once; to 'double-click', press and release the left mouse button twice in quick succession.

If you are asked to 'drag' (you will do this to move items on the screen or to select text), press the left mouse button and, holding it down, move your mouse. As you do so, a section of text will become highlighted, or the on-screen item you clicked on will also move. When the relevant text is selected, or the item has moved to the correct position, release the mouse button.

'Right-clicking' – that is, clicking with the right mouse button – anywhere on screen will activate a pop-up menu offering formatting functions and other options. Click on an option to activate or open it.

The keyboard
The most obvious use of the keyboard is for typing in text and data, but it is also possible to issue commands by using special combinations of keys (these keyboard commands are discussed on page 76).

It is also possible to use the arrow keys at the bottom of your keyboard to move your cursor around within a document. Most people find this more laborious than using the mouse.

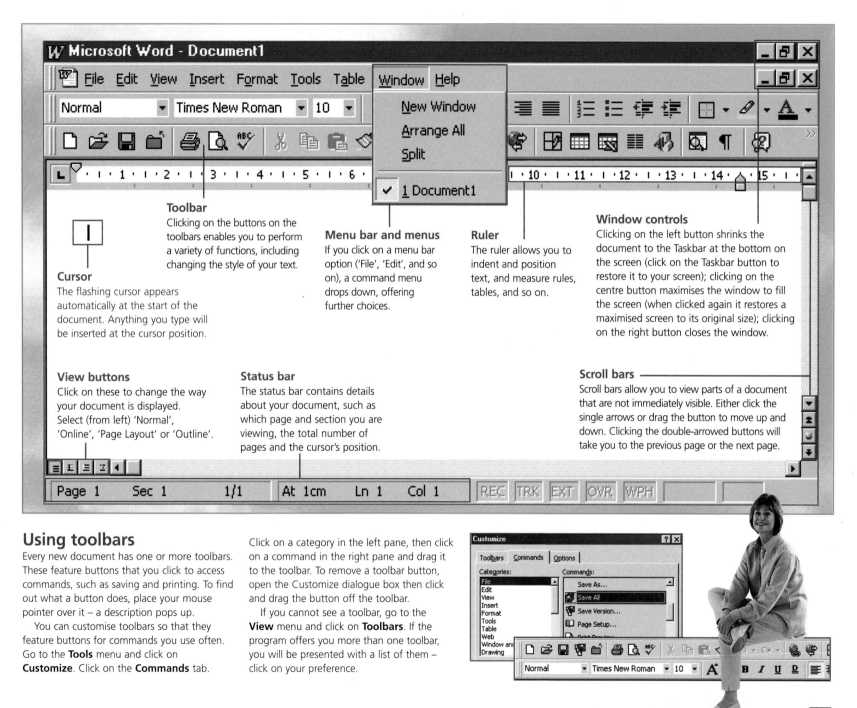

Toolbar
Clicking on the buttons on the toolbars enables you to perform a variety of functions, including changing the style of your text.

Cursor
The flashing cursor appears automatically at the start of the document. Anything you type will be inserted at the cursor position.

Menu bar and menus
If you click on a menu bar option ('File', 'Edit', and so on), a command menu drops down, offering further choices.

Ruler
The ruler allows you to indent and position text, and measure rules, tables, and so on.

Window controls
Clicking on the left button shrinks the document to the Taskbar at the bottom on the screen (click on the Taskbar button to restore it to your screen); clicking on the centre button maximises the window to fill the screen (when clicked again it restores a maximised screen to its original size); clicking on the right button closes the window.

View buttons
Click on these to change the way your document is displayed. Select (from left) 'Normal', 'Online', 'Page Layout' or 'Outline'.

Status bar
The status bar contains details about your document, such as which page and section you are viewing, the total number of pages and the cursor's position.

Scroll bars
Scroll bars allow you to view parts of a document that are not immediately visible. Either click the single arrows or drag the button to move up and down. Clicking the double-arrowed buttons will take you to the previous page or the next page.

Using toolbars

Every new document has one or more toolbars. These feature buttons that you click to access commands, such as saving and printing. To find out what a button does, place your mouse pointer over it – a description pops up.

You can customise toolbars so that they feature buttons for commands you use often. Go to the **Tools** menu and click on **Customize**. Click on the **Commands** tab.

Click on a category in the left pane, then click on a command in the right pane and drag it to the toolbar. To remove a toolbar button, open the Customize dialogue box then click and drag the button off the toolbar.

If you cannot see a toolbar, go to the **View** menu and click on **Toolbars**. If the program offers you more than one toolbar, you will be presented with a list of them – click on your preference.

The basics of word processing

Learn the essentials of working with text in documents

Once you have opened a new document in a word processing program, you can start typing in text. The great advantage that word-processing computers have over typewriters is that they allow you to revise and refine your text as much as you wish. You can also adjust the appearance of your text, its size, shape, colour and position on the page, and the spacing between individual letters, words and lines. You can even add special effects such as shadows. This is known as 'formatting'.

Becoming familiar with the terms used in word processing, and the basics of working with text, will enable you to create and modify documents with ease.

Setting up your document

Before you start typing you should first specify the size and orientation of the document, the size of its margins, and the size of paper you want to print on. To do this, go to the **File** menu and click on **Page Setup**. Click in the margin boxes and enter your settings, then click **OK**. (Your program will have default settings that you may not need to change.)

Page Setup		
Margins	Paper Size	Paper Source
Top:	2.54 cm	
Bottom:	2.54 cm	
Left:	3.17 cm	
Right:	3.17 cm	

Typing in text

To enter text, just type on the keyboard. As you type, the words will appear at the cursor position on your screen. When you reach the end of a line, the text will automatically flow on to the next line. To start typing on a new line before reaching the end of the current one, press the **Return** key on your keyboard and continue to type.

> I would like to raise several points:
> * Seventy people have confirmed that they are
> * Twenty people have confirmed that they are
> * Four people have yet to respond

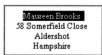

Highlighting text

To format a section of text you first need to select, or 'highlight', it. To do this, place your cursor just before the relevant section and press and release your left mouse button once (this is called 'clicking'). Press the mouse button again and, keeping it pressed down, move the mouse to the right (this is called 'dragging'). As you do this the text appears as white in a black bar. Release the mouse button once the relevant text is highlighted.

> Maureen Brooks
> 58 Somerfield Close
> Aldershot
> Hampshire

To highlight all the text in a document, press the **Ctrl** key and, keeping it pressed down, press the '**A**' key.

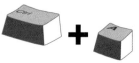

Formatting the text

Once text is highlighted it is ready to format, or style. Go to the **Format** menu and click on **Font** (in Works, click on **Font and Style**). A dialogue box appears offering formatting options. The Word dialogue box is shown here.

Fonts

Your word processing program offers a range of fonts (particular styles of type). To view the list of fonts, click on the arrows (this is called 'scrolling'). Click on your choice of font (it becomes highlighted).

Underline

You can underline text in a number of ways. Click on the arrow next to the Underline box, scroll through the options and click on your choice. If you do not want text to be underlined ensure **None** is selected.

Effects

You will be presented with a number of special effects that you can apply to text. To choose one, click in the relevant box (a tick will appear). Click the box again to remove the effect.

Font style

Once you have chosen a font, select a font style for it. Typically, you can choose whether your text appears in a regular format, or in italics or bold. To select a font style, click on your choice from the 'Font style' box.

Size

The size of text is measured in 'points' (pts). The greater the point size, the larger the text. However, point sizes are not uniform across all fonts, which means that 10pt text in one font may be taller than, say, 12pt text in another font. To alter a point size, scroll through and click on your choice in the Size box. A good rule of thumb is not to use text smaller than 8pt or 9pt, as it becomes difficult to read.

Colour

To alter the colour of text, click on the arrow next to the Color box, scroll through the colours and click on your choice. Remember that too many colours on one page can be overpowering.

Preview

The Preview pane shows you how your choices of font, size, and effects will look.

OK

Click **OK** to apply your formatting changes to the highlighted text.

Using the toolbar

Most of the styling options shown above also appear on the Formatting toolbar near the top of your window. If the toolbar isn't there (you may accidentally remove it), go to the **View** menu, select **Toolbars** then **Formatting** (in Works, go to the **View** menu and click on **Toolbars**).

Toolbars appear along the top of your window but can be dragged to anywhere on your document. Click on the toolbar (make sure you do not click on one of its buttons), then drag it to its new location. It appears with a Title bar bearing the name of the toolbar. To alter the shape of your repositioned toolbar, click on one of its edges and drag accordingly.

After highlighting your text click on the appropriate toolbar buttons. (To see what a toolbar button does, place your mouse pointer over the button – a small box describing its function pops up.)

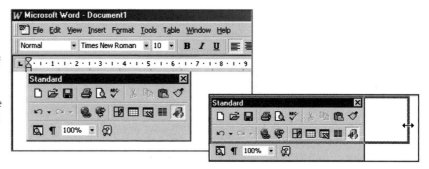

Laying out your document

Your word processing program allows you to adjust the structure of your documents, making them easier to read and drawing attention to important information.

Adding borders

To add a border around a section of text, to give it definition, highlight the relevant text (here, the company address) then click on the arrow beside the **Border** button on the toolbar. You will be offered a choice of styles. Click on your preference.

Paragraph indents

A simple way to distinguish where each new paragraph begins is to indent its first line. Click in the paragraph, go to the **Format** menu and click on **Paragraph**. In the Indentation section, click on the arrow beside the Special box and select **First line**. In the By box set the space required then click **OK**. (In Works, set the space in the 'First line' box then click **OK**.)

You can also indent entire paragraphs by highlighting them and clicking the **Increase indent** button on the toolbar.

Adding numbers and bullet points

To make lists easier to read, add a number or bullet point before each item. Highlight the list then click on the **Numbering** or **Bullets** button on the toolbar. The Numbering button automatically numbers points sequentially.

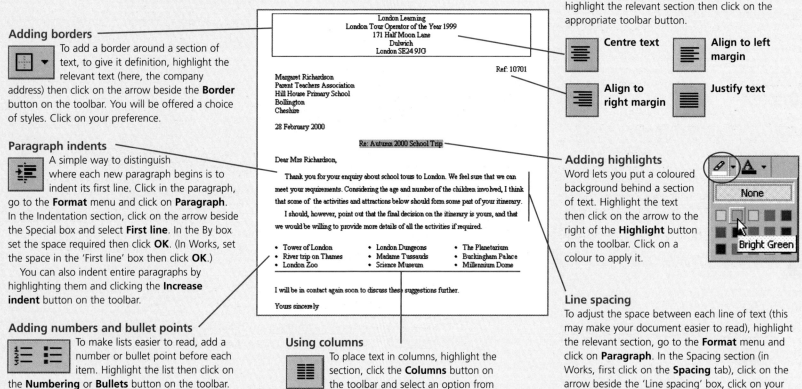

Using columns

To place text in columns, highlight the section, click the **Columns** button on the toolbar and select an option from the drop-down panel. (In Works you cannot place individual sections of text into columns.)

Aligning paragraphs

To position, or align, text in your document, highlight the relevant section then click on the appropriate toolbar button.

Centre text	**Align to left margin**
Align to right margin	**Justify text**

Adding highlights

Word lets you put a coloured background behind a section of text. Highlight the text then click on the arrow to the right of the **Highlight** button on the toolbar. Click on a colour to apply it.

Line spacing

To adjust the space between each line of text (this may make your document easier to read), highlight the relevant section, go to the **Format** menu and click on **Paragraph**. In the Spacing section (in Works, first click on the **Spacing** tab), click on the arrow beside the 'Line spacing' box, click on your choice then **OK**. (You can click on several options to see them in the Preview pane first.)

What if I make a mistake?

If you make a mistake, click on the **Undo** button on the Standard toolbar. (If the toolbar isn't there, go to the **View** menu, select **Toolbars** then **Standard**.) You can continue to click on it to undo previous commands. If you undo an action you then want to redo, click on the **Redo** toolbar button. (In Works, you can only undo the previous command. Go to the **Edit** menu and click on **Undo** or **Redo**.)

Moving or copying text

To move a section of text, highlight it and click on the **Cut** toolbar button. The text will disappear. Position the cursor where you want the text to reappear, click on the page, then click on the **Paste** button – the text will reappear in your document.

To copy a section of text so that it appears more than once in a document (you can also copy text from one document to another), highlight it then click on the **Copy** toolbar button. Position the cursor where you want the text to appear, then click on the **Paste** toolbar button.

You can also perform these functions by highlighting text then going to the **Edit** menu and clicking on an option.

Finishing touches

Once you have finished formatting and laying out your document, it's a good idea to check it for spelling and grammatical errors. Also, you can now add extra features, such as headers and footers.

Spelling and grammar check

When you type in text, some words may appear with a

> **Vennison stew with orange**
>
> Preparation time: 20 mins plus
> Cooking time: 1 hour

wavy red or green line underneath. A red line indicates a possible spelling error; a green line a possible grammatical error. When you have finished

typing your document, go to the **Tools** menu and click on **Spellings and Grammar** (in Works, click on **Spelling**). Or, press the **F7** key.

Your PC scans your document, selecting the underlined words for you to check and suggesting how to correct the 'error'. If you don't agree with any of the suggested changes click on **Ignore**; if you do agree, click on the relevant suggestion then on **Change**.

Spelling and Grammar: English (United Kingdom)

Not in Dictionary:

Vennison stew with orange

Suggestions:

Venison

☐ Check grammar   Options...   Undo

Thesaurus

To ensure your document reads well, open the Thesaurus function to find alternatives to repeated words, and suggestions for more suitable words.

To do this, highlight the word you would like to find an alternative for, go to the **Tools** menu and click on **Language** then **Thesaurus** (in Works, click directly on **Thesaurus**). Or, press the **Shift** key and, keeping it pressed down, the **F7** key.

The Thesaurus dialogue box will show a list of alternatives. Click on the appropriate meaning of the word in the Meanings pane, then on your choice of replacement word in the 'Replace with Synonym' pane. Click on **Replace**. If you don't think the alternatives are any better, click on **Cancel**.

Thesaurus: English (United Kingdom)

Looked Up:

comfortably

Meanings:

absolutely (other)

Replace with Synonym:

absolutely

absolutely
definitely
doubtless
positively
unequivocally
unquestionably
easily

Replace   Look Up   Previous   Cancel

Headers and footers

Word processing documents can include a section at the top and bottom of each page – known as headers and footers, respectively. Any text entered into these sections automatically appears on each new page of your document. This is useful if you want to include a title for your document at the top of each page, and the date or page number at the bottom.

To add text to these sections, go to the **View** menu and click on **Header and Footer** (in Works, **Header** or **Footer**). The cursor now appears in the Header section. Type in your text and style it. Then scroll down the document, click in the Footer section and do likewise.

To add a page number to the Footer, click in the Footer, go to the **Insert** menu and select **Page Numbers**. In Word, a dialogue box asks how you want the page number to be aligned, and whether you want it to appear on the first page or not. Only a figure is entered – you may want to type in 'Page' before it. In Works, the symbol *page* appears in the footer. In both programs, the page number automatically updates itself on each new page.

To return to normal view in Word, click **Close** on the Header and Footer toolbar. In Works, simply click on the main part of your document.

Header

Chapter 3 - Evaluatin

Footer

Page 1

Counting your words

If you are writing a long article or essay, it can be useful to know how many words you have written. Go to the **Tools** menu and click on **Word Count**. Word will also count the pages, paragraphs and even characters used. (In Works, you are given a total word count for your document, including footnotes, headers and footers.)

Word Count

Statistics:

Pages	4
Words	2,346
Characters (no spaces)	10,369
Characters (with spaces)	12,665
Paragraphs	59
Lines	196

☐ Include footnotes and endnotes

Close

Figuring out spreadsheets

Learn how to use spreadsheets for financial planning and budgeting

Of all the computer functions, spreadsheets are the hardest to get to grips with. But a small investment of time and effort will soon pay dividends, because once you have the hang of them, spreadsheets can perform quite complex financial calculations. You can, for example, set up a spreadsheet to work out the true cost of running your car, including such invisible outlay as depreciation and wear and tear. All you have to do is 'explain' the task to the program once: it will do all the arithmetic for you, month after month, year on year.

Opening a new spreadsheet

This book deals with the two most widely used spreadsheet programs: Microsoft Excel and the spreadsheet tool in Microsoft Works. To open a document in either program, go to the **Start** menu and select **Programs** then **Microsoft Excel** or **Microsoft Works**.

If you open Excel, a new blank document will automatically appear on screen. If you open Works, the Works Task Launcher will open. Click on the **Works Tools** tab, then on the **Spreadsheet** button, then on **OK**.

Saving your document

After opening a new document, go to the **File** menu and click on **Save As**. In the Save As dialogue box select a folder in which to save your document in the 'Save in' box, enter a file name, then click **OK**.

Another popular spreadsheet program is Lotus 1-2-3. The principles of using spreadsheets – as given here for Excel and Works – can also be applied to 1-2-3.

▶ OTHER PROGRAMS

Finding your way around

Identifying the various elements of your spreadsheet document will help you to navigate around it more easily, and so use it more effectively. Most elements are the same for all spreadsheet programs.

Understanding spreadsheets

A spreadsheet is a grid of 'cells'. The columns are like the columns in a ledger – you can use them to make lists of figures and perform calculations. Each column is identified by a letter of the alphabet, and each row by a number. So every cell has its own unique address, comprising the letter of the column and the number of the row it is in (A1, A2, and so on). You can type numbers, text or formulas into these cells. The formulas make it possible to get the program to do all the complicated and laborious arithmetic for you.

Using the Formula bar to input data

When you first open a spreadsheet, cell A1 is automatically selected as the 'active cell' – indicated by a thick black line around the cell – and you can type directly into it. To make entries into other cells, click on them first. As you make entries, they will appear in the Formula bar located below the toolbars. You can view and edit the contents of a cell in the Formula bar.

To the left of the Formula bar are two buttons (marked 'X' and '✔') that only appear after you type something in. If you make a mistake in your entry, click on the X button to cancel it; if it is correct, click on the ✔ button to enter it (or press the **Enter** or **Tab** keys).

What you can see

Spreadsheets look quite complicated. But once you understand how they work and how to find your way around them, they are easy to use. The documents displayed here are from Microsoft Excel. The main difference in appearance between these and Works documents is that there is only one toolbar in Works.

When using spreadsheets, the mouse pointer becomes a thick white cross, rather than the normal arrow head you will see elsewhere.

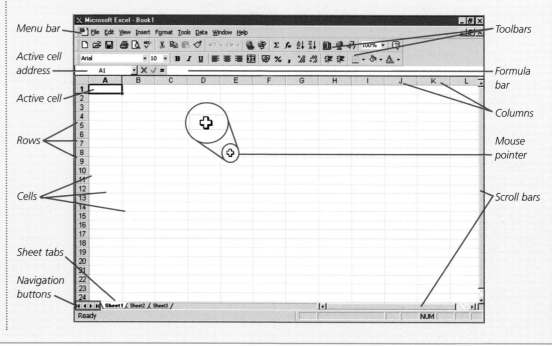

Menu bar — Active cell address — Active cell — Rows — Cells — Sheet tabs — Navigation buttons — Toolbars — Formula bar — Columns — Mouse pointer — Scroll bars

Moving around a spreadsheet

You can move from one cell to the next in several ways. You can either click on the next cell using your mouse, press the right arrow key (this is one of the four arrow keys on your keyboard), or press the **Tab** key (to move to a previous cell, press the **Shift** key and, keeping it pressed down, the **Tab** key).

In Excel, unless you want to move to a new row, do not press the **Return** key, as this will activate the cell below the one you are currently in.

Selecting cells

You can select cells for styling, cutting and copying in several ways. To select a column or row of cells, click on the grey column or row header. To select cells that are adjacent to each other, click on the first cell and, keeping the left mouse button pressed down, drag the cursor across or down the screen until the entire range of cells is selected, then release the mouse button.

If the cells you want to select are not adjacent, but are dotted throughout the spreadsheet, press the **Ctrl** key on your keyboard and, keeping it pressed down, click on each of the cells in turn.

Tips for using spreadsheets effectively

When you are dealing with numbers, it pays to give some thought to how to lay out the spreadsheet. When you type in information, be as careful as possible.

Adding titles and headings

To make it easier to identify your spreadsheet and navigate around it, it is helpful to enter a title at the top of the sheet, and to give separate headings to columns and rows. To do this, click on a cell and type in your text.

Adjusting column widths

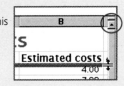

If an entry is too long for its cell, adjust the width of the column. Place your mouse pointer over the right-hand edge of the grey column header. When it becomes a double-headed arrow press the left mouse button and, keeping it pressed down, drag it to the desired width. Release the mouse button. You can make the column automatically adjust to include the widest entry in any of its cells by placing the mouse pointer in the same position and double-clicking.

Locking row and column headings

Often, column and row headings can disappear off screen when you scroll through large spreadsheets, making it difficult to keep track of which figures relate to what. To keep the headings viewable at all times, drag the small button at the top of the scroll bar down. This splits the worksheet into two independent panes, one to house the headings, one for the rest of the spreadsheet.

Enter identical data in multiple cells

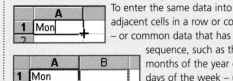

To enter the same data into adjacent cells in a row or column – or common data that has a set sequence, such as the months of the year or days of the week – use the Fill function.

Type an entry into the first cell. Place the mouse pointer in the lower right-hand corner of the cell. When it becomes a small black cross, press the left mouse button, keep it pressed and drag it over the cells you'd like filled. Release the mouse button.

To enter the same number into several columns and rows at once, select the cells, type in the number then press the **Ctrl** key and, keeping it pressed down, the **Enter** key.

Moving and coping data

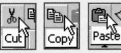

To move data in a spreadsheet, use the Cut, Copy and Paste commands. Select the cells you want to place elsewhere (the source range). To remove the source range, click the **Cut** toolbar button. The cells become selected. To leave the source range in its position and copy it, click the **Copy** toolbar button instead. Now click on the cell that you wish to be the top left-hand cell of the position where you want the moved information to appear (the target range). Click the **Paste** toolbar button.

Insert and delete columns and rows

Your spreadsheet design doesn't have to be set in stone and you can easily edit it according to your changing needs. For example, you can insert a new column or row. To do this in Excel, click on the grey column or row header (these contain either a letter or number) where you'd like your new one to be placed. Go to the **Insert** menu and select **Rows** or **Columns**. A new row or column will appear. To delete a row or column, click on its grey header, go to the **Edit** menu and select **Delete**.

In Works, all four commands – Insert Row, Delete Row, Insert Column and Delete Column – are found in the Insert menu.

Sorting by rows

Spreadsheet entries can easily be sorted, or prioritised. You can, for example, have items appear in order of expense. To do this, select the column(s) to be sorted. In Excel, go to the **Data** menu and click on **Sort**. In Works, go to the **Tools** menu and click on **Sort**. Both Excel and Works allow you to choose which column or columns (a maximum of three) you want to sort, and whether you want to list the results in ascending (A-Z) or descending (Z-A) order. Make your choices then click **OK**.

Formatting cells

Changing the style of the text or figures in your spreadsheet is a good way to help you to distinguish information quickly. Select the cell or cells to be formatted, go to the **Format** menu and click on **Cells**. In the Format Cells dialogue box click on the **Font** tab. Select a font, style, size and colour as desired, then click **OK**. Alternatively, select the cells then click on the relevant buttons on the toolbar.

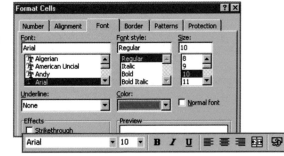

Performing calculations

It is the ability of spreadsheets to perform complex calculations which makes them such a powerful tool. It is worth the effort to learn how to use formulas correctly.

Adding figures

In Excel you can add together the contents of columns, rows or any combination of selected cells. Select the cells and their total is displayed on the Status bar at the bottom of the window.

Using the AutoSum function

Both Excel and Works have an AutoSum toolbar button to calculate figures. But they work in slightly differing ways.

In Excel, to add figures in adjacent cells in a column or a row, select the relevant cells then click the **AutoSum** button. The total will be displayed in the next cell of the column or row.

In Works, you must click on a blank cell in the column or row you want calculated, then click the **AutoSum** button. The cell references, or addresses, for the cells will appear in a formula. If they are correct, press **Enter**; if not, type in the correct cell references. The total will appear in your selected cell.

`=SUM(C3,C2,D3,D2,E3)`

In Excel, to add up figures in cells that are not adjacent to each other, click on an empty cell, then on the **AutoSum** button. The selected cell will display the legend '=SUM()'. Enter the cell references of the cells to be calculated. You can do this manually or by clicking on them, inserting a comma between each one. Each co-ordinate will be added to the formula automatically. Press the **Enter** key.

To add up figures in cells that are not adjacent to each other in Works, click on an empty cell then press the '=' key on your keyboard. Works now knows you want to enter a formula. Enter the cell references of the cells to be calculated, either manually or by clicking on them, inserting a '+' sign between each one. Press **Enter**.

To delete a formula in a cell press the **Delete** key.

Further functions in Excel

There are a number of preset functions in Excel that can take the effort out of spreadsheet calculations. Click on an empty cell to make it active and type in '='. Click on the arrow button between the Active cell address box and the Cancel button near the top of the window. A drop-down menu will appear. Click on an option and a dialogue box will appear, giving a brief description of the function it performs, such as the average value of selected cells, or depreciation of an asset (for example, a car) over a specified time period.

Further functions in Works

For other calculation functions in Works, click the **Easy Calc** button on the toolbar. A dialogue box appears, listing

common calculations and more specialised ones. Click on the **Other** button at the bottom of the box for a scrollable menu of the program's 76 preset functions with more detailed descriptions.

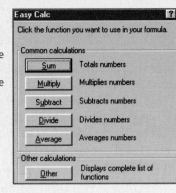

More complex equations in Excel and Works

You're not restricted to simple sums – you can create formulas for any type of calculation. Click on an empty cell and press the '=' key. Then type in the cell references of the cells to be calculated in your formula, separating them by the relevant 'operators' – the symbols for addition (+), subtraction (-), multiplication (*) and division (/). Press the **Enter** key.

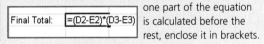

	A	B	C	D	
1	Item	Units ordered	Price per unit	Total	Di
2	Gloss Paint	6	£9.99	£59.94	
3	Brushes	4	£5.99	=B3*C3	

Spreadsheet programs automatically process some operators before others (for example, multiplication and division before addition or subtraction) so, to ensure that one part of the equation is calculated before the rest, enclose it in brackets.

Final Total: `=(D2-E2)*(D3-E3)`

Setting number formats

To help to prevent the accidental calculation of inappropriate data, it is advisable to format cells containing the same sort of figures: currency, dates, percentages, times, and so on. Select your cell or cells then go to the **Format** menu and click on **Cells**. In the Format Cells dialogue box click on the **Number** tab. A scrollable menu gives you a list of options. Click on an option (and the number of decimal places and, if a negative number, a style), then click **OK**.

An introduction to databases

Learn how to use database programs to keep records that you can sort

Databases are used for storing and organising large amounts of data about related topics. For example, you can create a database to catalogue your recipe collection and then search it to find all the lamb dishes or all the dishes using coriander.

A database's ability to organise and prioritise data in different ways also makes it suitable for storing names, addresses and contact details. If you forget someone's surname, you can search the database by first name only, by telephone code or by address.

But databases are more than just deposit boxes for information. They also make calculations. You can, for instance, enter the value of each item of your household contents, then add up the total value to provide a guide to how much you should insure your possessions for.

Working with fields

The building blocks of a database are fields. Each field represents a category of information. In an address database, they might be surname, first name, address, telephone number, and so on. To build a database, you must first create fields for it.

Membership No.	First name	Surname	Street address	Town

Creating records

Once the fields have been created you can begin to make your entries – each entry is known as a record. For each record, you fill in the fields. The database allows you to organise the records in a number of ways – for example, you can list them in alphabetical order or by date. You can also browse through the records, search for a particular entry and print out selected aspects.

First name: Gillian
Surname: Foster
Street address: 12 Hambley Gard
Town or city: London
Postcode: N24 7YT

Opening a new database

Click on the **Start** button and select **Programs** then Microsoft Works. The Works Task Launcher dialogue box will appear. Click the **Works Tools** tab, then the **Database** button. The First-time Help dialogue box appears. Click the button marked 'To create a new database'.

Building a database

When you open a new database, the Create Database dialogue box appears, in which you specify fields. Don't worry if you miss one out, or enter them in the wrong order, as you can edit your database later.

Setting up fields

As you enter field names you are given a chance to format them and choose a style for them.

Field name

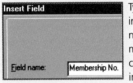

Type your field name into this box. Field names should not be more than 15 characters long (this includes spaces between words). The more fields you create, the greater the flexibility of your database. It is sensible, for example, to create separate fields for first and surnames so you can search by either category.

Try to enter field names in the order that you wish them to appear in your database. It's good practice to be as organised as possible at this stage.

Format

You have a choice of formats for your field names.

These relate to the type of information you are entering. The date field, for example, is automatically set up for the day, month and year. Select an option by clicking it. A small black dot indicates that the Format is active.

Choose the following formats for the appropriate information:

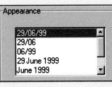

General This is the default setting for all field names. Text entries are aligned to the left, and numbers to the right.

Number This lets you specify the way that numbers are displayed. For example, you can select the number of decimal places, or whether negative numbers appear in red.

Date Select this to specify how dates are displayed – by month only, with or without the year, or with the month as text rather than a number.

Time Select either 'AM' or 'PM', and whether to include seconds as well as hours and minutes.

Text Use this if you want to display numbers as text rather than figures, or if you wish to include dashes or spaces (these are particularly useful when entering telephone numbers).

Fraction If you want to store fractions – 2¾, for example – choose this format. When entering data, type a space between the whole number (2) and the fraction (3/4) to let Works tell them apart. The decimal equivalent appears in the Entry bar when the cell containing a fraction is selected.

Serialized Choose this format to get Works to automatically add a serial number to each record. This unique number is useful if you need to sort records into the order in which they were entered.

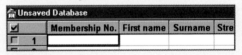

Appearance

You will be given style choices for how you want your number, date, time, fraction and serialised formats to appear. For example, you may want to include decimal values in your numbers, and to have months written out in full in dates. Scroll through the lists and click on your choice.

Add/Cancel

After you have created a field, selected a format and, if appropriate, an appearance for it, click on the **Add** button to create another field. When you have created all the fields for your database click on **Done**. Your database will appear in List View, with your field names as headings at the top of columns.

☑	Membership No.	First name	Surname	Stre
☐	1			

Database programs

Msworks

Microsoft Works includes a database tool. It also contains a selection of database Task Wizards (these are predesigned documents that you open and use as they are, or customise to your liking).

Microsoft Office

The Standard edition of Microsoft Office does not include a specific database program, but its spreadsheet program, Microsoft Excel, can perform many of the same tasks (see page 37).

Saving your database

When your database appears for the first time in List View, it is called 'Unsaved Database'. You should save it immediately with an appropriate name.

Click on the **Save** toolbar button or go to the **File** menu and click on **Save As**. A dialogue box appears. In the 'File name' box type in a name for your database. Click on the arrow beside the 'Save in' box to see the destinations to which you can save your file. Select a folder then click on **Save**. For more detailed information on saving documents, see page 38.

Getting around your database

Your new database appears in List View, which looks similar to a spreadsheet. There are three other ways to view your database, too. Become familiar with them before entering any records.

Different points of view

You can view your database in four different ways, each of which lends itself best to a particular use. All the views can be accessed via the View menu, or by clicking on the appropriate buttons on the toolbar.

List View

Immediately after you create your fields, your database is displayed in List View. This view allows you to see a number of records at the same time. It is useful when you simply want to browse your records, move data (copy and paste) from one record to another, or when entering a series of numbers or dates.

You can enter information into your database in List View by first clicking on a cell then typing your entry (it also appears in the Entry bar at the top of the window). List View is also used to display the results of any searches that you run (see opposite).

"233 Bedminster Bridge Rd

First name	Surname	Street address	Town or city	Postc
Gillian	Foster	12 Hambley Gard	London	N24 7Y
Paolo	Ianni	Flat 4, 7 Frith Str	London	WC1R
James	Knighton	233 Bedminster	Bristol	BS99 6
Ursula	Davidowicz	25 Ellesmere Ro	Birmingham	B45 2B
Peter	James	773 Long lane	Glasgow	G12 7G
Finola	Abrahams	12 Kings Road	Farnham	GU8 9T

Form View

Each record can be viewed separately using Form View. Most people prefer to enter information using this view – it means you can see the entries for all the other fields as you enter new data into the database.

Club database

First name: Gillian

Surname: Foster

Street address: 12 Hambley Garder

Town or city: London

Postcode: N24 7YT

Form Design

In Form Design you structure the look of Form View. You can rearrange fields and their adjoining field boxes. You can also add colours to text, select different fonts, and add borders and

Club database

The Electric Club

Membership

First name: Gillian   Surname: Foster

Street address: 12 Hambley Gardens

images. To move field names around the page, click on them and drag them into place.

To adjust the size of field boxes so that adjoining field names are large enough to hold all the information you want to include, click on the bottom right-hand corner of a field box and, with the left mouse button pressed down, drag it diagonally across the page.

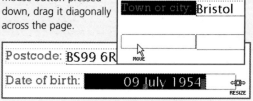

Town or city: Bristol

MOVE

Postcode: BS99 6R

Date of birth: 09 July 1954

RESIZE

Report View

A good database allows you to extract data. Through Report View you can design and print out a report that organises your information by related subjects. It also lets you perform calculations on fields, such as the total of subscription fees club members have paid to date.

Club database - Money owed

Membership No.	Surname	Fees paid/owed
00004	Davidowicz	-62.50
00020	Amir	-37.30
00006	Abrahams	-25.00
00013	Gonzalez	-25.00
00003	Knighton	-12.50
00008	Morden	-12.50
00015	Leger	-12.50
00023	Porter	-12.50
	SUM:	
		-199.80

Inputting your records

You can enter data into your database in either List View or Form View.

In List View, click on the relevant cell and start typing. To move to the next field, or cell, either click in it using your mouse, or press the **Tab** key on your keyboard. (To return to a previous field, or cell, press **Shift** and **Tab**.) Unlike with spreadsheets, pressing the Return key will not move your cursor to the next cell or row in a database.

In Form View, click the field box adjoining the field name and type your data. Press the **Tab** key to move to the next field (or the next record when you come to the end of the current one), and the **Shift** and **Tab** keys to return to a previous field, or record.

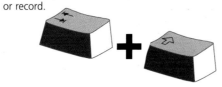

Navigating through forms

In Form View and Form Design you can view other records by clicking on the appropriate arrows displayed on each side of the current record name at the bottom of the window.

The arrows immediately to the left and right of the current record will take you to the previous and next records respectively. The arrows to the outside of these take you straight to the first and last records.

Date of birth: 04 April 1979

Phone No.: 0171 200 4512

|◀ ◀ Record 1 ▶ ▶| Zoom 50%

Finding information and sorting your records

Databases allow you to prioritise and organise your information as you please, and to search for specific entries quickly and easily.

Finding information

A single database in Microsoft Works can store up to 32 000 records. To locate a record quickly, you can initiate a search. In List View go to the **Edit** menu and click on **Find**. The Find dialogue box appears on screen. In the 'Find what' box type in a key word or words (be as specific as possible), select the **All Records** option then click **OK**. The records containing your key word will appear in a list. To return to your full list of records, go to the **Record** menu, select **Show** then **All Records**.

You can search in Form View in the same way but the records are displayed one at a time. To move between them, click the arrows at the foot of the screen.

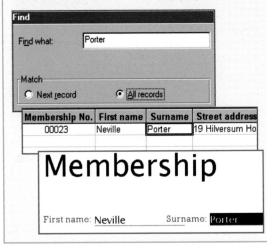

Sorting records in your database

You can use the Sort function in Works to re-order your database. Go to the **Record** menu and click on **Sort Records**. In the Sort Records dialogue box you can choose to have your records prioritised by up to three fields. For example, by first sorting by 'Date of birth' in ascending order, the oldest person in your database will appear at the top of the list, and the youngest person last. If you then sort by 'Surname' in ascending order, those who share the same date of birth will then be listed alphabetically. Sort a third time by town in ascending order, those who share a similar birthday and name will be listed alphabetically by town.

Click on the arrows beside each Sort box, scroll through the lists and select your choice of field. You have the option of sorting records in Ascending or Descending order (Ascending lists entries A to Z, or 1, 2, 3...; Descending lists entries Z to A, or 10, 9, 8...).

Editing your database

After you have created a database, you can add and delete information, and perform calculations.

Inserting new records

To insert a new record between existing records, click on the row number where you want to insert it in List View. Go to the **Record** menu and select **Insert Record**. To delete a row, click on the row number, go to the **Record** menu and select **Delete Record**.

Adding and moving fields

To add a new field, click the field heading where you'd like it to appear in List View. Go to the **Record** menu and select **Insert Field**. Choose to insert it before or after the selected one. A dialogue box appears in which you give the new field a name. Click **OK**. To delete a field, click its heading then go to the **Record** menu and select **Delete Field**.

To move a field, click on the field heading in List View. Move the mouse pointer to the edge of a highlighted cell. When it changes to a 'drag' pointer, drag the field to its new location. To move a record, click on the row heading and do the same.

Calculating data

You can perform calculations on values in two or more fields and display the results in another. If you have fields for 'Price' and 'Deposit', create a third called 'Total Due'. Click its heading and type '=Price-Deposit' in the Entry bar to show the balance.

	=Price-Deposit	
Database 1		
Price	**Deposit**	**Total Due**
£2,000.00	£500.00	£1,500.00

Microsoft Excel as a database

Microsoft Excel can be used to perform database functions. Instead of entering field names, headings are typed into the spreadsheet, in cells along the same row. Records are entered into the rows below. (Records must be numbered manually, so create a heading for 'Record No'.)

To look at a sub-set of your data, use AutoFilter. Go to the **Data** menu and select **Filter** then **AutoFilter**. Each column appears with a menu arrow on the right. Click the arrow on the menu

you want to sort, then select **Custom** from the drop-down menu. Now set your criteria. For example, in a 'Fees paid/owed' column, you can select records to see only those people who owe money. In the Custom AutoFilter dialogue box specify records for which the fees paid/owed are less than '0', then click **OK**. To return to the full database, go to the **Data** menu and select **Filter** then **Show All**.

Fees paid/owed
-£12.50
-£62.50
-£25.00
-£12.50
-£25.00
-£12.50
-£37.30

Membership details

Record No: 0001
Surname: Coady
First names: Emma
Date of birth: 26/05/68
Registration: 03/02/85
Address: Flat 6, Sherbourne Drive, Putney, London (previously Flat 3, Warholl Mansion Block, Bern Street, Putney, London)
Telephone No: 0181 879 7865 (work 0171 354 7689)
Occupation: Nurse
Club rating: 5

Saving and printing

Transform your work into printed documents

Your computer stores work in much the same way as a conventional filing system. The documents that you create on your PC are kept in folders. Within the folders are sub-folders that help you organise the different areas of your work. For example, if you create a folder for office work, you could then create sub-folders for business correspondence and accounts. As with any filing system, it's vital to organise it well right from the start.

You should first decide which folders you are likely to need. Begin by creating a folder for each family member. You can then decide which sub-folders to create. In a well-ordered system it becomes an easy matter to save and retrieve your work – far easier, in fact, than with a traditional paper-filled filing cabinet.

Printing is easy

Printing your PC files (these are the documents you create, rather than the folders in which you store them) is one of the most useful skills you can master on your computer. Depending on the type of printer you have, you can print on a variety of paper sizes and weights (thicknesses). You can print out sticky address labels and even print directly onto envelopes.

By using the many font styles, colours and graphics available on your PC, it's possible to produce printed work that looks professional.

As soon as you create a new document, save it. Continue to save it as you work. This way, should your PC crash, your work will not be lost.

SAVING YOUR WORK

Save As

Save in: My Documents

Desktop
My Computer
3½ Floppy (A:)
(C:)
My Documents
3dl1_f (D:)
Network Neighborhood
My Documents
My Briefcase
Internet Locations (FTP)
Add/Modify FTP Locations

File name: Letter to Liz

Save as type: Word Document

Save

1 To save a file, click on the **Save** toolbar button or go to the **File** menu and click on **Save As**. A dialogue box appears. In the 'File name' box type in the file's name. Click on the arrow beside the 'Save in' box to see the destinations to which you can save your file.

Auto saving

The more often you save files, the less work you risk losing if your computer crashes. You can set some programs, including Word, to save files automatically at regular intervals. Go to the **Tools** menu and click on **Options**. Click on the **Save** tab. Click next to 'Save AutoRecover info every:' and set a time interval. Finally, click **OK**.

☑ Save AutoRecover info every: 10 minutes

Save Word files as: Word Document (*.doc)

*If a sub-folder is selected but you wish to return to the main folder (moving up one level), click on the **Up One Level** button. To return to a main drive, click on the arrow beside the 'Save in' box, scroll through the list that appears and click on the drive.*

Up One Level

Bright idea
*You can print multiple copies of a long document and have the pages collated in order. In the Print dialogue box click on the box beside Collate. Enter the number of copies you want then click **OK**.*

The procedure for printing documents is more or less the same, irrespective of which program you are working in. Here, a Word document is printed.

▶ PRINTING YOUR WORK

Save As

Save in: My Documents

New Folder

Current Folder:

C:\My Documents

Name: Letters

Create New Folder

OK

Cancel

Save As

Save in: Letters

Letters
File   Edit   View   Go

Back   Forward   Up

Address C:\My Documents\Le

Letter to Liz

File name: Letter to Liz

Save as type: Word Documen

Print

Printer
Name: Apple LaserWriter
Status: Busy
Type: Apple LaserWriter
Where: \\`LaserWriter\LaserWriter 8500
Comment:

Page range
○ All
○ Current page   ○ Selection
○ Pages:
Enter page numbers and/or page ranges separated by commas. For example, 1,3,5–12

Print what: Document

Options...

Copies
Number of copies:
☑ Co

Print

Print: All pages in rang

OK

2 To create a sub-folder within, say, the My Documents folder found on your Desktop, click on the

Create New Folder toolbar button. In the New Folder dialogue box type in a name for the folder then click **OK**.

3 Your sub-folder appears in the main folder. Double-click on it, and it appears in 'Save in' box. Now, click on **Save** to save your

document into it. The document name now appears on the file's Title bar, and an icon for the Word file appears in the new sub-folder.

Go to the **File** menu and click on **Print**. In the dialogue box you are offered several options, such as printing multiple copies

and printing a range of pages. Click **OK**. To print without seeing the dialogue box, click on the **Print** toolbar button.

Setting your page
You can adjust how your document prints out. Go to the **File** menu and click on **Page Setup**. Click on the **Paper Size** tab. Scroll through the 'Paper size' box and click on your choice. If you do not want your document to print out as Portrait, select the Landscape option in the Orientation section. Click **OK**.

Page Setup

Margins   Paper Size   Paper Sc

Paper size:
A4

Width: 21 cm

Height: 29.7 cm

Orientation
○ Portrait
○ Landscape

Print preview
To check how your document looks before printing, click on the **Print Preview** toolbar button or go to the **File** menu and click on **Print Preview**. To return to your original document layout, click **Close**.

W Microsoft Word - Letter to Liz (Previe
File Edit View Insert Format Tools Ta
75%

4th June 1999

Dear Liz,
It was so nice
leave it six months agai
up with my correspond

How your computer works

Discover what happens inside your PC when you switch it on

When you switch on the system unit of your PC it has to complete several automatic operations before it is able to process the commands you will subsequently input via your keyboard and mouse.

To ensure that the operating conditions are as they should be, all your hardware components, such as your memory and keyboard, are checked to make sure that they are undamaged and are able to communicate with each other and with your software.

This process is called 'booting up'. It takes only a minute, but it's the most important minute of your PC's working day. Unless the hardware and software communicate properly, nothing else on your PC will work.

Your computer's memory
The basic functions of your computer are governed by different types of 'memory'.

RAM
Random Access Memory (RAM) is the memory used by your computer temporarily to store the files and programs you are working on. It can process your commands extremely quickly. This type of memory only works when the computer is switched on; when it is turned off, anything left in RAM is lost.

ROM
Read Only Memory (ROM) holds basic details about the computer and a small, self-test program that runs every time you switch the computer on. ROM is part of your computer's 'identity', and is retained when your PC is turned off. You can't change or remove what's stored in the ROM, which is why it's called 'read only'.

CMOS
Complementary Metal Oxide Semiconductor (CMOS) memory stores your computer's settings, such as which type of hard disk it uses. The CMOS also remembers the date and time. It is powered by a small battery that recharges itself when the computer is switched on (switch it on at least once a month for an hour or two).

BIOS
The Basic Input/Output System (BIOS) memory controls your computer hardware. The BIOS tells the operating system which hardware to expect to come into operation and how it is arranged. It is as if your computer were a chef, and the BIOS his assistant, checking he has all the necessary ingredients. The BIOS is stored within the ROM.

Watch out
If your PC was not shut down properly the last time you used it, a message will flash up the next time you switch it on. If this happens, allow your PC to boot up, then restart it immediately. This ensures that the shut-down mistake has no lingering after-effects.

Close-up
In addition to switching on your system unit, you may also have to turn on your monitor, and any other peripheral units, such as a modem or printer, if they have separate power sources.

When you switch on...
The first two minutes after you switch on are vital to the performance of your computer. Here's what happens after you press the power button.

The start-up routine
The first sound you will hear is the whirr of the fan. This regulates the temperature inside the system unit and operates for as long as the computer is switched on. You should avoid covering the air vents on your PC as this may cause overheating.

```
Award Plug and Play BIOS Extension   v
Copyright (C) 1998, Award Software, In
  Detecting IDE Primary Master   ... Qu
  Detecting IDE Secondary Master... CR
```

The first task the computer performs when you switch it on is the POST (Power On Self Test) routine. This checks that important components, such as the hard disk, are available, and detects any serious disk errors. The POST will often 'beep' when it has finished.

Working from memory
The computer then reads the BIOS (this allows it to communicate with memory, the hard disk and the monitor). The BIOS will often send simple messages to the screen, and will look up the computer settings and the date and time from the CMOS.

```
INTEL(R) CELERON(TM) CPU at 333A MHz
Memory Test : 65536K OK
```

The BIOS then starts each component of your computer – you may see the memory counting up on screen. You will also hear the hard disk start to whirr, as the information it stores is read.

These are the essential preliminary operations that start up each hardware element so they can communicate with each other. The on-screen text messages that appear briefly before Windows starts show that this process has been completed successfully.

Loading Windows
The Windows operating system is then read from the hard disk, and loaded into the RAM memory. Your PC will first read special configuration files containing important information, such as the country your computer is located in (this allows it to use the correct language and time settings). During this time the Starting Windows screen is displayed.

As the rest of the Windows program is read from the hard disk and transferred into RAM you will hear the

hard disk making a noise as its 'arm' moves over the disks. One of the last things Windows does before it has finished loading and initiating itself is to play a sound. It reads a sound file from the hard disk and directs the sound output to the speakers. This is done partly to test the speakers and partly to test that Windows is working properly. The Windows Desktop is then displayed ready for you to use (see below).

From now on, every command you input into your computer – either by moving and clicking the mouse or via keystrokes on your keyboard – passes through the RAM. The ROM is only ever used by the computer during its booting-up phase.

The hard disk
The hard disk is a series of magnetised metal disk platters. They are read by a small arm that passes over them – a little like an old-style record player. However, the arm never touches the disks – it skims thousandths of a millimetre above the platters, which you can hear spinning.

Ready and waiting
After your computer has checked through your hardware and software, you will be presented with the basic Desktop that tells you the computer is ready for use. Icons displayed on the Desktop include a folder to contain different users' documents, shortcuts to Internet software and the Recycle Bin.

How software works

Learn how the operating system, programs and your PC's hardware interact

No matter how powerful your PC, it is an inert box of chips and wires until it is told what to do and think. Computers function only when they are given instructions. Software is the electronic 'brain' that gives your PC these instructions. The most fundamental piece of software on your computer is the operating system. The operating system on most PCs is Windows. Just as your brain coordinates your thoughts with your movements, so Windows controls all the actions, from printing a page to closing a window, that you ask your PC to do.

From DOS to Windows

The original operating system for PCs was DOS (Disk Operating System). To use this system you needed to know the language, and you typed in commands one by one. These commands were quite complicated, and meant that DOS was difficult for most beginners to use.

In Windows 95 and 98, the DOS system is still accessible as a program called MS-DOS Prompt. If there is a fault with Windows, computer specialists can use this facility to execute text-based DOS commands to control the way the computer works at the most basic level.

```
Microsoft(R) Windows 98
   (C)Copyright Microsoft Corp 1981-1998.

C:\WINDOWS>xcopy c:\windows\*.* c:\winbac
```

Using Windows requires no knowledge of computer languages. It has a Graphical User Interface (GUI – pronounced 'gooey') that allows you to operate your PC by moving your mouse pointer around the screen and clicking on buttons, menus and images. All Windows-compatible programs and additional hardware can be accessed through the Windows system.

Windows gets updated regularly and contains new features and improvements with each upgrade. The current standard is Windows 98.

Bright idea
Before buying a new program check the packaging to see how much RAM it needs, and make sure that your computer has memory to spare (see below).

The Taskbar that runs along the bottom of your Desktop shows you which programs you have open – each is displayed as a separate button. In this Taskbar, Word, Excel and Outlook Express are open.

How does Windows work with other programs?
Understanding what happens when you open a program within Windows will help you operate your computer more effectively.

The role Windows plays
Application programs (so-called because they're designed to be applied to a specific task) rely on Windows to provide a basic level of communication with the computer's hardware. This 'middleman' role does away with the need to duplicate the same basic features into every application. This lets programmers concentrate on making sure programs do their job as well as they can.

So, for example, when you save files and the Save As dialogue box appears on screen, this is an element of Windows, not of the program you are using.

What happens when you switch your PC on?
When you switch your computer on, Windows starts automatically. Its program code is read from the hard disk then loaded into the computer's RAM memory.

If no software other than Windows is loaded, all you can do on your PC is see which files are on your hard disk, adjust your PC's settings and run some very basic programs. For most other tasks, you have to call on application programs.

Even Windows accessories, such as Internet Explorer, Paint and WordPad, are separate programs dedicated to their own jobs of Web browsing, calculating with numbers, and simple word processing, respectively. (For more information on specific programs you are likely to use, see page 22.)

Opening programs in Windows
When you open programs they too are loaded into the computer's RAM memory. They then draw on Windows' facilities to communicate with your computer's hardware.

Windows allows you to run several programs at once, and to move easily between them. For example, if you wanted to edit then insert a picture into a Microsoft Word document you were working on, you could open the Paint program, edit the picture, then insert it into the Word document. At the same time, you could be researching the subject of the document on the Internet using the Internet Explorer program.

The importance of memory
As each new program is opened it loads up into the computer's RAM memory, alongside the other software already running. This is why it's important that your computer has lots of RAM (at least 32 Mb). If you don't have enough to run a particular program, your computer stores the excess data on its hard disk, in a temporary 'scratch file'. However, this makes all the programs you have open run much more slowly. (To find out how to add more RAM to your PC, see page 346.)

When you have finished working with a program you should close or exit it (do not just minimise it to the Taskbar). The program then unloads from the RAM, freeing it up for use by other programs. This may also speed up the operation of the other programs that remain open.

Checking your RAM
To find out how much RAM you have on your PC, right-click on **My Computer** and click on **Properties** from the pop-up menu. Click on the **Performance** tab.

The first figure, Memory, tells you how much RAM your PC has in total. The second figure, System Resources, refers to a special area of RAM that Windows uses to keep track of programs it is running. With Windows alone running, this figure is about 80 per cent. System Resources rarely, if ever, run out, but with many programs running, your PC may slow down.

Storing all your data

How to make space for everything you need

Your computer's hard disk is where all your programs and documents are stored. The more programs and documents you have, the less disk space there is in which to store them. As the hard disk fills up, your computer will slow down. Disposing of unwanted documents in the Recycle Bin, and uninstalling software that you no longer use, will help to conserve hard disk space (for more details, see pages 54-55). However, eventually you may need to use extra storage devices.

Your first choices

Most computers contain a floppy disk drive, located in the system unit. Floppy disks can store about 1.44Mb of data each – that's equivalent to about 60 one-page letters or one digital image scanned in at a low resolution.

Although floppy disks are still a popular way of moving files – between home and office, for instance – their lack of storage capacity makes them a poor way of storing data. It's also worth noting that shared floppy disks are the most common source of viruses, so storing valuable data on them can be risky (this doesn't apply if you are using new disks).

Your computer almost certainly has a CD drive as well as a floppy drive. Most CD drives can only read pre-written CDs, but it is already possible to buy a drive that will 'write' information onto a CD. Such a drive would allow you to store as much as 600Mb of data on a single CD. That is a capacity equivalent to more than 400 floppy disks. But writable drives are expensive, and they may be made redundant by future developments.

Which storage device?

These devices are all suitable for storing large quantities of information. If you need to transfer data to other PCs, make sure each PC has the same type of drive.

DVDs

High-capacity CDs are now available in the form of DVDs (Digital Versatile Discs). These discs look exactly like CDs but can store up to 4.5 Gb of information – that's sufficient to store an entire feature film. But at the moment, most DVDs like CD-ROM drives, can only read – not write – information.

Zip disks

These are one of the most popular storage devices available, with each disk able to hold 250 Mb of data. Some PCs now come with a built-in Zip drive. Because of their popularity and widespread use, Zips provide a great way of sharing files with other PC users.

Super disks

Super disks look like floppy disks but can hold up to 140 times more data. The Sony HiFD super disk, for example, offers 200 Mb of storage, while the Imation SuperDisk offers 120 Mb. Another major point in their favour is that the super disk drive is able to read floppy disks.

Jaz disks

Jaz disks can hold up to 2 Gb of data and Jaz drives work much faster than Zip drives. But they are more expensive than Zips, and so are less widely used.

Tape drives

This is the oldest form of technology for storing large computer files. Nowadays, they are used mainly for creating back-up files of your work in case you lose the originals. They are too slow for everyday use, and the wide variety of different types available makes them unsuitable for exchanging files.

Connecting a drive

The storage devices described on this page are separate, external items that need to be connected to your system unit in order to function as data storage devices.

The type of connection varies: some types plug into the parallel port, but others may require a special expansion card to be fitted inside the computer. Read the instruction manual for your device.

Supplementary hardware

Extend your computer's capabilities with added devices

Once your computer knowledge and confidence grows, you will be eager to expand your PC's capabilities. A wide range of devices is available that will make working with your computer even more interesting and enjoyable.

If you're itching to get on to the Internet or send e-mail (electronic mail), buying a modem should be at the top of your shopping list. If you like to use images in your work, buying your own scanner will prove more cost-effective than paying for your photos to be scanned at a bureau or copy shop. However, it's worth remembering that not all images need to be scanned. Digital cameras will allow you to transfer digital images direct to your PC, no scanner required.

It's also possible to buy video cameras that attach to your computer. As well as being fun, you can hold video conferences with colleagues who have cameras.

Hardware can also be bought to make the most of existing on-screen entertainments. The new generation of joysticks, for instance, really take game playing to a new dimension.

These extras can be built up over time. You need not buy everything on the same shopping trip.

With added hardware, you can really make the most of your computer, turning it into a complete home office or entertainment centre

Modems

There are two main types of modem: **Internal** modems are installed inside the system unit in one of the spare 'expansion' slots at the back.
External modems sit outside your computer, on your desk, and plug into one of the serial ports at the back of the system unit.

Once you have a modem you can connect to the Internet, send e-mails, and send and receive faxes, using your computer as a fax machine.

Scanners

A scanner will transform your paper images and photo prints into graphic files that you can then edit and use on your PC. The most versatile kind of scanners are 'flatbed' scanners. They can scan not only individual sheets of paper, but also pages from books without

damaging the binding. Picture quality is described in terms of resolution, measured in dots per inch (dpi). The more dots that make up an image, the higher the resolution and the better the quality of the image. Buy a scanner with a resolution capability of at least 300 dpi.

Digital cameras

Digital cameras look similar to ordinary cameras, but take photographs without using any film. The picture is stored as a graphic file that you can transfer directly to your computer through a connection lead. Good-quality digital cameras are quite expensive, but it's worth remembering that you won't need to buy film and get it developed, and you don't need a scanner.

Joysticks

If you're a fan of computer games, a joystick is essential. Many home PCs come with their own joystick, but you can also buy joysticks with extra feature buttons and better grips. They plug into a port in your system unit. The best joysticks are those that also provide feedback – recoiling as you fire guns, or shaking as you drive over rocks – but these 'force feedback' devices only work with games software that supports them. It's also possible to buy steering wheels and pedals for driving games.

Video cameras

If you mount a small video camera on the top of your computer you can conduct video conferences. These

small cameras are also used for the WebCam sites on the Internet. Bear in mind that video conferencing requires a powerful PC, and without special high-speed phone lines, the picture can be jerky and the sound can stutter.

Microphones

Most microphones are fine for common uses – recording a narration, for instance – but it is now possible to use a microphone with speech-recognition software. This means that you don't have to type: you just speak your thoughts, and the words appear in your document. However, this software is still quite new and, unless you spend a long time teaching it to recognise your voice, may give poor results.

Installing drivers

Additional hardware usually needs extra software. At the very least, you will need a driver for it; a driver is a piece of software that allows Windows to control the added hardware.

Most hardware comes with a set-up program that will copy the driver to your computer's hard disk. You may have to add the driver

yourself: go to the **Start** menu, select **Settings** and click on **Control Panel**. Click on the **Add New Hardware** icon. Windows will then ask you to select the hardware device you are installing. When prompted to choose a driver file you need to insert the floppy disk or CD that came with the hardware and click the button **Have Disk**.

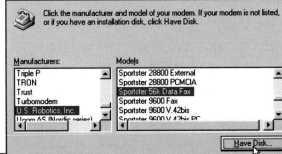

More software for your PC

Extend the uses of your computer with extra programs

When you bought your PC, a selection of software will have been included. Common packages include Microsoft Works, Microsoft Office 97, Lotus SmartSuite and Corel WordPerfect Suite. Each of these contains a number of programs that allow you to perform a range of functions such as word processing and spreadsheet work. The software that comes with your computer is known as bundled software.

Although this bundled software allows you to perform many different tasks on your PC, you're bound eventually to want to use more specialised or advanced software. If music is a hobby, for instance, you may be interested in a particular composing package; and if you have children, you may want a selection of games to play. You will also want to use virus-checking software to be sure your computer is kept free from viruses.

Checking the requirements

Before you buy a new piece of software, check the information on the packaging to ensure it runs on your version of Windows. The written details should also tell you how much memory (RAM) and hard-disk storage space it requires, then make sure your computer has sufficient of both.

To see how much disk space you have available, double-click on **My Computer**, then double-click on **[C:]** drive. Right-click in the window and select **Properties** from the pop-up menu. To see how much RAM is built into your PC, go to the **Start** menu, select **Settings** then **Control Panel**, then double-click on **System**.

Close-up
When buying goods by mail order through a magazine advertisement, check that the magazine operates the Mail Order Protection Scheme (MOPS). This offers consumers protection if the software doesn't perform the tasks claimed of it.

Watch out
Copying programs from friends is not obtaining software for free – it's stealing. Unless you have purchased a licence, you are breaking copyright laws and could be prosecuted.

'Free' software

You don't always have to buy new software for your PC. Some of it can be obtained free, if only for a limited period.

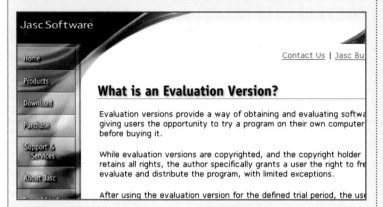

Jasc Software

Home | Products | Download | Purchase | Support & Services | About Jasc

Contact Us | Jasc Bu

What is an Evaluation Version?

Evaluation versions provide a way of obtaining and evaluating softwa giving users the opportunity to try a program on their own computer before buying it.

While evaluation versions are copyrighted, and the copyright holder retains all rights, the author specifically grants a user the right to fre evaluate and distribute the program, with limited exceptions.

After using the evaluation version for the defined trial period, the use

Freeware, shareware and evaluation software

Freeware describes software that's available completely free. Most of the programs have been written by PC enthusiasts and are of good quality.

Shareware and evaluation software are offered free for a limited period (usually 30 days), after which you will not be able to operate the program.

If you want to continue to use a shareware program you must pay a fee (usually much lower than the price of similar, shop-bought packages). To continue using evaluation software, you must purchase a full copy.

Sources of software

Specialist PC stores and electrical shops are good places to start, but the other sources outlined below may save you money.

Downloading programs

It's possible to download shareware, freeware and evaluation software from the Internet. Locate a dedicated Web site (do a search for 'shareware'), then follow the on-screen instructions on the site.

Your PC will tell you how long the download will take – anything up to a few hours for a big program. After it has downloaded, disconnect from the Internet and double-click the program's icon to install it.

PC magazines

Look out for free, cover-mounted CD-ROMS on PC magazines. Some CDs will hold 'full product' or complete programs, while others will offer demonstration or shareware versions.

Buying mail order

Mail order or 'direct' software vendors offer competitive pricing over high street retailers. Look at the adverts in PC magazines to compare prices. Software can be downloaded from the Internet or dispatched by post.

Which software?

There are literally thousands of programs available to computer users. As well as sophisticated games, you can learn how to redesign your home and garden, teach yourself a new language, or master a new skill such as typing.

Filing your work

Learn how to name and save your files, and to organise your work efficiently

It can be far easier to locate your work in a well-organised filing system on your computer than it is in a normal paper filing system

Your computer is an electronic filing cabinet. Each piece of work is stored in folders (as are all the programs you use). Folders can be stored in other folders which are like the drawers in the cabinet. It is tempting to keep all your files on your computer Desktop where you can see them but, as with a real desk, it makes life easier if you tidy things away before the clutter gets out of hand.

Filing made easy

Don't worry that you will forget where you put files, because Windows makes it easy to find them. It is like having an efficient personal assistant – or it is as if your filing cabinet could tell you exactly what is in all its drawers.

You can access your computer's filing system through a handy facility called Windows Explorer. Through it you can move folders and files around, make new folders and even copy, or duplicate, folders and documents.

There are several ways to create folders. The method you use will depend on how you save your work.

CREATING FOLDERS

1 To create a folder in Windows Explorer, go to the **Start** menu, select **Programs** then click on **Windows Explorer**. In the left pane click on the drive or folder in which you want to create the new folder.

Naming your files

Always name your files logically so that, should you misplace one and not remember its full name, you can still activate a search for it. If several members of the family are using the computer, create separate folders in which each person can store work. Use your name or initials when naming documents so that you don't get confused as to whose 'Personal Accounts' are whose.

Bright idea
To rename a file or folder, click on it in Windows Explorer, go to the **File** *menu and select* **Rename**. *Type in the new name over the highlighted old name.*

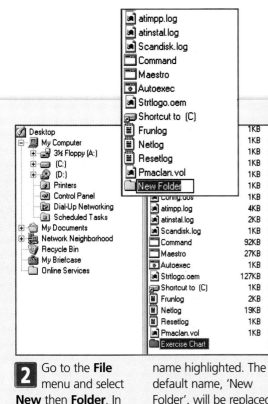

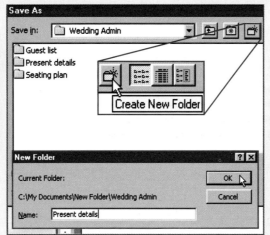

2 Go to the **File** menu and select **New** then **Folder**. In the right pane a new folder appears, with its name highlighted. The default name, 'New Folder', will be replaced as soon as you begin typing in the new name.

You can create folders in which to store work as you save documents. In the Save As dialogue box click on the **Create New Folder** button. In the New Folder dialogue box give the folder a name then click **OK**. Now double-click on your named folder and click on **Save**.

It is possible to create new folders by using your right mouse button. When you need to create a new folder click the right mouse button, select **New** then select **Folder**. The default name on the folder that appears will be replaced as you type in the new name.

Finding lost files

To find work you have misplaced, go to the **Start** menu, select **Find** then click on **Files or Folders**. In the Find: All Files dialogue box, type the file name, or as much of it as you can remember, in the Named box. Click on the arrow to the right of the 'Look in' box and click on **[C:]**. Click on **Find Now** to initiate the search.

Copying and moving files

Keep your documents in order

There will be occasions when you need to copy or move files. You may want to make a back-up of a document (a duplicate copy of a file to use in case your other one becomes damaged or lost), or transfer a file to another computer to work on. Perhaps you need to copy work onto a floppy disk, or you would simply like to store a file in a more appropriate folder on your computer. Whatever you want to do, Windows makes it easy.

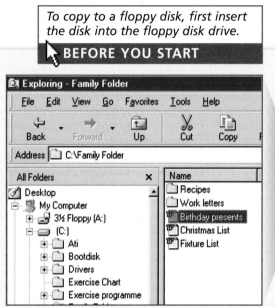

To copy to a floppy disk, first insert the disk into the floppy disk drive.

BEFORE YOU START

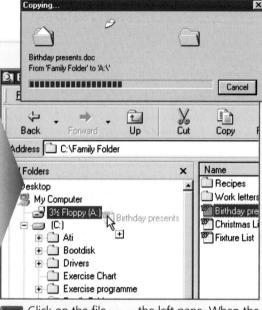

1 Go to the **Start** menu, highlight **Programs** and click on **Windows Explorer**. By clicking on the folders in the left pane of the dialogue box you can locate the file you wish to copy in the right pane of the box.

2 Click on the file and, keeping your finger pressed down on the mouse button, drag the file over to the 3½ Floppy [A:] drive icon in the left pane. When the drive icon becomes highlighted release the button. A dialogue box shows the copy operation in progress.

Watch out
Remember that dragging a file from one drive to another results in two copies of that file: the original on the source drive and a copy on the destination drive.
If you drag a file to another location on the same drive, the file will simply move to the new location, without a copy being made. To create two copies of a file within a drive, use the Copy and Paste commands in the Edit menu.

To copy a file onto your hard disk open **Windows Explorer** from the **Start** menu (see previous Step 1).

► BEFORE YOU START

Bright idea
*Save yourself time by copying or moving several files at the same time. Press the **Ctrl** key and, keeping it pressed down, click on each of the files or folders. Release the **Ctrl** key and move or copy them as usual.*

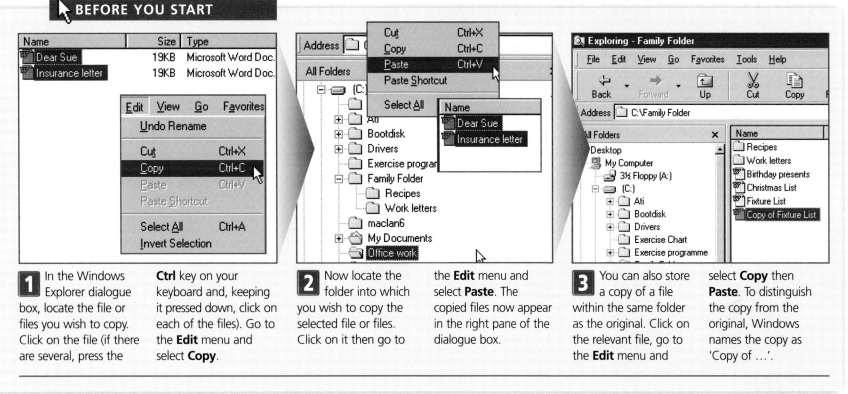

1 In the Windows Explorer dialogue box, locate the file or files you wish to copy. Click on the file (if there are several, press the **Ctrl** key on your keyboard and, keeping it pressed down, click on each of the files). Go to the **Edit** menu and select **Copy**.

2 Now locate the folder into which you wish to copy the selected file or files. Click on it then go to the **Edit** menu and select **Paste**. The copied files now appear in the right pane of the dialogue box.

3 You can also store a copy of a file within the same folder as the original. Click on the relevant file, go to the **Edit** menu and select **Copy** then **Paste**. To distinguish the copy from the original, Windows names the copy as 'Copy of …'.

Relocating files

Just as with a conventional paper filing system, it will often be necessary to move your files and folders to more suitable locations. Windows Explorer helps you do this. Click on the file or folder then, keeping your finger pressed down on the mouse button, drag the file or folder over to its new location. When the destination folder is highlighted, release the mouse button. The file or folder will then move.

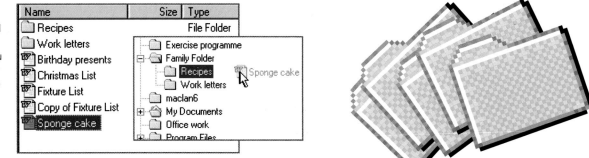

Maximising disk space

How to make the most of the space on your computer

Watch out
If you intend to delete (or restore) a folder from the Recycle Bin, remember that Windows will delete (or restore) the entire contents of the folder, not just the file you are interested in. Be sure you want to do this before proceeding.

Ensuring that your computer works efficiently means organising your folders and files effectively and using the available storage space properly.

As you create files and folders you will use more and more hard-disk space. This won't be a problem initially but, as the hard disk fills up, your computer may slow down as it searches for the correct file or folder, or performs a task. You will also find it more difficult to install new programs.

Deleting out-of-date folders and files, and uninstalling old software, will free up disk space, allowing your PC to run smoothly.

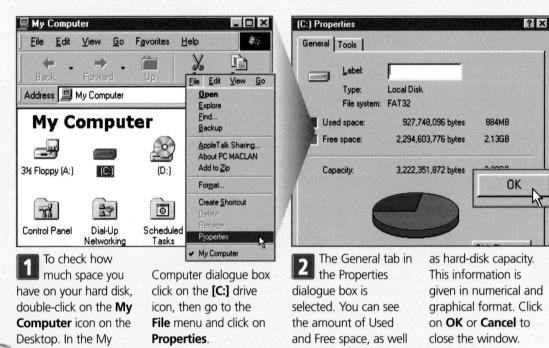

1 To check how much space you have on your hard disk, double-click on the **My Computer** icon on the Desktop. In the My Computer dialogue box click on the **[C:]** drive icon, then go to the **File** menu and click on **Properties**.

2 The General tab in the Properties dialogue box is selected. You can see the amount of Used and Free space, as well as hard-disk capacity. This information is given in numerical and graphical format. Click on **OK** or **Cancel** to close the window.

How much space do I need?

To keep your computer working efficiently, it's important that you keep a minimum of 100Mb of hard-disk space free. If you want to install new software, check how much disk space the software requires.

To do this, insert the software CD, set up the installation and look for the screen that lets you know how much space is required. If you don't have enough space available, quit the installation by following the on-screen instructions.

> *To delete files or folders, first go to the **Start** menu, select **Programs** and click on **Windows Explorer**.*

DELETING FILES

> *If you send a file to the Recycle Bin by mistake, Windows allows you to restore it to its original location.*

RESTORING FILES

1 Click on the file or folder you wish to delete. Go to the **File** menu and select **Delete**, or press the **Delete** key. A prompt box asks you to confirm your command. Click **No** to cancel or **Yes** to send the files or folders to the Recycle Bin on your Desktop.

2 Files in the Recycle Bin continue to take up space until the Bin is emptied. To completely remove an item from your computer, double-click on the **Recycle Bin**, click on the file, go to the **File** menu and select **Delete**. You will be asked to confirm your choice.

The Recycle Bin has a useful safety net if you make a mistake in deleting an item. To rescue a file from the bin, double-click on the **Recycle Bin** Desktop icon, click on the file, go to the **File** menu and select **Restore**. The item is then sent back to its original location.

Empty your bin
If you want to empty the Recycle Bin completely, go to the **File** menu and select **Empty Recycle Bin**. Confirm the command at the prompt.
An even quicker way in Windows 98 is to click on the blue text on the left-hand side of the Recycle Bin window.

Bright idea
To remove program files, use the special Uninstalling function described on page 56. Do not throw them in the Recycle Bin.

Tidying your hard disk

Learn how to uninstall software to create space on your PC

Over time, your PC's hard disk may become clogged up with programs you no longer use. Removing them is often the best way to create space on your hard disk and ensure it continues to run smoothly.

It is essential that programs are removed completely. Simply dropping them into the Recycle Bin is like pulling up a weed and leaving the roots behind.

Get it right

To ensure effective removal, some programs come with their own uninstall facility, located in the program folder. For the many that do not, use the Add/Remove Programs function in Windows.

The steps here are a guide only, as each uninstalling process is unique.

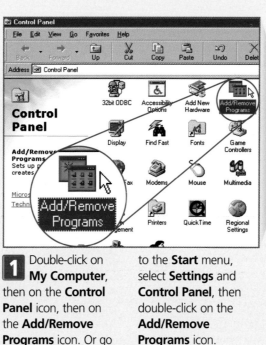

1 Double-click on **My Computer**, then on the **Control Panel** icon, then on the **Add/Remove Programs** icon. Or go to the **Start** menu, select **Settings** and **Control Panel**, then double-click on the **Add/Remove Programs** icon.

2 The Add/Remove Programs Properties dialogue box appears, with the Install/Uninstall tab selected. A list of all the programs that can be removed using this process is shown in a panel. Scroll through and click on the one you want to remove.

Watch out

Before uninstalling any programs, check that no-one else in the family wants to keep them. Then close down all active programs before starting the uninstall process.

Specialist uninstalling software

Some programs do not come with an uninstall option which means Windows will not put them into its Add/Remove Programs list. Other programs may be listed but then throw up problems while you are trying to uninstall them.

To deal with these programs, consider buying some of the specialist uninstalling software available. Most of this software is inexpensive and can sometimes be obtained as shareware (software distributed free for a trial period).

Bright idea
Before you uninstall any software, back up any related data that you wish to keep, and ensure that you still have the original installation disks or CD in case you want to reinstall the program later. If you have lost the originals, back up the programs on to a disk.

When you uninstall a program the Add/Remove facility may not remove shortcuts you have made to it in the Start menu. You can do this separately yourself.

▶ Removing shortcuts

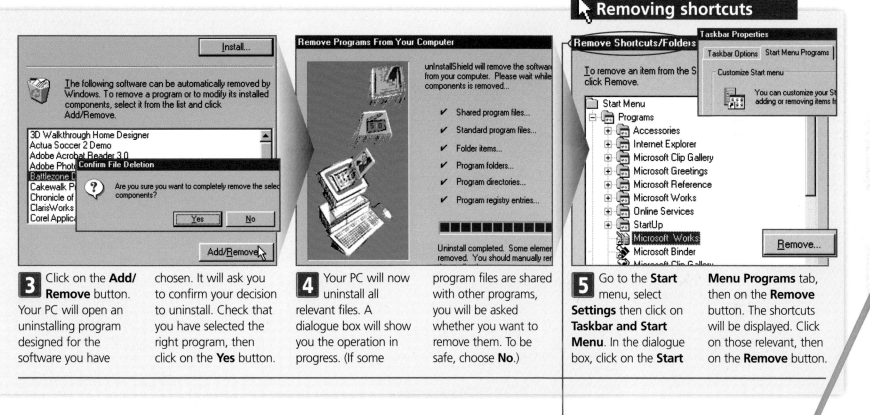

Install...

The following software can be automatically removed by Windows. To remove a program or to modify its installed components, select it from the list and click Add/Remove.

3D Walkthrough Home Designer
Actua Soccer 2 Demo
Adobe Acrobat Reader 3.0
Adobe Phot
Battlezone L
Cakewalk P
Chronicle of
ClarisWorks
Corel Applica

Confirm File Deletion

Are you sure you want to completely remove the selected components?

Yes   No

Add/Remove

Remove Programs From Your Computer

unInstallShield will remove the software from your computer. Please wait while components is removed...

✔ Shared program files...
✔ Standard program files...
✔ Folder items...
✔ Program folders...
✔ Program directories...
✔ Program registry entries...

Uninstall completed. Some element removed. You should manually re

Remove Shortcuts/Folders

To remove an item from the S click Remove.

Start Menu
Programs
Accessories
Internet Explorer
Microsoft Clip Gallery
Microsoft Greetings
Microsoft Reference
Microsoft Works
Online Services
StartUp
Microsoft Works
Microsoft Binder
Microsoft Clip Gallery

Taskbar Properties

Taskbar Options | Start Menu Programs

Customize Start menu

You can customize your St adding or removing items fr

Remove...

3 Click on the **Add/ Remove** button. Your PC will open an uninstalling program designed for the software you have

chosen. It will ask you to confirm your decision to uninstall. Check that you have selected the right program, then click on the **Yes** button.

4 Your PC will now uninstall all relevant files. A dialogue box will show you the operation in progress. (If some

program files are shared with other programs, you will be asked whether you want to remove them. To be safe, choose **No**.)

5 Go to the **Start** menu, select **Settings** then click on **Taskbar and Start Menu**. In the dialogue box, click on the **Start**

Menu Programs tab, then on the **Remove** button. The shortcuts will be displayed. Click on those relevant, then on the **Remove** button.

Deleting other shortcuts
You may have placed shortcuts in other areas of your hard disk. To remove them, click on the **Start Menu Programs** tab in the Taskbar Properties dialogue box, then click the **Advanced** button. Windows Explorer will open. Search through it for other shortcuts you want to remove. Right-click on any you find, then click on **Delete** from the pop-up menu.

Exploring - Programs

File Edit View Go Favorites Tools Help

Back   Forward   Up   Cut

Address C:\WINDOWS\Start Menu\Programs

All Folders

Start Menu
Programs
Accessories
Internet Explorer

Accessories

Open
Quick View
Add to Zip

Send To

Cut
Copy

Create Shortcut
Delete

Understanding computer viruses

Take the right precautions to keep your computer healthy

Vigilance pays when it comes to viruses. Make sure you install an anti-virus program on your computer and run it regularly

Viruses are computer programs that are designed to cause harm rather than good. Once inside your PC they can cause all sorts of problems, from making unwanted messages appear on your screen, to causing programs to crash, or your printer to stop working. In very rare cases, they can even delete all the data on your hard disk.

There are several ways a virus can infiltrate your computer, the most frequent being from floppy disks. Once a floppy disk has caught a virus from one PC, it can pass the infection on to every computer that it is used in. Another common way of picking up viruses is by downloading infected software from the Internet.

Anti-virus software

But no matter how your computer catches a virus, you probably won't be aware of it until something goes wrong and damage has been done. However, you can take precautions and limit the risk of catching a virus.

The first step is to buy an anti-virus program, such as McAfee's VirusScan. It is also sensible to subscribe to an update service, so that your PC will be protected against new viruses. This is often free for a year or so.

Then it's a matter of using your common sense. Don't put a floppy disk in your computer without running your anti-virus software first. And set up a weekly routine for checking your hard disk.

How viruses infect your PC

Identifying the different sorts of virus, and knowing how they spread from one computer to another, will help you keep your PC infection-free.

TYPES OF VIRUSES

File virus

A file virus infects program files. Once the affected program is running, it can infect other programs on your hard drive or on a floppy disk inserted in the A: drive.

| Microsoft Access | Microsoft Binder | Microsoft Booksh... | Microsoft Excel |
| Microsoft Word Setup | Microsoft Word | MS Access Workgrou... | Mscreate |

	A	B
1		
2		
3	**January Bills**	
4		
5	Mortgage	£ 524.00
6	Loan	£ 131.00
7	Phone	£ 35.00
8	Gas	£ 26.00

Macro virus

A macro virus infects individual documents. It affects files created in programs that use macro programming language, such as Microsoft Office's Word and Excel programs. The most common macro virus is known as Concept. Once the Concept virus infects your computer, it clings to the 'save' operation, passing on the infection to each and every document you save.

Boot and partition sector viruses

Boot and partition sector viruses infect the system software; that is, the special parts of the hard disk that enable your computer to start, or 'boot' up. These viruses may prevent you getting your computer working at all. They work by removing your PC's start-up instructions and replacing them with their own set of instructions. You may need specialist help if your computer catches this type of virus.

THE WAYS VIRUSES ARE SPREAD

Floppy disk

Always be wary of floppy disks as they are made to move files or programs between computers. The more machines that a disk is used on, the greater the chances of the disk picking up a virus and passing it on. Jaz and Zip disks can carry viruses in the same way as a floppy disk.

3½ Floppy (A:)

E-mail

Despite rumours to the contrary, you cannot catch a virus by simply opening and reading e-mail messages. However, be wary of opening a file attached to an e-mail as the file itself may carry a virus. As a general rule, do not open up files attached to unsolicited e-mail.

CD-ROM

You are safe with a CD-ROM (except in the extremely unlikely event that it was made with a virus). 'ROM' stands for Read Only Memory, which means it will not accept viruses – or, indeed, any other kind of information. However, with recordable or rewritable CDs you need to take the same precautions as with a floppy disk.

Wkssteccd4 (D:)

Internet

Don't download software of dubious origin from the Internet. Use a reputable company, such as Corel, Norton, Microsoft or McAfee.

Watch out

Be careful when buying software on a disk. Ensure it comes from a reputable source and that the packaging has not been tampered with. If the disk has been used there is a chance that it carries a virus. Remember, pirated software is illegal and greatly increases the chances of catching viruses.

Key word

Computer bug *A computer bug is different to a virus in that bugs are accidents or mistakes in programming, rather than programs specifically designed to cause harm.*

Safeguarding your hard disk

Creating a rescue disk will give you a safety net against hard disk failure

There is a very slim chance that one day your PC will refuse to start up. This is one of the most worrying computing problems that you can encounter, and potentially the most difficult to solve, because you need to get the computer to start up before you can fix the fault and retrieve your work.

A start-up problem may occur if your hardware sustains physical damage. But it is more likely that your computer has failed to access the files it needs to get itself up and running (see page 332 for reasons why this might happen). You can prepare for this eventuality of disk failure by creating a 'rescue' disk.

Helping your PC to start

The rescue disk contains the files your computer needs to operate at the most basic level, known as DOS. Normally, your computer would access these files on its hard disk. When it fails to do so, it can use the files on the rescue disk instead.

As long as your PC will start with the DOS system, a computer specialist should be able to retrieve your files, diagnose and fix hard-disk problems, and access your Windows CD-ROM for extra help.

Creating a rescue disk is easy – it takes less than five minutes. All you need is one floppy disk onto which you can load the essential files.

Bright idea
Even if you manage to get things going again with a start-up disk, you may have lost files which are irreplaceable. It's at this point that you will wish you had made a recent back-up. For instructions on how to back up your files, see pages 52 and 359.

Once you have started your PC with a rescue disk you can attempt to retrieve files yourself or have a computer specialist talk you through the process.

MAKE A RESCUE DISK

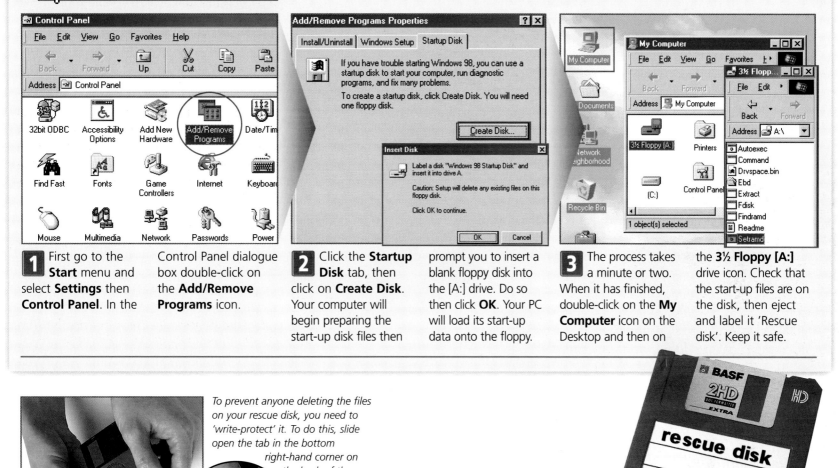

1 First go to the **Start** menu and select **Settings** then **Control Panel**. In the

Control Panel dialogue box double-click on the **Add/Remove Programs** icon.

2 Click the **Startup Disk** tab, then click on **Create Disk**. Your computer will begin preparing the start-up disk files then

prompt you to insert a blank floppy disk into the [A:] drive. Do so then click **OK**. Your PC will load its start-up data onto the floppy.

3 The process takes a minute or two. When it has finished, double-click on the **My Computer** icon on the Desktop and then on

the 3½ **Floppy [A:]** drive icon. Check that the start-up files are on the disk, then eject and label it 'Rescue disk'. Keep it safe.

To prevent anyone deleting the files on your rescue disk, you need to 'write-protect' it. To do this, slide open the tab in the bottom right-hand corner on the back of the floppy disk.

Defragmenting and scanning the hard disk

How to help your computer to perform at its best

Taking care of your computer means ensuring that the hard disk is working at its optimum level. Defragmenting and scanning the hard disk on a regular basis will help. Defragmenting makes sure large files can be stored in such a way that access to them is as easy and quick as possible. Scanning checks the hard disk and floppy disks for errors.

Windows has two useful tools – Disk Defragmenter and ScanDisk – that carry out these tasks. You need to use the tools every week or so. Windows 98 has a further function, called a Maintenance Wizard, which launches Disk Defragmenter and ScanDisk as part of an automatic maintenance schedule.

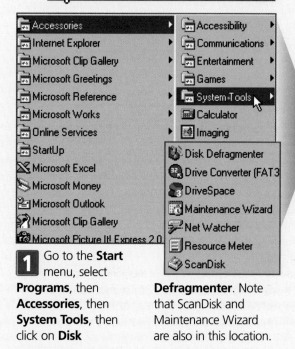

It can take up to half an hour to defragment your hard disk. Don't set the process in motion if you haven't got this time to spare.

DISK DEFRAGMENTING

1 Go to the **Start** menu, select **Programs**, then **Accessories**, then **System Tools**, then click on **Disk Defragmenter**. Note that ScanDisk and Maintenance Wizard are also in this location.

 Close-up
When you save a large file, your computer will often split it up into fragments and store it in different locations on the hard disk. Your computer can still find the file but it takes longer to do so. Disk Defragmenter rearranges the fragments of a large file so that they are stored next to each other. This makes it easier and quicker for your computer to access files.

Close-up
Whenever your computer has not been shut down properly, ScanDisk runs automatically the next time you switch it on.

Use ScanDisk to check your hard disk and floppy disks for errors. The process takes a minute or two.

SCANDISK

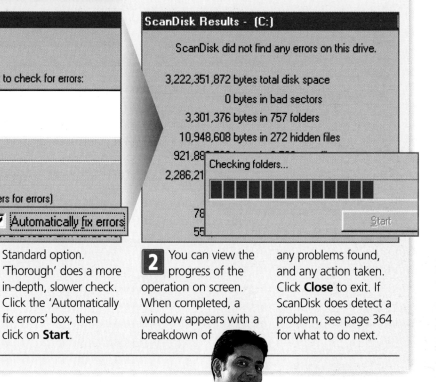

Select Drive

Which drive do you want to defragment?

Drive C	Physical drive
Drive A	Removable drive
Drive C	Physical drive

Copyright © 1988-1992 Symantec Corporation
Intel Application Launch Accelerator

Defragmenting Drive C

OK

■■■
10% Complete

ScanDisk - (C:)

Select the drive(s) you want to check for errors:

- 3½ Floppy (A:)
- [C:]

Type of test
- ● Standard
  (checks files and folders for errors)
- ○ Thorough
  (performs Standard t...

☑ Automatically fix errors

ScanDisk Results - (C:)

ScanDisk did not find any errors on this drive.

3,222,351,872 bytes total disk space

0 bytes in bad sectors

3,301,376 bytes in 757 folders

10,948,608 bytes in 272 hidden files

921,88...
2,286,21...

78...
55...

Checking folders...

■■■■■■■■■■■■

Start

2 In the Select Drive dialogue box choose which drive to defragment. Click **OK** to start the process. You can view the progress of the operation on screen.

1 Open ScanDisk (see previous Step 1) and click on the drive you wish to scan. In the 'Type of test' section click the Standard option. 'Thorough' does a more in-depth, slower check. Click the 'Automatically fix errors' box, then click on **Start**.

2 You can view the progress of the operation on screen. When completed, a window appears with a breakdown of any problems found, and any action taken. Click **Close** to exit. If ScanDisk does detect a problem, see page 364 for what to do next.

Let the Wizard help

Windows 98 allows you to schedule hard-disk maintenance automatically. To program your Maintenance Wizard, which will run Disk Defragmenter, ScanDisk and Disk Cleanup, follow these steps:
- Open Maintenance Wizard through the Start menu.

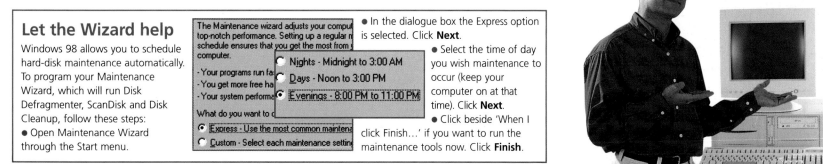

The Maintenance wizard adjusts your compu... top-notch performance. Setting up a regular m... schedule ensures that you get the most from ... computer.

- Your programs run fa...
- You get more free ha...
- Your system performa...

What do you want to ...
- ● Express - Use the most common maintena...
- ○ Custom - Select each maintenance settin...

- Nights - Midnight to 3:00 AM
- Days - Noon to 3:00 PM
- ● Evenings - 8:00 PM to 11:00 PM

- In the dialogue box the Express option is selected. Click **Next**.
- Select the time of day you wish maintenance to occur (keep your computer on at that time). Click **Next**.
- Click beside 'When I click Finish...' if you want to run the maintenance tools now. Click **Finish**.

Caring for your equipment

Cleaning hardware regularly will prevent problems in the future

Your computer needs simple but regular maintenance to stay in good condition. Problems such as your mouse seizing up, or the keys on your keyboard becoming stuck, can be easily avoided if you clean your equipment regularly. And keeping your work space clean and tidy will create a more pleasant environment for everyone to work in.

Simple measures include making a rule that you don't drink or eat at or near your PC, and that you protect it with a suitable dust cover when not in use. When cleaning, spare a few minutes to check that those 'spaghetti' wires are out of harm's way, too.

Kit yourself out

Have a cleaning routine that you carry out once a month. As with any type of cleaning, ensure that you have the correct materials for the job. Computer stockists offer a variety of cleaning products, but a multi-purpose cleaning kit is probably the best choice for the home user. A typical kit comprises PC wipes, PC buds, cleaning cloths, cleaning fluid and a cleaning card. You should also consider buying a dust spray.

Before you start cleaning, make sure that you turned your equipment off at the wall socket – it is never safe to use fluids with electricity.

Dust and stains on your screen can make it more difficult to look at

Watch out
Never use ordinary household spray polish or liquid spray cleaners on your keyboard. If liquid gets between or under the keys, it can damage the keyboard.

Bright idea
Before cleaning your keyboard, turn it upside down over a bin and shake it gently. Much of the debris that has slipped between and under the keys will fall out.

Cleaning your hardware

A few minutes of light maintenance every month is all that's required to keep your machine running at peak performance and in showroom condition.

The keyboard

Because your keyboard is an exposed component of your computer, dirt will inevitably accumulate between and under its keys. To remove it, wipe the keys with special cleaning buds or use dust spray to blow away dust. If you have them, work cleaning cards dipped in cleaning solution between the keys.

The printer

Check the paper paths of your printer to ensure they are clean and free from ink or toner. Use wipes to remove any spillage, but be careful not to get toner on your hands or clothes as it is difficult to remove. Don't touch the printing mechanism itself unless the print manual gives cleaning advice on this. Perform a print test (consult your print manual for instructions) to check on the ink or toner level. Replace print cartridges or toner as required.

Floppy and CD drives

Keeping your floppy disk and CD-ROM drives clean ensures that programs and files can be accessed smoothly and are less prone to data loss.

Specialist floppy and CD cleaning disks are available from computer stockists. Simply insert the appropriate cleaning disk and follow the on-screen instructions.

The monitor

It is important that you keep your monitor screen in pristine condition. Using a dirty, stained screen leads to unnecessary eyestrain. Use a PC wipe to keep the screen clean, clear and safe – the non-smear varieties are best for the job.

The mouse

Follow this simple routine to keep your mouse running smoothly and trouble-free.
1 Turn your mouse upside down and wipe the base firmly with a special PC wipe.
2 Twist the mouse-ball cover so that it opens and the ball falls out into your hand.
3 Clean the mouse ball by wiping it with a lint-free cloth. Dab it with sticky tape to pick up any dust or dirt particles that have accumulated on it.
4 Using a PC bud or your fingernail, remove dust and fluff from inside the mouse ball socket, concentrating on the three rollers that make contact with the ball.
5 Finally, return the ball to its socket and twist the mouse ball cover back into place.

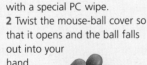

Welcome to the world of Windows

Fast and flexible – your PC's operating system lets you use your PC with confidence

To drive your car you don't need to know the intimate workings of an engine. It helps should you break down, but it's not essential. So it is with Windows. You don't need to know the layers of code that make it run, you just need to know the best way to drive it, while getting the most benefit.

Windows gets its name from the fact that every program – word processor, database, spreadsheet – operates inside its own window on your PC's Desktop.

Keeping your house in order

Windows is an 'operating system', the set of instructions which make sure your computer runs smoothly. It acts as a housekeeper, by keeping files in order, and allows your PC to perform basic jobs, such as printing.

You can personalise Windows to suit your needs by, for example, giving your computer its own wallpaper (a special picture or pattern that covers your Desktop).

Windows gives you a choice of wallpapers with which to decorate your Desktop

Key word
Start button This is where you can quickly access key functions, such as customising Windows controls. Click on the **Start** button and a menu pops up. Select an item by clicking on it.

Advances in Windows
Since Windows first appeared, it has been updated to keep pace with new technology. Windows 98 is the latest version but Windows 95 is still widely used.

The Desktops for each version are similar, with both containing a My Documents folder, Recycle Bin, Start button and Taskbar. Both versions can only run software compliant with Windows.

The main difference is that Windows 98 offers easy Internet access, through the Address and Explorer bars. The Web browser-like Back and Forward buttons (below) let you navigate through folders easily.

Windows 98 lets you connect to Internet sites by typing a Web address into the Address box. You have to be connected to do this.

*By clicking on the **View** menu, then **Explorer bar**, Windows 98 lets you quickly access Internet search engines and favourite Web sites.*

Changing face of PCs
In the days of DOS – the PC operating system before Windows – the way to print a file, say, was by typing in intricate commands in computer language (above).

```
C:\>printletter
```

The birth of Windows 3.1, then Windows 95 and 98, literally changed the face of PCs. The visual nature of Windows lets you see exactly what you are doing on your PC's Desktop.

The mouse became the new steering wheel. It allows you to move and organise files by picking them up and dropping them into the folders which you have created and named.

The Start button and Taskbar introduced in Windows 95 meant that you could find files, open programs and use Windows' many tools in just a few moves of the mouse. Windows 95 also included Windows Explorer (above), a valuable tool that lets you see and manage your files and drives in one window. It is still used in Windows 98.

Bright idea
Help is always at hand. Click the **Start** button and select **Help** from the pop-up menu, or use the Help drop-down menus (available in almost every window). Alternatively, simply press the **F1** key on your keyboard to get assistance relevant to the program you are using.

Getting to grips with windows

Organise your Desktop for maximum efficiency and ease of use

Your computer's Desktop is much like a conventional desk in that it holds files, folders, documents and tools. These are all represented on your PC by icons.

By double-clicking on any icon you will open it. The opened icon – whatever it represents – will appear as a separate window on your Desktop, and its size, shape and position can all be set by you.

Having several windows open on your Desktop at once can be just as confusing as having a pile of papers scattered all over your desk. But there are ways to keep your work area tidy and boost your efficiency.

Controlling the size of windows
The buttons in the top right-hand corner of a window help control its appearance.

The Minimise button
Click on the **Minimise** button to shrink the window to a button on the Taskbar. Clicking on the Taskbar button will restore the window to the Desktop.

The Maximise button
Click on the **Maximise** button to expand the window to fill the whole screen. When a window is maximised, the button changes to a Restore button. Click on this to restore the window to its original size.

The Close button
Click on the **Close** button to close a window or program.

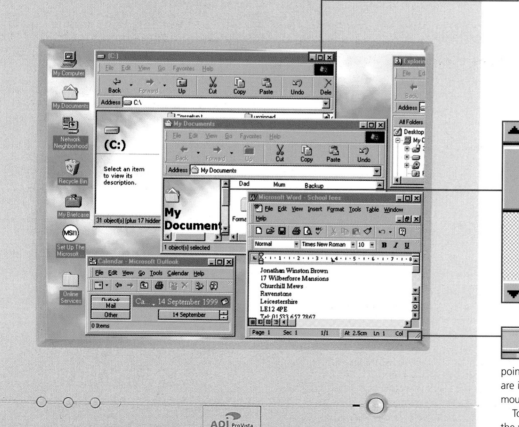

Scroll bars
Often, you won't be able to see all the contents of a window. When this happens, scroll bars appear to the right of, and/or bottom of, the window.

To view the window's contents, click on the arrows at each end of the scroll bar, or click on the slider itself and, keeping your finger pressed down on the mouse button, drag it along.

Resizing windows
To adjust the height or width of a window, click on any of the window's edges (the mouse pointer will change to a double-headed arrow when you are in position). Keeping your finger pressed down on the mouse button, drag the window in or out.

To resize the width and height at the same time, click on the window's corner and drag it diagonally.

Short cut
You may find it easier and quicker to maximise windows by double-clicking on the Title bar that runs across the top of them.

Bright idea
*If several windows are open and you need to see your Desktop, right-click on the **Taskbar** and click on **Minimise All Windows** from the pop-up menu. To restore the windows to your screen, click on **Undo Minimise All**.*

Arranging windows on your Desktop

Windows is extremely flexible when it comes to organising open folders and documents.

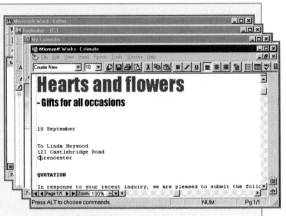

Working with windows

Ideally, it is best to have just one or two windows open on your screen at any one time. This not only keeps your Desktop tidy, but also makes it less likely that you will file documents in the wrong place.

Tiling your windows

You can arrange your windows so that you can see the contents of each one at the same time. Individual windows can be 'tiled' – that is, arranged in squares across your screen so that every open window is visible on the Desktop. (Think of a tiled wall or floor.)

Right-click on the **Taskbar** and select **Tile Vertically** or **Tile Horizontally**. Windows puts all your folders and open programs into a neat 'tiled' arrangement. To revert back to your former screen, right-click on the **Taskbar** and select **Undo Tile**.

Cascading windows

Another handy option is Cascade Windows, which arranges windows so that each one overlaps the one before, diagonally, from the top left-hand corner of your screen. This is useful if you have several windows open, as you will still be able to see the name of each one filed behind the other. Clicking on a cascaded window will bring it to the front of your stack.

To operate this function, right-click on the **Taskbar** then click on **Cascade Windows** from the pop-up menu. To revert back to your former screen, right-click on the **Taskbar** and select **Undo Cascade**.

Exploring with Windows

You can always see what's in a particular folder by double-clicking on it. But, to save you wading through a mass of folders to find a file, use Windows Explorer (go to the **Start** menu, select **Programs** then click on **Windows Explorer**).

This allows you to access all the contents of your PC from one window. The drives and folders appear in the left pane, while the contents of a selected folder or drive appear in the right pane. To select a folder, click on it.

Close-up
*To see what's behind a maximised window, press the **Alt** key and keep it pressed down. Now press the **Tab** key. Open windows appear as icons in a grey panel in the middle of your screen. Move along the icons by pressing the **Tab** key. When you release the keys the icon with the border around it opens up on screen.*

Personalising your Desktop

Decorate your PC to make it feel like part of the furniture

We all like to add individual touches to our houses. The colour that we paint our front door and the layout of our front gardens make us feel that our home truly belong to us. It is just as easy to put a personal stamp on Windows.

If, for instance, you don't particularly like the background colour or pattern of your Desktop – known as wallpaper – you can change it by selecting a different background from Windows' library of wallpapers. Options include red blocks, metal links and bubbles. You can easily change it again if you get bored with it.

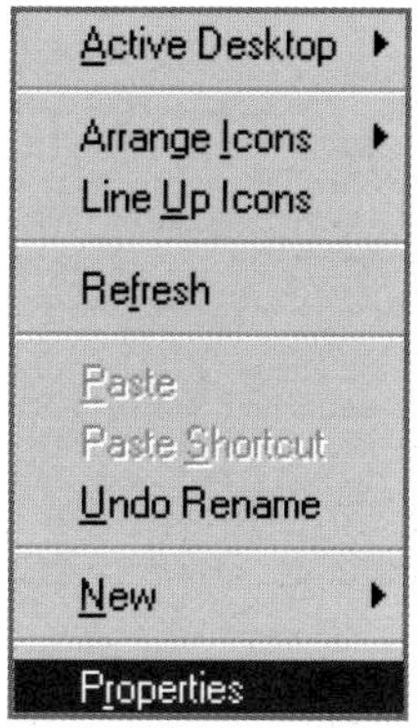

| Active Desktop ▶ |
| Arrange Icons ▶ |
| Line Up Icons |
| Refresh |
| Paste |
| Paste Shortcut |
| Undo Rename |
| New ▶ |
| Properties |

Wallpaper by design

To change your wallpaper, right-click anywhere on your Desktop and select **Properties** from the pop-up menu. In the Display Properties dialogue box the section headed 'Wallpaper' lets you choose from a list of wallpaper styles.

Scroll through the list, clicking on any that interest you to view them in the preview window. Click **Apply** to see them on the Desktop. When you've made your choice, click on it then click **OK**. If the image doesn't fit all your screen, go back into the Properties box and select the **Tile** option in the Display box to repeat the image over your Desktop. (In Windows 98 select **Stretch** to stretch the image across your screen.)

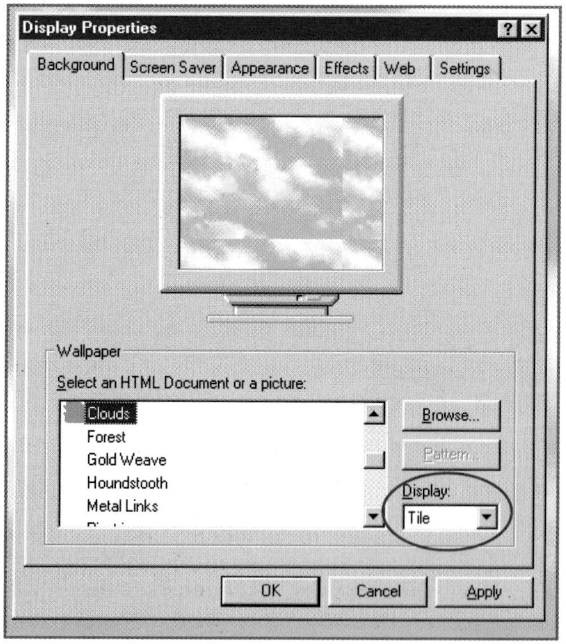

Display Properties

Background | Screen Saver | Appearance | Effects | Web | Settings

Wallpaper

Select an HTML Document or a picture:

Clouds
Forest
Gold Weave
Houndstooth
Metal Links

Browse...
Pattern...

Display:
Tile

OK | Cancel | Apply

Key word
Properties Nearly everything you see in Windows has its own properties, which give valuable information about your PC's resources and allow you to vary its settings. To see an item's properties, right-click on the object and select **Properties** from the pop-up menu.

Bright idea
To remind yourself of an important or amusing message or slogan, select the **Scrolling Marquee** screensaver. Type in your text and select a font, colour and style for it, along with the speed at which you wish it to travel across your screen.

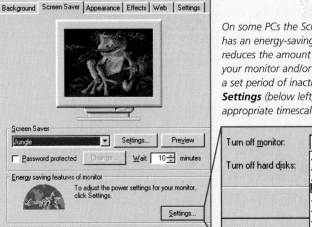

While you were away...

Screensavers appear when your PC is on but not in use. As well as being fun, they can also protect work from prying eyes.

To select a screensaver, right-click anywhere on the Desktop and select **Properties** from the pop-up menu. Click on the **Screen Saver** tab. Scroll through and select an option in the Screen Saver box. Click **Apply** to see it, then **OK** to set it. Set the length of time your PC waits before activating the screensaver in the Wait box.

*On some PCs the Screensaver tab has an energy-saving option that reduces the amount of power to your monitor and/or hard disk after a set period of inactivity. Click on **Settings** (below left) and select appropriate timescales from the list.*

More than just a Desktop

Themes is a feature that allows you to change wallpaper, colour schemes and sounds. It comes included with Windows 98 and as an optional extra with Windows 95.

To apply a theme, click the **Start** button, select **Settings**, and then click on **Control Panel**.

Double-click on the **Desktop Themes** icon. Scroll through and select a theme from the drop-down list at the top of the window. Click **Apply** to view it, then **OK**.

Setting passwords for users

If your PC has more than one user, each one can have his or her personalised version of Windows 98. This means they can access the PC without interfering with other users' settings. Each has their own wallpaper, document folders and Start menus. (Windows 95 does not have this full range of capabilities.)

Go to the **Start** menu, select **Settings**, then click on **Control Panel**. Double-click on the **Users** icon. A menu guides you, step by step. Enter a user name and password for each person who will need access to the computer.

Customising Windows controls

Tailor your computer's settings to make it work the way you want

When you are using your PC it's helpful to know that you can tailor Windows controls to suit your needs. For example, you can change the speed at which your mouse double-clicks, alter the size and shape of the mouse pointer, and change the appearance of your screen. Left-handed users can even swap the role of the mouse buttons.

Mouse settings

To customise your mouse settings, go to the **Start** menu, select **Settings** and click on **Control Panel**. In the Control Panel window double-click on the **Mouse** icon.

There are three tabs at the top of the Mouse Properties dialogue box – Buttons, Pointers and Motion.

Buttons allows left-handed users to swap the role of the mouse buttons; Pointers lets you choose a 'scheme', or style, for your on-screen pointer; and in Motion you can alter the speed at which your mouse pointer moves, choose whether it leaves a trail, and adjust the length of the trail.

If you are visually impaired, changing the shape and size of your mouse pointer will help you see it more clearly on screen

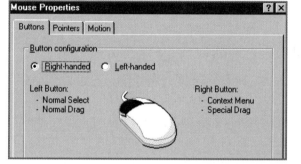

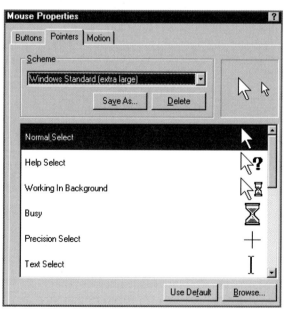

Bright idea
*Windows is aware of British Summer Time and can change the clock in spring and autumn. In the Date/Time Properties dialogue box click the **Time Zone** tab, then click in the 'Automatically adjust clock for daylight saving changes' box. Click **OK**.*

Date and time
The current time is displayed on the right-hand side of the Taskbar. To see the current date, place your mouse pointer over the time display. The date will pop up in a second.

To set the date or time, double-click on the Taskbar Clock. In the Date/Time Properties dialogue box, click on the relevant arrows to adjust the settings.

To set the time zone for your location, click the **Time Zone** tab in the Date/Time Properties box, then click on the arrow, scroll through and select your zone. Click **OK**.

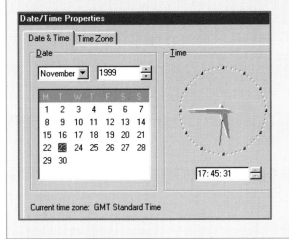

Accessibility Properties

Keyboard | Sound | Display | Mouse | General

StickyKeys
Use StickyKeys if you want to use Shift, Ctrl, or Alt key by pressing one key at a time.

☐ Use StickyKeys   Settings...

FilterKeys
Use FilterKeys if you want Windows to ignore brief or repeated keystrokes, or slow the repeat rate.

☐ Use FilterKeys   Settings...

ToggleKeys
Use ToggleKeys if you want to hear tones when pressing Caps Lock, Num Lock, and Scroll Lock.

☐ Use ToggleKeys   Settings...

Disability options in Windows
Windows offers help to users with disabilities. Go to the **Start** menu, select **Settings** and click on **Control Panel**. Double-click on the **Accessibility Options** icon. These are some of the options available:
- If you are visually impaired, select the high-contrast viewing mode (above right). Click on the **Display** tab, then click in the Use High Contrast box. Click **OK**.
- If you are hard of hearing, set your PC to send out visual warnings and notifications. Click on the **Sound** tab then click in the Use SoundSentry box. Next, click on **Settings** and select a warning from the 'Warning for windowed programs' box. Click **OK**. For SoundSentry to

*To prevent pressing the Caps Lock key and typing in your text in capital letters, use ToggleKeys, which will alert you with a warning sound. In the Accessibility Properties dialogue box click the **Keyboard** tab, then click in the Use ToggleKeys box. Finally, click **OK**.*

Control Panel

File Edit View Go Favorites Help

Back · Forward · Up   Cut Copy Paste Und

Address Control Panel

Control Panel

Accessibility Options
Changes accessibility options for your system.

32bit ODBC | Acce... Optio... | Add New... | Add/... Progr... | Date

Desk... Them... | Display | Find Fast | Fonts | Gan Cont

Inter... | Keyb... | Mail a... | Mode... | Mou

Multi | Netw | Pass | Power | Print

Microsoft Home

work, sound should not be assigned to the warning or notification you want to be alerted to. To disable sounds, click on the **Sounds** icon in the Control Panel. Click on the warning or notification in question from the Events list then, in the Sound Name box, scroll through and click on **None**. Click **Apply** and then **OK**.
- If you have trouble moving your mouse, clicking on the **Mouse** tab, then on the Use MouseKeys box, lets you use the numeric keypad on the right-hand side of your keyboard to move your mouse pointer.

Date/Time Properties

Date & Time | Time Zone

Date
November ▼ 1999

M	T	W	T	F	S	S
1	2	3	4	5	6	7
8	9	10	11	12	13	14
15	16	17	18	19	20	21
22	23	24	25	26	27	28
29	30					

Time

17: 45: 31

Current time zone: GMT Standard Time

Setting sounds
If your PC has a sound card (most new ones do) you can configure Windows to play any one of a number of built-in sounds.

Go to the **Start** menu, select **Settings** and click on **Control Panel**. Double-click on the **Sounds** icon then scroll through and click on an event from the Events list. Now click on the arrow to the right of the Sound Name box, scroll through and click on your preferred sound (for no sound, click on **None**). Click **OK**.

This sound (right) plays each time Windows opens.

Events:
Select
Show Toolbar Band
Start Windows
SystemDefault
Power Management
Critical Battery Alarm

Sound
Name:
Jungle Windows Start ▼

Preview:

Browse...   Details...

Close-up
*Windows 98 lets you decide how you open folders on your Desktop (with one click or two), and whether folders open within the same window or separate windows. Double-click on **My Computer**, go to the **View** menu and select **Folder Options**. In the dialogue box click beside 'Custom, based on setting you choose' and on **Settings**. Now click beside the settings you want and click **OK**.*

Create your own shortcuts

Fine-tune the way you work on your PC, and save yourself time and energy

Once you are familiar with the basic workings of Windows and you have a reasonable understanding of which programs and commands you use most often, you can begin using shortcuts to help you launch or activate them quickly.

You can create simple shortcuts to folders, documents and to almost anything else, including a printer, program and a drive. These can then be activated directly from the Desktop or Start button. You can also arrange for programs to launch when you start up Windows.

The Start menu

Being able to launch programs from the Start button is a real time-saver. To add extra programs to the menu, right-click on the Taskbar and click on **Properties** in the pop-up menu. In the Taskbar Properties dialogue box, click on the **Start Menu Programs** tab then click on **Add**. In the Create Shortcut dialogue box click on the **Browse** button. In the Browse dialogue box locate the relevant program by clicking on the arrow to the right of the 'Look in' box, scrolling through and clicking on relevant folders to open them. When you have found the program, click on it then click **Open**.

In the following dialogue boxes click on **Next**, **Next**, then **Finish**. Finally, click on **OK** in the Taskbar Properties dialogue box. The program will then appear in the Programs folder in the Start menu.

You can add a program to the Start menu by dragging the program icon onto it. The shortcut will then appear at the top of the Start menu, not in your Programs folder.

Desktop shortcuts from Start

Programs on the Start menu can be accessed even faster in Windows 98 by turning them into Desktop shortcuts. Go to the **Start** menu and select **Programs**. Right-click on the relevant program and, keeping the button pressed down, drag

the program onto the Desktop. A pop-up menu will appear. Click on **Create Shortcut(s) Here**. A shortcut icon will appear on your Desktop.

Bright idea
*In Windows 98, create a shortcut to the Internet. Right-click on the Taskbar, select **Toolbars** from the pop-up menu, then **Address**. Type a Web address into the bar that appears, and Windows will launch Internet Explorer and take you to the site.*

Create Desktop shortcuts for programs and documents

The quickest way to access programs and documents is directly from your Desktop. Creating Desktop shortcuts takes just a few seconds but saves hours of time.

Program shortcuts

To make a program shortcut in Windows, right-click anywhere on the Desktop. In the pop-up menu select **New** then click on **Shortcut**. In the Create Shortcut dialogue box click on the **Browse** button. In the Browse dialogue box locate the relevant program by clicking on the arrow to the right of the 'Look in' box, scrolling through and clicking on relevant folders to open them. When you have found the program, click on it then click **Open**. In the following two dialogue boxes click on **Next** then **Finish**.

The shortcut icon, which looks like the program icon but with a small black arrow on top, will appear on your Desktop.

To get rid of a shortcut from your Desktop, click on it and drag it onto the Recycle Bin. Don't worry that you are discarding the program itself, as the shortcut icon is simply a link to the main program which is safely stored in Program Files folder.

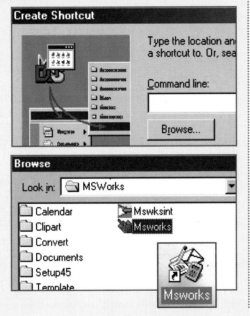

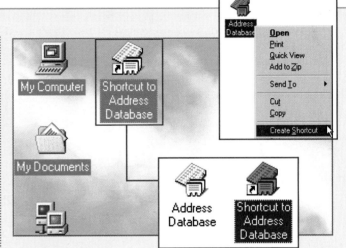

Desktop documents

If there are documents that you consult regularly, such as your address list, it's worth creating Desktop shortcuts to them.

To save you having to click through a series of folders every time you want to check an address, open the folder that the database is stored in, right-click on the **Address Database** icon and click on **Create Shortcut** from the pop-up menu. A shortcut file will appear in the same folder that contains Address Database. Click and drag it onto your Desktop. Double-click on it every time you want to access it.

The ultimate time-saver...

You can arrange for an often-used program to launch whenever Windows starts. Go to the **Start** menu, select **Programs** then click on **Windows Explorer**. Locate the program in the right pane then right-click on it. From the pop-up menu click on **Create Shortcut**. The shortcut icon appears in the right pane.

In the left pane of Explorer, click on the '**+**' sign beside the Windows folder, then the '**+**' beside the Start Menu folder and then on the '**+**' beside the Programs folder. Now, in the right pane, click on the program shortcut and, keeping the mouse button pressed down, drag it into the Start Up folder.

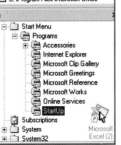

Quick keyboard commands

Save yourself time by using 'hot-keys' instead of your mouse

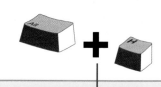

Nearly all the actions or commands you perform with your mouse can also be done by pressing 'hot-keys' – these are single keys or a combination of keys on your keyboard. For example, in Microsoft Word you can access the spelling and grammar facility by pressing one of the 'F', or function, keys at the top of your keyboard, or print by pressing the Ctrl and 'P' keys at the same time.

Using the hot-keys is quicker than using your mouse, especially if you do a lot of work from the keyboard, such as word-processing.

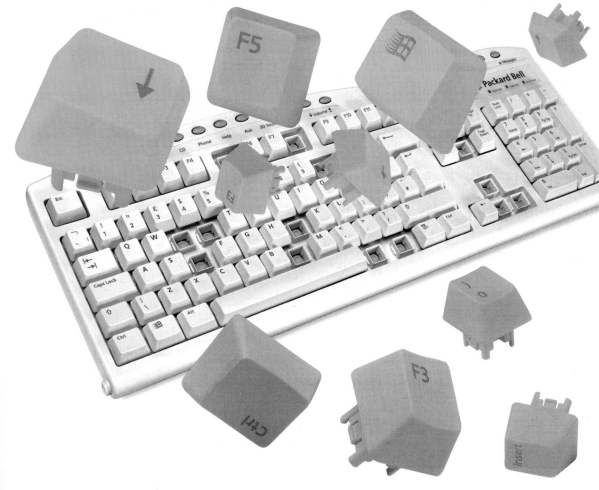

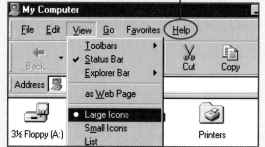

Selecting main menu options

The main menu bars in Windows and programs such as Word and Works look very similar. They contain common menus such as File, Edit and View. If you look carefully at the menu names you'll notice that one letter is underlined. These underlined letters indicate the keyboard shortcut that can be used to open the menus.

Instead of moving your mouse pointer over the menu name and clicking on it to open it, press the **Alt** key (immediately to the left of the Space-bar on the keyboard) and the underlined letter simultaneously.

In the My Computer window (see above) pressing **Alt** and '**F**' will open the **File** menu; **Alt** and '**E**' will open the **Edit** menu; and **Alt** and '**V**' the **View** menu.

Short cut
Most new keyboards have a Windows key – found between the Ctrl and Alt keys. Press it to open the Start menu and use the cursor keys to move around the menu items. Press the **Enter** *key to open a highlighted option or program.*

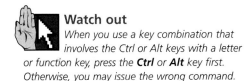

Watch out
*When you use a key combination that involves the Ctrl or Alt keys with a letter or function key, press the **Ctrl** or **Alt** key first. Otherwise, you may issue the wrong command.*

Key word
***Keyboard shortcut** This describes a key combination that replaces a mouse command. It can take the form of pressing just one key, such as a function key, or several keys, such as **Ctrl** + **F4**.*

How to select menu bar options

To select a menu from the menu bar in Windows or in a program, press the **F10** key. The first menu button – File – will become depressed. To move along the menu bar to access other menus, press the 'right' arrow key (one of four arrow, or cursor, keys at the bottom of your keyboard). The menu buttons will become depressed as you move through them.

To open a menu, select the menu name then press the 'down' arrow key. When the menu opens press the 'down' key again to move through the menu items. As you do so, each item becomes highlighted. Press **Enter** to select a highlighted item.

Using the function keys

The function keys along the top of your keyboard perform pre-assigned duties, or functions.

Press **F1** to access a program's Help facility. This helps you to solve software problems.

From the Window's Desktop, press **F3** to access the Find: All Files dialogue box. This allows you to search your hard disk to find a file.

You can use function keys in combination with other keys. To close a window or program, for example, press the **Alt** key and the **F4** key at the same time.

Moving around the Desktop

You can use keyboard shortcuts to move around your Desktop. For example, click on the **My Computer** icon then press the arrow keys to move around your various Desktop items (they become highlighted when selected). Press **Enter** to open a selected icon.

The same principle can be applied inside folders. Double-click on the **My Documents** icon then press the arrow keys to move around the folder's contents, pressing **Enter** when you want to open a file or folder.

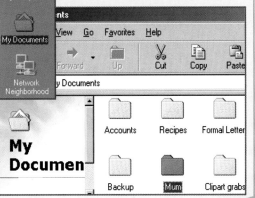

Important command keys

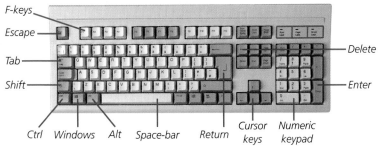

F-keys
Escape
Tab
Shift
Ctrl   Windows   Alt   Space-bar   Return   Cursor keys   Numeric keypad
Delete
Enter

Becoming a dab hand

If you have more than one window open, you can bring each one to the front of your Desktop using the **Alt** + **Tab** keys. Press **Alt** then **Tab** and a bar will appear with icons representing all the windows you have open. The uppermost window's icon will have an outline around it. To move to the next icon, press the **Tab** key. To bring that window to the front of your Desktop release the **Alt** key.

Windows built-in programs

Learn about these mini-applications and they'll soon become indispensable

Windows comes with a number of programs, known as Accessories. These are really useful and – even better – they don't cost a penny extra.

If you need to write a letter that can be read by computers that don't run Windows, you can use the Notepad text editor. If you have bought a scanner and want to 'touch up' or repair old photographs, you can experiment with Paint or Imaging. Once you familiarise yourself with Windows' accessory programs, you will be surprised how often you use them.

Where to find accessory programs

To find Windows' accessory programs, go to the **Start** menu, select **Programs** then select **Accessories**. A menu with the accessory programs will drop down.

These include a calculator, Imaging and Paint for image editing, and Notepad and WordPad for basic word processing.

The Accessories menu also contains other useful tools and facilities. For example, there are Internet tools to connect you to the Internet, and multimedia facilities to help you play video clips.

Bright idea
*If you're playing a music CD in your CD-ROM drive, you can view the track list through Windows Explorer. Go to the **Start** menu, select **Programs** and click on **Windows Explorer**. Double-click on **Audio CD [D:]** in the left pane. The track list appears in the right pane. Double-click on a track to play it.*

Close-up
*Notepad will only let you work in one font and font size per document. Go to the **Edit** menu and click on **Set Font**. Select a font and size. These will then be applied to the whole document.*

Everything you need from a word processor

WordPad is an effective word processor that has

many features in common with Word 97. It includes a toolbar that lets you do tasks quickly, has a good selection of fonts and font sizes and even lets you format text. The only important function it lacks is a spellchecker.

Notepad is far more basic. Referred to as a text editor, rather than word processor, it creates only plain text files. That is, files that lack formatting, such as bullet points or a mixture of fonts. Notepad is the program to use if you need your document to be readable on any type of computer.

For your entertainment

Windows can play both audio and video clips that you can find from sources such as the Internet.

To have music while you work (provided your PC has a sound card and speakers), insert an audio CD into your CD-ROM drive and it will play. To

control the CD-ROM drive, click on the **CD Player** button that appears on the Taskbar once the music starts. You then see the CD Player dialogue box. The Track box lets you select the play order.

Working with photographs and other images

Paint is a simple drawing package that lets you create your own images. You can also use it to edit pictures you have on your computer. For example, you may want to restore an old photograph by removing creases or you may want

to completely remove a small item.

The zoom feature makes it easy to edit in fine detail, pixel by pixel. Paint makes it easy to create and install personal wallpaper designs. When you are happy with your design, go to the

File menu and select either **Set As Wallpaper (Tiled)** or **Set As Wallpaper (Centered)**.

Imaging is a powerful variant of Paint. Aimed at more experienced users, it lets you edit scanned-in images in great detail.

Making all your sums add up

Calculator carries out basic addition, subtraction, multiplication and division.

To use it, click on **Calculator** in the **Accessories** menu. Then, either click the on-screen calculator keys using your mouse, or use the numeric

keypad on the right-hand side of your keyboard.

The Copy and Paste options in the Edit menu let you transfer numbers to other programs. If you want advanced functions, go to the **View** menu and click on **Scientific**.

Make the right connection

Share a printer, send faxes and e-mail, get on the Internet

One of the things that makes computers so useful is the fact that they can communicate with other electronic devices. Via cables and telephone lines, your computer can 'talk' to printers, faxes – and to other computers. There are many ways you can use the fact that so many pieces of equipment are on 'speaking terms'. You can share a printer with another computer user; you can send and receive faxes without the need for a separate fax machine; you can use e-mail – the fastest and cheapest way to send a message to the other side of the world; and most excitingly of all, you can link to the vast, global computer network which makes up the Internet.

Making the link

If you want to communicate with a distant computer (or its owner), then you need to send your messages via a modem and down a phone line. If you just want two computers in the same place to be able to share a printer or a scanner, then you can join them physically with a connector cable (see *Sharing resources*, right). In this way you can also move files from one computer to another.

To send and receive faxes, you need to have the right sort of modem (see right). You also need a mini-application that comes as standard with Windows 95 and 98.

To use the Internet you need a modem, and an account with a service provider (see right, and page 90). You can then use your PC as a postal service, a travel agent, a book-shop, a library, or a meeting point for people from all over the world.

Key word
Modem A modem takes digital data from one computer, then translates it into sound and sends it down a telephone line to another modem. This modem then converts it back to digital data.

Close-up
An Internet Service Provider (ISP) gives you your Internet connection. Some provide just the basic telephone connection and e-mail services, but the biggest also provide on-screen magazines and shopping facilities.

Ways to get connected

The world of computer communications is easy to use although it may seem daunting at first.

Sharing resources
Two computers in the same house can be linked to each other with a cable. You might want to do this if, say, you need to share a printer. First, make sure that the computers are connected by a cable, and that the lead is fitted into the same serial or parallel port on each computer. Then go to the **Start** button and select **Programs**, then **Accessories**, then **Communications** and finally **Direct Cable Connection** (in Windows 95, go to **Accessories** and **Direct Cable Connection**). Windows will then take you through the connection process.

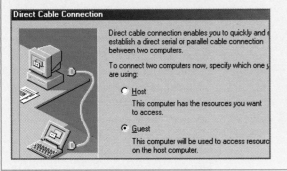

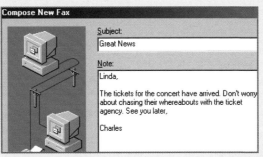

Sending and receiving faxes
You'll only ever have to set up your computer once in order to send and receive faxes. To get started, make sure that your modem can handle faxing (it has to be a fax modem) and that you have suitable fax software. Both Windows 95 and 98 come with a program, called Microsoft Fax, that makes faxing from your Desktop possible. Any document that can be printed can be faxed, including spreadsheets and graphic images.

Once you're set up, you can send faxes to other fax machines and computers. You can read incoming faxes on your screen or print them out. If you intend to do a lot of faxing, it may be worthwhile arranging through your phone company for a second phone line, with its own number, to be installed. (For more details on using your PC as a fax, see page 84.)

Connecting to the Internet
Access to the Internet allows you to tap into the huge well of information resources and services. In order to use the Internet you need a modem and an account with an Internet Service Provider (ISP) – an account with one ISP, 'rdplus.net', is available for free on the CD-ROM supplied with this book. This and other ISPs will provide you with the necessary telephone connection. ISPs also supply various on-line services of their own. (For more details on connecting to the Internet, see page 90.)

Sending and receiving e-mail
E-mail usually comes as an added extra when you arrange an account with an ISP, and you will be given your own personal e-mail address. Using the Internet you can send an e-mail message to another computer anywhere in the world in seconds, and usually for the price of a local phone call. (For more details on e-mail, see page 92.)

Connecting to another location

If you want to connect your computer to another one outside your home, and both PCs have a modem, it's possible to use a service called Dial-Up Networking.

Go to the **Start** menu, select **Programs**, then **Accessories**, then **Communications** then **Dial-Up Networking**. Click on the **Make New Connection** icon. Follow the on-screen set-up instructions. Once connected you can send and receive files. You don't need an account with an ISP to use this type of Dial-Up Networking.

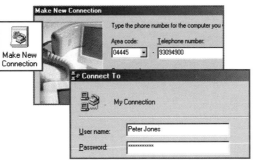

Choosing and setting up a modem

Link up to the outside world with a device to suit your way of working

A modem (the name is short for modulator-demodulator) is the piece of equipment that enables your PC to link to the Internet, and send or receive faxes and e-mail via your telephone line.

There are two types of modem – external ones that sit on your desk and are plugged into the rear of your system unit, and internal modems that are fitted inside a spare expansion slot in your computer's system unit. Many new computers now come with internal modems already fitted. If your PC doesn't, and you want to 'connect' with the outside world, you need to buy and install a modem.

Inside or out?

Internal modems are more difficult to install as you need to remove the cover from your system unit and fit it inside. However, they tend to be cheaper than external modems. Also, internal modems do not require a separate power supply, they don't use up a spare serial port and they don't use up any valuable extra space on your desk.

On the other hand, external modems are much easier to install because you simply plug them in. They also have indicator lights so you can tell how they are working – for example, a light shows when the modem is receiving information.

Watch out
New 56Kbps modems should have few compatibility problems as they operate under one 'industry standard', called V.90. Older modems operate under the K56FLEX or X2 standard. If you want to use the Internet and have an older modem, call your Internet Service Provider to check it is compatible with their modems.

Making the right connection

Before buying, consider all the modem options, and the needs of everyone who uses your PC.

Buying guide

When choosing a modem, check the speed at which it operates (to use the Internet you need at least a 33.6Kbps modem) and whether it can handle faxing. Make sure it can be upgraded with new software too. There's no point buying one that can't be upgraded – your needs may change in time and you may want to have a faster connection.

Whichever model you buy, a good, clear instruction manual that takes you through the installation process step by step and contains 'help' sections can make the whole process trouble-free. If your modem set-up is to include fax-management facilities, choose a modem that includes the relevant software. And if you buy an external modem, check you have a complete set of connection leads, including one to connect to the phone socket.

External modems

To install an external modem, first shut down your PC and disconnect the power at the mains socket. Attach the modem to your PC

with your modem cable (look in your modem and computer manuals to check which ports you plug the cable into). Plug the phone line connector into the modem and the phone socket, then plug the power adaptor into the modem and into a wall socket. When you switch on your PC, Windows will recognise that you have connected a new piece of hardware and ask you to insert the driver disk. Follow the on-screen instructions.

Internal modems

To install an internal modem, shut down your PC and disconnect the power. Carefully remove the cover from your system unit. Discharge any static electricity by touching the metal of your PC's case. Locate an empty expansion slot for the modem (look in your PC manual).

Remove the metal 'blanking' plate that's screwed to the back of the PC's case next to the expansion slot you have chosen. Keep the screw handy. Hold the modem card by its edges and, being careful not to touch any of its chips, gently push the card into place and secure it with the screw you removed. Replace the system unit's cover and plug the phone connector into the modem port at the rear of the system unit and the phone socket in the wall. When you switch on, Windows will recognise that you have a new device. Follow the on-screen instructions.

How to check for a modem

To see if you already have an internal modem installed, go to the **Start** menu, select **Settings** then click on **Control Panel**. In the Control Panel window double-click on **Modems**. If a modem is installed, its name will appear in the Modems Properties box.

Standards and speeds

The speeds at which modems can send data down a phone line is constantly improving. Today, the fastest modem can receive data at 56Kbps (kilobits per second), although this speed is rarely achieved because of interference down phone lines. But even the fastest modem can send data at an average of only 33.6Kbps.

If you intend to use the Internet (left), it is recommended that you use a modem that can receive data at speeds of 33.6Kbps and above.

Using your PC as a fax machine

With the right connection, your computer can send and receive faxes

If you have a modem that can cope with sending and receiving faxes (and most new modems can), Windows allows you to use your PC as a fax machine. This is a great benefit as it means you save both space around your desk and, best of all, the money you would otherwise have spent on a separate fax machine.

Once Windows is set up for faxing, you will see that it's as easy as printing a document. When you send a fax your computer stores the data as an uneditable image file. After the modem dials the destination number, it sends the fax image down the telephone line to the fax machine or computer at the other end.

Similarly, faxes you receive are images, made up of thousands of dots. You can view these fax images on your computer screen and print them out. You can also buy software that turn these dot-based images into text. You can then edit faxes that have been sent to you.

Remember that all sorts of documents can be faxed, including pictures and spreadsheets. Anything that can be printed can be faxed.

Set up Windows' fax software

Windows comes with two special utilities – Windows Messaging and Microsoft Fax – that allow you to use your computer as a fax machine.

If your computer runs Windows 98, you must install these utilities from the Windows 98 installation CD. After inserting the CD, double-click on drive **D:**, click on the **Browse This CD** option, then on the **tools** folder. A series of windows will appear – click on **oldwin 95**, then **message**, then **intl**. The two icons within the intl window – **wms** and **awfax** – represent Windows Messaging (wms) and Microsoft Fax (awfax). Double-click on each and follow the instructions to install.

If your computer runs Windows 95, add these utilities by going to the **Start** menu, selecting **Control Panel**, clicking on **Add/Remove Programs** and choosing **Microsoft Fax** from the Windows Setup tab.

 When your fax system is set up successfully, an Inbox icon appears on your Desktop. When you double-click on the **Inbox** icon for the first time, the Inbox Setup Wizard will run (below). This will identify the modem you are using and will ask for your name and fax number, which you need to fill in before you can send faxes. Once your Inbox is activated, incoming faxes appear as messages in your Microsoft Exchange box.

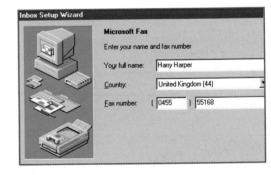

Inbox Setup Wizard

Microsoft Fax

Enter your name and fax number

Your full name: Harry Harper

Country: United Kingdom (44)

Fax number: (0455) 55168

Watch out
Always make sure that your modem is connected to the phone line when you are sending or receiving a fax. When you are receiving a fax, your fax software will detect the call. It will either pick it up automatically or leave it for you to pick up, depending on the set-up you have chosen.

Bright idea
If you are using Word and want more help with faxing, you can run the Fax Wizard. Go to the **File** *menu, select* **Send To** *then click on* **Fax Recipient**. *Here you can choose to send a fax with or without a cover sheet, or just a cover sheet with a note.*

Faxing direct

To send simple faxes in Windows, go to the **Start** menu, select **Programs**, then **Accessories**, then **Fax** and click on **Compose New Fax**. A 'wizard' runs (right) to help you.

At the opening box, click **Next**. Now, fill in the name and number of the person you want to send the fax to and click the **Add to List** button, then **Next**. You'll then be asked if you want to send a fax cover sheet (this contains your contact details and space for a brief message). Select the 'Yes. Send this one' or 'No' option, then click **Next**.

In the dialogue box complete the purpose of the fax in the Subject box

and type your message in the Note box (above). Click on **Next**. The following dialogue box asks if you want to include one or more files with your message. If the only thing you are sending is the message in the Note box, click **Next**, then **Finish** to send the fax. If you want to include an attachment

(a document from another program, such as Word, that can be attached to the fax and sent) click **Add File**. Browse through your hard disk for the document you want to fax, then double-click on it (its name will appear in the 'Files to send' box). Windows opens and transmits the document when the fax is sent.

Sending faxes from programs

Microsoft Word provides a selection of pre-styled fax cover sheets. To open one, go to the **Start** menu, select **Programs** and click on **Microsoft Word**. Now go to the **File** menu and click on **New**. Click on the **Letters and Faxes** tab.

Select a style of fax – you have a choice of Contemporary, Elegant or Professional – and click **OK**. If you only have a short message to send then type it into the space provided. If you have a few pages of text to

transmit, it's best to copy and paste the text into the form from the relevant word processing file. When you are ready, go to the **File** menu and select **Print**. Change the Printer setting to **Microsoft Fax**, then click **OK**. The Microsoft Compose New Fax Wizard will run (left).

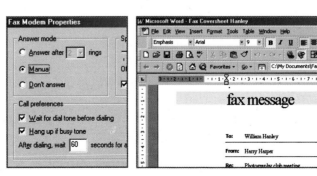

If you want to fax a spreadsheet or database file that can't be easily pasted onto a cover sheet, open the file, go to the **File** menu and select **Print**. As before, in the Printer Name box select **Microsoft Fax**. The Microsoft Fax Wizard will take you through the faxing process, step by step.

You can also attach a database or spreadsheet file when faxing direct by using the **Add File** step (see *Faxing direct*, left).

Incoming faxes

To receive a fax, double-click on the **Inbox** Desktop icon, go to the **Tools** menu, select **Microsoft Fax Tools** then **Options**.

Click on the **Modem** tab (the name of your modem appears in the 'Available fax modems' box). Click on **Properties**. In the dialogue box, set the modem to pick up calls either manually or

after a set number of rings. If you are using the same phone line for voice and fax calls, select the Manual option. This way, when an incoming call is detected, a dialogue box will appear asking whether you want to pick up the call. Click **Yes**. The fax appears in your Windows Messaging Inbox, located in the Inbox. Double-click to open.

The Internet

The Internet and the World Wide Web (the collection of Web sites created by businesses, societies and individuals), is expanding at a staggering rate. Users can now find information on almost any subject. The Internet also allows users, for the price of a local telephone call, to send messages in the form of e-mail (electronic mail) across the world. Find out how to connect to the Net, then go and explore this vast storehouse of information.

Getting connected to the Internet allows you to explore the worlds of travel, finance, education, medicine, history and much more. You will even make new friends and contacts in the process

In this section

The Internet Explained

Find out how to gain access to the Internet and navigate around it. This chapter also explains how to search for information quickly, successfully and safely, how to send and receive e-mail, and how to make purchases without putting your account details at risk.

Using the Internet

Learn in detail how to search for specific information and explore facilities on-line. Whether bidding for antiques in an on-line auction, doing historical research, or playing chess with a friend overseas, this chapter takes you through the process, step by step.

Enter the world of the Web and discover what it can help you do: from shopping and chatting, to research and study

Welcome to the Internet

A meeting place, shopping centre, travel agent and library in one

The Internet is made up of a network of millions of computers throughout the world that allow people to access a wide range of information and services. It comprises the World Wide Web, through which people access this information, and facilities such as electronic mail (e-mail), chat areas, forums and newsgroups.

E-mail is a major feature of the Internet. Messages are typed into a computer then sent via a phone line to other e-mail users thousands of miles away – all for the cost of a local phone call. If you have a particular interest, forums and newsgroups provide an opportunity to exchange opinions and ideas. Many Internet Service Providers (the companies that provide connection to the Internet) set up discussion areas in which you can comment on issues of interest to you.

A spider's web of information

The World Wide Web (WWW or Web) is the public face of the Internet. It is a vast conglomeration of Web sites, made up of Web pages. The text and images you see on the Internet are part of a Web page.

Web pages are written in a computer language called HTML, or HyperText Markup Language, that allows pages to be linked together. A collection of linked pages forms a Web site, which in turn can be linked to other sites around the world, forming a global spider's web of connected sites.

All Web sites have unique addresses. These act like phone numbers, connecting your computer to the computer that holds the Web page you want to view.

To find your way around the huge tangle of Web sites – or 'surf the Net' – you need a Web browser. This is a piece of software that allows you to view pages and move around the Web. The two main Web browsers are Netscape Navigator and Microsoft Internet Explorer, and both are easy to obtain free of charge.

Once you are on-line, the Web is your oyster. You can use it to buy goods, including books, CDs, food and clothes, to book holidays, to research any subject, and even to play computer games. For key areas you can explore on the Web, see opposite.

All you need to connect to the Internet is a modem and an account with an Internet Service Provider

The world at your fingertips

Once connected to the Net, you are ready to explore the potential of the World Wide Web. This is made up of a collection of Web sites that promote a multitude of subjects and interests.

Travel

Use the Web to access travel guides, check the latest weather reports, book flights and accommodation, view exchange rates, and find out what other visitors thought of a destination.

Research

Whether you are studying for a qualification or pursuing a personal interest, there are Web sites to help you. You will even find on-line encyclopedias. (See pages 122, 126 and 132 for research projects on the Internet.)

Health and medicine

The Web is an invaluable resource when it comes to health matters (but it is not a substitute for going to the doctor). You can find out about medical conditions, research treatment options and even get on-line advice – but not a diagnosis – from doctors and other health experts.

The media

The Web allows you to access the latest news from newspapers, magazines and broadcasting companies. Many of these services are free. With the correct software you can watch live television broadcasts from the other side of the world. You can get news of events before they reach the TV news bulletins or the papers.

Shopping

You can buy virtually anything on the Internet – from new shirts to a new home. The Internet also has on-line shopping malls designed to bring together Web sites for shoppers in one place. (To find out how to shop on the Internet, see page 108.)

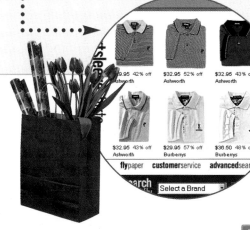

What you need to get on-line

To surf the Net you must have a PC, a modem and an Internet Service Provider

Getting connected to the Net is easy and inexpensive. You need a modem or other connecting device (see opposite). This is your link to the Net. You also need an account with an Internet Service Provider (ISP). An rdplus.net account is available free of charge on the CD-ROM with this book.

An ISP acts as a gateway to the Internet. It allows you to browse the World Wide Web and send and receive e-mail. It will also store any Web pages you have created, making them accessible to other users of the Internet.

Some ISPs are global Internet organisations such as CompuServe or America Online (AOL); others services are operated by supermarkets, bookshops, banks – even football clubs. Finding an ISP to suit your needs is the most important aspect of getting on-line.

Types of Internet Service Provider

The term ISP is used to describe all the companies that provide you with access to the Internet. However, these companies offer differing levels of service.

● Internet Access Providers (IAPs) offer a very basic package. These companies give you a connection and Web-browsing software, such as Internet Explorer, and an e-mail program, and provide technical help over the telephone. An example of an IAP is Freeserve.

● Online Service Providers (OSPs), like IAPs, provide a gateway to the Internet and e-mail handling. They differ in that they offer an extra level of service – or 'content' – including special news, information and entertainment channels, shopping services, chat rooms and topic-based newsgroups or forums. OSPs often have a home page designed to make using the Internet accessible to newcomers. AOL (America Online) is one of the best-known OSPs.

Key word
Web browser *This is a piece of software
that acts as your window on the Internet.
Your ISP will provide you with this in its start-up pack.
Microsoft Internet Explorer and Netscape Navigator
are two popular browsers.*

Questions to ask about ISPs

Some ISPs are expensive and some are free.
But the cost of connection is not the only
factor you need to consider.

Ways to pay

There are different ways of paying for Internet access. It's
worth noting that, in addition to any fee to an ISP, you
have to pay a telephone charge (normally at the local
rate) every time you connect and stay on-line.

● **Flat rate** This is a monthly charge that allows
unlimited use of Internet services.

● **Pay as you go** Some OSPs charge a small, flat rate
then an additional charge based on the number of hours
you spend on-line each month. This might be attractive
to users who connect infrequently.

● **Free** Using the CD-ROM with this book, you can install
the rdplus.net ISP for no fee. High-street stores and supermarkets, among others, offer a similar service. Companies
that offer free ISPs are able to do so by charging for
technical support or carrying adverts.

Do you get any added extras?

If you want added content, in the form of business pages,
chat rooms, shopping services and so on, make sure that
the content you get suits your needs. If you are interested
in business, choose an ISP that is strong in this area.

Find out whether you get e-mail access, and how
many e-mail addresses you can have. Having more than
one means that each family member can have their own
address and send and receive e-mail from the same PC.
Or, if you work from home, you could have one e-mail
address for personal mail and another for business use.

Find out whether you are allocated any Web space
on which to set up your own Web site. If so, how much
space do you get and is it free?

Ask whether your telephone calls to the support
helpline are free or charged at the local call rate. Some
ISPs that offer 'free' services charge premium rates for
support calls. Some ISPs offer 24-hour-a-day support.
Above all, ask if technical support is available when you
are most likely to need it – when first connecting up.
Check on the ISP's reliability: will you get through at
the first try or will the line be engaged? Does the ISP
have enough modems to handle
Internet traffic at peak usage times?

Get a real feel with a free trial

Many ISPs offer a free trial of their
services, usually for thirty days. If
you take up a trial offer make sure
that all sections of the service are
user-friendly. Are you impressed
with the standard of content? And
how easy is it to send and receive
e-mail through the ISP? (See page
92 for details
on how to
use e-mail.)

Modem or ISDN?

The most popular way of connecting to the
Internet is via a modem plugged into a
standard telephone connection. A modem
sends information to – and receives it from –
the Internet. Currently, the fastest modems can
download data at a speed of 56 Kbps (kilobytes
per second). For more information on modems,
see page 82.

The main alternative to a modem is an ISDN
link. ISDN (Integrated Services Digital Network)
is a digital phone line that can carry data at a
guaranteed speed of 64 Kbps – this speed can
be boosted with special software. For an ISDN
connection you need to install a separate,
digital phone line. ISDN can also operate along
an existing phone line, but you have to buy an
expensive adaptor.

BT Highway also operates at 64 Kbps and is
a much cheaper alternative to ISDN. It doesn't
require a separate phone line, but you do need
an adaptor for your regular phone line.

Send and receive e-mail

Using your PC to revolutionise the way you keep in touch

In addition to the World Wide Web, the Internet also provides electronic mail, or e-mail. Many people find that e-mail is the single most useful feature of the Internet.

E-mail functions at a staggering speed. A message can reach a computer on the other side of the world in minutes, and all it costs is the price of a quick local phone call. And because it's operated from your Desktop, it's very convenient too.

Every e-mail program has its own look, but all operate in a similar way. Here, we have used Microsoft Outlook Express, which is available on the CD-ROM with this book.

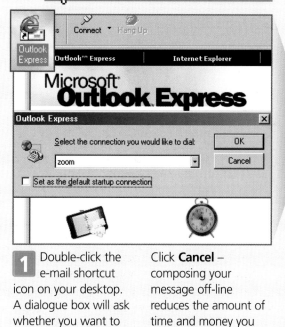

To save yourself time, set up a shortcut on your desktop to launch your e-mail program. For details on how to do this, see page 74.

BEFORE YOU START

1 Double-click the e-mail shortcut icon on your desktop. A dialogue box will ask whether you want to connect to the Internet.

Click **Cancel** – composing your message off-line reduces the amount of time and money you spend on-line.

Working off-line

Composing e-mail messages can take time, and doing it while you are connected to the Internet can be costly in terms of phone bills. Luckily, almost all e-mail programs allow you to write messages off-line (that is, without connecting to the Internet). When you click on the **Send** button, your PC will connect to the Internet (go on-line) and your message will be sent.

Close-up
E-mail addresses take the form of name@somewhere.com. 'Name' refers to the sender's name, and 'somewhere.com' refers to the host computer where mail is stored until it is collected by the recipient. Your ISP will provide you with an e-mail address.

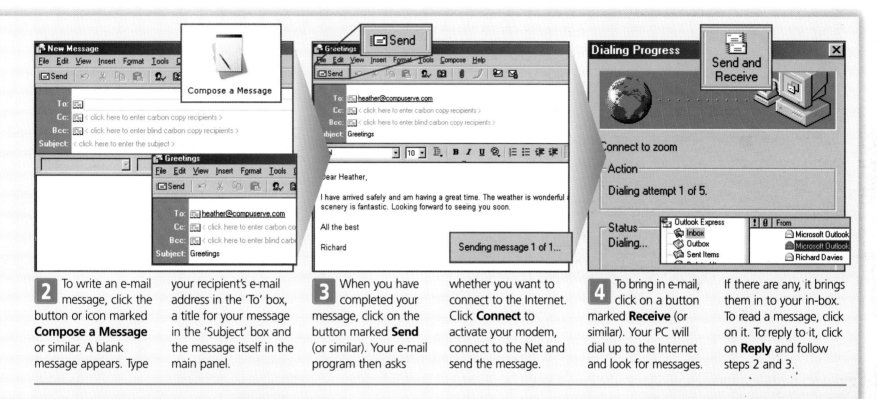

2 To write an e-mail message, click the button or icon marked **Compose a Message** or similar. A blank message appears. Type your recipient's e-mail address in the 'To' box, a title for your message in the 'Subject' box and the message itself in the main panel.

3 When you have completed your message, click on the button marked **Send** (or similar). Your e-mail program then asks whether you want to connect to the Internet. Click **Connect** to activate your modem, connect to the Net and send the message.

4 To bring in e-mail, click on a button marked **Receive** (or similar). Your PC will dial up to the Internet and look for messages. If there are any, it brings them in to your in-box. To read a message, click on it. To reply to it, click on **Reply** and follow steps 2 and 3.

Sending attachments

You can send pictures and other files with e-mails. Look out for an Attachment option. Click on it and a box will appear in which you find and select the file to be attached (for more information on finding files, see page 50). Click **Open** or **Attach** and then **OK**. An indication that the file has been attached will appear on your message. The recipient receives this as a separate file which they click on to open.

Address books

In some e-mail programs, every time an e-mail is sent, the sender's address is stored in the address book. To save having to type the address every time, click on the **Address Book** button, select the name from the **Name** list and click on the **Send Mail** button. The New Message box appears with the recipient's details. Type your message and click on **Send**.

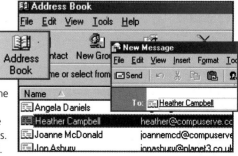

Starting out on-line

Set up your Web browser and you are ready to surf the Net

Many people are daunted by the idea of venturing onto the Internet. But, in fact, going on-line for the first time is a simple matter. It is no more difficult than installing a new piece of software.

To connect to the Internet you need a modem and an Internet Service Provider (ISP) – see pages 82 and 90 respectively. You also need a Web browser. This is a piece of software that opens the door through which you enter the world of the Web. Once your browser is set up, you can explore the fascinating world beyond.

Understanding Web browsers

A Web browser is a piece of software that allows you to access Web sites and navigate between them. All Web browsers are the same in principle. They contain an address box, in which you type a Web address, and an area in which Web pages are displayed.

Two of the most popular browsers are Microsoft Internet Explorer and Netscape Navigator. If you bought your PC in 1999 or later, Microsoft Internet Explorer will almost certainly have come preinstalled on your system. (If you can't see it loaded, consult your manual for installation instructions.)

Whether or not your PC came with its own browser, your ISP may also provide you with one in its start-up kit. For example, rdplus.net (available on the CD-ROM with this book) offers Microsoft Internet Explorer, while others offer Netscape Navigator. Some ISPs, such as AOL and CompuServe (see opposite), provide you with their own specially designed Web browser. You can have more than one Web browser, just as you can have more than one word processor or spreadsheet program.

When your ISP software first loads, look for a button that says 'Internet', 'Browse the Internet', 'Explore' or something similar. Clicking on this will start up the browser.

*Windows 98 has an Internet Wizard to help you get connected. Double-click on the Desktop's **Connect to the Internet** icon and follow the on-screen instructions.*

GETTING ON-LINE

Get to know your way around your Web browser

Your browser gives the Internet a face and allows you to view all its resources. Learning to use it effectively will make surfing the Net more enjoyable and rewarding.

Most browsers have a main menu, similar to that found in Microsoft Word or Works. Through the menus you can print Web pages, configure your ISP settings and access help facilities.

The Address box is where you type Web addresses. Click on **Go** (or press the **Return** or **Enter** keys) to download the Web page.

Use the Back and Forward buttons to navigate backwards or forwards through downloaded pages. Some browsers clearly label them Back and Forward.

Online Service Providers (see page 90) will list their content, usually in a panel on the left of the page. Click on these to access them.

Look for a toolbar containing buttons that allow you to set up automatic links to your favourite Web sites, organise your e-mail, and so on. To see what a button does, place your mouse pointer over it – a label will pop up.

Most browsers include some form of search facility to help you find information. Type a key word or words into the search box then click on **Find** (or press the **Return** or **Enter** keys).

This is the main viewing area, into which Web pages are downloaded and displayed.

Some ISPs, including CompuServe, have special areas where members can meet to exchange information.

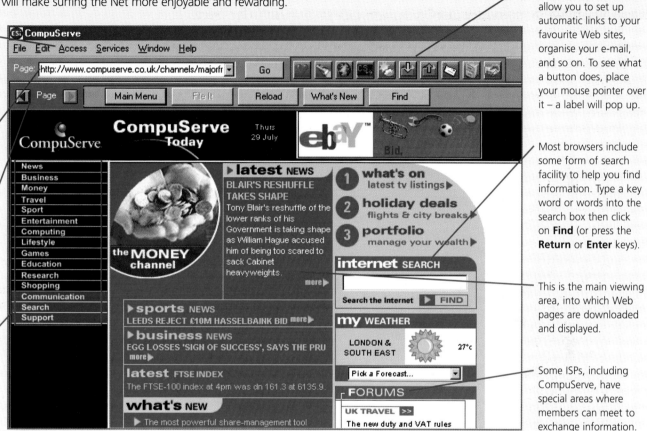

Web addresses explained

Every Web address is unique, in the same way that your telephone number is. In fact, it's helpful to think of a Web address as a telephone number, whereby you 'dial' the site's address to view it.

The 'www' in a Web address tells you that the site belongs to the World Wide Web. After the 'www' you are told the domain name (this 'points' to the computer that holds the Web site) and where that computer is located

('.uk', for the UK; '.au' for Australia; and so on).

Addresses do not always end in the country of origin. If you see '.com' at the end, for example, this indicates that the site is commercial. If you see '.gov', the Web site is a government agency.

For many pages, extra text appears after the domain name. This shows the location of the pages on the Web site.

Page: www.thisisuseful.co.uk

How to find information

Exploring the Internet is easy once you know where to start

Once your Internet connection is up and running you are ready to explore the World Wide Web. The quickest way to find information is to type the Web address of a relevant site into your browser's address box and press the Return key on your keyboard. The site's first page (known as the home page) will appear on screen.

If you do not know the address you can track down information using a search engine, which will search for key words or categories that you select, then present you with a list of sites to visit. The key to effective use of the Internet is knowing how to narrow your searches so that the number of sites yielded is manageable. Remember, the time you spend on-line costs money, so it pays to be efficient in your searching.

> Be as specific as you can in your search and tell the search engine exactly what you are looking for. You can get tips on better searching from the engines themselves.

USING A SEARCH ENGINE

1 Connect to the Internet. In your Web browser's address box type the address of a search engine (here, www.lycos.co.uk). Click on **Go**. The site's home page will appear in a few seconds. Type your key words into the search box and click on **Go Get It!**.

Which search engine?

The Web site at www.searchenginewatch.com explains how the main search engines work and how efficient they are. Here are the addresses of some popular search engines:

- www.altavista.com
- www.excite.co.uk
- www.hotbot.com
- www.lycos.co.uk
- www.northernlight.com
- www.yahoo.co.uk

Your Internet Service Provider might also have its own search facility (see page 90).

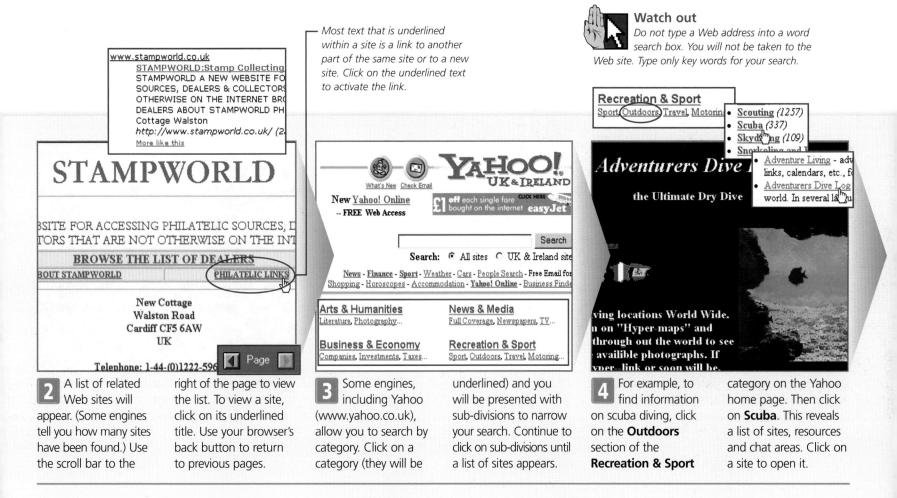

— *Most text that is underlined within a site is a link to another part of the same site or to a new site. Click on the underlined text to activate the link.*

Watch out
Do not type a Web address into a word search box. You will not be taken to the Web site. Type only key words for your search.

2 A list of related Web sites will appear. (Some engines tell you how many sites have been found.) Use the scroll bar to the right of the page to view the list. To view a site, click on its underlined title. Use your browser's back button to return to previous pages.

3 Some engines, including Yahoo (www.yahoo.co.uk), allow you to search by category. Click on a category (they will be underlined) and you will be presented with sub-divisions to narrow your search. Continue to click on sub-divisions until a list of sites appears.

4 For example, to find information on scuba diving, click on the **Outdoors** section of the **Recreation & Sport** category on the Yahoo home page. Then click on **Scuba**. This reveals a list of sites, resources and chat areas. Click on a site to open it.

Search by batch

Most search engines present their list of sites in batches (usually of 10). When you reach the bottom of the first batch in Lycos, click on **2** for the next batch, and so on.

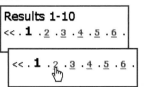

Information collected for you

Some Web sites hold databases of information that make searching easy. For example, Bigfoot (www.bigfoot.com) lists individual e-mail addresses, and Deja (www.deja.com) indexes all the messages sent to newsgroups.

Deja has its own search engine that will find topics of discussion for you. Type, say, 'New York Hotels', into the search box and press **Return** and you'll find recommendations for accommodation in New York from its index of users.

Your PC can use more than one search engine at a time. Copernic is a program that collects results from many search engines. Download it free of charge from the Internet.

SERIOUS SEARCHING

Watch out
Make sure your Internet connection is running before you double-click on the Copernic icon. Otherwise, you will not be able to use it.

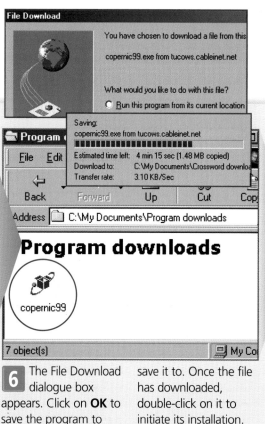

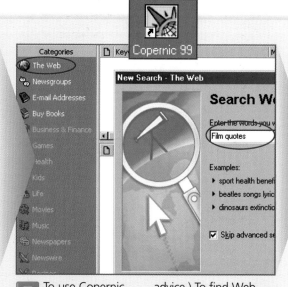

5 Type the Copernic address (www. copernic.com) into your browser's address box and click on **Go**. Click on the **Get Free**
Software button on the home page. Select a geographical location to download from by clicking on the place nearest you.

6 The File Download dialogue box appears. Click on **OK** to save the program to your hard disk. Then specify which folder to
save it to. Once the file has downloaded, double-click on it to initiate its installation. Follow the on-screen instructions.

7 To use Copernic, connect to the Internet, then double-click on its Desktop icon. (You may need to register – follow the
advice.) To find Web data, click on **The Web** category. Type a key word into the box that appears then click the **Search Now** button.

Bookmarking Web pages

Browsers allow you to record the addresses of favourite Web sites you have visited, which saves you having to remember the addresses and means you don't have to spend time on-line searching for the sites again. As long as you are connected to the Internet, a click on a bookmarked address will open up the site.

The process of bookmarking Web sites is similar in all browsers (look out for a facility called 'Bookmarks', 'Favorites' or 'Favorite

Places' on your browser's toolbar). To bookmark a site through CompuServe, first open the site then go to the **File** menu and click on **Add to Favorite Places**. The Define Favorite Places dialogue box appears with the address of the site you are visiting. Click **OK**.

To access this site again, click on the **Favorite Places** button on the CompuServe toolbar. A box appears with a list of your bookmarked addresses. Click on the relevant address to load the site (you must be connected, of course).

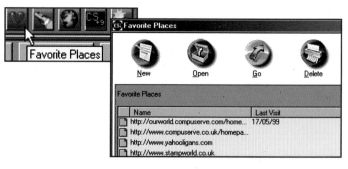

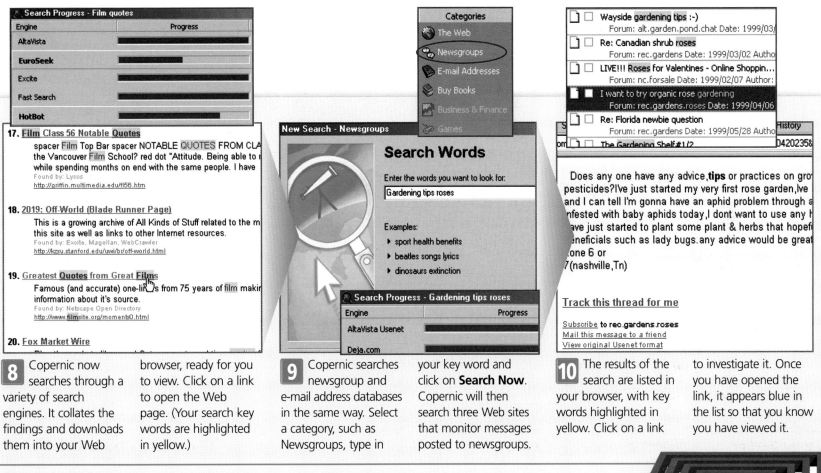

Search Progress - Film quotes

Engine	Progress
AltaVista	
EuroSeek	
Excite	
Fast Search	
HotBot	

17. **Film Class 56 Notable Quotes**
spacer Film Top Bar spacer NOTABLE QUOTES FROM CLA
the Vancouver Film School? red dot "Attitude. Being able to
while spending months on end with the same people. I have
Found by: Lycos
http://griffin.multimedia.edu/fl56.htm

18. **2019: Off-World (Blade Runner Page)**
This is a growing archive of All Kinds of Stuff related to the m
this site as well as links to other Internet resources.
Found by: Excite, Magellan, WebCrawler
http://kzsu.stanford.edu/uwi/br/off-world.html

19. **Greatest Quotes from Great Films**
Famous (and accurate) one-liners from 75 years of film makir
information about it's source.
Found by: Netscape Open Directory
http://www.filmsite.org/moments0.html

20. **Fox Market Wire**

Categories
- The Web
- Newsgroups
- E-mail Addresses
- Buy Books
- Business & Finance
- Games

New Search - Newsgroups

Search Words

Enter the words you want to look for:

Gardening tips roses

Examples:
▶ sport health benefits
▶ beatles songs lyrics
▶ dinosaurs extinction

Search Progress - Gardening tips roses

Engine	Progress
AltaVista Usenet	
Deja.com	

☐ Wayside gardening tips :-)
  Forum: alt.garden.pond.chat Date: 1999/03/
☐ Re: Canadian shrub roses
  Forum: rec.gardens Date: 1999/03/02 Autho
☐ LIVE!!! Roses for Valentines - Online Shoppin...
  Forum: nc.forsale Date: 1999/02/07 Author:
☐ I want to try organic rose gardening
  Forum: rec.gardens.roses Date: 1999/04/06
☐ Re: Florida newbie question
  Forum: rec.gardens Date: 1999/05/28 Autho
☐ The Gardening Shelf#1/2

Does any one have any advice,**tips** or practices on gro
pesticides?I've just started my very first rose garden,Ive
and I can tell I'm gonna have an aphid problem through a
infested with baby aphids today,I dont want to use any h
ave just started to plant some plant & herbs that hopef
eneficials such as lady bugs.any advice would be great
one 6 or
(nashville,Tn)

Track this thread for me

Subscribe to rec.gardens.roses
Mail this message to a friend
View original Usenet format

8 Copernic now searches through a variety of search engines. It collates the findings and downloads them into your Web browser, ready for you to view. Click on a link to open the Web page. (Your search key words are highlighted in yellow.)

9 Copernic searches newsgroup and e-mail address databases in the same way. Select a category, such as Newsgroups, type in your key word and click on **Search Now**. Copernic will then search three Web sites that monitor messages posted to newsgroups.

10 The results of the search are listed in your browser, with key words highlighted in yellow. Click on a link to investigate it. Once you have opened the link, it appears blue in the list so that you know you have viewed it.

Close-up
Don't forget to use links to track down information. Links are a key part of the World Wide Web. They appear as underlined text on a Web page and let you jump directly from one site or page to another. Most Web sites have links to other similar sites, so you may find the information you want browsing from one to the next.

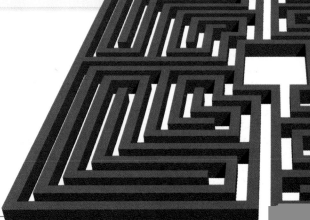

Security on the Internet

How to ensure users of your PC are protected when on-line

Internet newcomers are naturally concerned about security. They worry about whether it's safe to send credit card details over the Internet, or whether children will come across undesirable material. Concerns over the privacy of e-mail and the unauthorised issue of e-mail addresses are also common.

All these concerns are valid, but there are measures you can take to guarantee the integrity of the sites your family visits, and that your own personal details are kept confidential.

Keeping it safe and sound

Whether shopping, browsing or e-mailing, there are ways to guarantee your security on the Internet.

Shopping and security

If a shopping Web site states that it uses 'encryption' technology to transfer credit card details (a complex almost unbreakable scrambling system), there should be no security problem. However, a good Web site will also offer alternative methods of payment, such as issuing an invoice, offering to call you and take details over the phone, or faxing or posting an order form.

| Book Search | Browse Categories | Bestsellers | Computer Books |

help Q&A

Security Guarantee

None of the customers who has shopped at Amazon.co.uk has r‍ a credit or debit card as a result of purchases made with us. We the transaction security we offer on our site that we back every security guarantee.

Here is why shopping at Amazon.co.uk is safe:

1. Our secure server software encrypts **all your personal in** credit or debit card number, name and address. The encry characters you enter and converts them into bits of code transmitted over the Internet

Address | http://www.netnanny.com/

Download | Products | Company | News | Links | Jobs

Enter to win!

BIOPASSWORD.
undeniably identified
Enhanced password
protection at your
fingertips!

Coming Soon!

PC Nanny

Protect your Desktop!

Educate Emp...

Buy Net Nann...

Submit a Sit...

Technical S...

Produ...

Watch out

It is possible, but very unlikely, that your e-mail could be intercepted as it is sent across the Internet. However, anyone who uses your PC could read your e-mail once it has been received, which is a good reason for being discreet in what you write.

Children and the Internet

The best way to protect children from coming across undesirable material on the Internet is to use special software. Programs, such as Cyber Patrol and Net Nanny, block access to sites known to have unsavoury content.

You can also get software that creates a log of all the sites that have been visited from your PC, and so keep a check on what your children have seen. You can also use the History button on your Web browser to do a similar job (see below).

In Windows 98 you can set up a 'Content Advisor' ratings system to control how much of Web sites a person can view according to its levels of language, nudity, sex and violence. To do this, go to the **Start** button and select **Settings** then **Control Panel**. Double-click the **Internet** icon, then click the **Content** tab and the **Enable** button.

Internet Properties

General | Security | Content | Connection | Programs | Advanced

Content Advisor
Ratings help you control the Internet content that can be viewed on this computer.

Enable... | Settings...

Content Advisor

Ratings | General | Advanced

To specify which sites users are allowed to see, select a category, then adjust the slider.

Category: RSACi
  Language
  Nudity
  Sex
  Violence

Rating:

Level 4: Wanton and gratuitous violence

With the Ratings tab selected, click on each category then set a rating level. Setting all categories at 'Level 1' effectively bars all access to the Web, apart from the most child-friendly sites. Click **OK** when you have finished.

When you first click on the **Enable** button you'll need to set a supervisor password. You must type it in every time you change the Content Advisor settings, so don't lose it.

Viruses and the Internet

Computer viruses can seriously damage your PC. The best way to avoid getting a virus from the Internet, or from any other source, is to use an anti-virus utility.

For added security when downloading files, ensure the 'Always ask before opening' box is ticked on your virus scanner. Only disable this function if you are confident that a file or file type is safe to open.

There is also a risk of infection from 'macro viruses' that enter your PC via e-mail attachments.

If you are buying anti-virus software, try to choose a package that automatically scans incoming messages and attachments.

In Word 97 you can put up another barrier to macro viruses. Go to the **Tools** menu and click on **Options**. Click on the **General** tab and put a tick in the 'Macro virus protection' box.

Options

Track Changes | User Informati...
View | General | Edit

General options
☑ Background repagination
☐ Help for WordPerfect users
☐ Navigation keys for WordPerfec...
☐ Blue background, white text
☐ Provide feedback with sound
☑ Provide feedback with animation
☐ Confirm conversion at Open
☑ Update automatic links at Open
☑ Mail as attachment
☑ Recently used file list: 4
☑ Macro virus protection

Safeguard your e-mail address

Sometimes, your e-mail address is obtained by companies or individuals who send you junk e-mail, known as 'spam'. You can try to avoid this by omitting your e-mail address from forms that you fill in, either by hand or on the World Wide Web.

Only give your e-mail address to individuals of your choice. Good Internet trading companies should give you the option of withholding your address, even to reputable, third-party vendors.

Address | http://msn.co.uk/defa...

History

History
Week of 19/04/99
Monday
Tuesday
Today
  home.microsoft.com
  investing.lycos.com
  msn.co.uk

History button

A simple way to keep an eye on the Web sites that have been visited from your PC is to use the History button that comes with Internet Explorer. When you press it, a log of all sites that have been accessed will appear to the left of the Explorer window.

To set the number of days that the History button monitors, go to the **Start** button and select **Settings**, then **Control Panel**. Double-click on the **Internet** icon. With the General tab selected, go to the 'Days to keep pages in history' box and input the number of days that suits you.

Explore the world of multimedia

Use your computer to watch video clips and listen to the radio

The term multimedia describes the capability of modern computers to deliver many different kinds of information at once: the elements of multimedia are pictures, text, animations, sounds and video.

On a well-designed Web site, multimedia enhances the level of information and enjoyment. For example, you might find a short clip to accompany a film review, or a live radio feed at a news site. There are also many badly designed sites, where the use of multimedia results in a kind of indigestible visual porridge. As you learn to 'surf', you will encounter many examples of the best and worst of multimedia.

Sights and sounds on the Internet
In order to enjoy the extra dimension of multimedia, you may need to add extra features to your browser.

Bring your Web browser up to speed
All Web browsers, including Microsoft Internet Explorer and Netscape Navigator, can handle basic forms of multimedia. However, to view video clips and animation on some sites you need mini-programs called plug-ins. These can vary in sophistication but the best, such as Shockwave, can play film clips and animations.

The most popular plug-ins concentrate on playing sound, video and animation stored in different formats. RealPlayer from RealNetworks (www.real.com) and Shockwave from Macromedia (www.macromedia.com) are among the most widely used. You can download plug-ins from the Web; several sites, including the Plug-In Plaza (www.browserwatch.Internet.com), have lists of plug-ins.

Key word
Plug-in *This is a piece of software that adds new features to your Web browser. After a plug-in has been installed, your browser will use it automatically whenever necessary.*

Watch out
Don't get too carried away listening to Internet radio. There's not much point paying to listen to your favourite local or national station over the Net when you can listen to it free through an ordinary radio set.

Downloading a plug-in
Connect to the Internet as usual. When the home page loads, type 'www.real.com' into the address box and click on **Go** or press the **Return** key. When the next page loads, look for the icon illustrating the free version of RealPlayer to download. Click on it.

Follow the steps to download the software: you will need to fill in a registration form and select a location to download from (this depends where in the world you are).

When you click the option to download you will be asked if you want to run the program or save it to your disk. Choose to save it. You will then be asked to specify a file location (it might be worth creating a new folder called 'Download' on

your hard disk in which to save it before you begin). When you have done this a screen will appear showing how the download is progressing.

Installing a plug-in
To install RealPlayer, double-click on the downloaded file on your hard disk then follow the on-screen instructions. When installation is complete, a shortcut icon to RealPlayer will appear on your Desktop. Double-click on it to open it

then look at the Net video channels available. Select a channel and wait for the screen to load. Remember, your Internet connection needs to be running in order for you to view a video clip.

Listen to the radio
Once you have the RealPlayer plug-in installed you can listen to live Internet radio broadcasts. This helps people keep in touch with local news and music around the world. Visit 'www.csi.ukns.com' and 'www.timecast.com' for a list of latest broadcasts.

To listen to broadcasts your PC must have speakers and a sound card (a piece of hardware that slots into your system unit and helps translate digital output into sound).

Turn off to speed up
Multimedia files can often be very large, which means that a Web page with lots of multimedia elements in it can take a long time to open. If you would rather not have these elements present when you are using the Web, you can instruct your browser not to download them.

Go to the **Start** button and select **Settings** then **Control Panel**. Double-

click on the **Internet** icon. Click the **Advanced** tab then use the scroll bars to move down to the Multimedia section.

Note that some items have ticked boxes beside them. To get rid of the ticks, click in the boxes (you do not need to get rid of the tick in the 'Smart image dithering' box). Click **Apply**, then **OK**. Next time you access a Web page, it will appear without sound or images.

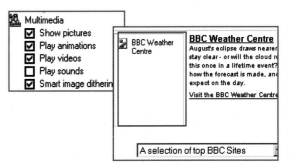

Meet new people

Use the World Wide Web to make new friends and contacts

One of the most exciting things about the Internet is that it brings all types of people together. People who share similar interests can keep in touch via e-mail by subscribing to mailing lists; others who want to chat in 'real time' (messages appear on the other person's computer screen as you type them), can log into chat rooms and 'talk'.

A growing section of the Internet, called Usenet, is made up of thousands of discussion groups. Here, people post messages that can be replied to, thereby initiating a discussion. Obtain a list of the main discussion groups from your Internet Service Provider (ISP).

Work out which hobbies or topics you wish to discuss and resolve to limit your chat time. Chatting is addictive and can run up your phone bill.

▼ BEFORE YOU START

CompuServe
File Edit Access Services Window Help
Page: www.liszt.com

Lis

topica   Archive your email
           Your subscribers

Since the 1970s, people have been joining "mailing lists" to talk ab intro if you're new. We've also got a Usenet newsgroups director even more friends

Most recent update: 181 new lists added to

Liszt has joined forces with Topica! Read all

I. **Search Liszt's main directory of 90,095 mailing lists:**

1 If you want to exchange information about hobbies and interests, you first need to find a suitable mailing list.

Open your Internet connection, type 'www.liszt.com' in your browser's address box, then click on **Go** or press the **Return** key.

What's on the Liszt Web site

The Liszt Web site lists thousands of mailing lists and chat services that exist on the Internet, and so is a good place to start your search for people who share your hobby or interest. You can use it to locate Usenet news groups, chat services and other Internet resources, too.

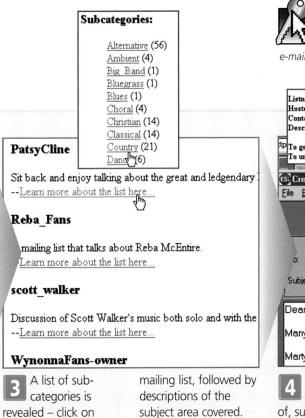

Subcategories:

Alternative (56)
Ambient (4)
Big Band (1)
Bluegrass (1)
Blues (1)
Choral (4)
Christian (14)
Classical (14)
Country (21)
Dance (6)

Key word
Mailing list Subscribers to mailing lists are kept informed about their particular interest through e-mail. When a message is sent, it goes to all members.

Listname: PatsyCline
Hosted at: onelist.com
Contact person: Jplinn3866@aol.com
Description: Sit back and enjoy talking about the great and ledgendary Patsy C

To get more info: mail the command *info PatsyCline* to Jplinn3866@aol.com
To unsubscribe: mail the command *unsubscribe PatsyCline* to Jplinn3866

Create Mail
File   Edit

Send   Send Later   File It

Name: Jplinn3866@aol.com
Address: >INTERNET:Jplinn3866@ao

Subject:

Dear JP I'm a big Patsy Cline and Country music fan. Could

Many thanks,

Marty Peters

II. **...or click on any topic to browse**
Liszt Select:

Books (102 lists)
   Writing, Science Fiction, Life and Works of...

Computers (250 lists)
   Hardware, Database, Programming ...

Education (112 lists)
   Distance Education, Academia, Internet ...

Humanities (254 lists)
   Philosophy, History, Psychology ...

Music (216 lists)
   Bands, Singer-Songwriters, Genres ...

News (50 lists)

Arts (20
   Crafts,

Business
   Financ

Culture
   Gay, J

Health
   Medic

Internet
   WWW

Nature
   Anima

Politics

PatsyCline

Sit back and enjoy talking about the great and ledgendary
--Learn more about the list here...

Reba_Fans

mailing list that talks about Reba McEntire.
--Learn more about the list here...

scott_walker

Discussion of Scott Walker's music both solo and with the
--Learn more about the list here...

WynonnaFans-owner

2 The site's home page lists its various directories. The Liszt directory categorises its information by subject, alphabetically. To search for mailing lists on, say, country music, click the **Genres** link under the Music category.

3 A list of sub-categories is revealed – click on **Country**. On the new page the words in bold denote each separate mailing list, followed by descriptions of the subject area covered. There may be an underlined link to further information.

4 If you find a list you like the sound of, subscribe to it. Do this by clicking on an e-mail link or on a **Subscribe** button.

Once you subscribe you can send e-mails to fellow members and receive members' messages in your own e-mail 'In' box.

Newsgroups

Newsgroups are made up of people who share the same interest. There are more than 30,000 Newsgroups in existence, covering all kinds of subjects. Ask your ISP for a list of groups it recognises. Web sites such as www.deja.com and www.supernews.com offer an introduction to the world of newsgroups. But be warned: the information you find in newsgroups is not always accurate or even true.

Key word

Chat room This is an area of a Web site set aside for people who want to chat in real time (that is, messages appear on screen as soon as they are typed, allowing an immediate response).

It's a convention in chat rooms for users to write a brief profile of themselves. This is usually a few words, giving details of your age, interests and location.

> Play rugby (badly) and football (worse)
> Big fan of Liverpool FC. Interested to
> hear from other supporters worldwide.

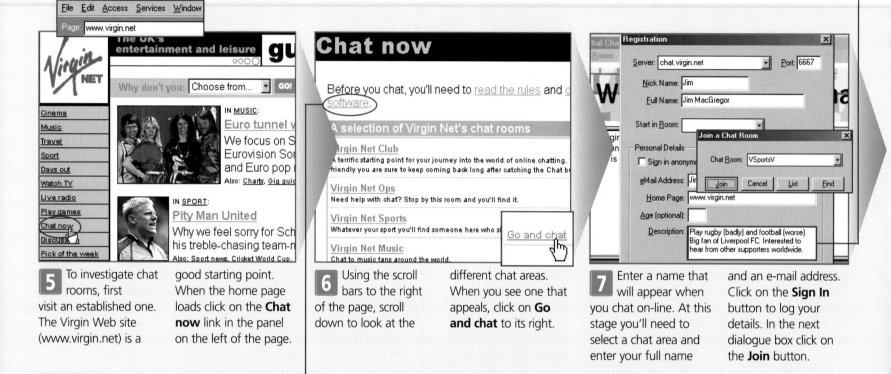

5 To investigate chat rooms, first visit an established one. The Virgin Web site (www.virgin.net) is a good starting point. When the home page loads click on the **Chat now** link in the panel on the left of the page.

6 Using the scroll bars to the right of the page, scroll down to look at the different chat areas. When you see one that appeals, click on **Go and chat** to its right.

7 Enter a name that will appear when you chat on-line. At this stage you'll need to select a chat area and enter your full name and an e-mail address. Click on the **Sign In** button to log your details. In the next dialogue box click on the **Join** button.

Chatting through Virgin

To chat through the Virgin Web site you need to download special software. Click on the **download the software** link and follow the on-screen instructions – make sure you click on the correct version (for Windows). The program's 'exe' file will be saved to your Desktop.

To install it onto your hard disk, close down your Web browser, double-click on the icon on your Desktop and follow the on-screen instructions. You will then be able to start the program from your Start menu. Alternatively, just click on a chat room on the Virgin site and the program will load automatically.

Before you chat, you'll need to read the rules and download the software.

A selection of Virgin Net's chat rooms

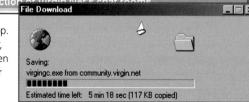

File Download

Saving:
virgingc.exe from community.virgin.net

Estimated time left: 5 min 18 sec (117 KB copied)

When messages are typed into the chat screen, the name of the sender appears just before the message. To avoid confusion, the messages you type won't have your name before them.

Watch out
When you are communicating with others over the Internet remember to think about your own personal privacy. Never divulge personal information such as your address and phone number to anyone unless you know them or feel sure you can trust them.

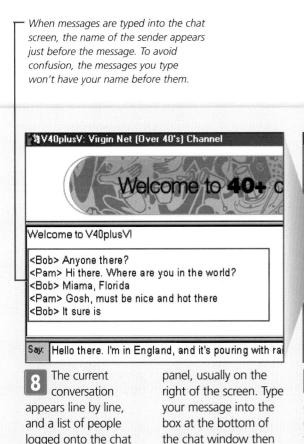

8 The current conversation appears line by line, and a list of people logged onto the chat area at that time is in a panel, usually on the right of the screen. Type your message into the box at the bottom of the chat window then press **Return** to send it.

9 To find out more about who you are chatting to, double-click on their name to open their profile box. It's common for people to have private chats in a separate window. If you don't want this, specify 'No private chats' in your description box when you first log on.

10 To join a new room, create a chat area of your own or leave a room, go to the **Rooms** menu and click on your choice. Another way to end your chat is to click on the close window button in the top right-hand corner of the window.

Room hopping
If you want to hold conversations on various topics in one session, you can log into more than one chat room at a time. First go to **Rooms** menu in the chat room's menu bar and click on **List All Rooms**. Simply double-click on one of the rooms listed to enter it.

chat.virgin.net - list of all rooms

Rooms: 219   Refresh

Room	Members	Topic
VEducationV	2	Virgin Net (Education) Channel
VEntertainmentV	2	Virgin (Entertainment) Channel.
VFootballV	2	Virgin Net (Football) Channel
VFriendlyV	2	Friendly people to talk to
VGamesV	2	Virgin Net (Games) Channel.
VHealthV	2	Virgin Net (Health) Channel. .
VMusicV	2	Virgin Net (Music) channel. .
VNewsV	2	Virgin Net (News) channel.
VOnlineGamesV	2	A Place to set up/discuss Online Games. .

Shopping on the Internet

Buying what you want is just a question of point and click

On-line shopping is one of the fastest growing areas of the Internet. Users have access to a far wider range of goods than can be bought in local shops. Many people prefer on-line shopping because of the convenience – no parking or queues, 'shops' open 24 hours a day, seven days a week, and goods are delivered to the door.

The prices of goods offered over the Internet are extremely competitive. Even after paying for delivery they can work out cheaper than shopping by conventional means.

In this project we show you how to buy a book and a piece of computer hardware. Use the steps as a general guide to buying any goods on-line.

Make sure your modem is plugged into a power supply, and that the modem cable is plugged into a phone line. Then switch it on.

▶ BEFORE YOU START

1 Connect to the Internet. In your Web browser's address box type in the address of an Internet shopping site (here, www.amazon.co.uk). Click on **Go** (or press the **Enter** or **Return** key) then wait for the site's home page to appear on screen.

Popular shopping sites

Addresses for popular shopping sites include:
- www.amazon.co.uk (books)
- www.cdnow.com (music)
- www.outpost.com (computer equipment)
- www.interflora.com (flowers)
- www.lastminute.com (tickets and travel)
- www.barclaysquare.com (superstore)

Bright idea
When you buy over the Internet make a note of information such as the date of purchase, item, cost, contact phone number or e-mail address. This makes follow-up queries easy.

*When you click on the **Add to Shopping Basket** button you are not committed to buy at this point. You are simply collecting items.*

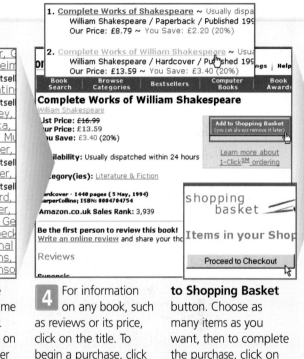

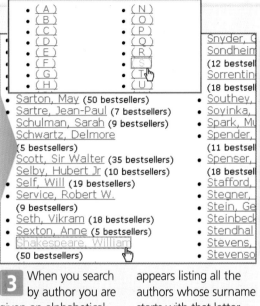

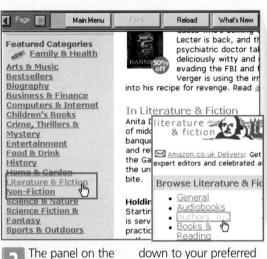

2 The panel on the left of the page lists different categories of books. Use the scroll bar to the right of the page to scroll down to your preferred category. Click on it, then wait for the new page to appear. To explore the category click on a subject.

3 When you search by author you are given an alphabetical list. Click on the initial letter of the surname of the author. A page appears listing all the authors whose surname starts with that letter. Scroll down and click on the name of the writer you're interested in.

4 For information on any book, such as reviews or its price, click on the title. To begin a purchase, click the title then the **Add to Shopping Basket** button. Choose as many items as you want, then to complete the purchase, click on **Proceed to Checkout**.

Making a quick search
On the Amazon home page you will see a search box near the top-left of the page. Type in the author, title, or subject of the book and click on **Go!**. A list of relevant books appears, which you can browse or buy.

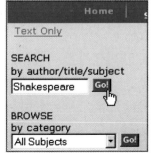

Quick browsing
The Shopping Basket lists all the books you've selected to buy, and the number of copies of each. If you decide not to buy a book you have selected, change the number in the quantity box to zero.

To continue browsing, click on the **Amazon.co.uk Home** button, or click on the browser's **Back** button to return to previous pages.

Items in your Shopping Basket

Proceed to Checkout	Amazon.co.uk Home

Quantity and Title Information:

Available immediately

1   *Reader's Digest New Gardening Year:* Hardcover
List: £19.95 ~ Our Price: £15.96 ~ You Save: £3.99 (20%)

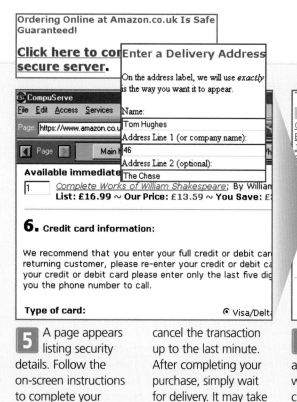

Ordering Online at Amazon.co.uk Is Safe Guaranteed!

Click here to co **secure server.**

Enter a Delivery Address

On the address label, we will use *exactly* is the way you want it to appear.

Name:
Tom Hughes

Address Line 1 (or company name):
46

Address Line 2 (optional):
The Chase

CompuServe
File Edit Access Services
Page https://www.amazon.co.u

Page | Main M

Available immediate

1 | *Complete Works of William Shakespeare*; By William
List: **£16.99** ~ Our Price: **£13.59** ~ **You Save: £**

6. Credit card information:

We recommend that you enter your full credit or debit car returning customer, please re-enter your credit or debit ca your credit or debit card please enter only the last five dig you the phone number to call.

Type of card: ⊙ Visa/Delt

Using the Internet to buy computer hardware can save you money. We used the Lycos search engine, at www.lycos.co.uk.

COMPUTER HARDWARE

Address | http://www.lycos.co.uk/

LYCOS ONLINE

Search Services
Classifieds
Business Directory
Jobs
Search Options
Translation
Pictures&Sound

Lycos Browser –
Download it now!

Shopping Centre
Lycos Shopping Network

Online Computer Store – click here

The Internet's Number One Music S

Click here for the **Internet Booksh**

Get Lycos in:
Germany, Belgium, Switzerland, Spain, France, Italy, Netherlands

Order Tracking
Personal Profile

product search [   ] GO!

GoLive 4.0

Outpost.com OVERNIGHT DELIVERY English
The Cool Place to Shop for Computer Stuff! Order by Midnight, Get it Tomorrow. Click for details

Customer Service | Shopping Cart | Privacy & Security | product search [   ]

Hardware Mac PC
Software Mac PC
Accessories Mac PC
Showcases

Store Map
OutpostAuctions.com

New Arrivals
Top Ten Mac
Top Ten PC
Bargain Basement
PC Steals & Deals
Game Outpost
Software Downloads

SAVINGS ON THESE GREAT DEALS..

Racer Tower 333 w/ 3 year Warranty
$499.95 GO!
While Supplies Last!

Apple iMac Blueberry or Grape!
$1099.95 GO!

For 30 other Great Specials! Click Here

GoLive 4
$289

Rio

Scanmaker X
$89
after R

FRE
Overni
Domes
Shippi

4 day delivery.

$499.95 **Click To Buy!**

New!

outpost.com/cgi-bin/bv.cgi?BV_Engin

---

5 A page appears listing security details. Follow the on-screen instructions to complete your purchase. You can cancel the transaction up to the last minute. After completing your purchase, simply wait for delivery. It may take just a few days.

6 In your Web browser's address box type www.lycos.co.uk then click on **Go** or press **Enter**. When the page appears scroll down to the Shopping Centre and click on **Online Computer Store**.

7 You can either type in the name of the item you are interested in, or click on the category buttons to explore what's available. Place items in your 'shopping basket' by clicking on the **Click To Buy** button.

Bright idea

If you are reluctant to send financial details over the Internet, look for an option to fax, telephone or post your order.

Buying abroad

Sometimes it can be cost-effective to buy goods abroad. Certain items of clothing and PC equipment, for example, can be bought more cheaply from the United States – even after adding import duty and sales tax. The buying process is essentially the same, but there are a few extra things to watch out for.

Information about shipping charges varies from site to site. For the one visited in Steps 6-10, click on the **Help** button to access the information.

Outpost.com Internat
Help [Shi
Back to Shopping Shipping
View your Cart Outp
Home appr
We'r
time
▶ How to Shop an a
▶ How to Place an Order (usu
▼ Shipping Information **Ship**
● Domestic Shipping prod
● International Shipping
● APO/FPII Addresses

Watch out
Make sure that equipment bought in the US is compatible for UK use (a lot of electrical equipment is not). You are unlikely to get technical support or a warranty for hardware shipped to the UK from the US. PC software should be universally compatible.

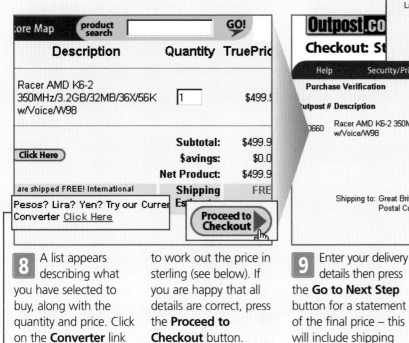

Billing Information (as it appears on your cr

First Name	Tom
Last Name	Hughes
Address	The Chase
	High Street
City	Bicester

ore Map | product search | [ ] | GO!

Description	Quantity	TruePric
Racer AMD K6-2 350MHz/3.2GB/32MB/36X/56K w/Voice/W98	1	$499.9

Subtotal:	$499.9
$avings:	$0.0
Net Product:	$499.9
Shipping	FRE

Click Here

are shipped FREE! International

Pesos? Lira? Yen? Try our Currer Converter Click Here

Proceed to Checkout ▶

Outpost.com
Checkout: St

Help | Security/Privacy | Store Map

Purchase Verification

utpost # Description | Qua

0660 | Racer AMD K6-2 350MHz/3.2GB/32MB/36X/56K w/Voice/W98

Shipping to: Great Britain
Postal Code OX10 2AI

DHL | **Go to Next Step ▶**
$95.00

Outpost.com
Checkout: Step ☑ ☑ ☑

Help | Security/Privacy | Store Map

ayment Options

I'd like to use the following credit card:

VISA | MasterCard | AMERICAN OPTIMA | | K |

● | ○ | ○ | ○ | ○

Credit Card # 04555 7878722222

Expiration Date: 03 ▾ / 2001 ▾ (MM/YYY

For other payment options, please contact our sales de at 1-877-OUTPOST or 1-860-927-2 | **Submit Order ▶**

8 A list appears describing what you have selected to buy, along with the quantity and price. Click on the **Converter** link

to work out the price in sterling (see below). If you are happy that all details are correct, press the **Proceed to Checkout** button.

9 Enter your delivery details then press the **Go to Next Step** button for a statement of the final price – this will include shipping

charges. (The price is in US dollars so you have to use your browser's **Back** button to use the currency converter.) Click on **Go to Next Step**.

10 Input your credit-card details (the vendor uses encryption technology to scramble your card number while it is being sent over the

Internet), and press the **Submit Order** button. You will receive confirmation. Then simply wait for your goods to be delivered.

Select your currency: | **Convert amount:**

| |
| Ukraine Hryvnia |
| Ukraine Karbovanets |
| United Kingdom Pound |
| Uruguayan Peso |
| Utd. Arab Emir. Dirham |
| Vanuatu Vatu |
| Venezuelan Bolivar |
| Vietnamese Dong |

499.95

314.731 British Pound

Submit | Close Window

*To use the currency converter type in the amount you want converted in the 'Convert amount:' box, click on your choice of currency in the 'Select your currency' pane, then click on **Submit**. Another window will appear giving you the converted sum.*

Find and buy an antique

Use the Internet to seek out new items for your collection

The Internet is an excellent source of information for collectors of almost anything, from records and model cars to paintings and antiques.

For keen collectors of antiques the World Wide Web opens up a completely new way of shopping and dealing, and many auction houses now run 'virtual auctions' on-line. Collectors can also find a wealth of detail on their favourite craftsmen and women, designers and painters. And they can share information with other enthusiasts, arrange sales and purchases, and simply enjoy chatting about their hobby.

BEFORE YOU START

Make a list of the categories or key words to search by. If one search doesn't yield many sites you can search again without wasting time. Remember to switch on your modem.

1 Connect to the Internet. In your Web browser's address box type in the address of a search engine and press the **Return** key.

Either type a key word in the search engine's search box (here, Antiques) and click on **Search**, or click on a relevant category.

Popular search engines

The addresses for popular search engines are:
- www.altavista.com
- www.hotbot.com
- www.lycos.co.uk
- www.yahoo.co.uk
- www.excite.co.uk
- www.northernlight.com

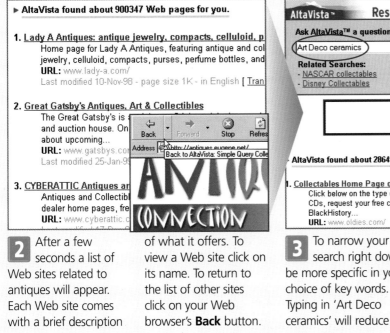

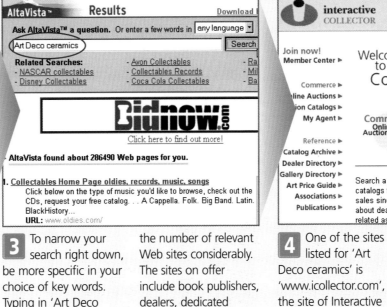

2 After a few seconds a list of Web sites related to antiques will appear. Each Web site comes with a brief description of what it offers. To view a Web site click on its name. To return to the list of other sites click on your Web browser's **Back** button.

3 To narrow your search right down, be more specific in your choice of key words. Typing in 'Art Deco ceramics' will reduce the number of relevant Web sites considerably. The sites on offer include book publishers, dealers, dedicated enthusiasts and experts.

4 One of the sites listed for 'Art Deco ceramics' is 'www.icollector.com', the site of Interactive Collector. This offers information about antiques, collectables and auctions. Through it you can bid on-line and learn about galleries and exhibitions.

Virtual auctions

On-line auctions operate along similar lines to traditional auctions. Goods are previewed (often as photos on the site) then bidding begins. When bidding closes, after a specified period of days or weeks, arrangements are made for the highest bidder to receive the goods.

Most on-line auction houses are bona fide, but there are some that are fraudulent. The real ones will happily answer queries and supply any information that you need. Find out how they handle transactions and whether there are additional charges.

Surfing the Internet

You can browse Web sites – or 'surf the Net' – in several ways. You can open any site by typing its address in the browser's address box and pressing **Return**, or clicking on its underlined link in another site. Alternatively, you can use the browser's toolbar buttons to move backward and forward through pages and sites.

Close-up
With Internet Explorer you can search and browse for Web sites within a single window. When you display the search Explorer Bar, the frame to the left displays the search engine and search results. Click on a site listed on the left and it will appear in the right frame.

5 If you want information relating to a specific artist, type the name into the search engine's search box, enclosed in speech marks, for example "Clarice Cliff". AltaVista will look for the two words as a phrase, and only show sites that match it.

6 There are some excellent resources on the Web for Clarice Cliff fans. The site at 'www.claricecliff.com' is designed for collectors, and provides lots of useful information, as well as being a forum for chat and discussion.

7 Another Clarice Cliff site, at 'www.storenet.co.uk', operates as a virtual showroom, allowing you to view and buy items from a catalogue. If you want to revisit a page, right-click on the browser's **Back** button then click on the page you want to view.

Picture search

If you are looking for a specific image you will find Image Surfer useful. This facility indexes images rather than Web sites. Type 'http://isurf.interpix.com/' into your address box (there is no 'www' in the address), then press **Return**. In the search box type key words to describe what you are looking for, or click on a category.

Short cut
*You can access the Internet from the Taskbar in Windows 98. Right-click on the Taskbar, select **Toolbars** from the pop-up menu, followed by **Address**. Type in a Web address (URL) in the address box that appears then press **Enter**.*

8 There are many sites that you can use to 'talk' to other collectors. The most popular have their own discussion areas. For antiques, go to 'www.bbc.co.uk/antiques'. This is the home page for the BBC Antiques site. Click on **Forums** to visit the chat areas.

9 Before you enter a Forum you have to register by filling in your e-mail address and a password in the box provided and clicking on the **Get Talking** button. Now click on your choice of topic from the Antiques Forum list on the left-hand side of the page.

10 You will see messages displayed on screen. To reply to one, click on **reply**. To start a discussion, click on the **new message** button, then type your note in the box that appears. To see what's been discussed on a topic, click on the **threaded** button.

Using search engines well

Each search engine has its own way of allowing you to narrow or broaden your searches for information. Look for pointers to special help sections on a search engine's home page that will teach you about searching successfully.

Set up a family Web site

You can make your personal mark on the World Wide Web

One of the most exciting Internet projects you can do is to create your own Web site. It is a great chance to send a message to an audience of millions.

A well-planned personal Web site can be used to promote a club or society, or to communicate with people of similar interests.

You can design your site while working off-line using Word. Then, in a matter of minutes, you can connect to the Internet and publish the pages using the Web Publishing Wizard available in Windows 98

If you are using Windows 95, you will need a separate Web publishing program. After that anyone can visit your pages whether you are on-line or not: the site is there for all to see.

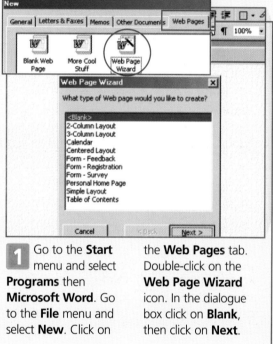

You need Web space and a Web address from your ISP (see page 90). You also need Word's Web Page Authoring option (see below) and the Web Publishing Wizard that comes with Windows.

BEFORE YOU START

1 Go to the **Start** menu and select **Programs** then **Microsoft Word**. Go to the **File** menu and select **New**. Click on the **Web Pages** tab. Double-click on the **Web Page Wizard** icon. In the dialogue box click on **Blank**, then click on **Next**.

Install Web Page Authoring

If the Web Pages tab is not shown, you must install this element of Word. To do this, close your programs, go to the **Start** menu and select **Settings**, **Control Panel**, then **Add/Remove Programs**. Select **Office** from the program list, click **Add/Remove** and insert your Office CD-ROM. Click **Add/Remove** again then, in the Options pane of the next dialogue box, click in the Web Page Authoring (HTML) box (a tick will appear). Click **Continue** to install it. Now go to Step 1.

Watch out

Some of the dialogue boxes and options shown may differ from those on your PC. This can be caused by the options chosen while installing Windows or Office, or by software updates received over the Net. This will not affect your ability to complete the project.

Key word

Home page This refers to the page that provides the point of entry to a collection of linked pages in a Web site. However, a home page can also stand alone, without links.

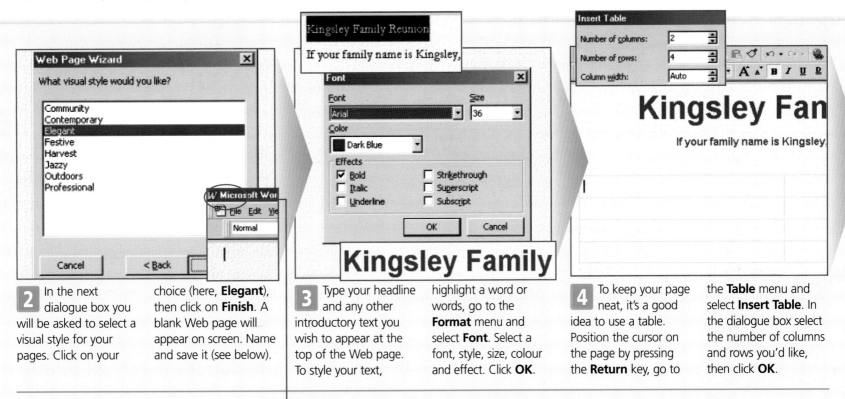

2 In the next dialogue box you will be asked to select a visual style for your pages. Click on your choice (here, **Elegant**), then click on **Finish**. A blank Web page will appear on screen. Name and save it (see below).

3 Type your headline and any other introductory text you wish to appear at the top of the Web page. To style your text, highlight a word or words, go to the **Format** menu and select **Font**. Select a font, style, size, colour and effect. Click **OK**.

4 To keep your page neat, it's a good idea to use a table. Position the cursor on the page by pressing the **Return** key, go to the **Table** menu and select **Insert Table**. In the dialogue box select the number of columns and rows you'd like, then click **OK**.

Saving your page as HTML

Web pages are created in a language called HTML (HyperText Markup Language). But you do not need to know the language because Microsoft Word will create the HTML for you.

When your blank page appears, go to the **File** menu and select **Save as HTML**. If this option is not offered, select **Save As** and then choose **HTML Document** in the 'Save as type' box. Create a new folder to save it to, and name the document 'home'. When saving a file for use on the Web, always give it a one-word name, typed in lower case (servers using the UNIX operating system won't recognise file names with capital letters or spaces).

To edit your page, open Word, go to the **File** menu and select **Open**. Then use the dialogue box to locate the page. To view your page in your browser, and test links before publishing, double-click on the file icon.

Why use a table?

A table can be used as the framework for your Web page. Without a table it is difficult to position your text and pictures precisely. For this project two columns have been chosen, one for pictures and one for text. Four rows were chosen to accommodate the projected content of the page.

Make sure that the cursor is positioned exactly where you want the table to appear.

Watch out
When you insert your table, you will not at first be able to see it. To make the table visible, go to the **Table** menu and select **Show Gridlines**.

Bright idea
Word offers a variety of design elements to use when creating your Web pages. More backgrounds, buttons and rules can be obtained from the Web and disks cover-mounted on PC magazines.

5 To adjust the width of a column, place the mouse pointer over the column edge. When it changes to a double-headed arrow, press the left mouse button and drag the line across to the required width.

6 To place text in the table, click in the relevant column and row and simply type it in. The row height will adjust automatically to accommodate your entry. Style the text as in Step 3.

7 To insert a picture in the table, click in the relevant column and row (here, in the first row of the first column). Go to the Insert menu and select **Picture**, then **From File**. This lets you import scanned pictures stored on the hard disk.

Preparing images

In order for your Web pages to carry the maximum amount of information and be downloaded quickly, pictures should use as little memory as possible. It's best, then, to use small images saved in a compressed format. To do this, you'll need an image-editing package such as Paint.

Open the image, go to the **Image** menu and select **Attributes**. Set the image to 200 pixels high and reduce the width by a similar degree (this reduces the memory required by the image file). Click **OK**.

Go to the **File** menu and select **Save As**. In the 'Save as type' box, select either **JPEG** (Joint Photographic Experts Group) or **GIF** (Graphic Image Format). JPEG is the best format for images with graduated colours; GIF is more suitable for images with solid colours. Pictures saved in these formats are compressed to use less memory. Name and save the file in your Web folder.

If the images files you are using are not already held in your publishing folder, you must save them in it. This is important as they need to be here when you publish.

The Web is made up of millions of linked pages. You can also add links from your home page to other pages that you have created or to other sites on the Web.

LINKING PAGES

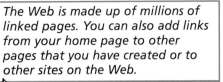

On the 25th March 2000, my grandfather George Kingsley w 100 years old. To mark this ev would like to gather together a of the Kingsley family as possi have contacted all the cousins relatives that I know of, but m grandfather is certain that there many more family members tha have lost touch with - or don't know about! For instance he ca remember hearing about an un who emigrated to America in th 19th Century and another cousi moved to Australia early last c

The Kingsley Family Photo Album

This is my wife Anne Kingsley, and our two children Laura (6) and Jack (4). The picture wa taken at Teignmouth in Dorset where we had our summer holiday this year.

This is me, John Kingsley and yes I'm the one with the glasses!

of the Kingsl have contacte relatives that grandfather is many more fa have lost tou know about! remember he who emigrate 19th Century moved to Au

s my grandfather, George sley, aged 16. If you notice ny family resemblance, get in touch!

ught that this Web site might help find a few of these long relatives, so if you're out there - let us know! **Click here to see** e information on the family. If you recognise any of your

Insert Format Tools Table
Break...
Page Numbers...
Date and Time...
AutoText ▶
Field...
Symbol...
Comment
Footnote...
Caption...
Cross-reference...
Index and Tables...
Picture ▶
Text Box
File...
Object...
Bookmark...
Hyperlink... Ctrl+K

8 The Insert Picture dialogue box appears. In the 'Look in' box find the folder that contains your images. Click on the image you wish to import, then click **Insert**. The image appears in the table. To resize the picture, click on it, then click and drag a corner handle.

9 To create another page for your site, first open another blank Web page as in Step 1. Save it in the same folder as your first page. Insert a table, type in your text then style it in a similar way to your previous page.

10 To link this second page to your home page, you need to set up a 'hypertext' link. Open the home page, highlight a word or words you want to act as the link, then go to the **Insert** menu and click on **Hyperlink**.

Key word
Link A set of words or an image which, when clicked on, takes the user to another page on the World Wide Web. Text links usually appear underlined and in different coloured type.

Close-up
*To remove a link, highlight the words that activate the link, go to the **Insert** menu and select **Hyperlink**. In the Edit Hyperlink dialogue box click on the **Remove link** button.*

Once you have designed your pages, Windows has a Web Publishing Wizard that takes you through the process of connecting to the Internet and publishing them.

PUBLISHING YOUR PAGES

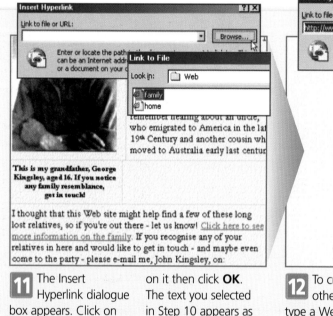

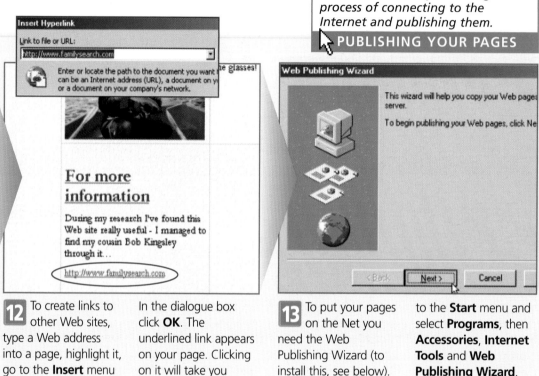

11 The Insert Hyperlink dialogue box appears. Click on the **Browse** button to locate the second page. When you find it, click on it then click **OK**. The text you selected in Step 10 appears as an underlined link. Click on this to see the linked page.

12 To create links to other Web sites, type a Web address into a page, highlight it, go to the **Insert** menu and select **Hyperlink**. In the dialogue box click **OK**. The underlined link appears on your page. Clicking on it will take you directly to that site.

13 To put your pages on the Net you need the Web Publishing Wizard (to install this, see below). To start the Wizard, go to the **Start** menu and select **Programs**, then **Accessories**, **Internet Tools** and **Web Publishing Wizard**. Click **Next** to continue.

Installing the Web Wizard

To install Microsoft's Web Publishing Wizard, go to the **Start** menu and select **Settings** then **Control Panel**. Double-click on the **Add/Remove Programs** icon. A dialogue box appears. Click on the **Windows Setup** tab. Double-click on the **Internet Tools** box. In the Components pane click in the Web Publishing Wizard box so that it is ticked. Click **OK**. Click **OK** again and then follow the instructions to insert your Windows CD-ROM and complete the installation.

Watch out

Make sure you are connected to the Internet before you complete the instructions in the Web Publishing Wizard and click on Finish. Otherwise the Wizard will not be able to publish your pages.

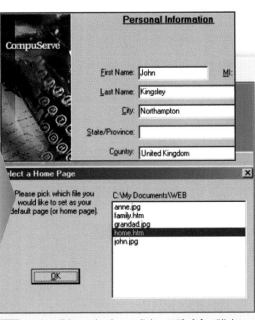

Kingsley Family R

If your family name is Kingsley, we want to hea

14 Click on the **Browse Folders** button and select the folder containing your Web pages and images. Click on **Next**. You will be asked for the name of the server to which you are publishing (here, CompuServe's Our World). Click on **Next**.

15 You will be asked further questions, including your Web address. Work through the screens, clicking **Next** as you go. Finally, click on **Finish**. Click on the file you wish to be your home page (here, **home.htm**) then click **OK**. Your pages will now be uploaded.

16 Now open your Web browser and type the Web address for your pages into the address box. Click on **Go** (or press **Enter** or **Return**). After you connect to the Web your home page will be located and displayed – just as Web users across the globe will see it.

Key word

Server *This refers to the computer that holds your Web pages. When you publish your Web pages you are transferring them to that computer. This means that you do not have to be on-line yourself for someone to see your pages.*

Do research on the Net

Use today's technology to learn about our yesterdays

The World Wide Web is a great tool for historical research. Whatever your field of interest, there are almost bound to be sites, discussion groups and library resources dedicated to that topic.

If, for example, you are interested in the First World War, you will find thousands of resources on the Web. Some will be pages produced by amateur historians, some will be educational sites aimed at children, some will be highly academic.

The first step is to do a search. Here we use a search engine called Northern Light, but you can use any one you like, and pick your own path through the wealth of information on the Great War.

Make a note of which direction you want your search to take. Be as specific as possible to limit the number of 'hits'. For example, search for 'Somme' rather than 'battles'.

BEFORE YOU START

1 Connect to the Internet as usual. In your Web browser's address box type in the address of a search engine then click **Go** or **Enter**. The engine's home page will appear. Type a key word or words into the search box then click on the **Search** button.

Popular First World War sites
Addresses for interesting war sites include:
- www.historyoftheworld.com (useful collection of links)
- www.encyclopedia.com (free on-line encyclopedia)
- www.worldwar1.com (reference works and discussions)
- www.opengroup.com (large database of books)

Key word
A home page is the opening page for any Web site. It will tell you what the site includes and provide links to the various parts of the site.

📄 **Documents that best n**

1. Doctrine, Technology, and War 1
   85% - Articles & General info: D
   D. Watts Air & Space Doctrinal Sy
   Alabama 30 April-1 May 1996 1. In
   Military site: http://www.cdsar.a

...on - RAF History - W
   66% - Articles & General info: Royal Wings - Royal Air Fo
   Information - RAF History - World War 1 Click Here to Visit to
   They mingle not with their... 12/09/98
   Commercial site: http://www.royalwings.co.uk/information.
   World_War_1/index.htm

15. Internet Addresses - World War 1
    66% - Directories & Lists: Internet Addresses - World War
    Internet Addresses GENERAL TIMELINE BIOGRAPHIES TRI
    WARFARE POETRY PAINTINGS CAUSES SOMME WOMEI
    WEAPONS GENERAL Great War... 06/02/97
    Educational site: http://www.highdown.berks.sch.uk/ subjec
    Ww1/1eft2.htm

16. Canada at War 1
    66% - Articles & Ger

114. The World War I Links Page
     58% - Directories & Lists The
     55 min 32 sec Abstract   Books Music... 09/06/98
     experienced by... 01/06   **Commercial site:** http://www.h
     Canadian site: http://   ww1.htm

Scots at War
Saint-Pierre et Miquelon F
Trenches on Web
US National Cryptologic I

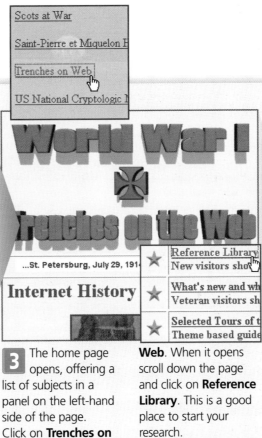

...St. Petersburg, July 29, 1914

Internet History

★ Reference Library
  New visitors sho

★ What's new and wh
  Veteran visitors sh

★ Selected Tours of t
  Theme based guide

Biographies: Index

2 After several seconds a list of Web sites will appear. A search for 'World War I' yields more than one million items, including sites on women's roles in the war, picture archives and eye-witness accounts. Scroll down and click on **The World War I Links Page**.

3 The home page opens, offering a list of subjects in a panel on the left-hand side of the page. Click on **Trenches on Web**. When it opens scroll down the page and click on **Reference Library**. This is a good place to start your research.

4 Through the Reference Library you can access huge amounts of data, including biographies, maps, artwork and even sound recordings of the period. Click on one of the buttons at the foot of the home page to access an area of your choice.

Results by category

The search service Northern Light groups together related Web sites by category. This is extremely useful as it means you don't have to trawl through thousands of sites to find ones you may be interested in.

After your initial search it organises the sites found into Custom Search Folders – these folders, or categories, appear on the left of the page. After you do a search, click on a category. Only the sites that conform to that category's specifications will be listed.

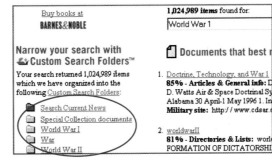

Buy books at
BARNES&NOBLE

Narrow your search with
📁 **Custom Search Folders™**

Your search returned 1,024,989 items which we have organized into the following Custom Search Folders:

📁 Search Current News
📁 Special Collection documents
📁 World War I
📁 War
📁 World War II

1,024,989 items found for:
World War 1

📄 **Documents that best n**

1. Doctrine, Technology, and War 1
   85% - Articles & General info: D
   D. Watts Air & Space Doctrinal Sy
   Alabama 30 April-1 May 1996 1. In
   Military site: http://www.cdsar.e

2. worldwarII
   81% - Directories & Lists: worl
   FORMATION OF DICTATORSHI

Remember to use your Web browser's Back and Forward

Back · Forward

buttons to revisit Web sites and pages you have opened since going on-line.

Bright idea
When you come across interesting or informative sites, bookmark them (see page 98). This way you can revisit them quickly, without having to type their address into your Web browser's address box.

Back

Virgil's photos - World War I
66% - Articles & General info: Vi
Iphotographs Below is a table of con
and photo caption with... 07/17/97
Personal page: http://jabberwock.v

World War I photographs

Below is a table of contents to a photo album, listing page nu
with a link to each. The page numbers link to image maps;
directly to the JPEG. The photos are from my grandfather, V
a ship's baker 1st class on the USS Henry R. Mallory. [The
prevents the detail of the stripes from scanning

After discussing the photo album with my aunt, we conclu
belonged to my grandmother, Millie, who also wrote the cap
on 3 things: 1) the captions are in her handwriting; 2) the
meaningful order; 3) most of the captions are in quotation ma
she asked Virgil and quoted his answ

As I said, you can jump to a photo directly from this page, or
and browse just like a regular photo album.

Narrow your search with
Custom Search Folders™
Your search returned 1,012,132 items
which we have organized into the
following Custom Search Folders:

- Search Current News
- Special Collection documents
- World War I
- War

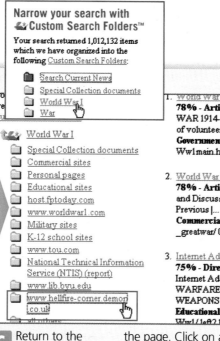

World War I
- Special Collection documents
- Commercial sites
- Personal pages
- Educational sites
- host.fptoday.com
- www.worldwar1.com
- Military sites
- K-12 school sites
- www.tou.com
- National Technical Information Service (NTIS) (report)
- www.lib.byu.edu
- www.hellfire-corner.demon.co.uk

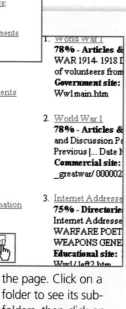

1. World War I
78% - Articles &
WAR 1914- 1918 D
of volunteers from
Government site:
Ww1main.htm

2. World War I
78% - Articles &
and Discussion Pe
Previous |... Date N
Commercial site:
_greatwar/ 000002

3. Internet Addresse
75% - Directorie
Internet Addresse
WARFARE POET
WEAPONS GENE
Educational site:
Ww1 / left2 htm

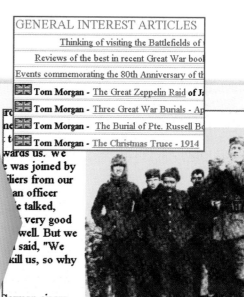

GENERAL INTEREST ARTICLES
Thinking of visiting the Battlefields of
Reviews of the best in recent Great War book
Events commemorating the 80th Anniversary of th
Tom Morgan - The Great Zeppelin Raid of J
Tom Morgan - Three Great War Burials - Ap
Tom Morgan - The Burial of Pte. Russell Bo
Tom Morgan - The Christmas Truce - 1914

wards us. we
e was joined by
iliers from our
an officer
e talked,
very good
well. But we
said, "We
kill us, so why

German cigars -
ery good ones
m. One of the
been opened

*Fusiliers and Germans -
No-Man's Land, Christmas Day, 1914*

5 To find other sites of interest, click on your Web browser's **Back** button to return to the Northern Light site. Click on another site, such as **Virgil's photos**. This fascinating photo album tells the story of an American soldier in the First World War.

6 Return to the page that listed the sites from your initial search. Look at the Custom Search Folders on the left of the page. Click on a folder to see its sub-folders, then click on one that interests you (here, **www.hellfire-corner.demon.co.uk**).

7 Now you can explore this site. Click on, say, **The Christmas Truce – 1914** for an account of that famous incident. When you have finished you can follow another link or use your browser's **Back** button to return you to your search results.

The Northern Light search service classifies the Web sites it lists in terms of their country of origin or whether they are commercial, educational or government sites.

114. The World War I Links Pa
58% - Directories & Lis
Books Music... 09
Commercial site: http://
ww1.htm

115. The Spirit of the Vikings
58% - Directories & Lis
the Vikings search page...
Norwegian site: http://

Printing a Web page
To print out a Web page for future reference, go to the **File** menu on your browser's menu bar at the top of the screen and click on **Print**.

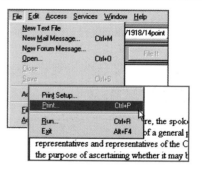

File Edit Access Services Window Help
New Text File
New Mail Message... Ctrl+M
New Forum Message...
Open... Ctrl+O
Close
Save Ctrl+S

Print Setup...
Print... Ctrl+P
Run... Ctrl+R
Exit Alt+F4

/1918/14point
File It

re, the spoke
of a general p
representatives and representatives of the C
the purpose of ascertaining whether it may b

22. IPL Pathfinder: World War I History
59% - Articles & General info: IPL Pat
the Internet Public Library Pathfinder: W
Introduction There are huge amounts of
World... Date Not Available
Non-profit site: http://ipl.org/ref/QUE

◆ the Internet Public Library

Pathfinder: World War One Hist

Introduction

There are huge amounts of available resources on World War One. Thousan
published since the conflict, and now the World Wide Web also offers hundr
resources, much less a starting point, can be very difficult.

This pathfinder was created to help Internet users find reliable information ab
personal knowledge or for
resources are excellent star
to understand the full comp

The World War I Document Archive
The document archive includes doc
http://www.lib.byu.edu/~rdh/w
The Versailles Treaty
This site features the full text of the Ver
bibliography; maps, charts, photos, an

Print Sources

There is an enormous amo
of Congress classification s

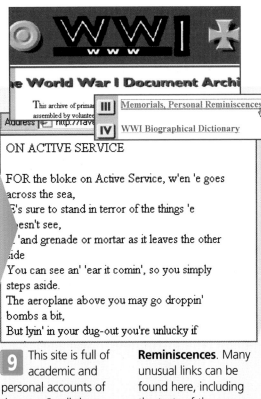

IV WWI Biographical Dictionary
V WWI Image Archive
VI Special Topics and Commentary Ar
VII WWI Sites: Links to Other Resour

III Memorials, Personal Reminiscences
IV WWI Biographical Dictionary

This archive of prima
assembled by voluntee
Address http://fave

ON ACTIVE SERVICE

FOR the bloke on Active Service, w'en 'e goes
across the sea,
'E's sure to stand in terror of the things 'e
doesn't see,
'and grenade or mortar as it leaves the other
side
You can see an' 'ear it comin', so you simply
steps aside.
The aeroplane above you may go droppin'
bombs a bit,
But lyin' in your dug-out you're unlucky if

War Albums

Commanders

Individuals

8 Scroll down and click on **IPL Pathfinder: World War I History**. This opens the Internet Public Library, a particularly helpful facility with useful links to other sites. Scroll down and click on **World War I Document Archive**.

9 This site is full of academic and personal accounts of the war. Scroll down and click on **Memorials, Personal Reminiscences**. Many unusual links can be found here, including the texts of the songs that were sung by the men in the trenches.

10 If you are interested in images to do with the First World War, return to the WWI Document Archive opening page and click on **WWI Image Archive**. The archive is divided into such categories as maps, medals and photographs.

Saving pictures

To save an image onto your hard disk, right-click on the image and select **Save Picture As...** from the pop-up menu that appears. Click on the arrow beside the 'Save in' box, scroll through and select a folder in which you want to save the image. Give the image a name in the 'File name' box then click **Save**.

Open Link
Open Link in New W
Save Target As...
Print Target
Show Picture
Save Picture As...
Set as Wallpaper
Copy

Save Picture
Save in: My Documents
World War 1 Research
File name: German Soldiers   Save

Primary school learning

Help your children expand their knowledge through the Net

The World Wide Web is, among many other things, a learning resource. It is full of material that can enhance children's understanding of their school subjects and of the world around them. There are thousands of educational sites, along with related sites that both parents and children will find useful. This project shows you a selection – some are bright and breezy interactive sites, others contain details of the National Curriculum.

Using the Internet for education is fun, and it equips primary-age children with learning skills they are likely to use throughout their school years, and beyond.

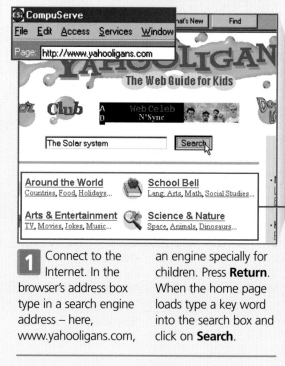

Make a daily study plan so that you can work out exactly which subjects are to be studied and when. This way, you can limit time spent on-line.

► BEFORE YOU START

1 Connect to the Internet. In the browser's address box type in a search engine address – here, www.yahooligans.com, an engine specially for children. Press **Return**. When the home page loads type a key word into the search box and click on **Search**.

Searching by category

In addition to a search box, some search engines let you search by category. You narrow your search by clicking on subdivisions that have been made already. This is useful for children who might misspell key words.

Close-up
Keep a record of a Web site's address by adding it to your Web browser's Favorites or Bookmarks file (see page 98). Once entered, all you need do to view the site is click on the entry instead of typing in the Web address every time.

*Click on the **Back** button to revisit sites and pages already viewed since you have been on-line.*

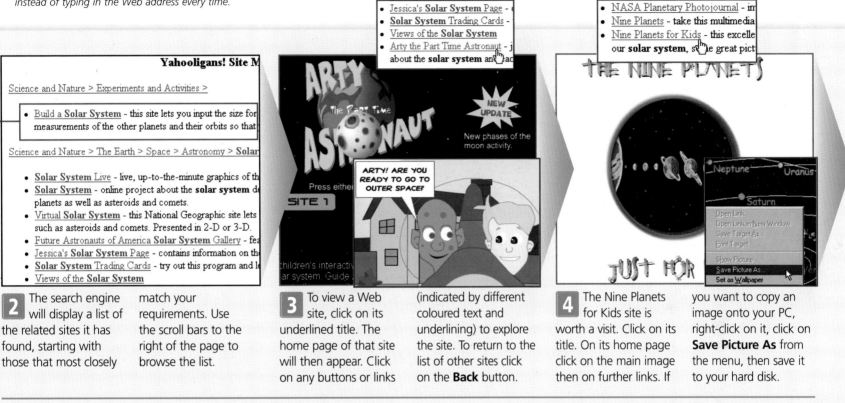

2 The search engine will display a list of the related sites it has found, starting with those that most closely match your requirements. Use the scroll bars to the right of the page to browse the list.

3 To view a Web site, click on its underlined title. The home page of that site will then appear. Click on any buttons or links (indicated by different coloured text and underlining) to explore the site. To return to the list of other sites click on the **Back** button.

4 The Nine Planets for Kids site is worth a visit. Click on its title. On its home page click on the main image then on further links. If you want to copy an image onto your PC, right-click on it, click on **Save Picture As** from the menu, then save it to your hard disk.

Most search engines provide a brief description of the contents of a Web site. This helps you to decide whether the site is likely to be useful or not.

Useful educational sites

You may find these Web sites and search engines particularly useful for children under 11:
- www.bbc.co.uk/education (contains a dedicated section to primary school learning)
- www.quia.com (fun and games for all ages)
- www.freezone.com (kids can build home pages)
- www.nationalgeographic.com/world/index.html (visit the Kids Network)

Bright idea
*Teach children how to read long Web pages off-line (using a Web site without staying on the phone line) to keep your phone bill down. If you're using Internet Explorer, go to the **File** menu and click on **Work Offline**.*

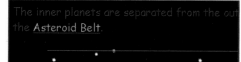

The inner planets are separated from the out the Asteroid Belt.

Click on the rocket to find about our nine planets!

are in relation to each other. Can you see ti y in the very bottom, left-hand corner? Plut tiny planet in the very top, right-hand corner

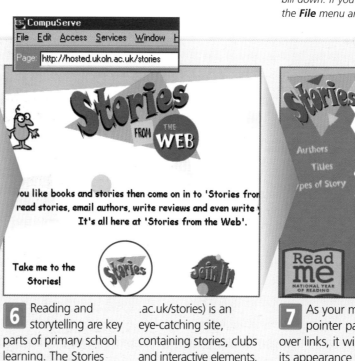

5 Remember to explore all links to other areas within the same site or to related sites. However, do not forget that time spent on the Internet costs you money.

6 Reading and storytelling are key parts of primary school learning. The Stories From The Web site (http://hosted.ukoln .ac.uk/stories) is an eye-catching site, containing stories, clubs and interactive elements. Click on the **Stories** for a good read.

7 As your mouse pointer passes over links, it will change its appearance to a hand sign. The site organises stories by Authors, Titles and Types of Story – clicking on a section header opens the link.

---

*When you find a page that contains useful information, you may want to print it. Click on the text first, then go to the **File** menu and click on **Print**.*

The Stories From The Web site offers guidelines for both parents and children. It also has an e-mail address should you want to contact the site administrators.

As you read stories on The Stories From The Web site, a page counter in the top right-hand corner of the screen will help you keep track of how far you have got.

Well-organised Web sites such as the one below will give you a guarantee that their pages and the sites they contain links to are child-friendly and safe.

Grown-Ups! Click here to find out more about Our Activities.

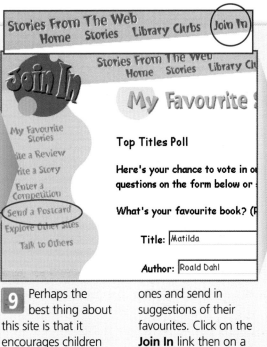

8 The stories appear on screen, page by page. You have to click on the **Read On** button to start and then the

Next Page button to turn the pages – a page counter in the corner tells you how many pages the book has.

9 Perhaps the best thing about this site is that it encourages children to write their own stories, review new

ones and send in suggestions of their favourites. Click on the **Join In** link then on a section from the panel on the left of the page.

10 Learning is easier when it's fun. The MaMamedia site (www.mamamedia.com) contains lots of

movement, colour and energy. This is definitely one to work through and enjoy, maybe as a break from homework.

The Send a Postcard section allows youngsters to select a special picture from the site's image library to send as an e-mail to a friend.

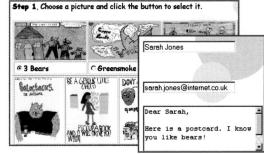

Watch out
To prevent children accessing unsuitable material on the Internet, consider buying a Web-screening program, such as Net Nanny or Cyber Patrol (see page 100).

Close-up
Links to other Web pages and sites usually appear underlined and in a different colour from the body text of a page. A mouse pointer will always change to a pointing hand when it passes over a link. A single mouse click opens a link.

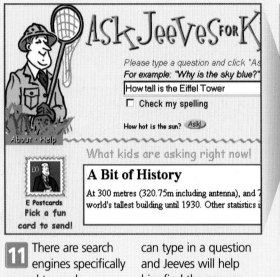

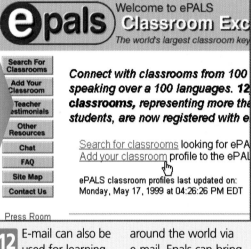

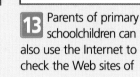

11 There are search engines specifically geared towards children. Ask Jeeves For Kids (www.ajkids.com) is one example. A child can type in a question and Jeeves will help him find the answer by listing Web sites that might contain relevant information.

12 E-mail can also be used for learning. Epals (www.epals.com) is a Net-based organisation that links schoolchildren from around the world via e-mail. Epals can bring together pupils of a similar age who are studying similar types of subject.

13 Parents of primary schoolchildren can also use the Internet to check the Web sites of prospective secondary schools. EduWeb (www.eduweb.co.uk) is a good place to start.

Navigating between windows

Sometimes, when you click on a link to another site, a new window opens in front of the original window. If you want to return to the original site, you have to make the original window 'active'.

To make the original window active, minimise or close the new window then click on the original window (clicking the **Back** button in the new window will not be effective).

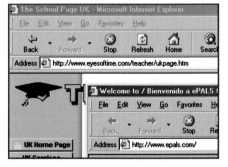

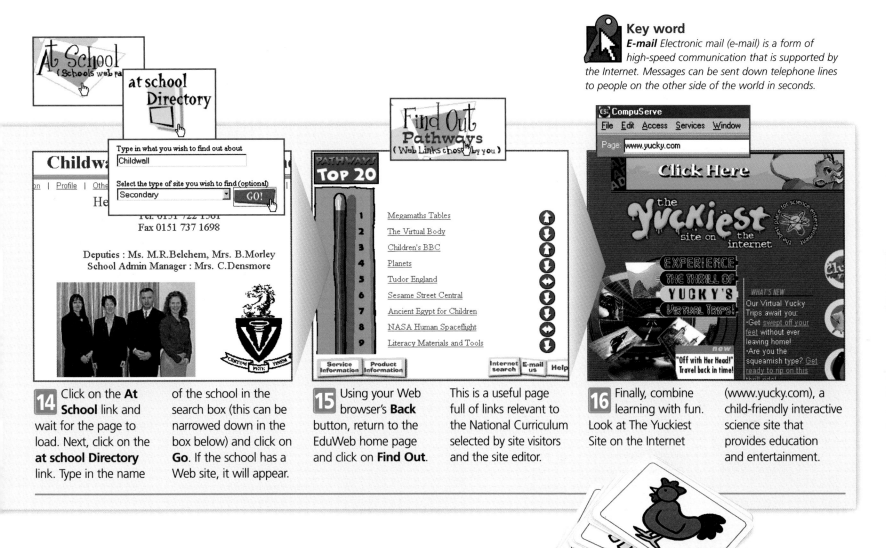

Key word
E-mail Electronic mail (e-mail) is a form of high-speed communication that is supported by the Internet. Messages can be sent down telephone lines to people on the other side of the world in seconds.

14 Click on the **At School** link and wait for the page to load. Next, click on the **at school Directory** link. Type in the name of the school in the search box (this can be narrowed down in the box below) and click on **Go**. If the school has a Web site, it will appear.

15 Using your Web browser's **Back** button, return to the EduWeb home page and click on **Find Out**. This is a useful page full of links relevant to the National Curriculum selected by site visitors and the site editor.

16 Finally, combine learning with fun. Look at The Yuckiest Site on the Internet (www.yucky.com), a child-friendly interactive science site that provides education and entertainment.

Secondary school learning

Gather material to help you study for your examinations

The Internet is a valuable aid to learning and study. In addition to helping with research for everyday school work, students can find lots of useful material that relates to GCSE and A-level syllabuses.

Certain sites offer the chance to browse past examination papers, take part in question-and-answer sessions, and chat with other students on-line. And when it comes to preparing for exams, students can get help setting up revision timetables.

Not all Web-based learning is geared towards specific exams, though. Language students can hone their skills by reading on-line foreign-language magazines, and everyone can find resources to help with all areas of study.

First make a list of the subject areas you wish to study, then make a note of appropriate key words and phrases to search by.

BEFORE YOU START

1 Connect to the Internet. In your Web browser's address box type the address of a search engine (here, www.infoseek.com),

then click on **Go** or press the **Return** key. After a few seconds the search engine's home page will load and appear on screen.

Close-up
Although the full address for Web sites includes 'http://' before the 'www...', you don't need to type this into the Address box. For most Web sites, you can simply start the address with 'www'.

The Infoseek search engine highlights every occurrence of your key word to help you make your choice of Web sites.

Search

| GCSE revision | Web sites ▾ | Find |

Search options | How to search | ⊙Oguardian™ is off | Powered by Infoseek

Web search results 1 - 10 of **2,796,220** results most relevan

Next 10 > | Hide summaries | Sort by date | Ungroup results

BBC Education - GCSE Bitesize Revision
BBC Education - **GCSE** Bitesize
83% Date: 4 Feb 1999, Size 7.3K, http://db.bbc.co.uk/education-bitesize/pkg_main
Find similar pages

GCSE Revision
WELCOME TO THIS SITE YOU ARE NEEDED TO MAKE THIS SITE
USEFUL SOURCE OF INFORMATION. AFTER VIEWING THIS SITE
SUBJECT NOT ALLREADY COVERED (OR ...
81% Date: 20 Feb 1998, Size 1.1K, http://www.homeusers.prestel.co.uk/rdale/revis
Find similar pages

GCSE Revision. Tips on how best to revise for GCSE examinati
A guide on **GCSE Revision**. How best to revise for **GCSE** exams.
79% Date: 4 May 1998, Size 8.7K, http://members.xoom.com/gcse/index.html
Find similar pages

BBC Schools Online

🖐 **Primary Resources**
Literacy and Numeracy

🍎 **Seco**
GCS

Welcome to BBC Schools Online
Lively, interactive learning resources for home and at school. Please choose eit
Resources, Secondary Resources or H

Modern World History

GET SHOCKWAVE
Get S
from

VIEW WITHOUT SHOCKWAVE
View
Shoc

BBC Scho

🖐 **Primary Res**
Literacy and N

Online Learning res

● English
● Maths
● Geography
● History

Shockwave technolo
you interactive anim
exercises. For the b
experience, we stro
recommend that yo
latest version of Sh
installed. Alternative
view the site withou
elements.

Watch out
When you do a word search, be as specific as you can. A search for, say, 'GCSE exams', might get unsuitable sites such as those containing people's CVs listing GCSE passes. See page 96 for advice on searches.

Welcome to AngliaCampus

AngliaCampus is th
service. Written exc
Curriculum by a team
thousands of

Sample a small selection from our Secondary
● Art: From the Real to the Surreal
● Geography: Coastal Landforms
● History: The Arab/Israeli Confli
● Maths: Concepts

Lizard Point, Cornwall

population a
reflect both
movements
coast, like th
is a comple
system. Into
in the form o
waves, wind
sediment re
the coast its
sea by rivers
include the
and sedime
and the sea
coastal feat

The major f

---

2 Type a key word or phrase into the search engine's search box and click on **Find** or press **Return**. A list of related Web sites will appear on screen. The number of sites found is listed at the top of the page. To open a particular site, click on its address.

3 A good place to start for general study is the BBC Web site (www.bbc.co.uk/ education/schools). Click on the link for **Secondary Resources**. This contains information on each subject in the National Curriculum. Click on a subject to open it.

4 Some sites, such as AngliaCampus (www.angliacampus.com) are subscription sites, whereby users have to pay a fee to access services and information beyond the 'guest' facilities. You are given sample content to help you decide whether it's worth subscribing.

Extra software

In order to interact with this particular site you need a Shockwave plug-in. If you don't already have this, you can download it by clicking on the button on the page. (See page 102 for more information on plug-ins.)

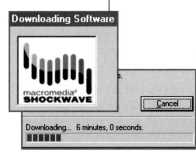

Downloading Software

macromedia® SHOCKWAVE

Cancel

Downloading... 6 minutes, 0 seconds.

Subscribing tips

Well-managed Web services such as AngliaCampus will offer you the choice to sign up either on-line or by fax. Read their terms and conditions very carefully. If you are asked to pay on-line you should be informed that the server is secure, and that your credit-card details cannot be viewed by unauthorised parties.

▸ Sign Up: All you need to becom an AngliaCampus subscriber.

angliacampus

To sign up with AngliaCampus follow these simpl

1 ▸ View the Terms and Conditions online or as a Wo document.

2 ▸ Download and print out the order form as an Acr PDF **or** Word document.

If you don't have Acrobat, you can download it fr

Welcome to How Stuff

How Stuff Works is a great place to come to learn about ho
around you. Have you ever wondered how the engine in you
what makes the inside of your refrigerator cold? Then **How**
A new article gets added every week, so visit often and sign
get the latest news. Here is the complete list of articles and f

Engines and Motors

- How Car Engines Work - Ever wonder what
  happens to the gasoline once you fill the

How a Car Engine Wor

by Marshall Brain

Have you ever opened the hood of your car and wondered what was go
here? Car engines can look like a big confusing jumble of metal, tubes
the uninitiated. You might want to know what's going on in there simp
ousity. After all, you ride in your car every day - wouldn't it be nice to
ks? Or maybe you are tired of going to the mechanic and having him
are totally meaningless to you and then charging you $750 for it. Or
u are buying a new car, and you hear funny words like "3.0 liter V6" a
erhead cams" and "tuned port fuel injection". What does all of that me

f you have ever wondered about this kind of stuff, then How Stuff Worl
help out with this complete guide to how gasoline engines work. Enjoy!

The Beginning

A car is one of the most complicated objects that a person sees during
of parts, all of them functioning reliably together day in and day out. How
car engines are very simple and once you understand them many differe

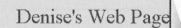

Denise's Web Page

Written examination

Practical examination

gail's Party

ar Day Out

The Birthday Party

The Tempest

Twelfth Night

I'm a Drama teacher at *Bishop Va
West Wales* (UK). For the past few
to help them in their preparation f
examinations, and it occurred to n
that these notes may well prove us

I make them available to you in no
find them useful, great! If you find
or if you have any suggestions or e
denise@killay.demon.co.uk

Other useful sites with theatre/drama/educational content and links:-

---

5 Another site packed with useful information is Schoolzone (www.schoolzone.co.uk). On the home page click on **Surf Schoolzone** to see a comprehensive A-Z list of useful links to other pages. Click on them to explore their content.

6 A great site to find out the workings of just about anything is How Stuff Works (www.howstuffworks. com). It covers a range of subjects, from car engines to tornadoes, and offers an extensive question-and-answer section, too.

7 Search engines will help you find sites that are written by enthusiastic academics but are not linked from larger sites. For example, www.killay.demon.co.uk contains a drama teacher's notes for various plays, plus tips on how to answer written exam questions.

Keep yourself posted

It's not just links to other Web sites that are underlined on Web pages. Links to e-mail addresses are, too. Look out for free subscriptions to educational newsletters, which you can receive via e-mail.

How Stuff Works!

to come to learn about how things work in the world
ered how the engine in your car works, or what gears do
igerator cold? Then **How Stuff Works** is the place for y
eek, so visit often and sign up for the **HSW Newsletter**
mplete list of articles and features:

Free HSW Newsletter!

Many people have written to say, "I love **How Stuff W**
time you add a new article so I don't miss it???" This s
your email address below and press the button. You w
and will receive the monthly HSW newsletter describin
added to HSW every month!

Attention parents

Chatting on-line can be addictive. If you allow your children to chat to other students on the Web, it's sensible to limit the time they spend doing so, as you would do when they are on the telephone.

There are several on-line timer programs that help you keep tabs on time spent chatting and the cost. You can even set an alarm to go off when your chosen budget has been reached. Try Internet Timer by Rat Software (www.ratsoft.freeserve.co.uk).

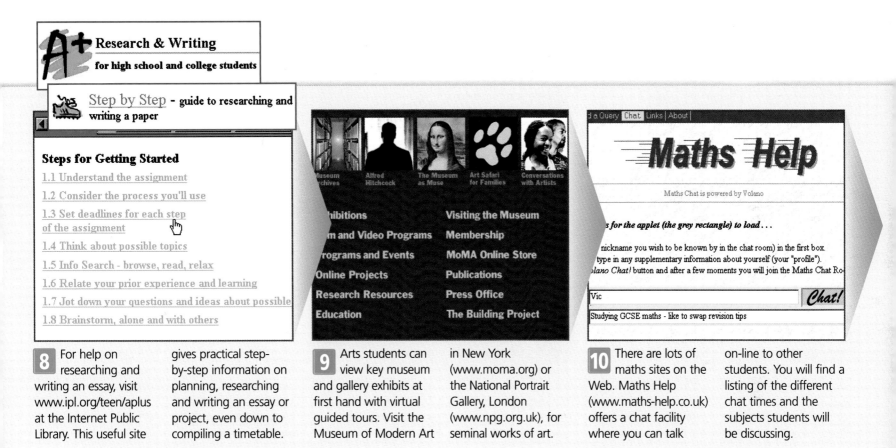

A+ Research & Writing
for high school and college students

Step by Step - guide to researching and writing a paper

Steps for Getting Started

1.1 Understand the assignment

1.2 Consider the process you'll use

1.3 Set deadlines for each step of the assignment

1.4 Think about possible topics

1.5 Info Search - browse, read, relax

1.6 Relate your prior experience and learning

1.7 Jot down your questions and ideas about possible

1.8 Brainstorm, alone and with others

Exhibitions | Visiting the Museum
m and Video Programs | Membership
rograms and Events | MoMA Online Store
Online Projects | Publications
Research Resources | Press Office
Education | The Building Project

Museum rchives | Alfred Hitchcock | The Museum as Muse | Art Safari for Families | Conversations with Artists

d a Query | Chat | Links | About |

Maths Help

Maths Chat is powered by Volano

s for the applet (the grey rectangle) to load . . .

nickname you wish to be known by in the chat room) in the first box.
type in any supplementary information about yourself (your "profile").
olano Chat! button and after a few moments you will join the Maths Chat Ro

Vic | *Chat!*

Studying GCSE maths - like to swap revision tips

8 For help on researching and writing an essay, visit www.ipl.org/teen/aplus at the Internet Public Library. This useful site gives practical step-by-step information on planning, researching and writing an essay or project, even down to compiling a timetable.

9 Arts students can view key museum and gallery exhibits at first hand with virtual guided tours. Visit the Museum of Modern Art in New York (www.moma.org) or the National Portrait Gallery, London (www.npg.org.uk), for seminal works of art.

10 There are lots of maths sites on the Web. Maths Help (www.maths-help.co.uk) offers a chat facility where you can talk on-line to other students. You will find a listing of the different chat times and the subjects students will be discussing.

Don't lose your focus

It's easy to become sidetracked when going through search results. Be disciplined about assessing each page quickly and deciding whether a site is likely to contain useful information about the subject you are researching. If it does, save the site as a bookmark or a favourite (see page 98). Then click the **Back** button to return to the results page.

Useful educational sites

You may find these Web sites and search engines particularly useful for children aged 11-16:
- www.dictionary.com (on-line spelling and grammar guide)
- www.virtualschool.co.uk (tuition and revision courses)
- www.studyweb.com (general educational resource)
- www.dfee.gov.uk/iyc/ (further education advice)

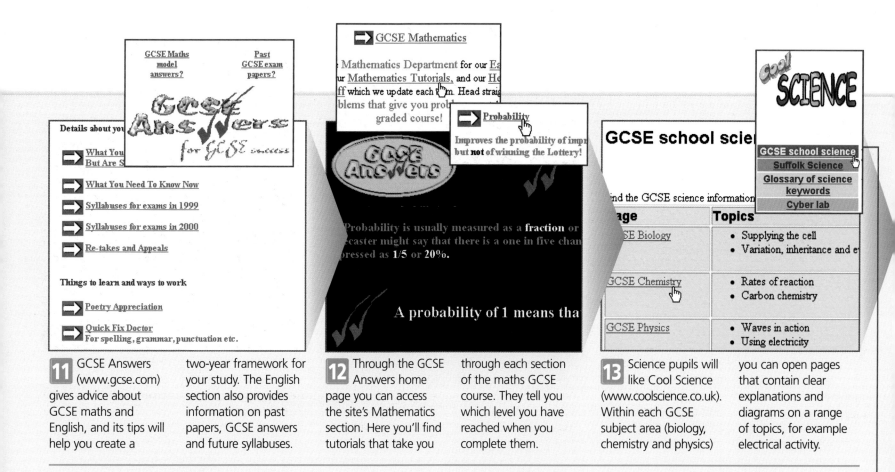

GCSE Maths model answers?   **Past GCSE exam papers?**

GCSE AnsWers for GCSE success

Details about you

→ What You...But Are S...

→ What You Need To Know Now

→ Syllabuses for exams in 1999

→ Syllabuses for exams in 2000

→ Re-takes and Appeals

Things to learn and ways to work

→ Poetry Appreciation

→ Quick Fix Doctor
For spelling, grammar, punctuation etc.

→ **GCSE Mathematics**

...e Mathematics Department for our Ea... ...ur Mathematics Tutorials, and our He... ...ff which we update each ...m. Head straig... ...blems that give you prob... ...graded course!

→ **Probability**

Improves the probability of impr... but **not** of winning the Lottery!

GCSE Answers

...Probability is usually measured as a **fraction** or ...ecaster might say that there is a one in five chan... ...ressed as **1/5** or **20%**.

A probability of 1 means tha...

Cool SCIENCE

GCSE school scie...

| GCSE school science |
| Suffolk Science |
| Glossary of science keywords |
| Cyber lab |

...ind the GCSE science information...

...age	Topics
...SE Biology	• Supplying the cell • Variation, inheritance and e...
GCSE Chemistry	• Rates of reaction • Carbon chemistry
GCSE Physics	• Waves in action • Using electricity

11 GCSE Answers (www.gcse.com) gives advice about GCSE maths and English, and its tips will help you create a two-year framework for your study. The English section also provides information on past papers, GCSE answers and future syllabuses.

12 Through the GCSE Answers home page you can access the site's Mathematics section. Here you'll find tutorials that take you through each section of the maths GCSE course. They tell you which level you have reached when you complete them.

13 Science pupils will like Cool Science (www.coolscience.co.uk). Within each GCSE subject area (biology, chemistry and physics) you can open pages that contain clear explanations and diagrams on a range of topics, for example electrical activity.

Losing a link

Web sites come and go on the Internet all the time. You might sometimes click on a link and get a message saying that the page either no longer exists or that 'A connection with the server cannot be established' (this often means the page no longer exists). So be prepared for the occasional disappointment.

Closing windows

When you click on the Glossary in the Cool Science site a second window will open. To close it, either click on the close window symbol in the top right-hand corner or click on the **Close this window** button.

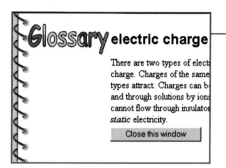

Glossary electric charge

There are two types of elect... charge. Charges of the same types attract. Charges can b... and through solutions by ions... cannot flow through insulator... *static* electricity.

Close this window

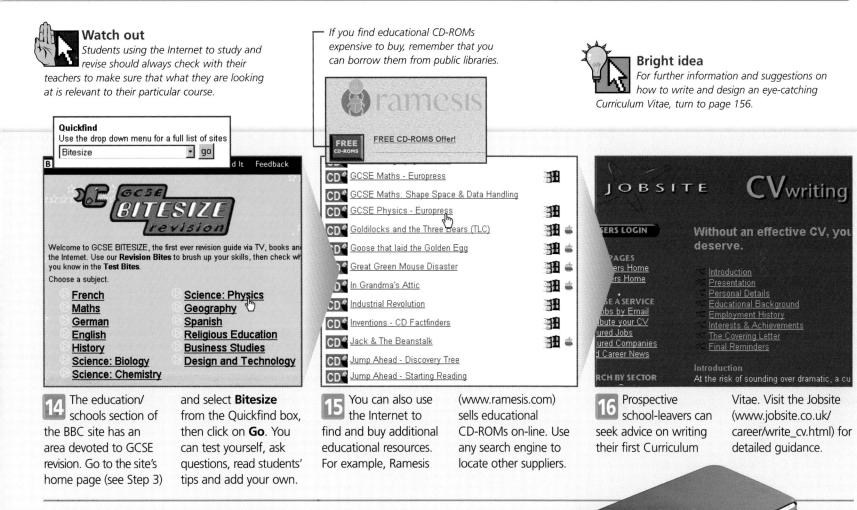

Watch out
Students using the Internet to study and revise should always check with their teachers to make sure that what they are looking at is relevant to their particular course.

If you find educational CD-ROMs expensive to buy, remember that you can borrow them from public libraries.

Bright idea
For further information and suggestions on how to write and design an eye-catching Curriculum Vitae, turn to page 156.

Quickfind
Use the drop down menu for a full list of sites
Bitesize   go

14 The education/ schools section of the BBC site has an area devoted to GCSE revision. Go to the site's home page (see Step 3) and select **Bitesize** from the Quickfind box, then click on **Go**. You can test yourself, ask questions, read students' tips and add your own.

15 You can also use the Internet to find and buy additional educational resources. For example, Ramesis (www.ramesis.com) sells educational CD-ROMs on-line. Use any search engine to locate other suppliers.

16 Prospective school-leavers can seek advice on writing their first Curriculum Vitae. Visit the Jobsite (www.jobsite.co.uk/ career/write_cv.html) for detailed guidance.

Work off-line
If you find you're becoming engrossed in a single detailed Web page, remember that you can work off-line and so save the cost of your call. With Internet Explorer, for example, go to the **File** menu and click on **Work Offline**.

Games on the Internet

You'll never lack a playing partner when you're on-line

The Internet is an unrivalled source of entertainment as well as information. In fact, when it comes to computer games, the Internet is in a league of its own, as it not only provides the games but the players, too.

Many on-line games are adventure or action-based, but there are plenty of gaming sites catering to more diverse tastes. There are,

for example, a large number of chess-related services, some of which allow you to play against opponents from around the world in 'real time', that is, live over the Internet. If, however, you do not want to spend money connected to the Internet while you play, you can opt to play games by e-mail. You can also download games to play at your leisure.

When playing a board game by e-mail, choose a game for which you have a board at home – you need to move for you and your opponent.

► PLAYING GAMES BY E-MAIL

1 Connect to the Internet. To play a game of Monopoly by e-mail, visit the Monopoly Zone. In your browser's address box type 'http://members. xoom.com/CyberCPA'. When the page loads click on the **Chat Room** link. You will be guided step by step.

Explore the Monopoly Zone's sections for tips on playing and connecting to other Monopoly sites.

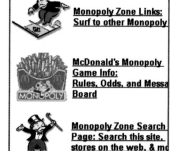

CompuServe

File   Edit   Access   Services   Wind

Page: http://www.excite.co.uk

Play By Mail Games [More Like This]

http://www.cus.ubu.br~ac.uk/~mark/pbm

Play By Mail & Play By Email Welcome to m
pages. I currently play in KJC Games QUES
Daniel Tho

Your Name: Tom

Play By Mail Games

Stock Name	Symbol				
				Stellar Warlords(tm)	
				Stocks & Bonds (3M game)	
Growth Corporation	Growth			Storm of the Eye	Sell
Metro Properties	Metro	0	+11	111	Nothing / Buy / Sell
Pioneer Mutual	Pioneer	4	-5	95	Nothing / Buy / Sell
Shady Brooks	Shady	7	-7	93	Nothing / Buy / Sell
Stryker Drilling	Stryker	0	+30	130	Nothing / Buy

Create Mail

File   Edit

[Send]   [Send Later]   [File It]

	Name	Address
To:	Alan Parker	Alan@Internet.co.uk
Subject:	Monopoly	

Dear Alan,

Thanks for being my first online Monopoly opponent.

Hopefully we can agree to play with the standard Monopoly rules
anything special you would like to add to the rules, can you let me

I look forward to hearing from you and making the first roll of the di

Best wishes,

Read Mail -

File   Edit

◄ ►

	Name	Address
To:	Alan	Alan@Internet.co
Subject:	Monopoly game	

Hi Alan,

I conform that I owe you rent of £50 for landing on Fe

roll a six and a three and land on Mayfair. I'll buy it.

Your move!

From: Gary

Subject: Monopoly   Date: 24/05/9

`I roll a four. Pass Go and collect £200`

`Over to you!`

1 recipient   Options:

---

2 Once you have selected your players, agree the official rules of the game with them by e-mail. If the game is likely to continue for several weeks and you may be absent for some of the time – to go on holiday, say – inform your opponents.

3 Once everything has been agreed you are ready to play. Exchange moves by e-mail and duplicate them on your board. If you are playing against several people, e-mails need to be sent to all players so that everyone can see all the moves played.

4 For other types of game, visit www.excite.co.uk. In its search box type 'Games by e-mail' then press **Return**. One of the results, Play By Mail, links to other e-mail gaming sites. This in turn links to a free e-mail game called Stocks & Bonds.

Registering details

In order to enter the Xoom chat area on the Monopoly site, you will be asked to register your name, e-mail address and a password. You may need a plug-in to gain access, too (see page 102).

User Name (required)	Mike Hardwick
Your Email Address (for FREE membership)	mike.hardwick@internet.co
Your Full Name	Mike Hardwick
Your Password	×××××××

Finding players

A good way to find opponents is through discussion groups. As a starting point, visit 'www.deja.com'. When the home page loads, type 'rec.games.chess.play-by-email' in the search box and press **Return** (make sure the discussions option is selected). When the results appear, click on any links to open them.

CompuServe

File   Edit   Access   Services

Page: http://www.deja.com

Search Deja.com

○ discussions   ○ ratings   ○ communities

rec.games.chess.play-by-em [Find]

Date	Subject		
05/23/99	Game		Har
05/23/99	Game	rec.games.chess.play-	Richa / Harg
05/22/99	One more game	rec.games.chess.play-	Jeff K
05/24/99	NEW! You have a	rec.games.chess.misc	rube

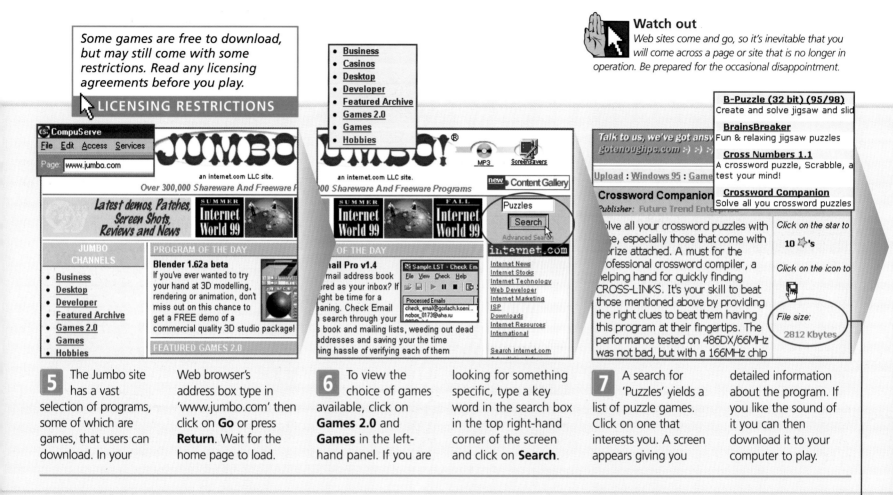

Some games are free to download, but may still come with some restrictions. Read any licensing agreements before you play.

LICENSING RESTRICTIONS

- **Business**
- **Casinos**
- **Desktop**
- **Developer**
- **Featured Archive**
- **Games 2.0**
- **Games**
- **Hobbies**

Watch out

Web sites come and go, so it's inevitable that you will come across a page or site that is no longer in operation. Be prepared for the occasional disappointment.

B-Puzzle (32 bit) (95/98)
Create and solve jigsaw and slid

BrainsBreaker
Fun & relaxing jigsaw puzzles

Cross Numbers 1.1
A crossword puzzle, Scrabble, a test your mind!

Crossword Companion
Solve all you crossword puzzles

5 The Jumbo site has a vast selection of programs, some of which are games, that users can download. In your
Web browser's address box type in 'www.jumbo.com' then click on **Go** or press **Return**. Wait for the home page to load.

6 To view the choice of games available, click on **Games 2.0** and **Games** in the left-hand panel. If you are
looking for something specific, type a key word in the search box in the top right-hand corner of the screen and click on **Search**.

7 A search for 'Puzzles' yields a list of puzzle games. Click on one that interests you. A screen appears giving you
detailed information about the program. If you like the sound of it you can then download it to your computer to play.

Software for free...

- **Shareware** is software that is distributed free for a limited period. When the license expires you should buy the program if you want to continue using it.
- **Freeware**, as the name suggests, is software that's distributed free of charge and can be used indefinitely. However, it often comes without any user support.
- **Demo/Sample software** is a reduced version of a commercial program. You use it to decide whether you want to buy the complete program.

File sizes

When you download a game file from the Internet you will usually be told the size of the file. A file of a couple of thousand kilobytes should take just seconds to download, but a file of several megabytes could take an hour or more. Games that contain lots of sophisticated graphics take the longest to download.

File size:

2812 Kbytes.

Bright idea
*Avoid deleting downloaded files after the programs
have been installed. If possible, back them up onto
a separate storage device, such as a floppy disk. The
installation programs may be needed again at a later date.*

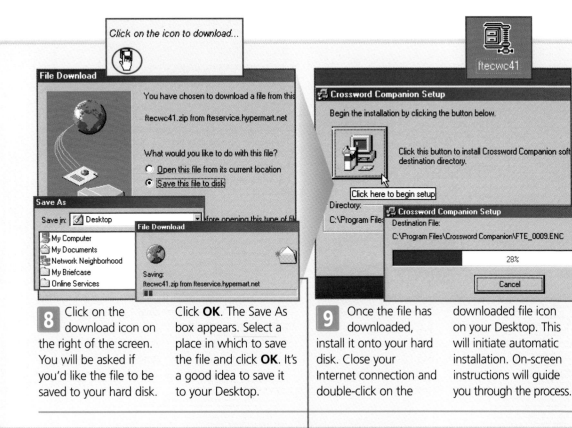

8 Click on the
download icon on
the right of the screen.
You will be asked if
you'd like the file to be
saved to your hard disk.

Click **OK**. The Save As
box appears. Select a
place in which to save
the file and click **OK**. It's
a good idea to save it
to your Desktop.

9 Once the file has
downloaded,
install it onto your hard
disk. Close your
Internet connection and
double-click on the

downloaded file icon
on your Desktop. This
will initiate automatic
installation. On-screen
instructions will guide
you through the process.

10 To open the
software, go to
the **Start** menu, select
Programs then click on
the program. With the
crossword solver

downloaded here, you
tell it the length of the
word you're looking for
and the category it falls
into. It then helps you
find the answer.

Watch the clock
You may be given an estimate for
how long the file will take to
download. But estimates are not
always accurate. You can get a
better idea of downloading time
by watching how quickly the clock
counts down. Remember that time
spent on-line costs money. Click on
the **Cancel** button if you change
your mind about downloading.

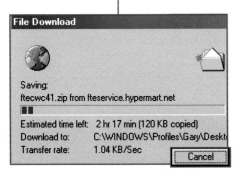

Added zip
Some programs
downloaded from the
Internet use a special
utility called WinZip
to compress several files into
a single one, making them
faster to download. For
more details on unzipping
files, turn to page 362.

Chess is a popular game on the Web. You play against a computer or a person in real time. Because you play on-line, set a time limit on individual moves to keep costs down.

▶ PLAYING CHESS ON-LINE

Bright idea
Before you begin playing a game of chess, print out a copy of the game rules and any tips you are given for on-line chess etiquette. Study them later at your leisure.

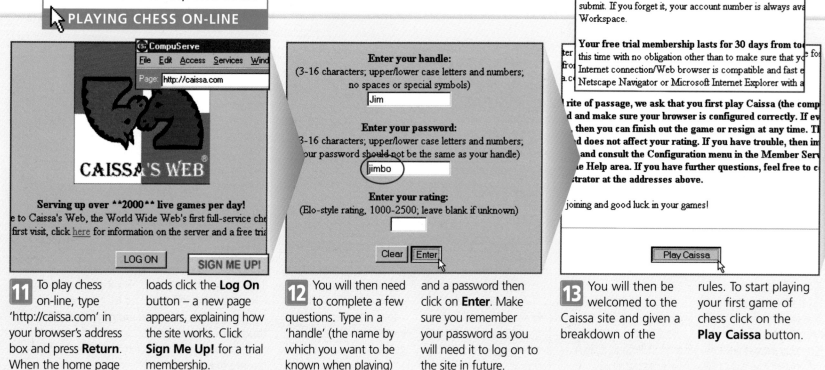

11 To play chess on-line, type 'http://caissa.com' in your browser's address box and press **Return**. When the home page loads click the **Log On** button – a new page appears, explaining how the site works. Click **Sign Me Up!** for a trial membership.

12 You will then need to complete a few questions. Type in a 'handle' (the name by which you want to be known when playing) and a password then click on **Enter**. Make sure you remember your password as you will need it to log on to the site in future.

13 You will then be welcomed to the Caissa site and given a breakdown of the rules. To start playing your first game of chess click on the **Play Caissa** button.

Try before you buy
Some Web-based chess services are free, but others, including Caissa's site (above), are membership services for which you have to pay a fee. Free trials help you to decide whether it's worth paying for these services or not.

Caissa's Web is a full-service, member-supported chess ser obligation trial membership of 30 days, after which we offer US$25 for a standard membership and US$50 for a premiu usage limitations or hourly fees.

On-line etiquette
When playing games on-line remember that you are often playing against other people – not a computer – and so the usual rules of social etiquette apply.

For example, you should not leave your computer without a mutual agreement to stop playing. One of the Caissa site's particular rules is that you should never prolong a game that you are clearly going to lose.

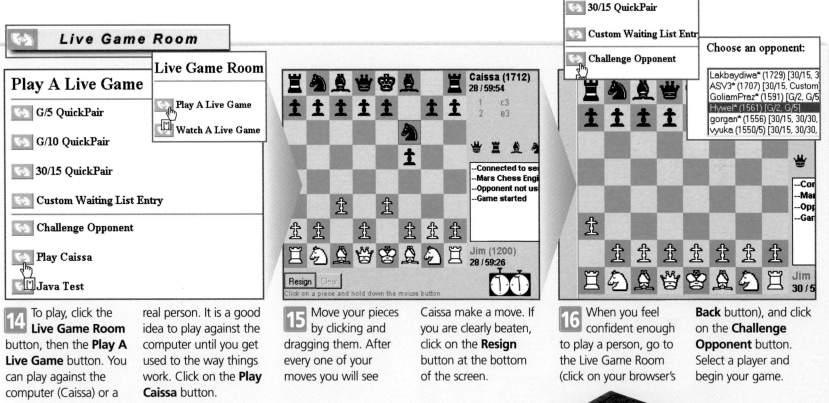

Live Game Room

Play A Live Game

- G/5 QuickPair
- G/10 QuickPair
- 30/15 QuickPair
- Custom Waiting List Entry
- Challenge Opponent
- Play Caissa
- Java Test

Live Game Room

- Play A Live Game
- Watch A Live Game

Caissa (1712)
28 / 59:54

| 1 | c3 |
| 2 | e3 |

--Connected to ser
--Mars Chess Engi
--Opponent not us
--Game started

Jim (1200)
28 / 59:26

Resign Clear
Click on a piece and hold down the mouse button

- 30/15 QuickPair
- Custom Waiting List Entr
- Challenge Opponent

Choose an opponent:

Lakbaydiwa* (1729) [30/15, 3
ASV3* (1707) [30/15, Custom
GoliamPraz* (1591) [G/2, G/5
Hywel* (1561) [G/2, G/5]
gorgan* (1556) [30/15, 30/30,
vyuka (1550/5) [30/15, 30/30,

--Con
--Mar
--Opp
--Gan

Jim
30 / 5

14 To play, click the **Live Game Room** button, then the **Play A Live Game** button. You can play against the computer (Caissa) or a real person. It is a good idea to play against the computer until you get used to the way things work. Click on the **Play Caissa** button.

15 Move your pieces by clicking and dragging them. After every one of your moves you will see Caissa make a move. If you are clearly beaten, click on the **Resign** button at the bottom of the screen.

16 When you feel confident enough to play a person, go to the Live Game Room (click on your browser's **Back** button), and click on the **Challenge Opponent** button. Select a player and begin your game.

Added insight

If you prefer to learn how the system works before you play a game, watch one first. Click on the **Watch A Live Game** button, which you can find on the Web site's Live Game Room page (see above).

Live Game Room ▼

Watch A Live Game

27 Active Games, **0** Tournament Games, **6** Games On Hold

White	Rating	Black	Rating	Speed
1chance	1528	alamn2	1525	30/30
Megan23	1725	abel	1559	30/30
RoyB	1600/1	Caissa	1689	30/60
Plasma	1445	Vitalij	1623	30/30

Practical
Home Projects

This section will guide you, step by step, through 40 practical projects over a range of subjects. Each task is self-contained – you require no prior experience of the program used. Suggestions are also made of ways you can bring the projects together to undertake more ambitious events, such as organising a reunion.

In this section

Wordpower

This chapter shows you how to create a variety of word-based documents, from a personal letterhead and formal letter, to a professional CV, address database and address labels.

Picture Perfect

A gallery of graphic images called ClipArt is supplied with Microsoft programs. Use these images to enhance your work. Alternatively, with a scanner, import your own pictures. You can use the Windows accessory program, Paint, to create pictures of your own.

Sounds Right

This chapter will show you how to maximise the sound facility of your PC and turn it into a mini-recording studio. With the right software you can learn to read music, and with a compatible instrument you can compose and orchestrate your own tunes.

Home Finance

From monitoring personal spending, predicting outgoings and helping you budget, to running larger group accounts, this chapter will make the task of tracking expenditure much easier.

Family Life

Use your PC to plan your domestic life, and also to make a record of your family's past and present. Make a family tree, a photo album, a recipe collection, a baby book; redesign a room, or organise a house move.

Better Leisure

This chapter shows you how to use your PC to increase your enjoyment of your interests. Gardening, sport, crafts, collecting antiques, travel: you can use your computer to enhance all these leisure activities in all kinds of imaginative and unexpected ways.

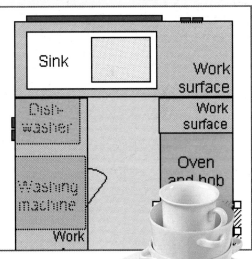

The range of programs supplied with your PC, or purchased through stores or the Internet, can tackle a wide range of projects

Design a letterhead

Create your personal stationery with an individual look

A personalised letterhead will add a touch of flair and individuality to all your correspondence. Once you have mastered the skills involved in creating a letterhead, you can follow the same principles to design letterheads for different occasions – one for business stationery, perhaps.

When you have created your letterhead, save it as a template that you can use again and again, whenever you write a letter. And if your details change – for example, if you move house or acquire an e-mail address or mobile phone number – you can easily alter them on your template.

Susannah Matthews
104 Chamberlain Avenue
Maidstone, Kent ME16 4LR
Telephone: 01622 442 7272

Dear Fiona

Decide what you are going to use your letterhead for. If it is for letters to family and friends, you can be creative with your choice of fonts.

▶ BEFORE YOU START

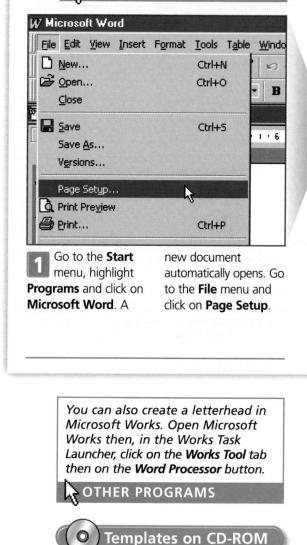

1 Go to the **Start** menu, highlight **Programs** and click on **Microsoft Word**. A new document automatically opens. Go to the **File** menu and click on **Page Setup**.

*You can also create a letterhead in Microsoft Works. Open Microsoft Works then, in the Works Task Launcher, click on the **Works Tool** tab then on the **Word Processor** button.*

▶ OTHER PROGRAMS

Templates on CD-ROM

Bright idea
If you have an e-mail address, remember to include it in your letterhead.

Page Setup

Margins | Paper Size | Paper Source | Layout

Top: 2.54 cm
Bottom: 2.54 cm
Left: 3.5cm
Right: 3.5 cm

Gutter: 0 cm

From edge
Header: 2cm
Footer: 1.25 cm

Preview

Apply to: Whole documen

Mirror margins

View Insert Format Too
- Normal
- Online Layout
- Page Layout
- Outline
- Master Document

Toolbars
✓ Ruler
Document Map

Header and Footer
Footnotes
Comments

File Edit View Insert Format To

Insert AutoText ▾

Header

Header
Susannah Matthews
104 Chamberlain Avenue
Maidstone, Kent ME16 4LR
Telephone: 01622 442 7272

Header
Susannah Matthews
104 Chamberlain Avenue
Maidstone, Kent ME16 4LR
Telephone: 01622 442 7272

Font

Font | Character Spacing | Animation

Font: Garamond
Garamond
Haettenschweiler
Impact
Letter Gothic
LinePrinter

Font style: Bold
Regular
Italic
Bold
Bold Italic

Size: 20
12
14
16
18
20

Underline: (none)
Color: Auto

Effects
☐ Strikethrough ☐ Shadow ☐ Small ca
☐ Double strikethrough ☐ Outline ☐ All caps
☐ Super
☐ Subsc

Preview

Susannah Matthews

---

2 In the Page Setup dialogue box type in sizes for the Top, Bottom, Left and Right margins, and distances between the top of the page and the Header, and the bottom of the page and the Footer. Equal-sized margins top and bottom, and left and right look neatest.

3 You are going to create your letterhead within the Header section of your document. Go to the **View** menu and click on **Header and Footer**. The cursor automatically appears in the Header section. Type in your name, address and telephone number.

4 Now highlight your name, go to the **Format** menu and select **Font**. In the dialogue box select a font, style and size, clicking on any to view them in the Preview window. Make your selection and click **OK**. Style your address in the same way.

Key word
Header and Footer *These terms describe the information that appears at the top (header) and bottom (footer) of each page of a document – for example, running titles, reference details and page numbers.*

Let the Wizard help

Microsoft Works has a useful device, called a Wizard, that can help you create personalised letterheads. When you open Microsoft Works you will find the TaskWizards tab automatically selected in the Works Task Launcher. In the Common Tasks folder displayed in the window, double-click on **Letterhead**. All you do then is simply follow the on-screen steps.

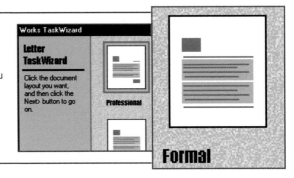

Works TaskWizard

Letter TaskWizard

Click the document layout you want, and then click the Next> button to go on.

Professional

Formal

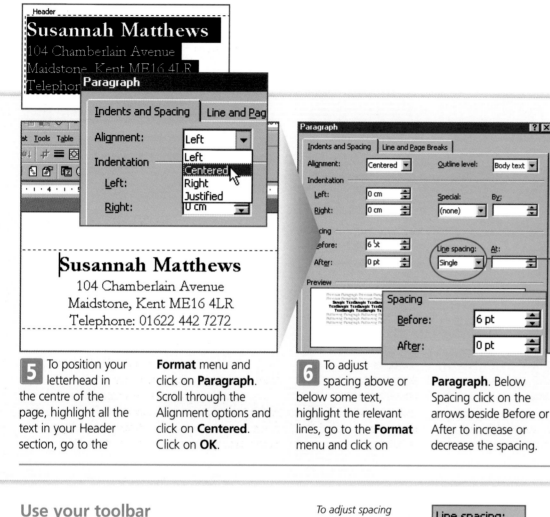

5 To position your letterhead in the centre of the page, highlight all the text in your Header section, go to the **Format** menu and click on **Paragraph**. Scroll through the Alignment options and click on **Centered**. Click on **OK**.

6 To adjust spacing above or below some text, highlight the relevant lines, go to the **Format** menu and click on **Paragraph**. Below Spacing click on the arrows beside Before or After to increase or decrease the spacing.

7 When you are happy with your design, save it as a template that you can use again and again. Go to the **File** menu and select **Save As**. Scroll through the 'Save as type' box at the bottom of the dialogue box and click on **Document Template**.

Use your toolbar

The toolbar buttons at the top of the screen help you style your text quickly. Highlight the text. Click on the relevant button to make it bold, to italicise it or to underline it. Change your text's position, too, by clicking on the left, centre or right alignment buttons.

To adjust spacing between lines, highlight the relevant text, go to the **Format** menu and click on **Paragraph**. Click on the arrow beside the 'Line spacing' box then click on a suitable measurement. Click **OK**.

Works template

To save your letterhead as a template in Microsoft Works, go to the **File** menu and select **Save As**. In the dialogue box click on the **Template** button in the bottom right-hand corner. In the Save As Template dialogue box type in a name for your template then click **OK**.

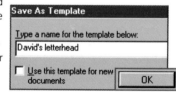

Bright idea
*Save yourself time by using automatic dating for your letters. Click where you want the date to appear in your document, go to the **Insert** menu and click on **Date and Time**. In the dialogue box click on your preferred style then click on **Insert**.*

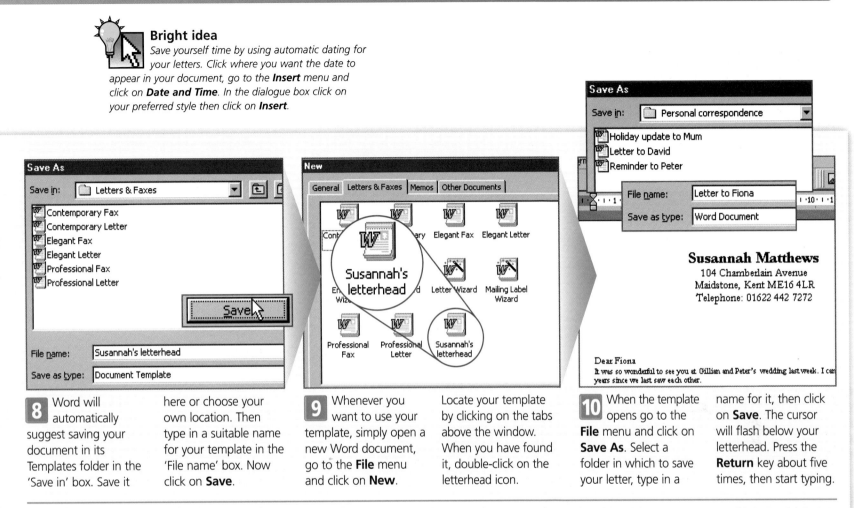

8 Word will automatically suggest saving your document in its Templates folder in the 'Save in' box. Save it here or choose your own location. Then type in a suitable name for your template in the 'File name' box. Now click on **Save**.

9 Whenever you want to use your template, simply open a new Word document, go to the **File** menu and click on **New**. Locate your template by clicking on the tabs above the window. When you have found it, double-click on the letterhead icon.

10 When the template opens go to the **File** menu and click on **Save As**. Select a folder in which to save your letter, type in a name for it, then click on **Save**. The cursor will flash below your letterhead. Press the **Return** key about five times, then start typing.

Changing your template
In Word, go to the **File** menu and select **Open**. From the 'Files of type' box select **Document Templates**. Double-click on your template in the Templates folder, make any changes to it then save it.

In Works, click the TaskWizards tab in the Works Task Launcher. Double-click on your letterhead in the User Defined Templates folder, make your changes, go to the **File** menu and select **Save As**. Double-click on the old file in the Templates folder to replace it with the new one.

Why not spruce up your letterhead with a graphic from the gallery that comes free with Word and Works? See page 188 to find out how.

OTHER IDEAS TO TRY

Jonathan Winston Brown
17 Wilberforce Mansions
Churchill Mews
Ravenstone
Leicestershire
LE12 4PE
Tel: 01533 657 787

Customer Services Manager
Torchlight Gas
High Street
Leicester
LE11 9PR

23 November 1999

Ref: TG00042/100

Dear Sir/Madam
Further to your letter dated 18 November, I would like to clarify a few points. Firstly,
I became a member of Torchlight Gas with the understanding that your standing
charge would be considerably less than my previous gas supplier. Secondly, your
promotional literature states quite clearly that low users – which I am – qualify for a
further discount of £10 per quarter.

As I informed you over the phone last week, the standing charge on my current bill is
£2 more than my previous supplier charged, and I see no evidence of a £10 discount.
Please could you clarify my position as soon as possible. I feel misled in changing my
supplier, and if this situation is not remedied soon I shall have no choice but to switch
back to British Gas.

Yours faithfully,

Send a formal letter

Give your business correspondence a professional look

Writing a formal letter can often seem a daunting task, but with a personal computer it couldn't be more straightforward. On all your correspondence make sure you include your name, address and the date on which you are writing. For formal letters it is also usual to include the name, company position and address of the person you are writing to.

It's also a good idea to include an official reference. If you are writing to your bank, for example, this could be your account number. When replying to a letter, take a look at it to see if a reference is included, and repeat that.

Assemble all relevant documents and make a quick note of the points you wish to make. Check that you are writing to the appropriate person to deal with your letter.

▸ BEFORE YOU START

Save As

Save in: [Formal Letters] ▼ 🔁 📇

Electricity Connection
Planning Application
School fees
Torchlight Gas

[Save]

File name: [Torchlight Gas]

Save as type: [Word Document]

1 Go to the **Start** menu, highlight **Programs** and click on **Microsoft Word**. Save your new document by going to the **File** menu and selecting **Save As**. Select a suitable location in the 'Save in' box, type in a file name then click on **Save**.

---

*You can also create a letterhead in Microsoft Works. Open Works then, in the Works Task Launcher, click on the **Works Tool** tab then on the **Word Processor** button.*

▸ OTHER PROGRAMS

Templates on CD-ROM

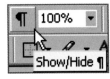

To see exactly how many line spaces you have used, click on the **Show/Hide** button on the toolbar.

Watch out
You are in danger of losing your work if you do not save it frequently. Make a habit of saving your letter every few minutes.

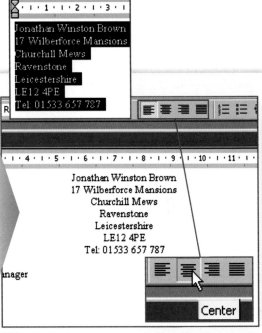

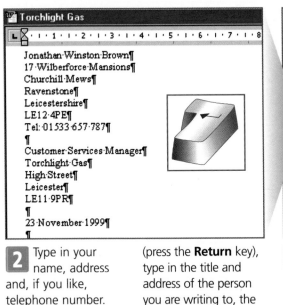

Torchlight Gas

Jonathan·Winston·Brown¶
17·Wilberforce·Mansions¶
Churchill·Mews¶
Ravenstone¶
Leicestershire¶
LE12·4PE¶
Tel:·01533·657·787¶
¶
Customer·Services·Manager¶
Torchlight·Gas¶
High·Street¶
Leicester¶
LE11·9PR¶
¶
23·November·1999¶

23 November 1999

Ref: TG00042/100

Dear Sir/Madam
Further to your letter dated 18 November , I would like to cl
member of Torchlight Gas with the understanding that your
an my previous gas supplier. Secondly, your promotional 1
which I am – qualify for a further discount of £10 per quar

As I informed you over the phone last week, the standing ch
previous supplier charged, and I see no evidence of a £10 di
position as soon as possible. I feel misled in changing my su
soon I shall have no choice but to switch back to British Gas

Yours faithfully,

Jonathan Winston Brown
17 Wilberforce Mansions
Churchill Mews
Ravenstone
Leicestershire
LE12 4PE
Tel: 01533 657 787

Center

2 Type in your name, address and, if you like, telephone number. Leaving a line space between each section (press the **Return** key), type in the title and address of the person you are writing to, the date and, if relevant, a reference number.

3 Leave one more line space then begin your letter. If you do not know the name of the recipient, address your letter to 'Sir/Madam' and sign it off at the end with 'Yours faithfully'. If you know the name of the recipient, sign off with 'Yours sincerely'.

4 To position your own details in the centre of the page, highlight your name, address and telephone number then click on the **Center** button on the toolbar.

Let the Wizards help

Microsoft Word and Microsoft Works have useful devices, called Wizards, to help you create your own formal letter.

In Word, open a new document then go to the **Tools** menu and select **Letter Wizard**. In Microsoft Works, the TaskWizards tab is automatically selected in the Works Task Launcher. In the list of Common Tasks double-click on **Letter**. For both programs, follow the on-screen steps.

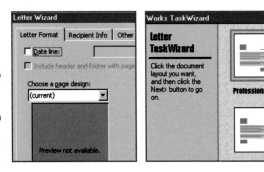

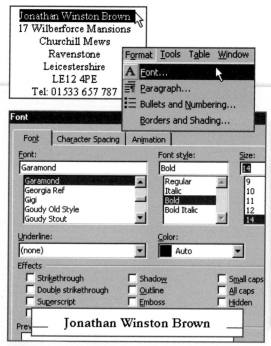

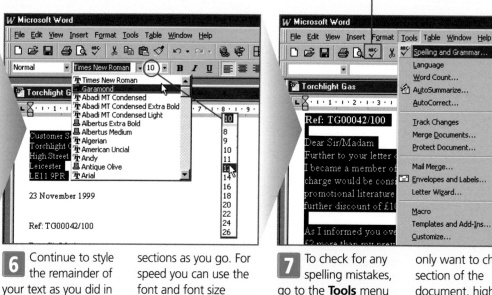

*Clicking on the **Spelling and Grammar** button on the toolbar will also bring up the Spelling and Grammar dialogue box.*

5 To style your letter first highlight your name at the top, go to the **Format** menu and select **Font**. In the dialogue box select a font, style and size, clicking on any that interest you to view them in the Preview window. Make your selection then click **OK**.

6 Continue to style the remainder of your text as you did in the previous step, highlighting individual sections as you go. For speed you can use the font and font size shortcuts on the toolbar as shown.

7 To check for any spelling mistakes, go to the **Tools** menu and select **Spelling and Grammar**. If you only want to check a section of the document, highlight the relevant text before going to the menu.

Select a font

If you know the name of the font you want to use, type its first letter in the Font box. All the fonts beginning with that letter will automatically appear at the top of the font window. This saves you scrolling through all your fonts.

Change the scale

If you want to magnify your document to see it in more detail, without adjusting the size of the type, you can change its scale by clicking on the arrow beside the Zoom toolbar function and selecting one of the options. If you can't see the Zoom function, you may need to maximise your window.

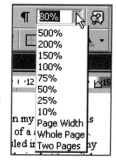

Bright idea
Before posting your letter read it through to check for errors then give it to a friend to proofread. Ask him if it is clear and makes sense.

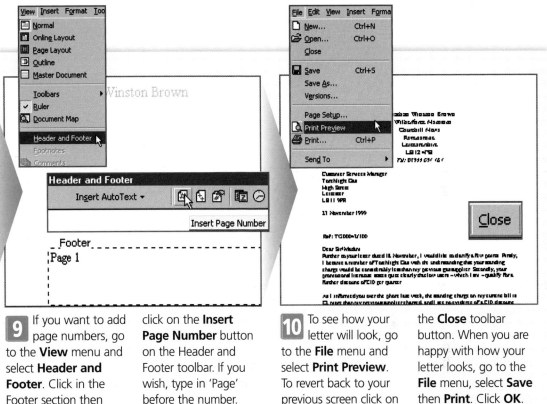

8 If Word questions a spelling, click **Ignore** or **Change** depending on whether the word is misspelled. If you can't think of the exact word you're looking for, use the Thesaurus. Go to the **Tools** menu, highlight **Language** and click on **Thesaurus**.

9 If you want to add page numbers, go to the **View** menu and select **Header and Footer**. Click in the Footer section then click on the **Insert Page Number** button on the Header and Footer toolbar. If you wish, type in 'Page' before the number.

10 To see how your letter will look, go to the **File** menu and select **Print Preview**. To revert back to your previous screen click on the **Close** toolbar button. When you are happy with how your letter looks, go to the **File** menu, select **Save** then **Print**. Click **OK**.

Make your point

If you are making a number of important points in your letter and wish to emphasise them, type each of them on a new line and put a line space between each one. Highlight each point in turn then click on the **Bullets** toolbar button.

- I did not become a member of yo therefore do not owe the full year

- I was recommended to the club b a reduced rate.

- I joined with my wife, which mea subscription.

Improve your service as

If you are the chief organiser of a tennis club, bridge club or amateur operatics society, your PC can make light work of the daily administration

At the heart of every successful club is a well-organised and unflappable secretary. It's the kind of job that requires attention to detail, an ability to prioritise a large number of tasks, and a head for figures.

The simplicity and flexibility of today's computer software makes such duties both enjoyable and much easier to manage.

A sensible starting point for any club secretary would be to set up a database containing members' personal details: addresses, contact telephone numbers, relevant abilities and so on. It's a good idea to create a standard membership form that can be stored on computer then printed out for prospective club members to complete.

Project planner

Create a folder named after your club. Add sub-folders for each area of administration.

Club administration
- Members
- Money
- Minutes
- Communications
- Publicity
- Results & events

a club secretary

Once you have a database set up, it's a simple task to produce address labels for club correspondence.

Using a second database, the secretary of a sports club can produce tables to show fixtures, results and club rankings.

Keeping club accounts and tracking membership fees are simple tasks once you set up a spreadsheet. You can use it for recruitment-based fiscal planning.

For communications with other organisations, create your own club stationery. You could design a club logo using Paint or another graphics program. The logo could then be used on club newsletters or, with the help of an outside supplier, on merchandise such as club ties and keyrings.

Consider compiling a pictorial club history on your computer. Somebody might like to write a short account that you could publish for members' interest.

And don't forget that many members will be on-line. If you compile an e-mail address book, you can send information on rankings, fixtures and social events to everyone at once. You could even post them on a club Web site which, of course, you could design and compile yourself.

With the introduction of on-line banking, monitoring your club accounts could not be simpler. And, provided there is the right software compatibility, you can download information straight from your bank to your spreadsheets and pay bills on-line.

Start the ball rolling

- Compile and collect all membership details and transfer them to your database
- Transfer a copy of the club's accounts to a spreadsheet on your computer
- Set up an on-line bank account
- Produce a club logo for all communications
- Arrange for all league/club information to be sent via e-mail to on-line members

Ideas and inspirations

Customise the following projects and ideas to suit the needs of your club. That way, you'll spend less time on administration, and far more time enjoying the club's benefits. Once you've set up the basic documents you need, maintaining them should be a quick and easy matter.

168 **Membership database**
Compile a handy reference document to keep a record of all your members' details.

272 **Club accounts**
Keep track of income and outgoings, and budget for projects, such as buying new equipment.

196 **Illustrate your stationery**
Liven up your correspondence with stationery that raises the profile of your club.

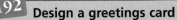

192 **Design a greetings card**
Send your members (or prospective members) cards for Christmas or to publicise a club event.

224 **Painting on your PC**
Design your own logo or artwork for stationery, club posters or Internet use.

Also worth considering…

With the paperwork now kept to a minimum, you might want to branch out onto the Internet.

116 **Design a Web page**
Refer existing and prospective members to your site and you'll save time fielding phone queries.

Write an eye-catching CV

Make the most of your experience and achievements

Your CV, or curriculum vitae, is intended to make a favourable impression on potential employers. As well as including details of all the companies you have worked for and how long you were employed by them, explain what your responsibilities were and what skills you have developed.

Keep your CV brief and to the point. If possible, try to fit it on a single page. Select a clear, easy-to-read font and don't be tempted to make the font size too small in an effort to squeeze everything in. Also, keep your CV's design simple, with well-defined sections that make it easy to extract information.

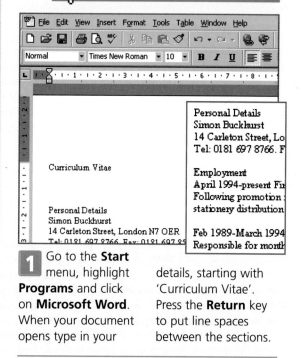

To make sure all your dates of employment are correct, collect your old P45 forms and refer to them as you type in your details.

BEFORE YOU START

1 Go to the **Start** menu, highlight **Programs** and click on **Microsoft Word**. When your document opens type in your details, starting with 'Curriculum Vitae'. Press the **Return** key to put line spaces between the sections.

*You can also create your CV in Microsoft Works. Open Works then, in the Works Task Launcher, click on the **Works Tool** tab then on the **Word Processor** button.*

OTHER PROGRAMS

Templates on CD-ROM

Watch out

*You may lose your work if you don't save it. Either go to the **File** menu and select **Save**, or press the **Ctrl** key and, keeping the Ctrl key pressed own, press the '**S**' key, too.*

*Remember to use the function keys on your keyboard for frequently used commands. Press **F7** to bring up the Spelling and Grammar dialogue box.*

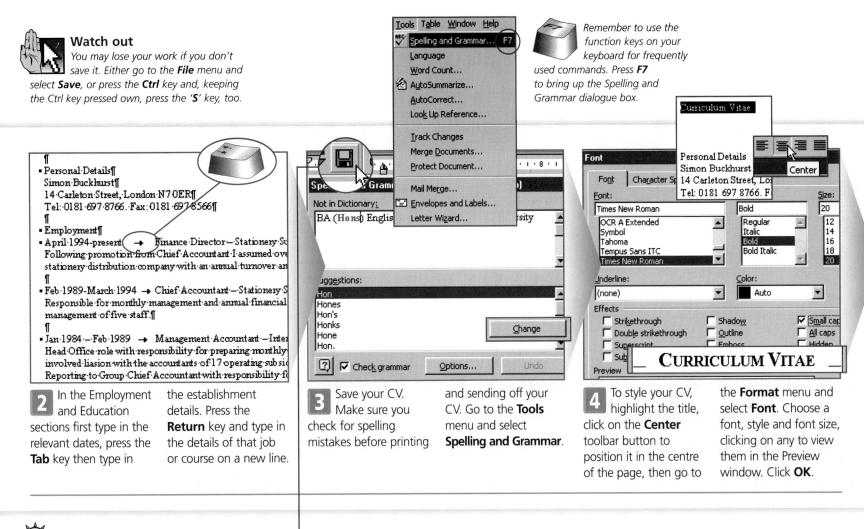

2 In the Employment and Education sections first type in the relevant dates, press the **Tab** key then type in the establishment details. Press the **Return** key and type in the details of that job or course on a new line.

3 Save your CV. Make sure you check for spelling mistakes before printing and sending off your CV. Go to the **Tools** menu and select **Spelling and Grammar**.

4 To style your CV, highlight the title, click on the **Center** toolbar button to position it in the centre of the page, then go to the **Format** menu and select **Font**. Choose a font, style and font size, clicking on any to view them in the Preview window. Click **OK**.

Bright idea

Type in your details under the following headings: 'Personal Details', 'Employment', 'Education', 'Computer Skills' and 'Hobbies and Interests'. List jobs and qualifications in chronological order, beginning with the most recent.

*Clicking on the **Save** toolbar button will bring up the Save As dialogue box. When you have located a suitable place in which to save your CV, type in a file name then click on **Save**.*

Let the Wizard help

Microsoft Works has a Wizard that can help you create a CV. Open Microsoft Works and the Works Task Launcher will appear on screen with the TaskWizard tab automatically selected. Scroll through the window and double-click on **Resume**. Follow the on-screen steps to create a CV designed to your specifications.

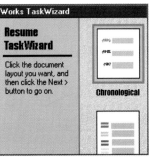

Bright idea
Be prepared! Update your CV on a regular basis, remembering to add details of any training courses, new interests and areas of responsibility.

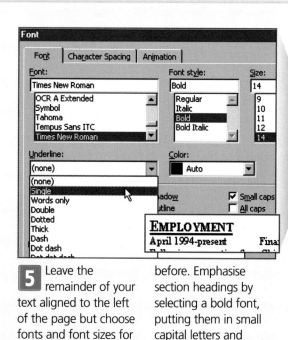

5 Leave the remainder of your text aligned to the left of the page but choose fonts and font sizes for it in the same way as before. Emphasise section headings by selecting a bold font, putting them in small capital letters and underlining them.

6 For each job and educational establishment, make the font size of the first line slightly larger than the subsequent lines, and choose a bold font style or a bolder font.

7 Highlight these lines in turn, go to the **Format** menu and select **Tabs**. In the Tabs dialogue box type in 5 cm as the 'Tab stop position'. Click **OK**. The second half of these lines will now appear neatly above each other. If necessary, adjust the spacing to suit your text.

Use your toolbar

For speed, use the Underline button on your toolbar to put a line beneath text. Simply highlight the relevant text then click on the button.

Bright idea
When you write your accompanying letter of application, use the same fonts as in your CV. Not only will your letter and CV complement each other, but they will also have a professional appearance. A potential employer may well form the impression that you pay attention to detail.

Short cut
To close the Print Preview window and revert back to the previous screen, press the Esc key on your keyboard.

After you have printed your CV for the first time and are happy with how it looks, use better-quality paper for the finished result.

FINISHING TOUCH

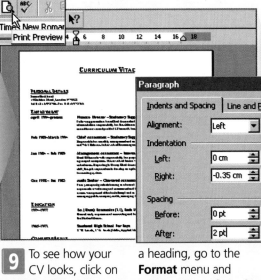

8 Now highlight the lines that describe what each job entailed, go to the **Format** menu and select **Paragraph**. In the Indentation section of the dialogue box, beside Left, type in the same measurement you used to set the tabs in Step 7. Click **OK**.

9 To see how your CV looks, click on the **Print Preview** button. To increase space below headings, press **Esc**, then highlight a heading, go to the **Format** menu and select **Paragraph**. In the Spacing section click on the uppermost arrow to the right of After.

10 To adjust line spacing, highlight the lines in question, go to the **Format** menu and select **Paragraph**. In the 'Line spacing' section scroll through the options available. When you are happy with your CV, go to the **File** menu and select **Save** then **Print**.

Add page numbers

To add page numbers in Word, go to the **View** menu and select **Header and Footer**. Click in the Footer section of your CV then, on the Header and Footer toolbar, click on **Insert AutoText** then on **PAGE**.

In Microsoft Works, click in the Footer section, go to the **Insert** menu and select **Page Number**. In the Footer section '*page*' appears. Highlight it and type in your page number. Subsequent pages update automatically.

Design a dinner party menu and place cards

Impress your guests with specially designed table decorations

Great food and good company are the key ingredients of a dinner party, but to make the evening really special, you need to pay attention to detail. One way to set just the right tone for your party is by designing and printing your own menus and place cards. Whether the mood is formal, fun, festive or themed, you will be able to find appropriate fonts, colours and ClipArt graphics on your computer.

Make sure you have the correct spellings of all the dishes on the menu, and a list of names of the guests you have invited.

BEFORE YOU START

1 To make menus, go to the **Start** menu, select **Programs** then **Microsoft Word**. Go to the **File** menu and click on **Page Setup**. Set the margins to 2.5 cm. Click the **Paper Size** tab. Select the Landscape option, then click **OK**. Set columns (see above right).

You can style text and add ClipArt in Microsoft Works but, because you can't place text in a table, it's difficult to size place cards precisely. However, this shouldn't spoil your design.

OTHER PROGRAMS

Templates on CD-ROM

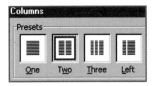

To set columns, go to the **Format** menu and select **Columns**. Select **Two** in the Presets section, then click **OK**.

Bright idea
Whenever you need to select the table – to change the colour of the border, for instance – press the **Alt** key and, keeping it pressed down, double-click anywhere in the table.

If you can't see your 'Return' symbols click on the **Show/Hide** toolbar button. (In Microsoft Works go to the **View** menu and click on **Show All Characters**.)

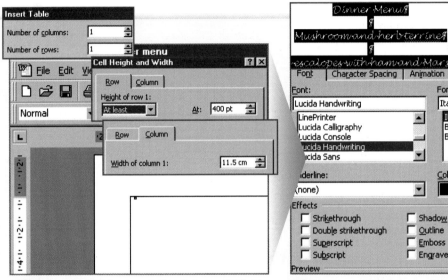

2 Go to the **Table** menu and click on **Insert Table**. Set the rows and columns to 1. Click **OK**. Return to the **Table** menu and select **Cell Height and Width**. In the Row tab select 'At Least' and '400 pt'. Click on the **Column** tab and set the width to 11.5 cm. Click **OK**.

3 Type your text into the table. Leave a line space between courses by pressing the **Return** key twice. Highlight the text and click on the **Center** toolbar button. Go to the **Format** menu and click on **Font**. Choose a font, style and size for your text then click **OK**.

4 To adjust the spacing between courses, highlight the first 'Return' symbol, go to the **Format** menu and click on **Paragraph**. In the 'Spacing section' click on the arrows to the right of the Before and After boxes until you are happy with the result. Repeat for all 'Returns'.

Checking your spelling

Any words that your computer doesn't recognise will appear on the screen with a wavy red line underneath. To check the spelling of these words go to the **Tools** menu and select **Spelling and Grammar**. But just because a computer doesn't recognise a word, it doesn't mean it doesn't exist. It's best to double-check in a dictionary.

Let the Wizard help

Microsoft Works includes templates for two types of menu (formal and informal) and four types of place card (jazzy, festive, informal and formal).

To use one of these, open Works then, in the Works Task Launcher, with the TaskWizard tab selected, click on **User Defined Templates** in the pane. A list of templates appears. Double-click on the relevant menu or place card to open it, then follow the on-screen instructions.

Bright idea
Instead of creating your own border through Word or Works, experiment with the more decorative borders and frames in the Microsoft ClipArt gallery.

For uniformity, design your place cards using the same ClipArt and fonts that you used in the menu.

DESIGNING PLACE CARDS

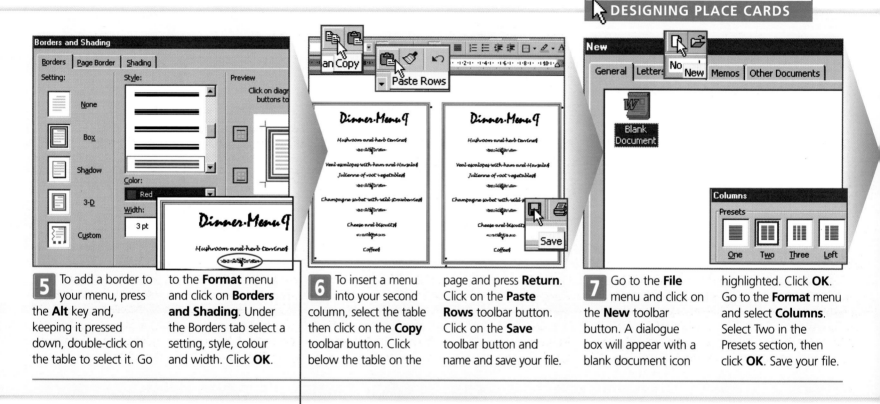

5 To add a border to your menu, press the **Alt** key and, keeping it pressed down, double-click on the table to select it. Go to the **Format** menu and click on **Borders and Shading**. Under the Borders tab select a setting, style, colour and width. Click **OK**.

6 To insert a menu into your second column, select the table then click on the **Copy** toolbar button. Click below the table on the page and press **Return**. Click on the **Paste Rows** toolbar button. Click on the **Save** toolbar button and name and save your file.

7 Go to the **File** menu and click on the **New** toolbar button. A dialogue box will appear with a blank document icon highlighted. Click **OK**. Go to the **Format** menu and select **Columns**. Select Two in the Presets section, then click **OK**. Save your file.

Adding ClipArt

Use ClipArt to enliven your menu. Click in the document, go to the **Insert** menu and select **Picture** then **ClipArt**. Click through the categories, click on an image you like then select **Insert image** from the pop-up menu. It will appear in your document. To learn how to size and position it, see page 188.

If you are placing divisions between courses, as here, you will not want the text to shape, or wrap, itself around the image. Go to the **Format** menu and select **Picture**. Click on the **Wrapping** tab, select **None** then click **OK**.
Now copy the ClipArt and paste it between each course using the Copy and Paste toolbar buttons.

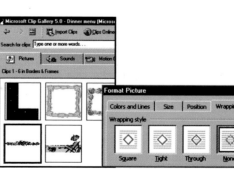

When you set the width of your columns, the spacing between the columns adjusts automatically.

Add a ClipArt image as before. See Step 5.

Close up
*Your place cards may not all fit on a single sheet of A4. To add another page to your document press the **Return** key at the end of the first page – a second page appears automatically.*

Cell Height and Width

Row | Column

Height of rows 1-2:
At least | At: 100pt

Row | Column

Width of column 1: 6 cm
Space between columns: 0.38 cm

Font

Font | Character Spacing | Animation

Font:
Baskerville Old Face

Augsburger Initials
Baskerville Old Face
Bauhaus 93
Beesknees ITC
Bernard MT Condensed

Font style:
Regular

Regular
Italic
Bold
Bold Italic

Size:
14

9
10
11
12
14

Underline:
(none)

Color:
Auto

Effects
☐ Strikethrough
☐ Double strikethrough
☐ Superscript
☐ Subscript

Preview

¶
¶
Nicholas·Vincent¤

an Copy

Paste Rows

¶
¶
Anthony Farthing¤

¶
¶
Melanie Swift¤

¶
¶
Ruth Wilson¤

¶
¶
Helen Maslin¤

8 In the **Table** menu click on **Insert Table**. Set columns to 1 and rows to 2. Click **OK**. In the **Table** menu select **Cell Height and**

Width. Select 'At least' in the 'Height of rows' box and set the height at 100 pt. Click the **Column** tab and set the width to 6 cm. Click **OK**.

9 Click in the lower of the two cells (so you can fold each card over). Press the **Return** key twice then type in a guest name.

Highlight it, go to the **Format** menu and click on **Font**. Select a font, size and style. Click **OK**. Click on the **Center** toolbar button.

10 To duplicate your card, select the table and click on the **Copy** button. Click below the table and press **Return** twice.

Click on the **Paste Rows** toolbar button. Highlight the name and type in your second guest's name. Repeat for other cards.

Bright idea
It's worth buying a small guillotine to cut your place cards after you have printed them out. Cutting with a guillotine rather than scissors will ensure the edges of your cards are neat and precise.

To help you organise the menu for your dinner party, why not set up a database of recipes? Turn to page 282 to find out more.

▶ **OTHER IDEAS TO TRY**

Create a family newsletter

Keep in touch with distant friends and relatives

A regular newsletter is a great way to keep family members in touch with each other. The first step is to ask your relatives whether they would like to contribute any news, such as a new job or a recently passed exam. They may even like to send in favourite recipes or poems they have written.

Impose a deadline and suggest they send anything to you on a floppy disk or, even better, via e-mail to save you typing in their text.

Once the contributions have arrived write your own stories to incorporate them. Finally, decide what you are going to call the family newsletter. It's tempting to use your surname in the heading, but remember that not all family members share the same name.

Prioritise your contributions. If there isn't enough space for all your news in the current edition of the newsletter, save some for the next.

▶ BEFORE YOU START

Page Setup

| Margins | Paper Size | Paper Source | Layout |

Top: 2 cm
Bottom: 2 cm
Left: 2 cm
Right: 2 cm

Gutter: 0 cm

From edge
Header: 1.25 cm
Footer: 1.25 cm

Preview

Apply to: Whole docum

☐ Mirror margins

1 Go to the **Start** menu, select **Programs** and click on **Word**. Go to the **File** menu and click on **Page Setup**. With the Margins tab selected, set the sizes for the Top, Bottom, Left and Right margins. Click **OK**.

Family News

Top marks!

Congratulations to Anna Taylor, Jim and Jo's daughter, for passing her degree in Spanish. She really deserved the 2.1 she got.

We went to her graduation in July at Birmingham Cathedral and I have to admit that I nearly burst with pride when she shook hands and received her degree from the Chancellor of her university.

Anna is planning to travel and work in Spain for a year, starting in Barcelona and travelling to the south coast in time for next summer's tourist season.

All the family will really miss Anna but I'm sure you'll join us in wishing her good luck and 'bon voyage!'

Making a splash

Our son, Paul Taylor, has been indulging in his favourite watery pastime – swimming.

This time it's in a good cause because his school is collecting money for the charity Children in Need, so Paul asked friends and neighbours to dig deep into their pockets and sponsor his watery antics.

His father, Jim, and I went along to watch his efforts along with plenty of other weary but devoted parents and were really pleased that he swam so well.

Children in Need will be pleased too when they receive the school's cheque for £267 to help their charity work, including Paul's contribution of £31.80. A valiant effort.

It's a girl!

Sally Stafford gave birth to Sarah Jane on 4th July. Congratulations! Mother and baby are doing well and the family hopes to come to England early next year. Better put the kettle on…

Fun in the sun

After all their effort, Jim and I felt that the kids deserved a holiday. So we had a fortnight in Majorca…

The neighbours kindly took Barney and he was quite happy to go as they feed him chocolate. We packed our bags (so much luggage!) and headed for the sun.

The children chose a hotel near the beach with a pool for Paul and his friend Sam and plenty of Spanish waiters for Anna and her friend Sue to practise their Spanish with

Now that the kids are older, we didn't mind leaving them at the hotel while we went exploring the island in a jeep. It really is quite beautiful but the hair-raising mountain roads took some negotiating.

We all returned, bronzed, relaxed and ready to argue about next year's break

Celebration!

Margaret Taylor will be celebrating her 100th birthday in December. To celebrate this wonderful event, we are holding a surprise party at her home in Sussex. Hope to see you there on the 8th

You can also create a newsletter using Microsoft Works. Open Works then, in the Works Task Launcher, click on the **Works Tools** tab then on the **Word Processor** button.

▶ OTHER PROGRAMS

Templates on CD-ROM

*To control how your text wraps around your ClipArt image, click on the **Wrapping** tab. Click on the **Tight** icon in the 'Wrapping style' section. Click **OK**.*

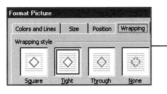

2 Type in your heading then press the **Return** key. Type in your articles, giving each its own title and leaving a line space between them (press the **Return** key).

3 Add a ClipArt image for fun (see below). When inserted and resized, go to the **Format** menu and click on **Picture**. In the Format Picture dialogue box click on the **Position** tab. Click on the 'Float over text' box to give you more control over your image, then **OK**.

4 Now highlight your heading, go to the **Format** menu and click on **Font**. Choose a font, style, size and colour. As this is an informal document, choose a fun font. For a distinctive effect, click in the Shadow box and select a dotted rule in the Underline box.

Add page numbers

To add page numbers in Word, go to the **View** menu and click on **Header and Footer**. Click in the Footer section of your document and, in the Header and Footer dialogue box, click on **Insert AutoText** then on **PAGE**.

In Microsoft Works, click in the Footer section, go to the **Insert** menu and click on **Page Number**. In the Footer section '*page*' appears. Works replaces this with the correct page number when you print your document.

Using images

To import ClipArt, place your cursor at the top of the document, go to the **Insert** menu, select **Picture** then click on **ClipArt**. Select an image from the gallery then click on the **Insert** icon. To resize your image, click on a corner and drag it diagonally with your mouse.

To import photos, scan them in, or get them scanned at a bureau, and save them on your PC (for details on scanning, see page 206). Go to the **Insert** menu, select **Picture** then click on **From File**. Find your photograph then click on **Insert**.

For more details on inserting and using ClipArt images and photos, see pages 188 and 212.

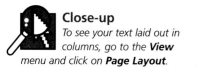

Close-up
*To see your text laid out in columns, go to the **View** menu and click on **Page Layout**.*

Bright idea
For a professional look, style all your headings using the same font, font style and font size. Use colour only in the headings as coloured text can be difficult to read.

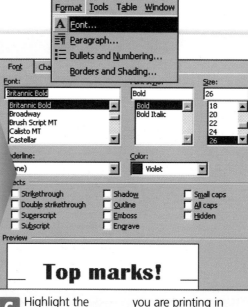

5 To create columns, place the cursor at the start of your first article, go to the **Format** menu and click on **Columns**. Select **Two**

in the Presets section. Set the column width and the spacing between the columns. Ensure the 'Line between' box is ticked then click **OK**.

6 Highlight the heading of your first article, go to the **Format** menu and click on **Font**. Select a font, font style and size. If

you are printing in colour, click on the arrow to the right of the Color box, scroll through and select a colour. Click **OK**.

7 Highlight and style the first paragraph of your first article in the same way. Choose a bold font style to make it stand out.

Highlight and style the remainder of the first article, selecting a regular font style.

Applying settings
To apply your column settings to the area of the document below the heading, click on the arrow to the right of the 'Apply to' box, scroll through and click on **This point forward**.

Columns in Works
To set columns in Microsoft Works, go to the **Format** menu and click on **Columns**. Set the 'Number of columns' and the 'Space between' them. Click in the 'Line between columns' box, then click **OK**. Note that all the text in your newsletter reflows into columns.

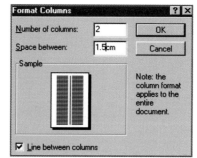

*In the Drop Cap dialogue box, click on the **Dropped** icon in the Position section. Select the number of lines you want it to drop by in the 'Lines to drop' box. Click **OK**.*

Drop Cap

Position

None   Dropped

Lines to drop: 3
Distance from text: 0 cm

If you want to produce a regular newsletter, save your first one as a template that can be opened and altered for each edition.

CREATE A TEMPLATE

Paragraph

Indents and Spacing | Line and Page Breaks

Alignment: Left   Outline level: Body text

Indentation
Left: 0 cm   Special: (none)   By:
Right: 0 cm

Spacing
Before: 0 pt   Line spacing: At:
After: 2 pt   Exactly   14 pt

Preview

Family News

Top marks!

It's a girl!

Fun in the sun

Making a splash

Save As

Save in: Templates

- Access
- Binders
- Databases
- Letters & Faxes
- Memos
- Other Documents
- Outlook
- Presentation Designs
- Presentations
- Spreadsheet Solutions
- Web Pages
- Illustrated stationary let
- Letterhead
- Normal

File name: Family Newsletter

Save as type: Document Template

8 To adjust line spacing, highlight your first article (not the heading), go to the **Format** menu and click on **Paragraph**. Apply settings in the dialogue box (see below). Style the rest of your articles in the same way.

9 To add a 'drop cap', place your cursor in the first paragraph, go to the **Format** menu and click on **Drop Cap**. Apply settings in the dialogue box (see above). Click **OK**. To check how your document looks, go to the **File** menu and select **Print Preview**.

10 Go to the **File** menu and select **Save As**. In the Save As dialogue box type in a name in the 'File name' box. Scroll through the 'Save as type' box and click on **Document Template**. Word will save your newsletter in its Templates folder. Click **Save**.

Adjusting line spacing

To adjust spacing between lines, click on the arrow to the right of the 'Line spacing' box and scroll through. If you know which point size you want, click on **Exactly** then select the size in the At box.

To increase the space between paragraphs, click on the uppermost arrow to the right of After in the Spacing section. Finally, click **OK**.

Spacing
Before: 0 pt   Line spacing:
After: 2 pt   Single

Single
1.5 lines
Double
At least
Exactly
Multiple

Preview

Finishing touch

Don't forget to add your name and contact details at the end of the newsletter, and explain how to submit articles for future editions.

Spare yourself having to make amendments later by making sure the details you are going to enter into your database are up to date.

BEFORE YOU START

1 Go to the **Start** menu, highlight **Programs** and click on **Microsoft Works**. In the Works Task Launcher double-click on **Address Book** in the Common Tasks folder. In the next dialogue box click the 'Yes, run the TaskWizard' button.

Make an address list

It can be easy to keep in touch with friends and contacts

One of the most useful things you can do with a database is make an address list. There are many advantages to doing this on your PC. You can easily update it when people move house or change their name; you can sort addresses to view just family, or just work colleagues, or just people who live abroad (handy when you are making Christmas card lists); you can search for individual words (if, say, you can remember that someone was called Jim but you have forgotten his surname). And you can always print it out if you need to.

*You can also create an address list in Outlook. Open Outlook and click on the **Contacts** icon in the left pane of the window. Press **Ctrl** and **'N'** at the same time to open the data entry form.*

OTHER PROGRAMS

Templates on CD-ROM

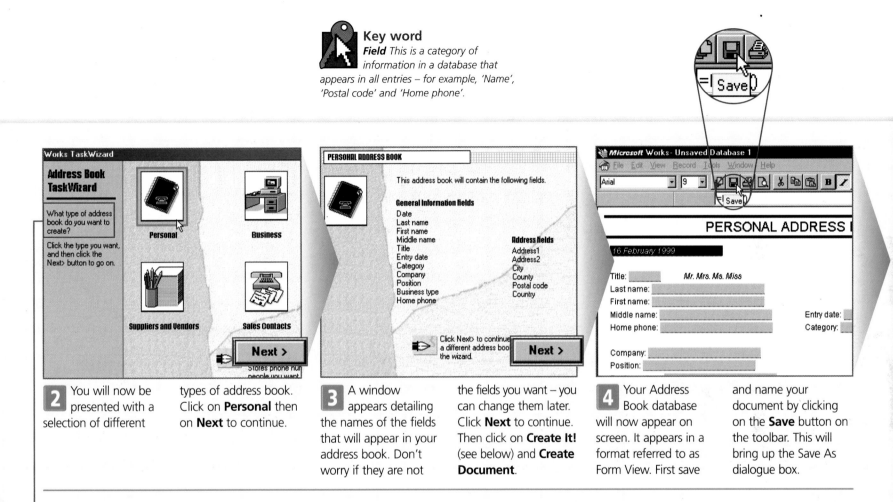

Key word

Field *This is a category of information in a database that appears in all entries – for example, 'Name', 'Postal code' and 'Home phone'.*

2 You will now be presented with a selection of different types of address book. Click on **Personal** then on **Next** to continue.

3 A window appears detailing the names of the fields that will appear in your address book. Don't worry if they are not the fields you want – you can change them later. Click **Next** to continue. Then click on **Create It!** (see below) and **Create Document**.

4 Your Address Book database will now appear on screen. It appears in a format referred to as Form View. First save and name your document by clicking on the **Save** button on the toolbar. This will bring up the Save As dialogue box.

There are six address book templates provided in Works, which you can edit to include the fields you need. The six templates are:

- **Personal** *For family and friends.*
- **Business** *For companies and people you work with.*
- **Customers or Clients** *Contact and credit details.*
- **Suppliers and Vendors** *Contact and credit details.*
- **Sales Contacts** *Potential customers and sales leads.*
- **Employees** *Contact and job details.*

Accessing your address list

You can access your address book at any time in Microsoft Works through the Address Book toolbar button.

After you click on the **Create It!** button, the next dialogue box asks whether you want the address book you are about to create to become the one that opens through the toolbar button. Click on the button beside 'Yes...', then click on **Create Document**.

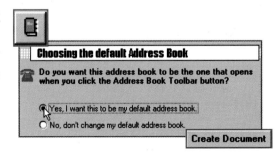

To move from field to field, press the **Tab** key. To move back, press the **Shift** key and **Tab** key simultaneously.

Form Design

Short cut
To move several fields at the same time, press the **Ctrl** key and, keeping it pressed down, click on the fields in turn. Release the **Ctrl** key and then drag your selection with the mouse.

---

16 February 1999

Title: Mr   *Mr. Mrs. Ms. Miss*
Last name: Rivers
First name: Simon
Middle name:
Home phone:

Company:
Position:
Business type:

Edit View Insert Format Tools Window Help

Cannot Undo
Cut   Ctrl+X
Copy   Ctrl+C
Paste   Ctrl+V
Paste Special...
Delete Selection
Go To...   Ctrl+G
Position Selection

PERSONAL ADDRESS BOOK

Mr. Mrs. Ms. Miss

name: Simon
ddle name:
Home phone: 00 65 833 8745

Company:
Position:
Business type:

File Edit View Insert Format Tools Window Help

Arial   9

2.8cm 5.3cm   "00 65 833 9745

PERSONAL AD

6 February 1999

Title: Mr   Mr. Mrs. Ms. Miss
Last name: Rivers
First name: Simon

Home phone: 00 65 83 9745
MOUE

---

5 Begin entering data. Click on the first field and type in the title of your first person. Click on successive fields and complete entering your details. When you reach the last field of one entry, press the **Tab** key to take you to the first field of the next entry.

6 To remove an unwanted field, click on the **Form Design** toolbar button. Click on the field you want to remove, then go to **Edit** menu and click on **Delete Selection**. You will be prompted to confirm the deletion. To add a field, see below.

7 You can rearrange the order of the fields, and reduce or increase the spacing between them. In Form Design click on a field and, keeping the mouse button pressed down, drag it to its new position.

Different views

There are three ways to view your address list:

 List View is best for quick reference as it allows you to view lots of entries at the same time.

 Form View displays one entry at a time and is the best for inputting data.

 Form Design lets you add/delete fields and alter their layout.

Adding fields

To add a field – for example, Work phone – click on the **Form Design** toolbar button. Place the cursor where you want the new field inserted, go to the **Insert** menu and click on **Field**.

In the Insert Field dialogue box, type in the new field name. Ensure that **General** is selected in the Format box and click **OK**.

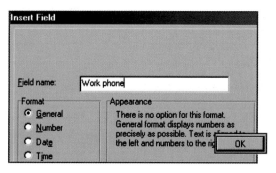

Insert Field

Field name: Work phone

Format
⊙ General
○ Number
○ Date
○ Time

Appearance
There is no option for this format. General format displays numbers as precisely as possible. Text is a... the left and numbers to the ri...

OK

Ascending sorts your records from A to Z. Descending sorts them from Z to A.

Ascending
Descending

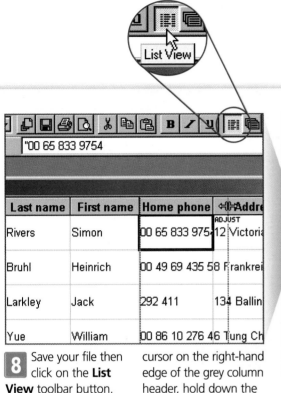

"00 65 833 9754

Last name	First name	Home phone	Addre
Rivers	Simon	00 65 833 975	12 Victoria
Bruhl	Heinrich	00 49 69 435 58	Frankrei
Larkley	Jack	292 411	134 Ballin
Yue	William	00 86 10 276 46	Tung Ch

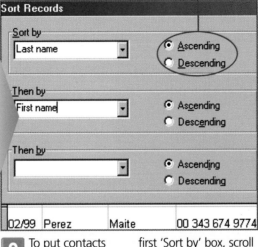

Sort Records

Sort by
Last name

Ascending
Descending

Then by
First name

Ascending
Descending

Then by

Ascending
Descending

| 02/99 | Perez | Maite | 00 343 674 9774 |

Pen-pal address list

✓		Date	Last name	First name	Home phone	
☐	1	03/99	**Bruhl**	Heinrich	00 49 69 435 5611	8 F
☐	2	03/99	Duchamps	Francoise	00 331 493 2240	67
☐	3	03/99	Jamil	Issi	00 91 33 673 8865	7 M
☐	4	03/99	Larkley	Jack		134
☐	5	03/99	Marlowe	Paul	Bold	Bri
☐	6	03/99	McIntyre	Kate	0131 794 4839	4 F
☐	7	03/99	Perez	Maite	00 343 674 9774	Ap
☐	8	03/99	Peters	Louise	00 61 9 867 1441	3 H

8 Save your file then click on the **List View** toolbar button. To adjust the width of a column to view your data better, place the cursor on the right-hand edge of the grey column header, hold down the left mouse button and drag the edge to the desired width.

9 To put contacts into alphabetical order go to the **Record** menu and click on **Sort Records**. Click on the arrow to the right of the first 'Sort by' box, scroll through and select 'Last name'. In the second box select 'First name'. Click the Ascending option then click **OK**.

10 You now have all the last names listed alphabetically. As 'Last name' is the most important field, give it more prominence by using bold type. Click on the 'Last name' column header to highlight the column, then click on the **Bold** toolbar button.

Setting up a date

Works automatically creates a date field for your address book, and enters the date on which addresses were made. In List View this entry initially shows as a series of symbols. Increase the field's column width to see the date, month and the year.

To change the format of the date, go to the **Format** menu and select **Field**. Click on a new style from the Appearance box, then on **OK**.

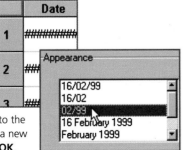

	Date
1	########
2	###
3	###

Appearance
16/02/99
16/02
02/99
16 February 1999
February 1999

Now that you have completed your address list, why not use it to print out address labels? See page 172 to find out how.

▶ OTHER IDEAS TO TRY

Make address labels

Save time and effort by printing your own labels

Computers come into their own when there are repetitive or time-consuming tasks to be done. Writing addresses on envelopes – at Christmas or for a charity mailshot – is one such task. Why not use your PC to create and print out address labels? It will spare you the tedium of doing it by hand, and you give your envelopes a professional look.

You can create labels with a wide variety of designs, text styles and sizes. You can also put a personal stamp on your mail by adding your own decorative images.

You must have the addresses you want to print compiled on a database. To do this, see Make An Address List *on page 168. You also need to buy sheets of sticky labels.*

▶ BEFORE YOU START

1 Go to the **Start** menu, select **Programs** then click on **Microsoft Works**. In the Works Task Launcher click on the **Works Tools** tab then on the **Word Processor** button. A new document will appear.

*You can also create address labels in Microsoft Word. Open Microsoft Word, go to the **Tools** menu and click on **Mail Merge**. Follow the steps in the Mail Merge Helper box.*

▶ OTHER PROGRAMS

Templates on CD-ROM

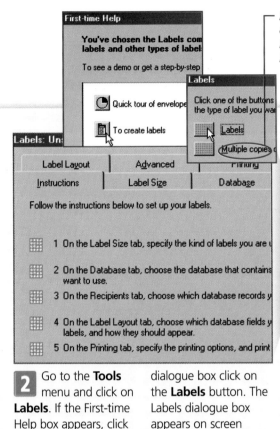

*If you don't have an address book database and just want to print single labels, click on the **Multiple copies** button. Follow the on-screen instructions.*

First-time Help

You've chosen the Labels com
labels and other types of label:

To see a demo or get a step-by-step

⊙ Quick tour of envelope

▣ To create labels

Labels

Click one of the buttons
the type of label you war

▦ Labels

▦ Multiple copies

Labels: Uns

| Label Layout | Advanced | Printing |
| Instructions | Label Size | Database |

Follow the instructions below to set up your labels.

▦ 1 On the Label Size tab, specify the kind of labels you are

▦ 2 On the Database tab, choose the database that contains
want to use.

▦ 3 On the Recipients tab, choose which database records y

▦ 4 On the Label Layout tab, choose which database fields y
labels, and how they should appear.

▦ 5 On the Printing tab, specify the printing options, and print

Labels: Unsaved Document 1

| Label Layout | Advanced | Printing |
| Instructions | Label Size | Database |

What size labels will you be using?

Choose a label size:

Avery L7160 (63.5mm x 38.1mm)
Avery L7161 (63.5mm x 46.6mm)
Avery L7162 (99.1mm x 33.9mm)
Avery L7163 (99.1mm x 38.1mm)
Avery L7183 (63.5mm x 72mm)

Hint: If your label size is not listed above, click the Custom button
correct dimensions.

Custom...   Next >

Labels: Unsaved Document 1

| Label Layout | Advanced | Printing |
| Instructions | Label Size | Database |

Which database has the information you want to use?

Choose a database:

🗃 (No Database)
🗃 Address - business.wdb
🗃 Address - friends.wdb
🗃 Eastern Recipes.wdb
🗃 Family Health Records.wdb

▦ Open a database not listed here

Hint: Click the View Database button to review the database to be sure
you want.

View Database...   Next >

2 Go to the **Tools** menu and click on **Labels**. If the First-time Help box appears, click on the **To create labels** button. In the next dialogue box click on the **Labels** button. The Labels dialogue box appears on screen with the Instructions tab selected.

3 Click on the **Label Size** tab. Check the reference number of the labels you've bought, scroll through the menu and click on the matching size in the list displayed. Click **Next** to continue. If your label size is not listed, click **Custom** to specify the dimensions.

4 Now click on the **Database** tab. The 'Choose a database' pane shows all the database files that you have created in Works. Click on the address list you want then click on **Next** to continue.

Close-up
Address labels come in a variety of sizes, each with their own reference number. You can buy labels that fill the whole of an A4 page. Specialist labels to put on floppy disks, videos, cassettes, etc, are also available. One of the most common address labels is the L7163 – you get 14 of them on an A4 page.

Searching for a database

▦ Open a database not listed here   Search for databases not listed in the dialogue box by clicking on the 'Open a database not listed here' button.

View Database...   You may have made several address lists – one for your family and friends, one for your business contacts, and one for the members of a social club. To check which one you want to use, click on **View Database**.

*If you want to change the order of your fields on your label, click on the **Clear All** button to start again.*

Add Field

New Line

Clear All

Labels: Unsaved Document 1

| Instructions | Label Size |
| Label Layout | Advanced |

Click the Edit button to go to the Word Processor to e
even add pictures to your envelope, label, or form lett

Edit...

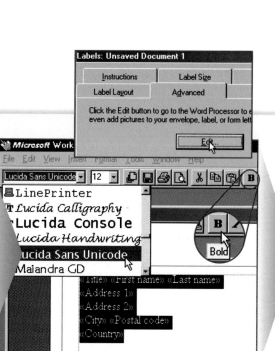

Labels: Unsaved Document 1

| Label Layout | Advanced | Printing |
| Instructions | Label Size | Database |

Which database records do you want to print?

- ⦿ All records in the database
- ◯ Current records visible in the database
- ◯ Currently marked records in the database
- ◯ Filtered records in the database

Current Filter: [(No Filters)]   Change Filter...

Hint: Click the View Database button to review your database or mark t
       you want.

View Database...   Next >

Labels: Unsaved Document 1

| Instructions | Label Size | Database |
| Label Layout | Advanced | Printing |

Which fields do you want on your labels?

Choose a field:
City
Postal code
Country
Title

Add Field

New Line

Clear All

Add fields one
a new line to m
way you want.

Label layout:
«Title»

Microsoft Work
File Edit View Insert Format Tools Window Help

Lucida Sans Unicode ▾ 12 ▾

▤ LinePrinter
𝑻 Lucida Calligraphy
ᴛ Lucida Console
Lucida Handwriting
Lucida Sans Unicode
ᴛ Maiandra GD

B

Bold

«Title» «First name» «Last name»
«Address 1»
«Address 2»
«City» «Postal code»
«Country»

5 Click on the **Recipients** tab. To print a label for everybody on your database, ensure the 'All records in database' option is selected. Then click on **Next**.

6 Click the **Label Layout** tab. In the 'Choose a field' list click on the field that you want to appear first on your label. Click **Add** **Field** and it will appear in the 'Label layout' pane. Repeat the process for all the other fields and then click on **Next**.

7 Click on the **Advanced** tab and then **Edit** to style your label. To change the font, highlight the text then scroll through and click on a font from the font shortcut on the toolbar. Click on the **Bold** toolbar button to put text in heavy type.

Select recipients

To print labels for a selection of people on your database, select the 'Currently marked records in the database' option, then click on the **View Database** button.

Select the people you want to print labels for by clicking in the box in the first column of their rows. If you select the wrong row, click on it again to deselect it.

- ◯ All records in the database
- ◯ Current records visible in the database
- ⦿ Currently marked records in the databa
- ◯ Filtered records in the database
- Current Filter: [(No Filters)]

Hint: Click the View Database
       you want.

View Database...

Home Address List 2

☑		Date	Last name	First name	
☑	1	02/99	Bruhl	Heinrich	00
☐	2	02/99	**Duchamps**	Francoise	00

*When you want a field to appear on a different line, click on the **New Line** button.*

Choose a field:
City
Postal code
Country
Title

Add Field

New Line

Clear All

Label layout:
«Title» «First name» «Last name»
«Address 1»
«Address 2»
«City» «Postal code»

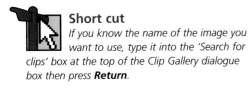

Short cut

*If you know the name of the image you want to use, type it into the 'Search for clips' box at the top of the Clip Gallery dialogue box then press **Return**.*

Watch out

Don't waste your sticky labels. Before printing do a test on a sheet of paper, then overlay the paper on your sheet of labels to check the fit. If necessary, add or remove line spaces to improve the fit.

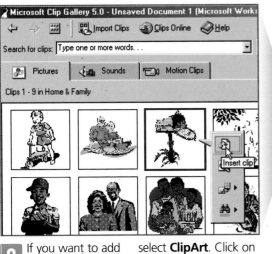

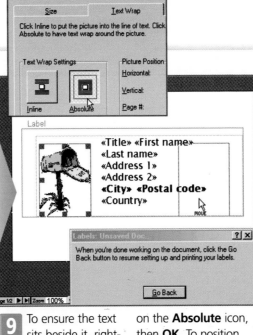

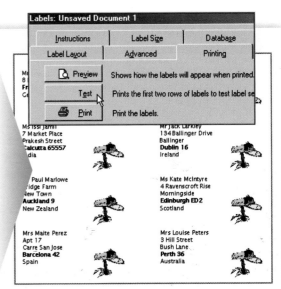

8 If you want to add a ClipArt image to your label, click on the point where you'd like the image to appear, go to the **Insert** menu and select **ClipArt**. Click on a category to view its contents. Click on the image you want then click on the **Insert clip** icon that appears.

9 To ensure the text sits beside it, right-click on the image and click on **Format Picture**. Click on the **Text Wrap** tab, then on the **Absolute** icon, then **OK**. To position the image, click on it and drag it accordingly. In the Labels dialogue box click on **Go Back**.

10 Click on the **Printing** tab. Click **Preview** to see how your labels look. Click **Test** to print the first two rows of your labels to check your settings are OK. If not, click on the **Label Size** tab and select a new size. When you are happy, click on the **Print** button.

Resizing images

Reduce or enlarge the size of your ClipArt image by clicking on one of the corner handles and dragging it across the screen.

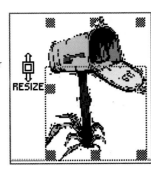

Bright idea

If you design a label that you think you might use again, remember to save it. You will be prompted to do so before you close the document.

175

Make a home

Let your computer take care of the

Project planner

Create a folder named after your business. Add sub-folders for each of its various aspects.

- Business
  - Clients
  - Suppliers
  - Finance
  - Product development
  - Publicity

Millions of people around the world have seized the opportunity to start their own business. There is a real thrill to be had from making a go of your own idea, from being your own boss and taking your financial destiny into your own hands.

But with this opportunity come new responsibilities: for accounting, correspondence, and publicity; for dealing with suppliers, your bank manager and the tax man, and – perhaps most importantly – for finding your next client.

In fact, most of your time could easily be taken up with anything

business work

details while you take care of the profits

other than realising your original business idea.

Your PC can reduce the time spent on many of these tasks. It can even help you to research your business idea before you invest heavily in it.

For correspondence and publicity you could design a logo using Paint or another drawing program. It's often easiest to design your stationery and produce correspondence from a template, and keep a record of all your communications either on your computer's hard disk or backed-up on portable disks.

You can use your PC's database program to create a client database and, from that, customer name and address labels.

Ensure you never miss an appointment by running your

business diary from your Desktop. If you use a car for work, you can work out your running costs to claim them as business expenses. And your spreadsheet program will make dealing with your accounts less of a headache.

With your PC you can design your own business cards, or you can advertise much farther afield with your own Web site.

You can also use the Internet to correspond by e-mail, compare competitors' prices and services, and surf the Web for trade leads – some companies even post supply requirements on Government sites set up to encourage trade.

Before long, your computer will establish itself as your most productive and versatile employee, leaving you more time to enjoy your work.

Minding your own business

- Research the market for your business
- Research prices/costings for your product and those of competitors
- Prepare a business plan
- Arrange/prepare start-up finances
- Seek an accountant's advice on running a business
- Officially register as a business

Ideas and inspirations

Below are some suggestions for limiting the time you spend taking care of your business and maximising its efficiency. The projects can be adapted depending on your own circumstances. If you have business partners, you may agree to divide the tasks between yourselves.

252 **Do your own accounts**
Organise your income, outgoings and overheads; project future expenditure and profit.

196 **Illustrated business stationery**
Increase the profile of your business and make communications more effective.

168 **Compile a client database**
Make sure you don't lose track of anyone by storing their details in an updatable record.

182 **Set up a business diary**
Keep track of your appointments and timetable a variety of tasks in an on-screen diary.

116 **Design your own Web page**
Advertise your products or services on the Internet and invite potential clients to e-mail you.

Also worth considering…

Use pictures as well as words to sell your product – to get the message home to potential clients.

220 **Create a press pack**
With the same techniques used to produce a photo album you can design a mailshot or brochure.

Design a business card

Make a good impression on colleagues, associates and friends

A well-designed business card can make a huge impact on potential clients and on your business. It reflects on your professionalism and its design can impart key aspects of your business. For example, a cake decorator who uses a picture of a traditional wedding cake and traditional fonts on their business card is likely to attract a different clientele than one who uses a picture of a more unusual cake and modern fonts.

A business card, or visiting card for social occasions, can easily be created using Word, and you can personalise it with your choice of text style and graphics. Alternatively you may wish to design a card for a society or association with which you are involved.

Think carefully about what information you want to include on your card, and double-check that all your contact details are correct.

BEFORE YOU START

Page Setup

| Margins | Paper Size | Paper Source | Layout |

Top: 2.54 cm
Bottom: 2.54 cm
Left: 1 cm
Right: 1 cm
Gutter: 0 cm

From edge
Header: 1.25 cm
Footer: 1.25 cm

☐ Mirror margins

Preview

Apply to: Whole docume

OK

1 Go to the **Start** menu, select **Programs** and click on **Microsoft Word**. Go to the **File** menu and click on **Page Setup**.

With the Margins tab selected, type in 1 cm for the Left and Right margins, so that two cards fit side by side on an A4 sheet. Click **OK**.

It is possible to style text and import ClipArt in Works' word processing program. However, Works cannot size your card effectively, and so is not a suitable alternative to Word.

OTHER PROGRAMS

When you adjust the width of your columns, the spacing between them adjusts automatically.

Close-up
When inserting your table, rulers should appear at the top and to the left of your document. If they do not, go to the **View** menu and click on **Ruler**.

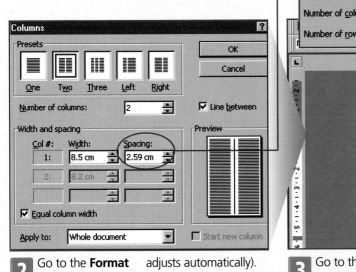

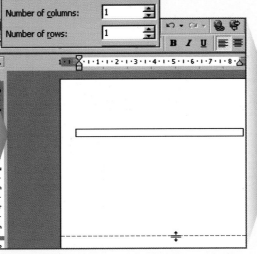

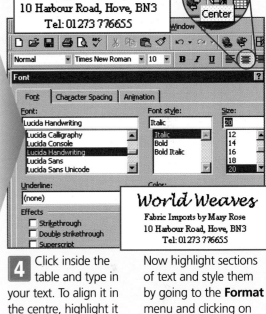

Center

2 Go to the **Format** menu and select **Columns**. In Presets, click on **Two**. In 'Width and spacing' make the Width 8.5 cm (Spacing adjusts automatically). Ensure the 'Equal column width' and the 'Line between' boxes are ticked (to tick, click in them). Click **OK**.

3 Go to the **Table** menu and click on **Insert Table**. Set the columns and rows to one. Click **OK**. A box appears. Move the mouse pointer over the bottom line. When it becomes a double-headed arrow, drag the line to the 5.5 cm mark on the left ruler.

4 Click inside the table and type in your text. To align it in the centre, highlight it then click on the **Center** toolbar button.

Now highlight sections of text and style them by going to the **Format** menu and clicking on **Font**. Select a font, size and style. Click **OK**.

Save your document

Soon after opening your new Word document, remember to save it. Go to the **File** menu and select **Save As**, or click on the **Save** toolbar button. Save your business cards into a suitable folder.

Watch out
It may be tempting to use an unusual font for fun, but make sure your text is legible. If your card can't be read easily, there's little purpose in having one in the first place.

Watch out
Position your ClipArt image so that there is an equal amount of space around it. This will look balanced and more professional.

5 Add a ClipArt graphic. Go to the **Insert** menu, select **Picture** and click on **ClipArt**. Click on the category you want, scroll through to find a suitable graphic, then click **OK**. The graphic appears above the table and the Picture toolbar pops up on screen.

6 In order to move your image around inside your table, click on it, go to the **Format** menu and select **Picture**. Click the **Position** tab and then check that the 'Float over text' box is not ticked. If it is, click in the box to untick it. Click **OK** to continue.

7 To alter the size of your ClipArt image, click on one of its corners and drag it across your screen to the desired size. To position the image in the centre of your card, click on it then click on the **Center** toolbar button.

Add space around your ClipArt
To add more space around your picture, click on it, then go to the **Format** menu and click on **Paragraph**. In the Spacing section click on the uppermost arrows beside Before and After to increase the spacing. Experiment until you get the effect you like.

Undoing changes
If you have experimented with spacing and formatting, but find you don't like the results, the quickest way to remove the changes is to click on the **Undo** button on the Word toolbar. Each click you make takes you back a stage in the development of your document.

Bright idea
Print your cards on card that is 250gsm or thicker to get the best results. Most printers only handle card up to 160gsm thick, so you should consider having the file printed at a print shop.

Close-up
*To remove a card, click on it, go to the **Table** menu and click on **Select Table**. Go back to the **Table** menu and select **Delete Rows**.*

8 To create several cards, simply copy and paste the original. Click anywhere inside the table, go to the **Table** menu and click on **Select Table**. Go to the **Edit** menu and select **Copy**. A copy of your business card is now stored in the computer's memory.

9 Click below the original table and press **Return**. Go to the **Edit** menu and select **Paste Cells**. A second card appears. Use the same process to fill the page with cards. When you reach the end of the first column, Word automatically moves on to the second column.

10 Once you're happy with the design of your cards, go to the **File** menu and select **Print**. Choose the page range and number of copies you want then click **OK**.

Professional results

If you want to have the card printed at your local print shop, save the document onto your hard disk then copy it onto a floppy disk.

Place your disk in the floppy disk drive, click on **My Computer** and click on **3½ Floppy [A:]**. Drag the icon of your saved business card document onto the window of the disk.

Business Card .doc
From 'Business Stationery' to 'A:\'

Create your own diary

Organise your life – use a computer to help you plan

Many people have such pressurised schedules that it is easy to lose track of everything that needs to be done. By creating a diary using the Microsoft Office program Outlook, you need never miss an appointment again.

Outlook allows you to enter appointments, events, meetings and tasks into your diary and view them by the day, week or month. It allows you to print out a schedule for your day, attach important documents to relevant entries in your diary, and it even reminds you of your appointments well before they catch up with you.

> *Ask your family or work colleagues if there are any events, tasks or appointments that you should add to your diary immediately.*

BEFORE YOU START

1 Go to the **Start** menu, select **Programs** then click on **Microsoft Outlook**. Click on the **Calendar** icon. A blank schedule for the day appears. It includes sections for each hour of the day, a view of the next two months and a blank list of tasks in the TaskPad.

> *You can make a calendar in Microsoft Works using a TaskWizard. Open Works then, in the Works Task Launcher, click on **Business Management** and then **Calendar**.*

OTHER PROGRAMS

Bright idea
The small arrows beside the name of each month in the daily or weekly view enable you to quickly move to the previous or following month.

Short cut
To add a new appointment when you are displaying your daily calendar, double-click at the new appointment time and enter the details.

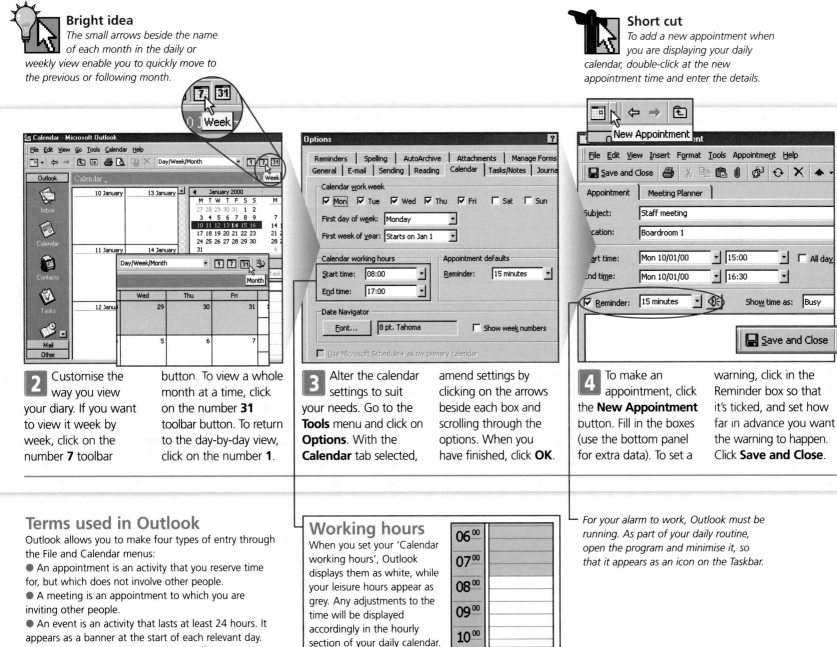

2 Customise the way you view your diary. If you want to view it week by week, click on the number **7** toolbar button. To view a whole month at a time, click on the number **31** toolbar button. To return to the day-by-day view, click on the number **1**.

3 Alter the calendar settings to suit your needs. Go to the **Tools** menu and click on **Options**. With the **Calendar** tab selected, amend settings by clicking on the arrows beside each box and scrolling through the options. When you have finished, click **OK**.

4 To make an appointment, click the **New Appointment** button. Fill in the boxes (use the bottom panel for extra data). To set a warning, click in the Reminder box so that it's ticked, and set how far in advance you want the warning to happen. Click **Save and Close**.

Terms used in Outlook
Outlook allows you to make four types of entry through the File and Calendar menus:
● An appointment is an activity that you reserve time for, but which does not involve other people.
● A meeting is an appointment to which you are inviting other people.
● An event is an activity that lasts at least 24 hours. It appears as a banner at the start of each relevant day.
● A task is a duty that you can check off on completion.

Working hours
When you set your 'Calendar working hours', Outlook displays them as white, while your leisure hours appear as grey. Any adjustments to the time will be displayed accordingly in the hourly section of your daily calendar.

For your alarm to work, Outlook must be running. As part of your daily routine, open the program and minimise it, so that it appears as an icon on the Taskbar.

*To delete a task from the TaskPad, click on the task then click on the **Delete** toolbar button.*

Short cut
*If you want to delete a task in your diary, click on the item then click the right mouse button. Click on **Delete** in the pop-up menu.*

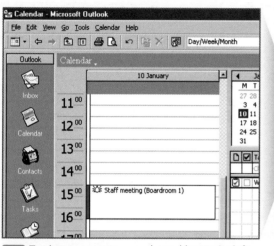

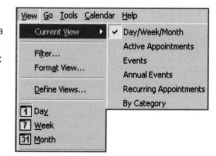

5 To view your entry, scroll through the relevant day's calendar. To move an entry to a new time, click on the coloured bar to its left and drag it to the new time, releasing the mouse button to put it in place.

6 To add a task in the TaskPad, double-click on **Click here to add a new Task**. Type in the details. Click **Save and Close**. When you complete the task, click on the box beside it.

7 To add an event, go to the **Calendar** menu and click on **New Event**. Enter the details in the window that appears. Click **Save and Close**. The event appears as a banner at the top of the relevant day or days.

Altering entries

To change an entry's duration, first click on it. Place your cursor over the top or bottom edge of the appointment box. When the cursor becomes a double-headed arrow, click and drag the edge of the box up or down.

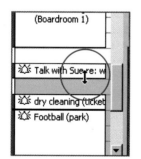

Different views

You can view your diary in a number of ways. Go to the **View** menu, select **Current View** then click on one of the options available.

Close-up
You don't need to save your diary as you would any other document – it will save itself when you close it. When you open Outlook again it will appear automatically.

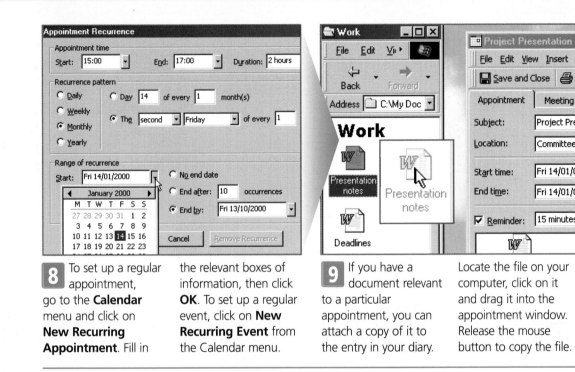

8 To set up a regular appointment, go to the **Calendar** menu and click on **New Recurring Appointment**. Fill in the relevant boxes of information, then click **OK**. To set up a regular event, click on **New Recurring Event** from the Calendar menu.

9 If you have a document relevant to a particular appointment, you can attach a copy of it to the entry in your diary. Locate the file on your computer, click on it and drag it into the appointment window. Release the mouse button to copy the file.

10 To print out a daily schedule, go to the **File** menu, select **Page Setup** then click on **Daily Style**. Select your Layout options (see below left) then click on **Print**. In the Print dialogue box click on **OK**.

Setting print options

In the Page Setup dialogue box you can set options for how you want your diary to print. These include printing the day over one or two pages, adding your list of tasks, choosing which hours of the day to cover, and which fonts to use.

Finishing touch

Add a title and date to your diary. In the Page Setup dialogue box click on the **Header/Footer** tab. Type your title in the Header section, and the date on which you created the diary in the Footer section (you can also add a page number and your name). Click on the **Font** button and choose a font and size in the dialogue box.

Form a pressure group to

Whether you're campaigning to save the rain forest or your local

Across a huge range of concerns – from the global movement to preserve the rain forests, to local campaigns petitioning for traffic-calming measures – the number of people involved with lobbying official bodies has never been greater.

Whether you are starting a new group or opening a local branch of an existing one, it is important to recruit and organise committed members, accrue campaign donations and maintain momentum. Many pressure groups are run by volunteers on slender resources. Your computer can help to make the best use of both.

Increasingly, pressure groups are turning to the Internet to formulate and publicise their campaigns. Researching topics on-line is an obvious starting point. Many educational facilities and research centres release reports via the Net, and the introduction of more 'open

Project planner

Create a folder named after your group. Add sub-folders to it for each mini-project.

Pressure group
- Research
- Contacts
- Communication
- Membership
- Publicity
- Money

make a difference

park, your PC can get the message across

government' in some countries has led to the publication on the Web of a vast quantity of official statistics and information which can aid a campaign.

Newsgroups also offer fertile ground for pressure groups. There are issue-specific noticeboards and forums, where information is traded and debates instigated by interested parties, such as members of other groups and contributors with expert knowledge. Any pressure group would do well to post its details and aims on suitable sites, both to attract members and donations and to collect new information.

And a Web site is the cheapest way to publicise a cause, and is

the only medium with a truly global reach. The cost of maintaining a site is minimal once it has been set up.

Beyond research and publicity, your computer can be used to manage your organisation or branch. You can set up a membership database in Microsoft Works, use a spreadsheet package to manage the group accounts, and produce newsletters and press releases using a word-processing program. You can also create a mailing list, an e-mail list and print address labels. Consider producing questionnaires or petitions using your database's Form Design feature, and lobby local politicians via e-mail.

Form your plan of action

- Arrange venue/date/agenda for launching group
- Publicise launch meeting
- Arrange a visiting speaker
- Appoint officers and detail responsibilities
- Organise street publicity, collect shoppers' signatures and recruit new members
- Plan local demonstrations/publicity campaign
- Design and produce publicity material and flyers

Ideas and inspirations

Adapt the following projects and ideas to enhance your pressure group's profile, attract new members and make the most of your existing members' time and your group's resources. You may even think of other ways to apply your new skills and your computer's capabilities.

96 Internet research
Find the facts to formulate your argument, or simply keep up to date with affiliated groups.

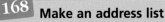

168 Make an address list
Create a handy, easy-to-manage reference file for all your membership and contact details.

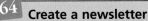

164 Create a newsletter
Keep your members updated about ongoing developments with a short publication.

34 Design a questionnaire
Use database software to gather information on members' opinions and concerns.

272 Accounts
Set up a spreadsheet to keep a close track of membership fees, donations and outgoings.

Also worth considering...

Once your pressure group is up and running, make regular mailshots easier on yourself.

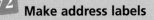

172 Make address labels
Use your membership database as the basis for time-saving printed stationery.

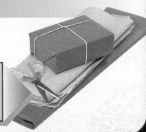

Watch out
Inserting ClipArt in Works is slightly different to Word. In Works all you need to do is go to the **Insert** *menu and select* **ClipArt**. *There is no Picture option.*

1 To insert ClipArt into a Word document, place the cursor where you want the image to go. Go to the **Insert** menu, select **Picture** and click on **ClipArt**. Click on the image category buttons to view them. Click on the **Back** button to go back to the main menu.

Using ClipArt images

Give a touch of creativity to your work by adding illustrations

ClipArt illustrations are predesigned graphic images or pictures that you can incorporate into any document to give it a professional look. A gallery of such images is included free with Word and Works.

The images are generally arranged in such categories as 'Christmas', 'Children' or 'Travel'. They can be used as logos, borders, dividers or just as decorative devices. You can also alter the look of an image, cropping it, framing it and colouring it as you wish.

It is not always easy to get the best, most polished results at the first attempt, so be sure to experiment with ClipArt. Soon you will be making your own greetings cards, wrapping, invitations and address labels.

A ClipArt gallery comes as standard with Word and Works. You can buy more ClipArt on CD-ROM or download it from the Internet. You can also scan in your own designs to use as ClipArt.

OTHER SOURCES

ClipArt on CD-ROM

Insert the image

See an enlarged preview of the image

Add image to Favorites or other category

Find images similar to the one chosen

*To see Word's Picture toolbar, go to the **View** menu, select **Toolbars** then click on **Picture**. To find out what an icon on the Picture toolbar does, place the mouse pointer over it and an explanatory note will pop up.*

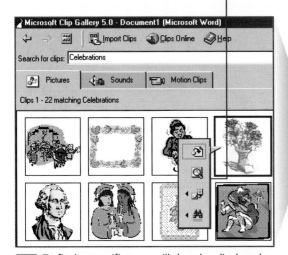

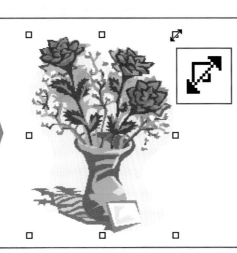

Square
Tight
Through
None
Top and Bottom

2 To find a specific image, type a key word into the 'Search for clips' box then press **Enter**. Any images matching your criteria

will then be displayed. When you click on an image that interests you, a toolbar appears giving you four options as shown above.

3 To insert the image into your document, click on the **Insert clip** button. To resize it, while keeping it in proportion, click on

one of the corner handles and drag it to the required size. To move the image, click on it and drag it to the correct position.

4 If you type text into your document, the words will appear either above or below the image, depending on where

you put the cursor. To position text at the side of the image, click on the **Text Wrapping** button on the Picture toolbar. Select **Square**.

Add to your images

To insert ClipArt from a CD, first insert the CD. Go to the **Insert** menu, select **Picture** and click on **From File**. In the dialogue box select your CD-ROM drive in the 'Look in' box. Scroll through the pictures and folders on the disk, clicking on any that interest you to view them. Click on the image you want, ensure the 'Float over text' box is ticked, then click on **Insert**.

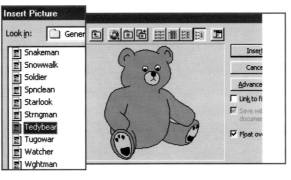

Using text in Works

In Microsoft Works you have two options when positioning text. It can either sit above and below the image (called Inline) or around the image (called Absolute). To make your selection, go to the **Format** menu and click on **Text Wrap**. In the Format Picture dialogue box click on one of the icons in the Text Wrap Settings section. To be able to move, or drag, the image you must choose Absolute.

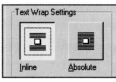

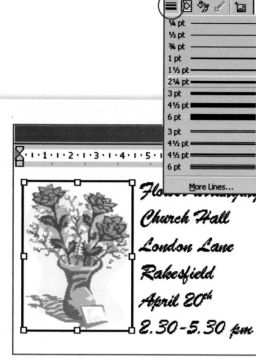

5 You can put a frame around the image. Click on the **Line** button on the Picture toolbar and select a line width from the menu. (It's possible to give your line a dashed effect by clicking on **More Lines** and choosing an effect in the Dashed box.)

6 To give your image a background colour, click on the **Line** button and select **More Lines**. In the Fill section click beside the Color box and select a colour. To get rid of your frame and background colour, select **No Fill** in the Color box and **No Line** in the Line Color box.

7 If you want to shape text closely around the image, click on the **Text Wrapping** toolbar button and select **Tight**. To adjust the wrap, click on **Edit Wrap Points** from the Text Wrapping menu. Click on the points that appear and drag them accordingly.

Using images with text

If you want to use text with ClipArt on a page of typescript, you need to 'float' the ClipArt over the text. This means that you can move the image in and around your text, and you can wrap text around it.

Click on the image, go to the **Format** menu and click on **Picture**. Click the **Position** tab. Ensure that the 'Float over text' box is ticked. If it is not, click in the box to tick it. You can now use the options under the **Wrapping** tab to position the text around the image. Click **OK** when you have finished.

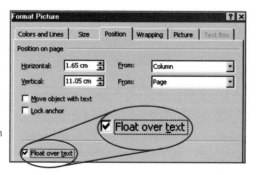

 *If you're unhappy with your image adjustments, click on the **Reset Picture** button on the Picture toolbar. The image will then look exactly the same as when you first inserted it.*

Bright idea
*In Word you can customise ClipArt. Click on the image, go to the **View** menu, select **Toolbars** then click on **Drawing**. On the Drawing toolbar, click on **Draw** and select **Ungroup**. Click off the image. You can now select an area of the image and change the colours as you prefer, and add 3D or shadow effects to your image.*

8 You can crop your image, that is, remove part of it. Click on the **Crop** toolbar button then on the image. Drag a handle into the image. Click on the **Crop** button to deactivate it. To restore the image, select the **Crop** button again and pull the handle back out.

9 If you select **None** from the Text Wrapping menu, the text will appear on top of the image. This can look a bit messy. Make the text stand out by reducing the vibrancy of the image. Click on the image, then the **Image Control** button and select **Watermark**.

10 To centre your text on top of the image, highlight the text and click on the **Center** button on the main toolbar. Then drag the image to sit below the text.

Changing the image
You can alter the way your ClipArt looks by clicking on the **Image Control** button on the Picture toolbar. You can choose more than one option at a time.
- **Automatic** gives a normal image and is the default setting.
- **Grayscale** produces a faint shaded monochrome image.
- **Black and white** gives a monochrome image.
- **Watermark** gives a faint colour image.

You can also adjust the brightness and contrast of the image using four buttons on the toolbar:

More contrast

Less contrast

More brightness

Less brightness

Design a greetings card

Send a personal message with your own special occasion cards

Making your own greetings cards allows you to combine a personal message with an appropriate – even unique – choice of image, and ensures that you always have the right card for any occasion.

On a Christmas card, for example, you could insert a series of photographs showing things that you and your family have done over the past year. And for birthday cards you could scan in and use pictures your children have painted (see page 224).

Anyone who receives personalised cards such as these will greatly appreciate all the thought and effort that has gone into producing them.

Look at your printer manual to find out the maximum thickness, or weight, of paper your printer can take. Consider mounting thinner paper onto card.

BEFORE YOU START

1 Go to the **Start** menu, select **Programs** and click on **Microsoft Word**. To name and save your document go to the **File** menu and click on **Save As**. Select a suitable location in the 'Save in' box, type in a file name, then click on **Save**.

*You can create greetings cards in Microsoft Works. Open Works then, in the Works Task Launcher, click on the **Works Tools** tab then on the **Word Processing** button.*

OTHER PROGRAMS

 Templates on CD-ROM

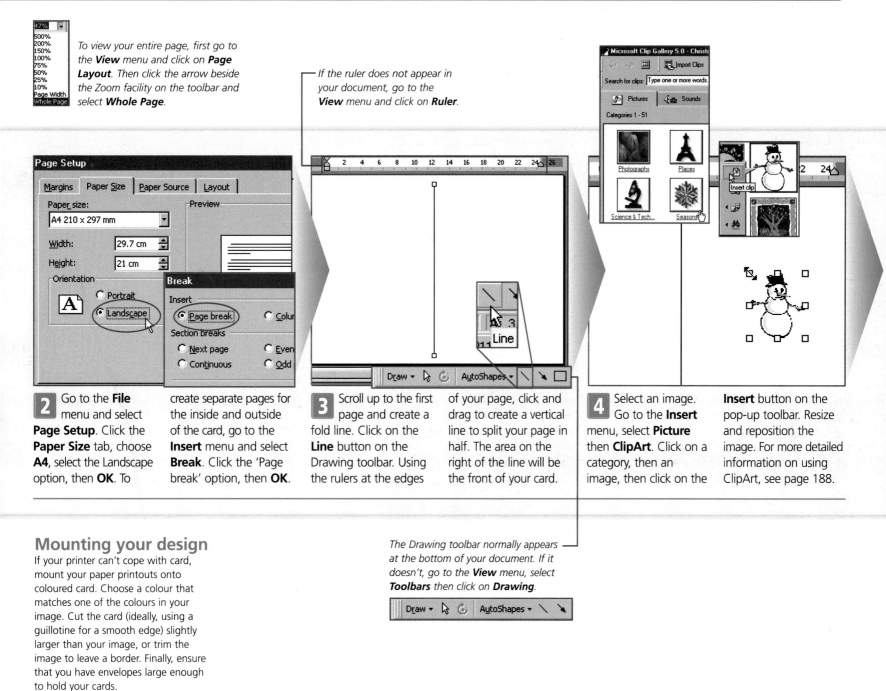

*To view your entire page, first go to the **View** menu and click on **Page Layout**. Then click the arrow beside the Zoom facility on the toolbar and select **Whole Page**.*

*If the ruler does not appear in your document, go to the **View** menu and click on **Ruler**.*

2 Go to the **File** menu and select **Page Setup**. Click the **Paper Size** tab, choose **A4**, select the Landscape option, then **OK**. To

create separate pages for the inside and outside of the card, go to the **Insert** menu and select **Break**. Click the 'Page break' option, then **OK**.

3 Scroll up to the first page and create a fold line. Click on the **Line** button on the Drawing toolbar. Using the rulers at the edges

of your page, click and drag to create a vertical line to split your page in half. The area on the right of the line will be the front of your card.

4 Select an image. Go to the **Insert** menu, select **Picture** then **ClipArt**. Click on a category, then an image, then click on the

Insert button on the pop-up toolbar. Resize and reposition the image. For more detailed information on using ClipArt, see page 188.

Mounting your design

If your printer can't cope with card, mount your paper printouts onto coloured card. Choose a colour that matches one of the colours in your image. Cut the card (ideally, using a guillotine for a smooth edge) slightly larger than your image, or trim the image to leave a border. Finally, ensure that you have envelopes large enough to hold your cards.

*The Drawing toolbar normally appears at the bottom of your document. If it doesn't, go to the **View** menu, select **Toolbars** then click on **Drawing**.*

Key word
WordArt This describes the Microsoft library of text formats that you can customise. All you need do is select a form of WordArt then type in your text. You can colour the text and style it however you wish.

Click and drag your WordArt into position. To resize it, click and drag on one of its corner handles.

5 If you want to add snowflakes, click on the **AutoShapes** button on the Drawing toolbar and select **Stars and Banners**. Click the shape you want, then click and drag to draw it. Use the white handles to resize the item, and the yellow one to alter its shape.

6 To add colour to your snowflakes, right-click on one of the flakes and select **Format AutoShape** from the pop-up menu. In the dialogue box the Colors and Lines tab is selected. Click the arrow beside the Color box in the Fill section and select a colour. Click **OK**.

7 Add a message to the front of the card. Go to the **Insert** menu, select **Picture** then **WordArt**. In the WordArt Gallery click on a style, then **OK**. A box appears asking you to type in your text. Do so, selecting a font, size and style at the same time. Click **OK**.

Create a frame

You can easily place a border around the front of your card. Click on the **AutoShapes** button on the Drawing toolbar, select **Basic Shapes** and then the Rectangle option. Click and drag on the document to create your frame.

Click on the **Line Color** toolbar button then click on **Patterned Lines** from the colour palette. Select a pattern, foreground and background colour, then click **OK**.

Click the **Fill Color** toolbar button and then click **No Fill** to ensure your ClipArt is visible.

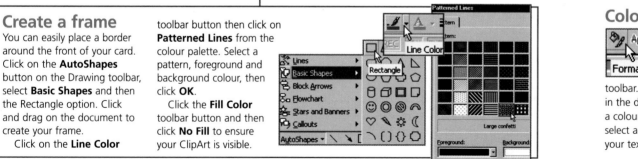

Colouring WordArt

To change the colour of your WordArt, click on the **Format WordArt** button on the WordArt toolbar. The Colors and Lines tab is selected in the dialogue box. In the Fill section select a colour for the text, and in the Line section select a colour and style for the outline of your text. Click **OK**.

To change a WordArt message, double-click on it and type in your new text. To change its format, click on the **WordArt Gallery** button on the WordArt toolbar, then double-click on the style you want. Your text will remain the same.

Use the alignment toolbar buttons to position text within your text box.

Before you print, remove the fold lines you have used as guides. Click on each of them and press the **Delete** key.

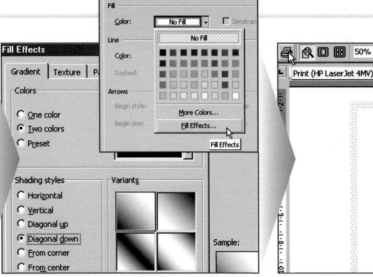

8 Scroll down to the second page and draw a fold line as in Step 3. Go to the **Insert** menu, select **Text Box** and click and drag to draw a box. Type in your text, highlight it, go to the **Format** menu and select **Font**. Select a font, size and style, then click **OK**.

9 To give the text box a background colour, double-click on the edge of the box. In the Fill section of the dialogue box click on the arrow beside the Color box and select **Fill Effects**. Under the Gradient tab, select your colours, shading style and variant. Click **OK**.

10 Now go to the **File** menu and click on **Print Preview**. If you are happy with your card, click the **Print** toolbar button. Print page 1 only, then place the paper or card back in the printer (you will need to experiment with orientation) and print page 2 on the reverse.

Remove the border around your text box before you print. Double-click on the edge of the box then, in the Line section of the dialogue box, click on the arrow beside the Color box and select **No Line**. Click **OK**.

Illustrate your stationery

Be creative with your personal and business correspondence

Using an image on your business stationery illustrates the nature of the business and adds a professional touch. On letters, compliments slips and business cards, a distinctive logo sends out an impressive message. On personal stationery, imagery can also reflect your personality and set a tone.

Your computer makes it simple to design and produce high-quality stationery. These pages cover business stationery, but the same principles apply for personal stationery. The word processing programs in Microsoft Office and Works offer a wide range of fonts, styles and colours, as well as ClipArt images. For personal stationery you could use an image of your house or a family coat of arms.

Make sure you have all the correct details at hand, especially postcodes and e-mail addresses.

BEFORE YOU START

Save As

Save in: Business Stationery

Business

Save

File name: Illustrated letterhead

Save as type: Word Document

1 Go to the **Start** menu, select **Programs** then click on **Microsoft Word**. After your document opens, save it as a letterhead, go to the **File** menu and click on **Save As**. Select a folder in which to save it in the 'Save in' box. Give it a file name. Click on **Save**.

You can also create stationery in Microsoft Works. Open Microsoft Works then, in the Works Task Launcher, click on the **Works Tool** tab, then on the **Word Processor** button.

OTHER PROGRAMS

Templates on CD-ROM

*To make it easy to position the image, go to the **Format** menu and click on **Picture**. Click the **Position** tab and ensure that the 'Float over text' box is ticked (click in it if necessary). For details on using ClipArt, see page 188.*

Key word

Template *This is a predesigned file. It is useful for any kind of standard document – invoices or letterheads, for example – where the basic look of the document is always going to be the same.*

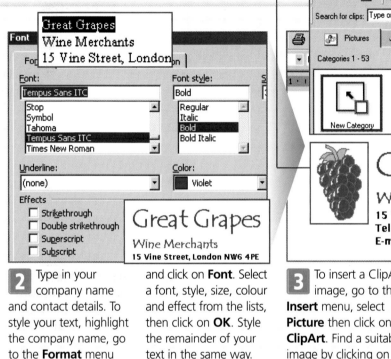

2 Type in your company name and contact details. To style your text, highlight the company name, go to the **Format** menu and click on **Font**. Select a font, style, size, colour and effect from the lists, then click on **OK**. Style the remainder of your text in the same way.

3 To insert a ClipArt image, go to the **Insert** menu, select **Picture** then click on **ClipArt**. Find a suitable image by clicking on the categories. Click on your image then click on the **Insert** button in the toolbar that appears. To resize and reposition your image, see above.

4 Go to the **File** menu and click on **Save As**. Scroll through the 'Save as type' box and click on **Document Template**. Word will suggest saving your document in its Templates folder in the 'Save in' box. Type in a name in the 'File name' box, then click on **Save**.

Inserting e-mail addresses

When you type in an e-mail address in Word, it will try to create a link to Microsoft Outlook, your e-mail software. To style the text as you wish, turn off this function. Go to the **Tools** menu and select **AutoCorrect**. Click on the **AutoFormat As You Type** tab. Click in the box beside 'Internet and network paths with hyperlinks' (this removes the tick), then click **OK**.

james@greatgrapes.co.uk

Let the Wizard Help

Microsoft Works has a useful device, called a Wizard, to help you create a letterhead. When you open Works, the Works Task Launcher dialogue box appears. In the Common Tasks folder displayed in the pane, double-click on **Letterhead** then follow the on-screen instructions.

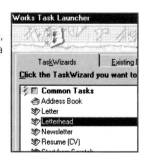

Once your letterhead is designed, create further items of stationery by copying and pasting the details.

▶ COMPLIMENTS SLIPS

Close-up
You cannot paste ClipArt into text boxes so, in order to copy and paste text from your letterhead template, you must delete the ClipArt first. When you close your letterhead template, do not save any changes.

*The Copy and Paste toolbar buttons allow you to duplicate text. Click and drag your mouse over the text in question to highlight it, then click on the **Copy** button. Click on the **Paste** button to place the text.*

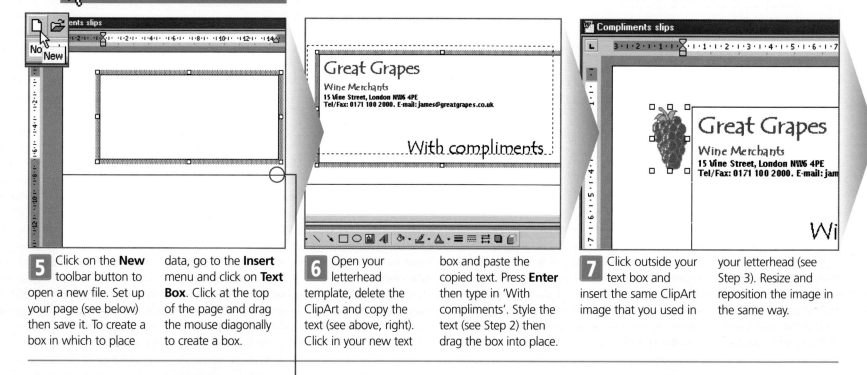

5 Click on the **New** toolbar button to open a new file. Set up your page (see below) then save it. To create a box in which to place data, go to the **Insert** menu and click on **Text Box**. Click at the top of the page and drag the mouse diagonally to create a box.

6 Open your letterhead template, delete the ClipArt and copy the text (see above, right). Click in your new text box and paste the copied text. Press **Enter** then type in 'With compliments'. Style the text (see Step 2) then drag the box into place.

7 Click outside your text box and insert the same ClipArt image that you used in your letterhead (see Step 3). Resize and reposition the image in the same way.

Setting up
You can fit three compliments slips onto one A4 sheet. To get the maximum print area, go to the **File** menu and click on **Page Setup**. Set the Top and Bottom margins to 0 cm. Click **OK**. A warning box appears, alerting you about small margins. Click **Fix**, then **OK**.

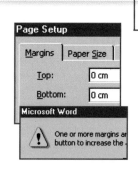

─ Adding guidelines
Divide your page into thirds with guidelines. To access the Drawing toolbar, go to the **View** menu, select **Toolbars** then click on **Drawing**.
 Click on the **Line** toolbar button. Move the cursor to just short of the 10 cm mark on the vertical ruler, then click and drag the cursor across the page. Draw the second line, starting just short of the 20 cm mark.

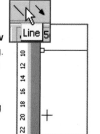

Short cut
If you ever need to change the details within your stationery, amend the text in your letterhead first, then copy and paste that text into your compliments slips.

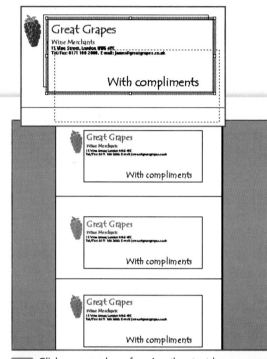

You do not want your guidelines to print out. To delete them, click on each of them in turn and press the **Delete** key.

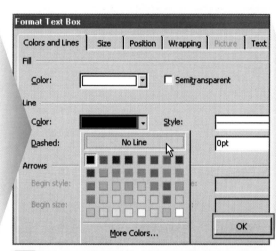

Your business card will carry the same information and graphics as your letterhead and compliments slip.

BUSINESS CARD

8 Click on an edge of the text box, right-click and select **Copy** from the menu. Click outside the box, right-click and select **Paste**.

Another text box appears in front of the first. Click on it and drag it down to the second slip. Repeat for the third slip and then your image.

9 To ensure the text box border does not print, click on the box, go to the **Format** menu and click on **Text Box**. The Colors and

Line tab is selected. In the Line section click on the Color box then on **No Line** and **OK**. Go to the **File** menu and click **Print**.

10 Now that you have designed your letterhead and a compliments slip, use a similar process

to create a business card. Creating a business card is explained in full on page 178.

Using Works

With Works, you enter text into a box which you can then move around the page.

Go to the **Insert** menu and click on **Drawing**. In the window that opens click on the **Rectangle** icon. Now click on the page and drag the cursor diagonally to draw a box (click on and drag a corner to resize).

Click on the **Text** button and type your text into the box. To style it, click on the sections, go to the **Text** menu and select the font and style you want.

Close the window to insert the drawing onto the Works page. Click on it and drag it to reposition it. Add ClipArt as described in Step 3.

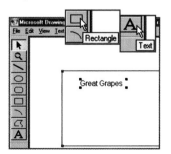

Decide what size you want your invitation to be. For convenience, it's a good idea to print two or four per sheet of A4 paper.

BEFORE YOU START

1 Go to the **Start** menu, select **Programs** and click on **Microsoft Word**. A new document appears. Save it by going to the **File** menu and clicking on **Save As**. Select a location in the 'Save in' box, type in a file name, then click on **Save**.

Create an invitation

Make a special occasion even better with your own design

Making your own invitation allows you to create a design that reflects the type of event you are organising – and the type of person you are arranging it for. If it is going to be a lively party, use bright colours and fun fonts. If it is for a more sober dinner party, choose more subtle colours and traditional fonts.

Before designing your invitation, make a note of the relevant information guests will need, including the date, time, location of the event – and any dress requirements.

You can create an invitation in Microsoft Works. Open Microsoft Works then, in the Works Task Launcher, click on the **Works Tool** tab then on the **Word Processor** button.

OTHER PROGRAMS

Templates on CD-ROM

Page Setup

Margins | Paper Size | Paper Source | Layout

Paper size:
A4 210 x 297 mm

Width: 21 cm
Height: 29.7 cm

Orientation
◉ Portrait
○ Landscape

Page Setup

Margins | Paper Size | Pape

Top: 0 cm
Bottom: 0 cm
Left: 3.17 cm
Right: 3.17 cm

⚠ One or more margins are set outside the printable area
button to increase the appropriate margins.

Fix | Ignore

Font

Font | Character Spacing | Animation

Font: Juice ITC
Imprint MT Shadow
Informal Roman
Jokerman
Juice ITC
Kino MT

Font style: Bold Italic
Regular
Italic
Bold
Bold Italic

Size: 48
26
28
36
48
72

Underline: (none)
Color: Red

Effects
☐ Strikethrough ☑ Shadow ☐ Small caps
☐ Double strikethrough ☐ Outline ☐ All caps
☐ Superscript
☐ Subscript

Preview

Shhh...

Shhh...
It's a surprise party
Andy's 30th Birthday
At: 24 Chapel Road

Roman Cut

Shhh...

It's a surprise

Andy's 30th Birthday

At: 24 Chapel Road, London
On: Saturday 9th December
Time: Please be there by 7.30pm
RSVP: Lynn 0171 444 2000

2 Go to the **File** menu and click on **Page Setup**. Click the **Paper Size** tab and make sure that A4 is selected in the 'Paper size' box. Click the **Margins** tab and set the Top and Bottom margins to 0 cm. Click **OK**. A warning box comes up, click **Fix** then **OK**.

3 Type in your text. To style it, highlight the first part, go to the **Format** menu and click on **Font**. Select a font, style, size, colour and effect, then click **OK**. Now style the rest of your text, or use the special graphics effect facility, WordArt.

4 The WordArt Gallery contains a selection of text designs that you can edit and customise for your own use. Highlight the relevant text then click on the **Cut** toolbar button. This removes the text from the page and keeps it in your PC's memory.

Close-up
If you want to design a classic, traditional invitation, choose from the following fonts: Baskerville Old Face, Book Antiqua, Brush Script MT, Copperplate Gothic Light or Garamond. For a more fun look, try: Beesknees ITC, Comic Sans MS, Curlz MT, Juice ITC or Lucida Handwriting.

Let the Wizard help
Microsoft Works has a Wizard that makes it even easier to design an invitation. Go to the **Start** menu, select **Programs** and click on **Microsoft Works**. In the Works Task Launcher the TaskWizards tab is selected. Double-click on the **Correspondence** folder in the window, then double-click on **Flyer**. Follow the on-screen instructions.

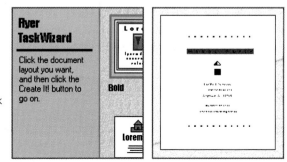

Flyer TaskWizard

Click the document layout you want, and then click the Create It! button to go on.

Bold

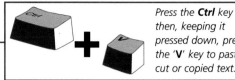

Press the **Ctrl** key then, keeping it pressed down, press the '**V**' key to paste cut or copied text.

You can exaggerate the effect of the WordArt shape by clicking on the yellow square and dragging it across the screen.

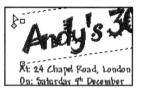

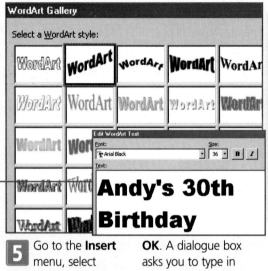

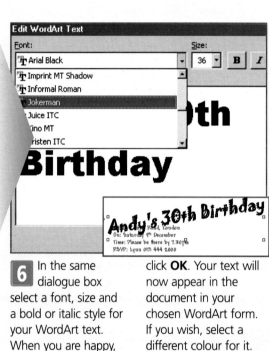

5 Go to the **Insert** menu, select **Picture** and click on **WordArt**. In the WordArt Gallery click on a style then click on

OK. A dialogue box asks you to type in your text. Hold down the **Ctrl** key then press the '**V**' key to paste in your line.

6 In the same dialogue box select a font, size and a bold or italic style for your WordArt text. When you are happy,

click **OK**. Your text will now appear in the document in your chosen WordArt form. If you wish, select a different colour for it.

7 To move WordArt, click on it and drag it. To resize it, click on one of its corner handles and, keeping the mouse button

pressed down, drag it across the screen. To create space for it, click at the end of the preceding line and press the **Return** key.

Letter spacing in WordArt

You can adjust the spacing between WordArt letters, or characters. Click on the **Character Spacing** button on the WordArt toolbar, then click on your choice from the pop-up menu.

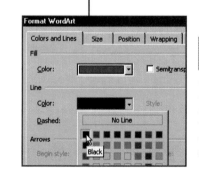

Colour in WordArt

To change the colour of your WordArt, click on the **Format WordArt** button on the WordArt toolbar. The Colors and Lines tab is selected. In the Fill section choose a colour for your text; in the Line section choose an outline colour (black gives a shadow effect). Click **OK**.

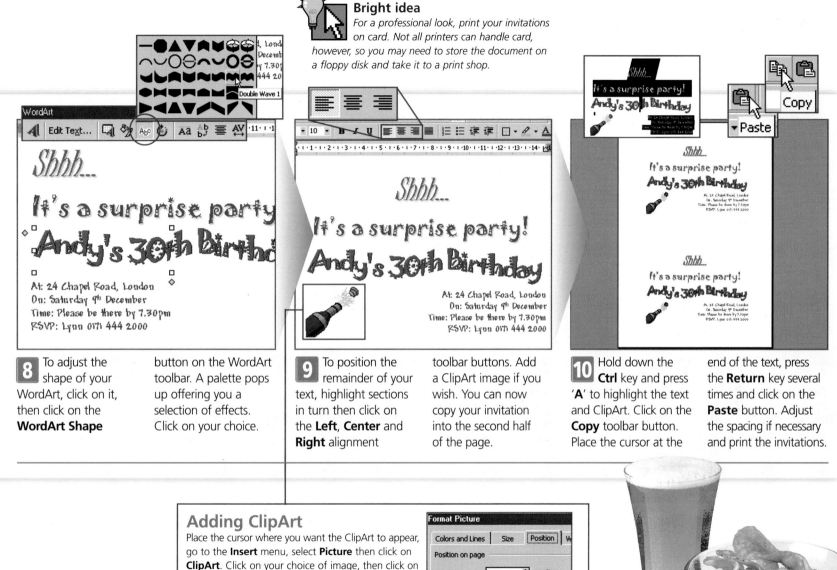

Bright idea
For a professional look, print your invitations on card. Not all printers can handle card, however, so you may need to store the document on a floppy disk and take it to a print shop.

8 To adjust the shape of your WordArt, click on it, then click on the **WordArt Shape** button on the WordArt toolbar. A palette pops up offering you a selection of effects. Click on your choice.

9 To position the remainder of your text, highlight sections in turn then click on the **Left**, **Center** and **Right** alignment toolbar buttons. Add a ClipArt image if you wish. You can now copy your invitation into the second half of the page.

10 Hold down the **Ctrl** key and press '**A**' to highlight the text and ClipArt. Click on the **Copy** toolbar button. Place the cursor at the end of the text, press the **Return** key several times and click on the **Paste** button. Adjust the spacing if necessary and print the invitations.

Adding ClipArt

Place the cursor where you want the ClipArt to appear, go to the **Insert** menu, select **Picture** then click on **ClipArt**. Click on your choice of image, then click on the **Insert clip** button on the pop-up toolbar.

Go to the **Format** menu and click on **Picture**. In the dialogue box click the **Position** tab and make sure that the 'Float over text' box is ticked. For details on how to manipulate your image, see page 188.

Plan the perfect party for

Use your computer to help organise your celebration

An informal get-together at home is one thing, but it is quite a different matter to arrange the kind of special party your friends and relations talk about for years after.

Silver weddings, landmark birthdays, marriages and christenings – these occasions do not come around very often, but when they do you want to be sure it all goes right. The preparations can take months and the planning will have to be meticulous. Venue, catering, entertainment, guests and accommodation – if people are coming a long way – must be booked and confirmed well in advance. You also need to plan the cost of it all.

One of the main areas in which your computer can help is in compiling a guest list. The

Project planner

Create a folder called 'Party'. Add sub-folders to it for each mini-project.

- Party
  - Guest list
  - Invitations
  - Letters to suppliers
  - Budget
  - Menus
  - Reminders

a special occasion

and ensure you have a day to remember

Microsoft Works database will store the contact details of guests and of key suppliers such as caterers. Use your PC's design capabilities to produce invitations, then address them instantly by making labels from your guest database. As people reply, input the information into the database for a record of confirmed numbers.

Using a database means you'll only have to compile the list once, and you can then use it to note details such as the number of people, who is bringing small children, and who is a vegetarian. Now you can estimate the number of people attending, and use a spreadsheet to prepare a budget. Allocate a sum for the cost of the venue and entertainment, and an amount per head for food. If you need to get in touch with and select caterers, DJs and so on, send out letters written in your word-processing program giving your requirements and requesting quotes. Use the word-processing program to create menus and place cards, too.

Now set up a planning spread-sheet in the form of a 'Celebration Countdown'. Use it to schedule remaining tasks.

Once everything is in place, you can relax and start looking forward to the big day.

Pay attention to detail

- Compile guest list
- Book venue
- Organise caterer
- Design and send out invitations
- Book disc jockey and Master of Ceremonies
- Compile 'Celebration Countdown'
- Write and send reminders/directions

Ideas and inspirations

These suggestions will get you started on organising your event. All the projects can be adapted depending on the nature of your occasion. For example, on your invitation you could include your e-mail address so guests can respond by computer.

168 Guest list and address labels
Set up a guest list to keep track of who you invite and use labels to mail your invitations.

200 Create an invitation
A little imagination – and the versatility of Word and Works – will ensure a good response.

150 Send a formal letter
Use Word to produce businesslike letters to suppliers, to check availability and prices.

272 Project-based budgeting
Compile a spreadsheet to help keep track of all your party's expenses.

310 Celebration countdown
In the same way you plan a holiday, create a spreadsheet to organise last-minute tasks.

Also worth considering...

Whether you have a caterer or are doing the food yourself, guests might like to see the menu.

160 Dinner party menu
If your party involves catering, you could save money by asking guests to select their choice in advance.

Add your own images

Scan in your favourite photographs to liven up your documents

There is no limit to the variety of images you can use in your documents. If you have a scanner, you can transfer photographs, or pictures from newspapers or books, to your own computer.

A scanner takes a digital copy of an image and, using its own special software, displays it on your screen. Once an image is saved in this form, you can manipulate it in any way you wish before placing it in a newsletter, invitation or card (but be aware that the use of printed material is covered by copyright laws).

The Epson GT-7000 scanner was used for this project. No matter which scanner you use, you will be able to follow the steps. However, consult your manual for specific guidance.

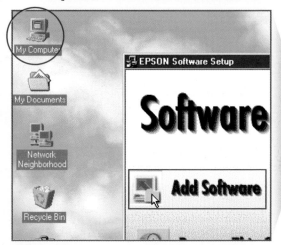

Connect your scanner to the system unit and unlock the scanning head (this has been locked to protect it in transit). Consult your manual.

BEFORE YOU START

1 Insert the software CD in your CD drive. Double-click on **My Computer**, then again on the **CD-ROM** icon. Click on **Add Software**. Follow the instructions. When the installation is complete, shut down your PC, turn on the scanner and restart.

Watch out
Most printed material is covered by copyright laws. Unless purely for your own use and you are not going to distribute it, it is not available for you to use freely. As a general rule, if you are designing a newsletter or poster, for example, you are breaching copyright laws if you use images from published sources without the copyright owner's permission.

*Most scanners will have an 'Easy' or quick-scan option that will do all the work for you. Click on the **Easy** button then, in the 'Image type' box, select the appropriate option for your type of image.*

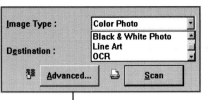

To make adjustments to the area to be scanned, place the cursor over one of the dotted lines and, when it becomes a double-headed arrow, click and drag the line to the required position.

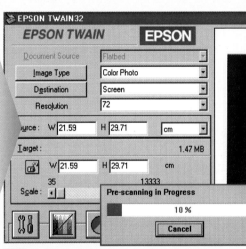

2 Place the photo in the scanner. Go to the **Start** menu, select **Programs**, then **Scanner**, then click on **Scanner utility**. Go to the **File** menu and click on **Acquire**. The main scanning window will appear.

3 Before you select any settings, preview your picture. This involves the scanner doing a quick, rough scan of the whole scanning area. If this is not done automatically, click on the **Preview** button. The image appears in a preview window.

4 To define the exact area you want scanned, click at an appropriate point in the top left-hand corner of the picture and drag the cursor down and to the right until the area is selected. A dotted line will appear around your picture as you drag the cursor.

Fitting a SCSI card

Many new scanners can be plugged directly into a computer's printer port. Others, however, require a special expansion card, known as a SCSI card, to be fitted into the system unit. SCSI stands for 'Small Computer Systems Interface'. The scanner cable plugs into the card port.

The PC expansion card slots are white in colour and about 8.5 cm long (see page 18 for directions). To insert a SCSI card, first remove the case from the system unit. Locate a free slot then, from the inside, remove the metal 'blanking' plate fitted at the back of your PC's case, next to the expansion slot you will use.

You will notice a screw that sits at the top of the plate. Remove it and put it to one side. Gently push the SCSI card into the slot, making sure the socket on its backing plate is facing outwards from the back of the PC. Secure the card by replacing the screw, then replace the case.

If you have a SCSI connection, and the only device your scanner is connected to is your PC, you must ensure the Terminator switch at the rear of the scanner is switched on. The terminator allows SCSI devices to 'talk' properly to each other. Check the scanner's manual for any other SCSI instructions.

Key Word

Resolution *This describes picture quality. Resolution is measured by the number of dots per inch (dpi) that make up an image. The greater the dpi, the better quality the picture, and the more memory it uses.*

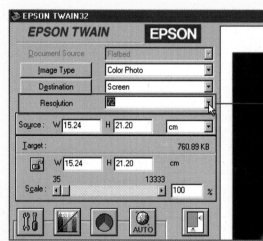

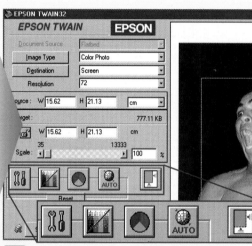

5 Now select your settings. Choose a resolution setting of 72 dpi (this will probably be the scanner's default setting). This means that your images will be good quality and won't use up a lot of memory.

6 Look for a set of tools that allows you to make further adjustments, such as increasing or decreasing brightness and setting the contrast between light and dark tones. Experiment with them to get an effect you like.

7 The **Image Controls** button (top), is an important tool for editing pictures. When you click on it a dialogue box containing several setting options appears. Adjust these settings to alter the image's appearance.

Conserving space

The amount of space your file uses relates both to the resolution at which the image has been scanned in and to its dimensions (height and width). By increasing just the resolution of this scan from 72 dpi to 200 dpi, the amount of memory it uses increases from 760 Kb to 5.73 Mb.

Exposure *either lightens or darkens the image*

Gamma *sets the contrast between dark and light tones*

Highlight *lets you apply light areas to the scan*

Shadow *lets you apply dark areas to the scan*

Threshold *scans grey shades as black or white*

Bright idea
Experiment with different settings until you get the look you want. Your image doesn't have to appear exactly as it did in its original context, and you can double the image's impact by editing it to suit your own material.

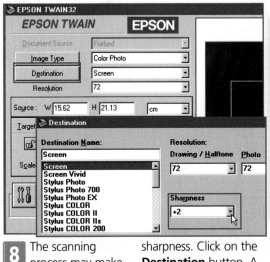

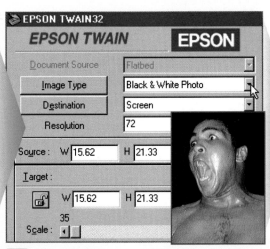

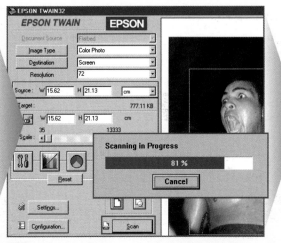

8 The scanning process may make your image appear a little blurred. Correct this by adjusting the sharpness. Click on the **Destination** button. A dialogue box will now appear. Select a value in the Sharpness box.

9 Although the image you are scanning may be in colour, you may want to view it in black and white. In the 'Image type' box select **Black & White Photo**. The monotone scan will appear immediately.

10 Once you have chosen your settings you are ready to scan your photo. Click on the **Scan** button. The scanner will make a noise as the head moves over the picture, reading the information. A dialogue box will show you how the scan is progressing.

Scanning a printed image

If you are scanning an image from a newspaper, you may find the scan appears slightly distorted. This arises from the hexagonal pattern of ink dots that printing produces.

You may find a 'de-screen' setting within your scanning controls that contains different settings in 'lpi' (lines per inch). For glossy, printed material select 133-200 lpi; for newspapers select 65-120 lpi. If you don't have these settings try to improve the scan by reducing the sharpness setting to lessen the distortion (see Step 8).

Ensure the Bitmap (.BMP) file format is selected in the File Format box. This means the scanned file can be imported into Word, Works and Paint, the Windows accessory program.

Use Paint's tool palette and menus to achieve different effects. To flip an image, for example, go to the **Image** menu and click on **Flip/Rotate**, then select either **Vertically** or **Horizontally**. For more details on picture editing, see page 212.

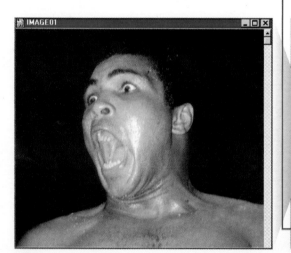

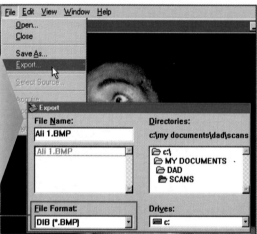

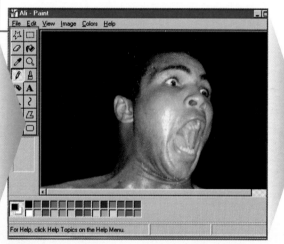

11 Once scanned, the image will appear in its own window. (If it appears behind the controls, minimise the control dialogue box to view it.) If you are not happy with the image, re-adjust the settings in the same way you did before. You may even need to re-scan it.

12 Now save your scan. To make sure it can be read by other software, you have to export it. Go to the **File** menu and click on **Export**. Name your file then locate a folder in which to save it by double-clicking on the folders in the Directories section. Click **OK**.

13 You can edit your image in the software that was supplied with your scanner or in Paint. Go to the **Start** menu, select **Programs**, then **Accessories**, then **Paint**. When it opens, go to the **File** menu and select **Open**. Locate your scan then edit it.

Create a wallpaper

You can scan in a photo and use it as wallpaper on your Desktop. Go to the **Start** menu, select **Programs**, then **Accessories** then click on **Paint**. Go to the **File** menu and click on **Open**. Locate your photo then click **Open**. Go to the **File** menu and select **Set as Wallpaper** (you have the option of tiling or centring it on the screen). Click **OK**.

*To crop the image, click on the **Crop** tool in the Picture toolbar then click on one of the side handles and drag it inwards. To resize the image, click on one of the corner handles and drag it diagonally.*

Now try placing your scan into a document to make, say, a card, a mini-magazine or a newsletter.

NEW PROGRAM

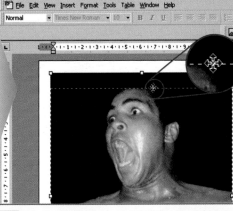

He's the greatest...

14 To place your scan in a Word document, first open the document. Place the cursor where you want the image to appear, go to the **Insert** menu, select **Picture**, then click on **From File**. Locate the scan through the 'Look in' box, then click **Insert**.

15 To move your image, place your mouse pointer over an edge. When it changes to a four-headed arrow, click and move it. To resize and crop the image, see above.

16 To add text, go to the **Insert** menu and select **Text Box**. The cursor will change to a large cross. Draw two boxes – one for the heading and one for a caption. Size them in the same way you did for the picture. Click on the boxes and type in your text.

Using photos in Works

To insert a photograph into a Microsoft Works document, you must first import the image into Paint, one of Windows' accessory programs.

Open Paint, go to the **File** menu and click on **Open**. Locate your scan, click on it, then click on **Open**. Click on the

Select tool then click and drag over the photograph. Go to the **Edit** menu and click on **Copy**.

Now click in your Works document, go to the **Edit** menu and click on **Paste**. To reposition the image, click on it and drag it; to resize it, click on a corner handle and drag it.

You will need to scan your picture in (see page 206) or get it scanned in at your local copy shop. Make sure it is saved in Bitmap (.bmp) format so that Paint can read it.

BEFORE YOU START

1 Go to the **Start** menu and select **Programs**, then **Accessories**, then **Paint**. Go to the **File** menu and click on **Open**. Locate and click on your image, then click **Open**. Go to the **File** menu and click on **Save As**. Save as a 24-bit Bitmap file.

Use Paint to edit images

The camera never lies, but your PC can embellish the truth

Looking over old photographs can evoke many treasured memories, so it can be quite upsetting when they become faded, torn or scratched. Fortunately, you can use Paint, one of Windows accessory programs, to help to restore the photograph to its original state. You can even use it to improve on the original image, removing 'red eye' and unwanted objects. And once you know the program, you can try creating special effects, such as adding elements of one photograph to another.

Paint comes with Windows and is a good place to start image editing. Advanced programs are available, including Adobe Photoshop, Corel Photo-Paint and JASC Paint Shop Pro.

OTHER PROGRAMS

Watch out
A scratch cannot be repaired using just one colour. As you work along the scratch, pick up colour from the surrounding area (see Step 3 for details).

Key word
Pixel *A computer image is made up of row upon row of tiny, coloured squares called pixels. Barely visible to the naked eye, they appear clearly when you enlarge your image using the View menu.*

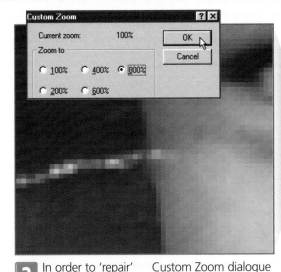

2 In order to 'repair' a scratch you need to magnify the image. Go to the **View** menu and select **Zoom** then **Custom**. In the

Custom Zoom dialogue box, click the 800% option, then **OK**. Now use the scroll bars to find an area of the image to work on.

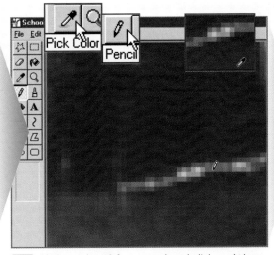

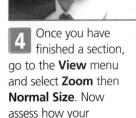

3 Click on the **Pick Color** tool. Click on an area of colour close to the blemish to 'pick up' that colour. Now click on the **Pencil**

tool and click and drag over the blemish. If the colour is not quite right, use the **Pick Color** tool to select another one. Repeat for other areas.

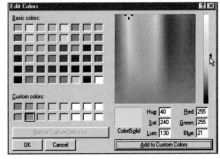

4 Once you have finished a section, go to the **View** menu and select **Zoom** then **Normal Size**. Now assess how your

changes look. To make further adjustments, repeat Steps 2 and 3. Once you are satisfied, go to the **File** menu and click on **Save**.

Losing red eye
One of the most common photographic problems is red eye, the result of using a flash. It is possible to correct this in Paint, but you will almost certainly have to use several colours in order to ensure the eye looks real. To broaden Paint's colour palette, see right.

Create new colours
To add a new colour to the standard palette available in Paint, customise an existing one.

Double-click on the colour you want to customise in the Color box. In the Edit Colors dialogue box click on the **Define Custom Colors** button. Click and drag the slider next to the graduated colour palette until

you get the right tone in the Color/Solid pane.

To save your colour, click on the **Add to Custom Colors** button. When you want to use it again, click on the Color box colour you customised. In the Edit Colors dialogue box the new colour will appear in the 'Custom colors' section. Click on it to select it.

Attributes

File last saved: 27/04/99 14:26
Size on disk: 1,100,934 bytes

Width: 660   Height: 556

Units
○ Inches   ○ Cm   ● Pixels

OK
Cancel
Default

Fonts
Lucida Sans   48   B I U

Anna, Max 197

Anna, Max 1972

5 To add a caption to your picture, go to the **Image** menu and click on **Attributes**. In the Height box, increase the value by about 100 pixels then click **OK**. Scroll down the window and you will see a section of white has been added at the base of the image.

6 Click on the **Text** tool, then click and drag across the white space to create a text box. Type in your caption. Use the text toolbar to select a font, font size and style for your text. If the toolbar doesn't appear, go to the **View** menu and click on **Text Toolbar**.

7 Once you are happy with your image, go to the **File** menu and select **Save**. Return to the **File** menu and select **Print** **Preview** to see how the file looks before printing. Either print it yourself or take it to a print shop for a higher quality result.

Family treasures

You'll get particularly good results when restoring old black-and-white photos in Paint. Use the same technique as for colour, and remember that the depth of grey will vary across the photo. You'll see the huge range of shades when you magnify the image.

Mistakes with text

Once you click outside the text box you can't select your text and alter it. If you realise in time, you can correct your last three actions or commands by going to the **Edit** menu and selecting **Undo**. This will reopen the text box for you to correct the mistake.

If you notice your error after you have completed three more actions, click on the **Select** tool and click and drag to draw a rectangle around the text. Go to the **Edit** menu and select **Clear Selection**. Then create a new text box and type.

Edit View
Undo
Repeat

Cut
Copy
Paste

Clear Selection

Select

You can use Paint to add elements of one photograph to another. Simply select and copy part of one picture then paste it into another.

WORK WITH TWO IMAGES

Bright idea
Where possible, paste an image on to a plain, rather than a multi-coloured, background. This makes disguising the manipulation much easier.

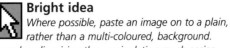

8 First scan in your two pictures. Open the file from which you want to copy an element. Click on the **Free-Form**
Select tool, then click and carefully drag the cursor around the section you want to copy. Go to the **Edit** menu and click on **Copy**.

9 Open the second file. Go to the **Edit** menu and click on **Paste**. The copied element appears in a white box. Click the
Paste Transparent tool to lose the background. Click on the pasted image and drag it into position. Click off it only when it is in position.

10 Use the colour-filling method in Steps 2-4 to remove the unwanted outline around the pasted
image and to blend the images into each other. When you are happy with the result, save the finished image.

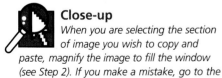
Close-up
*When you are selecting the section of image you wish to copy and paste, magnify the image to fill the window (see Step 2). If you make a mistake, go to the **File** menu, click on **Undo**, then start again.*

Tidying up
If you simply want to remove a detail from a photo, select the image, go to the **Edit** menu and click on **Cut**. To fill the gap left, click on the **Pick Color** tool then 'pick up' a colour from the surrounding area. Click the **Fill With Color** tool then click in the white space.

Design your own poster

Use graphics and text imaginatively to get your event noticed

When it comes to advertising an event, a colourful, eye-catching poster can really pull the crowds in. You can make a poster for almost any event, from a company dinner to a jumble sale. With a computer you don't need to be artistic to design an effective poster.

Posters should catch the attention of any passers-by and impart all the essential details of the event – the date, time, place, entry cost and purpose. If you use ClipArt, unusual fonts and WordArt (graphically enhanced text) be careful that you do not confuse readers with too many elements.

Check that all the information you want on your poster is correct, and think about which type of image will make the greatest impact.

BEFORE YOU START

1 Go to the **Start** menu, select **Programs** and click on **Microsoft Word**. Go to the **File** menu and select **Page Setup**. In the Page Setup dialogue box type in measurements for the Top, Bottom, Left and Right margins (at least 1 cm). Click **OK**.

*You can also design a poster in Microsoft Works. Open Microsoft Works then, in the Works Task Launcher, click on the **Works Tool** tab then on the **Word Processor** button.*

OTHER PROGRAMS

Templates on CD-ROM

Bright idea
There are certain fonts specifically designed for headlines. For example: Arial Black, Gills Sans Ultra Bold, Copperplate Gothic Bold and Eras Ultra. Try out any that have Black or Ultra in their name.

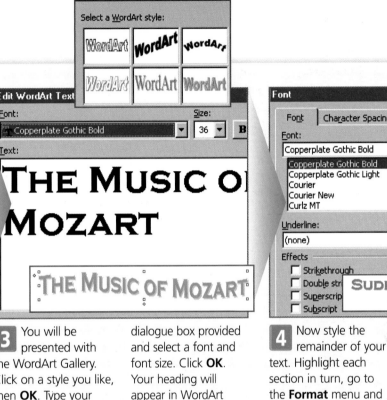

2 Type in your text. To position it in the centre of your document, highlight it then click on the **Center** toolbar button.

To insert WordArt, place your cursor where you want it to appear, then go to the **Insert** menu, select **Picture** and click on **WordArt**.

3 You will be presented with the WordArt Gallery. Click on a style you like, then **OK**. Type your heading into the

dialogue box provided and select a font and font size. Click **OK**. Your heading will appear in WordArt form in your document.

4 Now style the remainder of your text. Highlight each section in turn, go to the **Format** menu and click on **Font**. Select

your choice of fonts, styles and font sizes. You can also choose from a selection of different effects, including Embossing.

Choosing the page size

When you open a new document, the paper size is automatically selected as A4, and the orientation as portrait (upright). If you wish to change the size, click on the **Paper Size** tab in the Page Setup dialogue box. Click on the arrow to the right of the 'Paper size' box, scroll through and select your preferred size. To change the orientation, select the Landscape option.

Using WordArt

To move WordArt on the page, click on the image and drag it. To adjust its size, click on one of the handles and drag it across the screen. To exaggerate its artistic effect, click on and drag the yellow square.

In Microsoft Works, WordArt is more limited. After selecting WordArt in Works, go to the **Format** menu and click on **Rotation and Effects** to experiment with its appearance. To position text around it easily, click off the WordArt, go to the **Format** menu and click on **Text Wrap**. Then click on **Absolute**.

If the Picture toolbar does not appear, go to the **View** menu, select **Toolbars** and click on **Picture**.

5 To add space between text, place your cursor at the end of each section and press the **Return** key. For finer adjustments, highlight a section, go to the **Format** menu and click on **Paragraph**. In the Spacing section click on the uppermost arrow beside After.

6 To add a ClipArt image, place your cursor where you want it to appear, go to the **Insert** menu, select **Picture** and click on **ClipArt**. Type in the subject of your poster in the 'Search for clips' box and press **Return**. Click on an image then on the **Insert clip** icon.

7 Move and resize your image as desired. Add as many images as you like. To ensure text flows around an image, click on it. The Picture toolbar will appear. Click on the **Text Wrapping** button then click on one of the six options.

Importing images

If you want to use your own image from a CD-ROM or your scanned picture folder, go to the **Insert** menu, select **Picture** and click on **From File**. In the dialogue box scroll through and click on the location of your image. When you have located your image, click on it, then on **Insert**.

Cropping images

If you do not want to use all of the ClipArt image in your poster, crop out the unwanted parts. Click on the **Crop** tool in the Picture toolbar then click on and drag one of the picture handles. Drag the handles in or out to cut or restore the sides of your image.

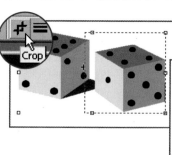
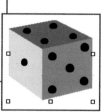

Watch out
A ClipArt image may be too large to fit where you want it to, in which case it will drop onto the next page. Reduce its size by clicking and dragging its picture handles then move it to your desired location.

8 The Square option allows you to position text neatly above, below and at either side of your image. Tight keeps the text close to the image. With Edit Wrap Points you define the exact path the text takes around the picture by moving the wrap points.

9 To add a border, go to the **Format** menu and click on **Borders and Shading**. Click on the **Page Border** tab. Choose a style, colour, width and setting. (If necessary, click on **Options** and set the gap between the border and the edge of the page.) Click **OK**.

10 To view your poster, go to the **File** menu and click on **Print Preview**. If you need to make any alterations, press the **Esc** key and edit as necessary. To print your poster, click on the **Print** toolbar button.

Inserting an indent

When you type in text to a new document it automatically aligns to the left of the page. However, you may prefer to have more space between the text and the left-hand side of the page. Do this by adjusting the left indent.

Highlight your text and click on the **Increase Indent** toolbar button until you get the look you want. Click on the **Decrease Indent** button (to its left) to reduce the indent.

Create a photo album

Make a browsable display of your favourite pictures

Most people take more photographs than they ever put into an album. As a result, everyone has memory-filled shoe boxes that rarely see the light of day.

If you scan your pictures into your PC, you can create a kind of virtual photo album. You can make backgrounds and add captions and dates. By using the PowerPoint program in Microsoft Office, you can make your pictures into a slide show. You can even add special effects such as music or your own narration.

Using your computer to store and display your photographs means that the originals can be tucked away and kept in perfect condition. And the images on your computer will never fade or become dog-eared.

To create a photo album your pictures need to be scanned. Scan them yourself (see page 206), or take them to a photographic shop. Alternatively, use a digital camera.

BEFORE YOU START

1 Go to the **Start** menu, select **Programs** then click on **Microsoft PowerPoint**. In the next dialogue box select the 'Blank presentation' option, then click **OK**. In the New Slide dialogue box click on one of the layout options – here, Title Slide. Click **OK**.

You can use the word-processing program in Microsoft Works to insert pictures, add titles and captions and print your album, but you cannot have an animated show.

OTHER PROGRAMS

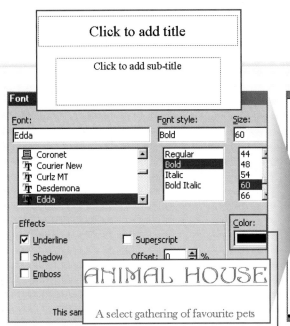

Font

Font: Edda

Font style: Bold

Size: 60

Coronet
Courier New
Curlz MT
Desdemona
Edda

Regular
Bold
Italic
Bold Italic

44
48
54
60
66

Effects

☑ Underline
☐ Shadow
☐ Emboss

☐ Superscript

Offset: 0 ⬍ %

Color: ▮

This sam

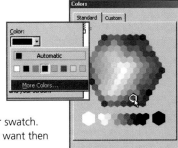

ANIMAL HOUSE

A select gathering of favourite pets

2 A page with text boxes for a title and subtitle appears. Click on the title box and type in the title of your album. Highlight your title, go to the **Format** menu and click on **Font**. Select a font, style, size, colour and effect. Repeat the process for your subtitle.

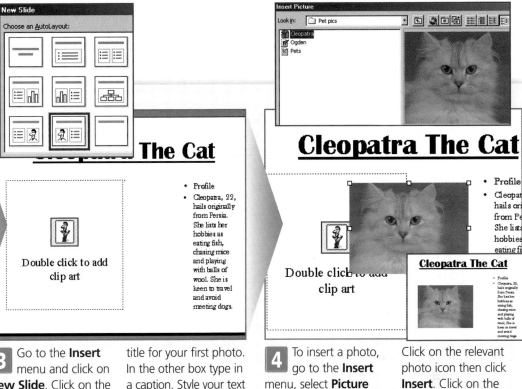

New Slide

Choose an AutoLayout:

The Cat

Double click to add clip art

• Profile
• Cleopatra, 22, hails originally from Persia. She lists her hobbies as eating fish, chasing mice and playing with balls of wool. She is keen to travel and avoid meeting dogs.

3 Go to the **Insert** menu and click on **New Slide**. Click on the 'ClipArt and Text' layout, then **OK**. Click on the title box and type in a title for your first photo. In the other box type in a caption. Style your text as before. Go to the **File** menu and click on **Save** to save your document.

Insert Picture

Look in: Pet pics

Cleopatra
Ogden
Pets

Cleopatra The Cat

Double click to add clip art

• Profile
• Cleopat hails ori from Pe She list hobbies eating fi

Cleopatra The Cat

• Profile
• Cleopatra, 22, hails originally from Persia. She lists her hobbies as eating fish, chasing mice and playing with balls of wool. She is keen to travel and avoid meeting dogs.

4 To insert a photo, go to the **Insert** menu, select **Picture** then click on **From File**. Locate the folder containing your photos. Click on the relevant photo icon then click **Insert**. Click on the picture on the page then drag and drop it onto the picture box.

Add colour

PowerPoint offers a variety of colour options for your text. Click on the arrow beside the Color box then click on **More Colors**. You will be presented with a colour swatch. Click on the colour you want then click **OK**.

Colors

Standard | Custom

Color: ▮

Automatic

More Colors...

To resize a text box, click on the bottom right-hand corner and drag it across the screen.

patra The Cat

Bright idea
Adding funny captions to your photos is a good way to liven up your slide show. Ask the family to come up with captions for some of the photos. You could even give a prize for the best one.

Bright idea
Cropping your pictures so that the main subject of the photo is at the centre of the image makes for a more eye-catching display.

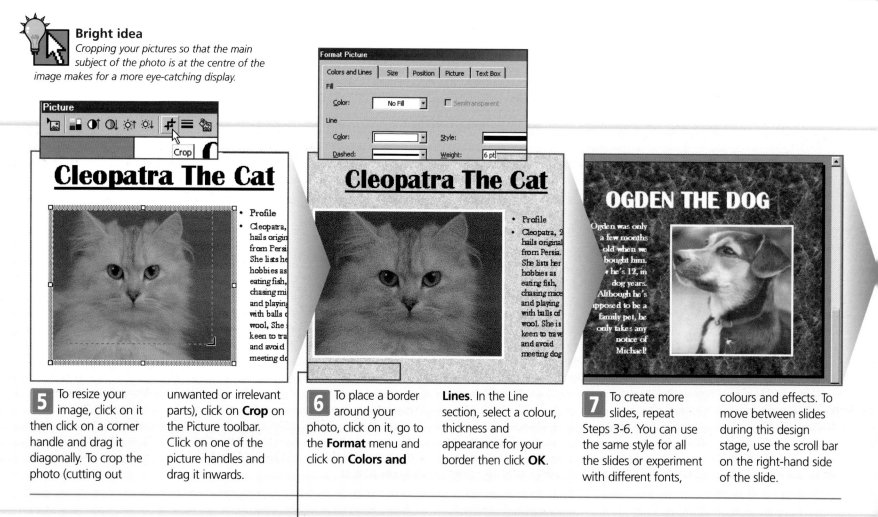

5 To resize your image, click on it then click on a corner handle and drag it diagonally. To crop the photo (cutting out unwanted or irrelevant parts), click on **Crop** on the Picture toolbar. Click on one of the picture handles and drag it inwards.

6 To place a border around your photo, click on it, go to the **Format** menu and click on **Colors and** **Lines**. In the Line section, select a colour, thickness and appearance for your border then click **OK**.

7 To create more slides, repeat Steps 3-6. You can use the same style for all the slides or experiment with different fonts, colours and effects. To move between slides during this design stage, use the scroll bar on the right-hand side of the slide.

Background colour

To give a slide a background colour, go to the **Format** menu and click on **Background**.

In the Background dialogue box click in the empty box in the Background Fill section. Click on a colour from the choices available then click on **Fill Effects**.

In the Fill Effects box click on the **Gradient**, **Texture** and **Pattern** tabs, making your selections as you go. Click **OK**. In the Background dialogue box, click **Apply**.

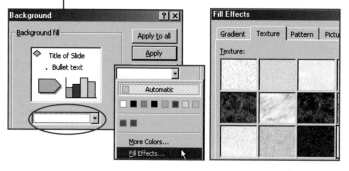

Making a narration

You can record a narration for your show. First, write down what you want to say, then ensure a microphone is connected to your PC. Go to **Slide Show**, click on **Record Narration** then **OK**. Make your narration, clicking the mouse to bring up the next slide. After the final slide, click the mouse and click **Yes** on the two prompts. To hear your narration, go to **Slide Show** and select **View Show**.

Bright idea
*PowerPoint also allows you to print out your slides, with an option to print up to six slides per page. Go to the **File** menu, select **Print** and click on the **Print what** box. Select **Handouts (6 slides per page)** from the drop-down menu and click **OK** to print.*

Using the special effects and animation available in PowerPoint, you can now create an entertaining show of your slides.

PUTTING ON A SHOW

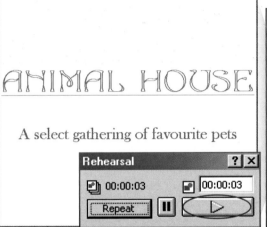

ANIMAL HOUSE

A select gathering of favourite pets

Rehearsal ? ✕
🔲 00:00:03   🔲 00:00:03
[Repeat] ❚❚ ▶

No Transition ▾   No Effect

Cleopatra The Cat

ANIMAL HOUSE

A select gathering of favourite pets

:06   1   :06   2

OGDEN THE DOG

MEET THE FAMILY!

Cleop   OGDEN THE

Ogden was only a few months old when we bought him. Now he's 12, in dog years. Although he's supposed to be a family pet, he only takes any notice of Michael!

8 Go to **Slide Show** and click on **Rehearse Timings**. Your first slide appears with a timer in the bottom right-hand corner. Click the arrowed Play button when you want the next slide to appear. If you are doing a narration, allow enough time on each photo.

9 When all your slides have been viewed, a prompt box appears. Click **Yes** and **Yes** again to go to Slide Sorter view. Your slides now appear in order, with their show times beneath. To change the order of your slides, click on one and drag it to a new position.

10 Once you are happy with your choice of slides, the viewing order and any special effects you have created, go to **Slide Show** and click on **View Show**. Your fully animated high-tech slide show will now run.

Adding effects

Your slides can appear on screen in a number of ways. To determine how, click on a slide in Slide Sorter view, click on the arrow beside No Transition and, from the drop-down menu, select a transition.

Your captions can appear in a number of ways, too. Click on the arrow beside No Effect and, from the drop-down menu, select an effect.

Now go to **Slide Show** and select **View Show** to see your special effects in action.

No Transition
No Transition
Blinds Horizontal
Blinds Vertical
Box In
Box Out
Checkerboard Across
Checkerboard Down
Cover Down
Cover Left

Fly From Bottom
No Effect
Appear
Fly From Bottom
Fly From Left
Fly From Right
Fly From Top
Fly From Bottom-Left
Fly From Bottom-Right
Fly From Top-Left

Painting on your PC

Create impressive works of art at the touch of a button

Fun, flexible and user-friendly, Paint is one of the most exciting accessory programs to come with Windows. Even if you have never picked up a real paintbrush, you can create a piece of art to be proud of. Use it to paint abstract designs or familiar scenes, then transform your pictures into such things as greetings cards or party invitations.

The program has a variety of paintbrushes, pencils and airbrushes. And you can mix any colour you want using the Color box. Another advantage that Paint has over conventional oils or watercolours is that you can easily make 'authentic' copies of your work.

You might want to make a quick pencil sketch of your picture to give you a rough guideline to follow as you work on your PC.

BEFORE YOU START

Attributes

File last saved: 15/04/99 17:19
Size on disk: 362,454 bytes

Width: 400   Height: 300

OK
Cancel
Default

Units
○ Inches   ○ Cm   ● Pixels

Colors
○ Black and white   ● Colors

Transparency
☐ Use Transparent background color
Select Color...

1 Go to the **Start** menu, select **Programs**, then **Accessories**, then **Paint**. Go to the **Image** menu and click on **Attributes**. Click on a measurement option in the Units section, then set the width and height of your canvas. Click **OK**.

Paint is the only graphics program available in Windows. But you can buy other, more sophisticated graphic packages – CorelDraw, for example – from computer shops.

OTHER PROGRAMS

Close-up
The Attributes default setting for your picture size is 400 x 300 pixels, which is approximately 10.5 cm by 8 cm (4 in by 3 in). A pixel is the smallest area of the canvas which you can colour in order to create a picture.

Watch out
*When you use the **Fill With Color** tool in an enclosed space, the colour will appear only in that area. If the area isn't entirely enclosed, the colour will leak onto the rest of the picture.*

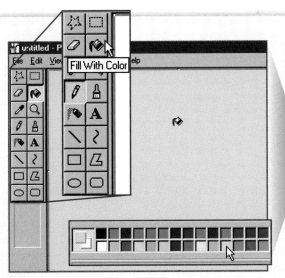

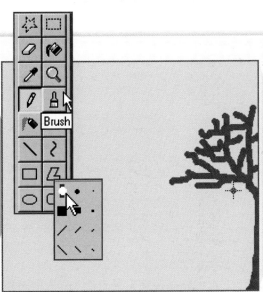

2 Start your picture by adding a background colour – you can then add other colours over this. Click on the **Fill With Color** tool then click on your choice of colour from the Color box at the bottom of the screen. Click on the canvas to add the colour.

3 Now begin painting. Select the **Brush** tool and click on a type of brush from the options below the Tool Box. Click on your choice of colour from the Color box. To make a brush stroke, click on the canvas and drag.

4 You can also use a spray-paint effect. Click on the **Airbrush** tool and click on a size of spray from the options below the Tool Box. Click on a colour from the Color box. Apply the colour as you did in Step 3.

Using the Tool box

Some tools, such as the brush tools, have a variety of styles which appear below the tool panel. Click on a style before using the tool. The functions of the tools are described below (the 'shape' tools are described on page 226):

 Free-Form Select Selects an irregular-shaped area. Click and drag the pointer to select.

 Select Selects a rectangular area. Click on the canvas and drag diagonally.

 Eraser/Color Eraser Acts just like a rubber. Click and drag the pointer over the area to clear it.

Fill With Color Places a solid colour in an area. Choose a colour and click on the relevant area.

Pick Color Picks up a colour from the canvas. Apply the colour elsewhere by selecting another tool.

 Magnifier Shows an area in close-up. Just click on the area. Also demagnifies magnified areas.

 Pencil Draws a thin, freehand line. Click and drag the pointer to draw.

 Brush Used for a brushstroke-style line. Select a style of brush then click and drag the pointer.

Airbrush Gives a spray-paint effect. Choose a spray radius then click and drag the pointer.

Text Inserts text into the picture. Click on the tool to draw a text box first, then add the text.

Line Draws a straight line. Select a thickness then click and drag the pointer.

Curve Used to draw a curve. You draw a line first then click on it and drag it to make a curve.

 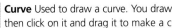

Key word
Background colour This is the colour of the backdrop to your canvas. You have as much control over this, as you do the colour of your subject.

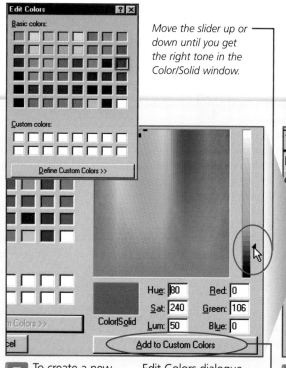

Move the slider up or down until you get the right tone in the Color/Solid window.

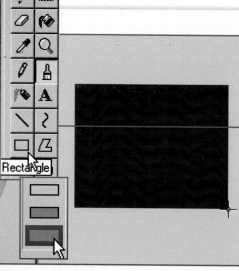

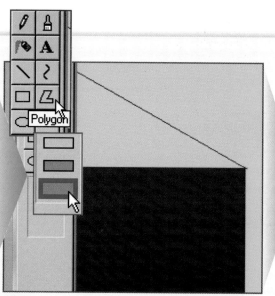

5 To create a new colour, customise an existing one. Double-click on the colour in the Color box. In the Edit Colors dialogue box click on the **Define Custom Colors** button. Create your colour (see above) then click **OK**.

6 To add a shape click on one of the shape tools (see below) then click on a style for it from the options below the Tool Box. Click on a colour from the Color box, then click on the canvas and drag to draw the shape.

7 To draw a triangle click on the **Polygon** tool. Click on the canvas and drag to create the first line. Release the button then click where you want the second side to end. A line will appear between this point and the first side. Repeat until the triangle is drawn.

*To save your new colour, click on the **Add to Custom Colors** button. When you want to use it again, click on the Color box colour you customised. In the Edit Colors dialogue box your new colour appears in the 'Custom colors' section. Click on the colour to select it.*

Shape tools

There are four shape tools to choose from – a rectangle, polygon (used to create irregular shapes), rounded rectangle and ellipse.

When you select a shape you are given three style options for it below the Tool box. The top one draws an outline with the colour of your choice; the middle one draws a coloured outline and fills the shape centre with the background colour; and the bottom one draws the shape and fills it with the colour of your choice.

Watch out
When you select a section of your canvas and move it, only click off it when you are happy with its new position. Once you click off it, you will not be able to move it again.

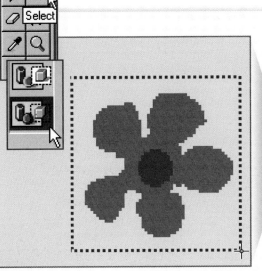

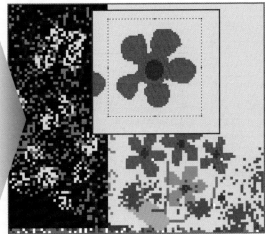

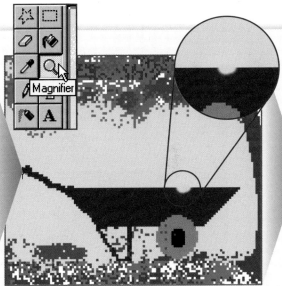

8 If you draw an item that you would like to repeat elsewhere on the canvas, click on the **Select** tool then click on the lower of the two options you are given below the Tool box. Click and drag over the item, go to the **Edit** menu and select **Copy**.

9 Return to the **Edit** menu and select **Paste**. The copied image appears at the top of the screen. Click on it and drag it to its new position. To change the colour of the item, click on the **Fill With Color** tool, select a different colour and click on the item.

10 Use the Magnifier to check for errors. For instance, you may have painted over part of another object. To undo this, click on the **Pick Color** tool and click on the correct colour on the canvas. Click on the **Brush** tool, select an option, then paint the area.

Stretch and skew

To stretch or skew part of your picture, go to the **Image** menu and click on **Stretch and Skew**. Experiment with measurements in either the Stretch or Skew sections.

Stretch and Skew

Stretch
Horizontal: 60 %
Vertical: 60 %

Skew
Horizontal: 0 Degrees
Vertical: 0 Degrees

OK
Cancel

Flip and rotate

To flip or rotate part of your picture, click on the **Select** tool and select the area in question. Go to the **Image** menu and click on **Flip/Rotate**. To change the way it faces select the 'Flip horizontal' option; to turn it upside-down select the 'Flip vertical' option; to move it around by increments of 90° select the 'Rotate by angle' option, then the relevant degree option.

Flip and Rotate

Flip or rotate
• Flip horizontal
○ Flip vertical
○ Rotate by angle
  ○ 90°
  ○ 180°
  ○ 270°

There are two types of text box:

With this box you can add a background colour. Click on **Fill With Color**, select a colour then click in the box.

This option gives a transparent text box, through which you can see the background colour.

Once you have created your picture, Paint allows you to save it and use it in a number of ways, including as Desktop wallpaper.

USING YOUR IMAGE

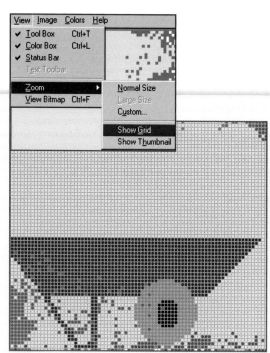

Come to our garden party!
Saturday 22nd May, 2pm
18 Elm Lane, Bramley
RSVP: 0113 765432

11 For precision corrections and drawing, magnify an area, go to the **View** menu, select **Zoom** then click on **Show Grid**. Now edit or draw, one pixel at a time.

12 To add text, click on the **Text** tool and select a box style (see above). Click and drag on the canvas to draw a box. Click on a colour from the Color box for your text, then start typing. To style text, highlight it, go to the **View** menu and select **Text Toolbar**.

13 Go to the **File** menu and click on **Save As**. Select a location and type a file name. To insert a Paint file into other documents, select **24-bit Bitmap** in the 'Save in' box. (To e-mail or add it to a Web page, choose either **GIF** or **JPEG**.) Click **OK**.

Correcting mistakes

There are various ways to correct errors:

 Undo You can undo up to three changes at a time by going to the **Edit** menu and clicking on **Undo** for each correction. As a shortcut, press the **Ctrl** and 'Z' keys simultaneously.

Erase Click on the **Eraser** tool and select a style option, then rub out the mistake on the canvas. Be aware that this rubs out all colour.

Paint over You can hide the error by painting over it. Click on the **Pick Color** tool, then click on the correct colour on the canvas. Select a brush and start painting over the error.

Edit by pixel Click on the **Magnifier** tool then click on the appropriate part of the canvas. Go to the **View** menu, select **Zoom** then **Show Grid**. Now edit individual pixels.

Close-up
You can set your Desktop wallpaper as either Centered or Tiled. The first option places the image in the centre of your screen with a plain surround. The second covers your screen by repeating the image.

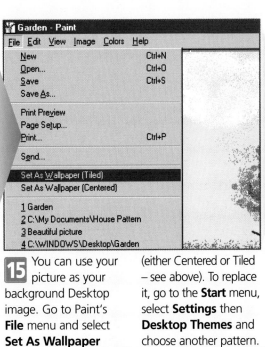

14 To use your image as ClipArt, open a word-processing document, go to the **Insert** menu, select **Picture** then **ClipArt**.

Click on **Import Clips**. Locate and click on your picture then on **Import**. The image appears in your gallery. Double-click on it to insert it.

15 You can use your picture as your background Desktop image. Go to Paint's **File** menu and select **Set As Wallpaper**

(either Centered or Tiled – see above). To replace it, go to the **Start** menu, select **Settings** then **Desktop Themes** and choose another pattern.

16 Printing from Paint follows the same rules as in other programs. Go to the **File** menu and click on **Page Setup** to set your

margins and orientation. From the **File** menu select **Print Preview** to check the look of your document, and **Print** to run out a copy.

Now you have mastered Paint's tools, you can go on to edit photographs and other images. Turn to page 212 for more details.

OTHER IDEAS TO TRY

Make your fête a day

There's no aspect of a fête (except the weather) that

A successful fête is a matter of pre-planning and organisation. The main thing is to be sure that everything comes together at the right moment. It is a serious job making certain that everyone has fun on the day.

There are so many things to think about that the first job is to delegate some of the work. Form a committee and assign roles: someone to deal with drumming up publicity in the press and on the radio; someone to approach businesses for sponsorship or material help; and someone to be fête treasurer (this is particularly important if yours is a fundraising or charitable event).

Now you have to decide on a venue, and on a beneficiary if you plan to donate the proceeds of the fête to charity. Someone on the committee should keep careful notes of the discussions, and these should be typed up and circulated soon after each committee

in a million

you can't plan on your computer

meeting. You may want to invite your community police officer, or someone from the local council to take part in one of the meetings.

By now, you will have set up a timetable database on which you record the tasks that need to be carried out and when. Tick tasks off as they are completed – that way you can use the sort facility to separate completed tasks from those yet to be done, and so plan a weekly schedule.

If you are seeking sponsorship or prize donations, you might like to create an event letterhead for your correspondence. If you have

e-mail or a fax-modem, then use them to keep in touch with all the clubs and organisations taking part in the fête. Meanwhile, use your PC to plan the location of all the stalls on the site.

As the day approaches, you can use your PC to create posters and flyers. By now you will know what the big attractions are and you can feature these on your publicity material (if you have asked a celebrity to open the fete, be sure that their photograph is on the poster).

Then relax and enjoy the day – by now you'll have earned it.

Event organiser

- Form an organising committee. Arrange either monthly or weekly meetings
- Agree a date and beneficiaries of the profits
- Provisionally book the venue
- Approach local businesses for sponsorship
- Contact the police/council to ensure date and venue are suitable
- Inform local press for advance and on-the-day coverage. Agree and implement publicity ideas

Ideas and inspirations

Listed here are a selection of projects you might want to use – or customise – to help you in the organisation of a successful community event. Allocate as much work as possible to other people, but keep a record of all developments on your computer.

182 **Timetable database**
Leave nothing to chance – produce a helpful diary of 'to do' tasks with your database.

146 **Event letterhead**
Correspond with stallholders and potential sponsors in a distinctive and memorable way.

216 **Design your own poster**
Publicise the date, time and venue of your event locally, together with details of its attractions.

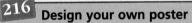

272 **Accounts spreadsheet**
Use a spreadsheet to keep track of all expenditure and income arising from your event.

294 **Stall planner**
Create a simple, overhead 2D plan of the venue and organise your space effectively.

Also worth considering...

If your timescale and responsibilities justify it, you may find the following project makes things easier.

164 **Create a newsletter**
Keep the key people involved in the event informed of developments and progress.

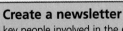

Introducing sound files

Have fun with the sounds that your computer makes

If your computer has a pair of speakers and a sound card (located inside your system unit), you can alter its 'tone of voice', or perform other tasks to do with sounds and music. For example, if your CD-ROM drive is not in use while you are working, you can use it to play music.

The addition of sound also maximises your enjoyment of computer games, and you can even use your PC's audio capabilities in conjunction with other software to make your own music.

It's also possible to add new sounds and assign them to tasks your computer performs, such as switching on or starting a piece of software. Windows even comes with a set of sound 'themes' which means you can change the entire acoustics of your system.

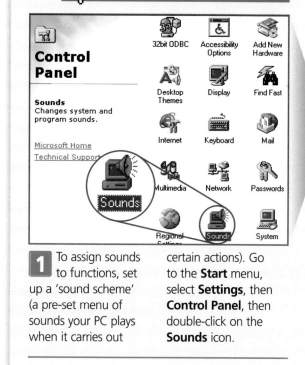

Ensure your speakers are plugged into the correct socket on the sound card (at the rear of your system unit) and that they are switched on.

BEFORE YOU START

Control Panel

Sounds
Changes system and program sounds.

Microsoft Home
Technical Support

32bit ODBC · Accessibility Options · Add New Hardware

Desktop Themes · Display · Find Fast

Internet · Keyboard · Mail

Multimedia · Network · Passwords

Regional Settings · Sounds · System

1 To assign sounds to functions, set up a 'sound scheme' (a pre-set menu of sounds your PC plays when it carries out certain actions). Go to the **Start** menu, select **Settings**, then **Control Panel**, then double-click on the **Sounds** icon.

Watch out
*When you select a different sound scheme you may be asked whether you want to save the previous scheme if you haven't already done so. Click **Yes**, type in a suitable name, then click **OK**.*

*To remove a sound from an event, click on the event and select **(None)** from the Name box in the Sound section.*

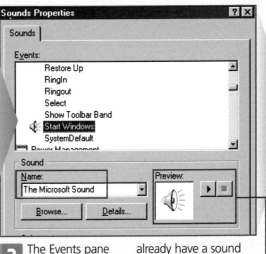

2 A Sounds Properties box opens. Click on the arrow beside the Schemes box and scroll through the options.

Click on any scheme, except 'No Sounds', to select it. The sounds you assign to individual events will be part of this overall theme.

3 The Events pane at the top of the window shows every action to which a sound can be assigned. Those with a speaker icon already have a sound assigned. To find out the name of the sound that has been assigned, click on the event then look in the Name box.

4 To assign a different sound, click on the relevant event, scroll through the options in the Name box in the Sound section and click on your choice. Click on **Save As**. A box will appear asking you to name your new scheme. Click **OK**.

Events on your PC
Assign sounds to the key events, or actions, that your PC performs:
● Start Windows
● Open program
● Program error
● Close program
● Maximise windows
● Minimise windows

To hear the sound assigned to an event, first click on the event then click on the arrow button beside the Preview icon.

Close-up
The most recent sound scheme you have saved will be loaded automatically when you switch on your PC. You won't have to reload it from the Control Panel.

You can have fun by recording your own set of sounds to assign to certain events. For this you will need a microphone.

Bright idea
Before opening Sound Recorder, make sure your microphone is switched on. If you don't want to record your own voice, record music or dialogue from another source, such as a videotape.

RECORDING SOUNDS

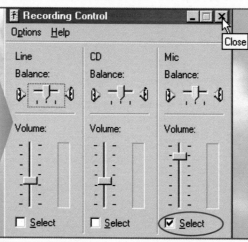

5 Go to the **Start** button and select **Programs**, then **Accessories**, then **Entertainment** and **Volume Control**.

In the Volume Control dialogue box go to the **Options** menu and select **Properties**. Click the Recording option then click **OK**.

6 The Recording Control dialogue box appears. Make sure the box at the base of the 'Mic (Microphone) Balance' section is

ticked. This tells Windows that you are going to use a microphone as your source. Then close the dialogue box.

7 To open the Microsoft Sound Recorder, go to the **Start** menu and select **Programs**, then **Accessories**, then

Entertainment and finally **Sound Recorder**. Your PC is now ready to record any sound you enter via the microphone.

Setting up for recording

Plug your microphone into the sound card at the rear of the system unit beside the speakers socket (your speakers should already be connected). The microphone socket will probably be marked 'mic', or have a picture of a microphone by it. If the microphone itself has an on-off switch, make sure it is turned on. If your microphone needs a battery (few do), make sure it has one.

Other sound sources

As well as recording your own sounds, you can download some from the Internet. In order for Windows to read them they need to be in .wav format – they will have .wav after their names.

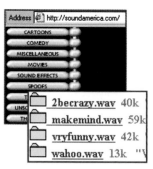

Watch out
If you switch off your speakers when you finish using your PC, remember to turn them on again when you want to hear sounds.

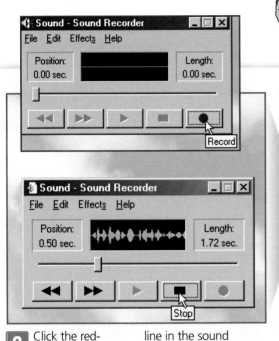

Record

Stop

Play

8 Click the red-dotted **Record** button and speak (or play a pre-recorded sound) into the microphone. The green line in the sound recorder distorts, giving a visual representation of the sound. When you have finished recording, click the **Stop** button.

9 To speed up, slow down, reverse, add an echo or alter the volume of your sound, go to the **Effects** menu and click on a relevant option. Click the **Play** button to preview your changes. To save your sound, go to the **File** menu and click on **Save As** (see below).

10 To assign your recorded sounds to events, open the Sounds Properties window (see Steps 1-4), and click on an event.

Click the **Browse** button and search through your hard drive to open your sounds folder. Select your sound and click **OK**.

Organising your sound files

Save all your sounds in the same folder so that it will be easy to find them. Create a new folder in My Documents, or put them in the Windows Media folder (double-click on **My Computer**, then **[C:]**, then **Windows**, then **Media**). This is the folder in which Windows automatically looks for sound files.

Link a music keyboard

Turn your PC into a musical instrument or recording studio

There are many ways to make music on your PC. With the correct software and a good sound card (you may already have one fitted in your system unit), you can generate sound without the need for separate instruments. You can record your voice and sample it, or use sound files from other sources such as the Internet or CDs.

You can link a keyboard to your PC using a connector called a Musical Instrument Digital Interface (known as a MIDI). This allows you to record your own tunes as you play them. You can then play back your music, edit and rewrite it, arrange and orchestrate it.

You can also buy software that allows you to write musical notation – a real advance over the long-winded business of writing compositions by hand on score paper.

To use a music keyboard you need a MIDI-compatible sound card, music software, speakers, an instrument with MIDI connections and MIDI-interface connecting leads.

BEFORE YOU START

1 Insert the music software CD in your CD drive. Your computer will automatically recognise it and begin to install it.

You may be asked which version of the software you wish to install. Select one according to your PC's specification.

For this project Cubase VST music software and a Yamaha PSR-220 keyboard have been used. Cakewalk is another popular type of software. Both can display and print music as a score. Whatever software you use, the basic steps here will apply.

OTHER PROGRAMS

Watch out

Combining MIDI with computer sound recordings uses a lot of your PC's resources. Using a low specification computer can slow the program down and cause other difficulties. There are versions of software for lower and higher specification PCs – choose the right one.

Close-up

In order for your keyboard to be able to communicate with your PC, you must set it up correctly. Follow the instructions in the music keyboard's manual to help you do this.

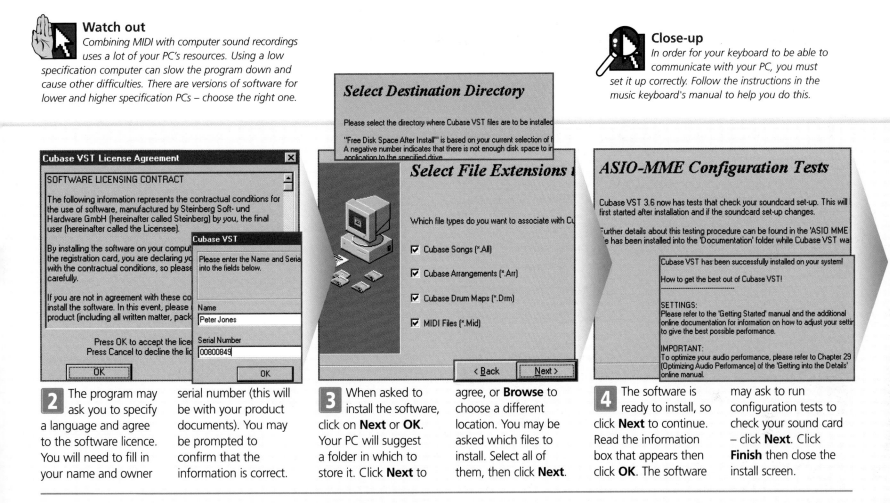

Select Destination Directory

Please select the directory where Cubase VST files are to be installed

"Free Disk Space After Install" is based on your current selection of f
A negative number indicates that there is not enough disk space to in
application to the specified drive

Select File Extensions

Which file types do you want to associate with Cu

☑ Cubase Songs (*.All)

☑ Cubase Arrangements (*.Arr)

☑ Cubase Drum Maps (*.Drm)

☑ MIDI Files (*.Mid)

< Back   Next >

Cubase VST License Agreement

SOFTWARE LICENSING CONTRACT

The following information represents the contractual conditions for the use of software, manufactured by Steinberg Soft- und Hardware GmbH (hereinafter called Steinberg) by you, the final user (hereinafter called the Licensee).

By installing the software on your comput the registration card, you are declaring yo with the contractual conditions, so please carefully.

If you are not in agreement with these co install the software. In this event, please product (including all written matter, pack

Press OK to accept the licer
Press Cancel to decline the lic

OK

Cubase VST

Please enter the Name and Serial into the fields below.

Name
Peter Jones

Serial Number
00800849

OK

ASIO-MME Configuration Tests

Cubase VST 3.6 now has tests that check your soundcard set-up. This will first started after installation and if the soundcard set-up changes.

Further details about this testing procedure can be found in the 'ASIO MME e has been installed into the 'Documentation' folder while Cubase VST wa

Cubase VST has been successfully installed on your system!

How to get the best out of Cubase VST!

SETTINGS:
Please refer to the 'Getting Started' manual and the additional online documentation for information on how to adjust your settin to give the best possible performance.

IMPORTANT:
To optimize your audio performance, please refer to Chapter 29 (Optimizing Audio Performance) of the 'Getting into the Details' online manual.

2 The program may ask you to specify a language and agree to the software licence. You will need to fill in your name and owner serial number (this will be with your product documents). You may be prompted to confirm that the information is correct.

3 When asked to install the software, click on **Next** or **OK**. Your PC will suggest a folder in which to store it. Click **Next** to agree, or **Browse** to choose a different location. You may be asked which files to install. Select all of them, then click **Next**.

4 The software is ready to install, so click **Next** to continue. Read the information box that appears then click **OK**. The software may ask to run configuration tests to check your sound card – click **Next**. Click **Finish** then close the install screen.

Setting up

Plug the MIDI lead into the sound card at the back of the system unit (this will probably be the joystick port and may be marked as such). The other end of the lead splits into two. The two jacks plug into the keyboard's 'MIDI Out' and 'MIDI In' sockets. If these ports are not marked, check with your software supplier. Now plug the keyboard into the mains socket and turn it on.

To combat software piracy, some software companies supply a special adaptor that must be plugged into the printer port.

Watch out
You may need to restart your computer before your software can finish installing. When it restarts, your PC's configuration will have changed and the software will be located in the Programs folder in the Start menu, or as a shortcut on your Desktop.

5 There may be a shortcut to your new software on your Desktop (double-click to open it). If not, go to the **Start** menu, select **Programs** then click on the program's name.

6 All MIDI software requires a 'device driver' to help it run. Because this is the first time you have opened your MIDI software, it will check your driver configuration. So, click **OK** to confirm that you want the driver tested.

7 Ensure everything is working as it should. Click **Audio 1**, go to the **File** menu and click on **Import Audio File**. Select your CD-ROM drive in the 'Look in' box. Double-click on **Quick Start Song**. Click on a file then on **Play**. If it plays, the software is OK.

What is MIDI?

MIDI stands for Musical Instrument Digital Interface. This is a technical standard that allows musical data to be sent between different computers and specially equipped musical instruments.

It does not record specific sounds but instead records information about which notes you want in your compositions in a universal language which any computer can translate and – if connected to a MIDI sound source – replay.

The transport bar

Cubase's transport bar works just like the controls on an ordinary Hi-Fi system. As well as the usual Stop, Play and Record buttons (in yellow, green and red respectively), plus Rewind and Forward, you can set the tempo and time signature (4/4 etc) and check MIDI input and output.

Close-up
Keyboards are effective at emulating the sounds made by other instruments and are the most common MIDI instruments. But there are other MIDI instruments you can record and play with – guitars and drums are also popular choices.

To return to the beginning of a tune, whether you are playing it or have just recorded it, double-click on the yellow **Stop** button. If you just want to play a part of the song, click **Stop** then drag the 'Song position line' back to where you want the playback to begin.

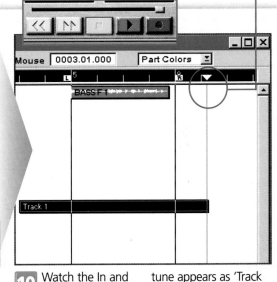

8 In order to hear what you are playing while you are making a recording, ensure the MIDI Setup is configured correctly. Go to the **Options** menu and click on **MIDI Setup**. In the dialogue box click in the Active box in the Midi Thru section. Click on **Exit**.

9 To make a MIDI recording, start a new song and click on **Track 1**. (Do not select Audio as this refers to the sound files on your hard disk.) Then click the red **Record** button on the transport bar, play your tune, then click on the yellow **Stop** button.

10 Watch the In and Out meters on the transport bar as you record to ensure your PC is receiving the keyboard's signal. Your tune appears as 'Track 1' in the arrangement window. Click the green **Play** button to hear it. Your PC and keyboard are now in harmony.

Get to know your keyboard
Keyboards have a range of different facilities. Like electronic synthesisers, some are more sophisticated than others. Some have two built-in libraries, one for instrument voices and another for rhythm styles. Some have facilities to construct and save their own rhythms. In addition to sound banks, your keyboard may have other useful features – for example, the ability to split the keyboard into two different voices, a built-in metronome to count off beats and keep time, automatic harmonisation and the facility to automatically alter the beat.

Compose your own music

Use specialist software to make music on your computer

Your PC can be a key compositional tool, helping you to create anything from a simple tune to a complex arrangement. In fact, with a sound card and/or MIDI instrument, you have access to a 'virtual' orchestra.

You don't need to be an experienced musician to enjoy composing music although, naturally, the more musical training you have, the more you can make of your PC's capabilities. Specialist software makes it possible for the novice to experiment with special effects, from simple fading in and fading out, to 'bending' and 'stretching' the sounds in ways that can't be achieved with a single instrument.

This project uses a MIDI keyboard and follows the creation of a simple arrangement composed of two piano parts which form a 'round', a rhythm track and a drum track.

Music software – an overview

Composition software, such as Cubase, allows you to record any number of musical strands – called Parts – separately, then play them back together at once as a single composition or arrangement. After you record your Parts you can then edit them, moving and lengthening notes, adding echoes and so on, to achieve the effect you want. (Edit mode also allows you to write musical notes on your screen and play them back through your sound card and/or MIDI instrument.)

Parts are recorded onto Tracks. Cubase has seven types – or classes – of Track, including Audio, MIDI and Drum. Audio Tracks are sound recordings kept on your computer's hard disk; MIDI Tracks are sequences of notes and chords; and Drum Tracks store sequences of drum beats. You can create any number of any class of Track you choose to build up the musical composition you want.

Working with MIDI

Using your software in conjunction with a MIDI instrument as well as your PC opens up more opportunities and yields better results. A MIDI keyboard allows you to record notes played on one type of instrument and play them back through another. For example, you can record a part played on a piano, then, by changing the keyboard setting, play it back on a harpsichord.

Recording vocals

You can record vocals onto Audio Tracks stored on your hard disk. But be aware that they take up huge amounts of memory, so you will need a large hard disk.

> *The arrangement in this project was composed using Cubase VST music software. Whichever software you use, the basic principles of composition are the same. Consult your manual for specific guidance.*

OTHER PROGRAMS

*If you'd like a metronome to keep time as you play your Parts, click on the **Click** button on the transport bar.*

To set up your music keyboard and software, and to familiarise yourself with the key elements of Cubase, see pages 236-239.

► BEFORE YOU START

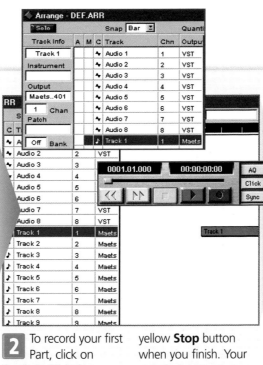

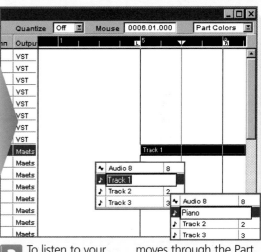

1 Go to the **Start** menu, select **Programs** then click on your music software. To check if it is receiving an external signal, play a note on your keyboard. If it is set up correctly, the red 'In' meter on the transport bar at the bottom of the screen will respond.

2 To record your first Part, click on **Track 1**. Click the **Record** button on the transport bar then play your tune. Click the yellow **Stop** button when you finish. Your new Part appears as 'Track 1' in the pane on the right of the arrangement window.

3 To listen to your Part, double-click the **Stop** button on the transport bar, then click the **Play** button. The 'Song position line' moves through the Part as it plays. To name the Track in the Track listing, double-click on the Track label and type in a title. Press **Enter**.

Understanding your arrangement window

When you open your program you will be presented with an arrangement window. This will contain a list of Parts. If you have MIDI Tracks already recorded, these may be named as different musical instruments. If you don't, they will most likely appear as a numerical list – Track 1, Track 2, and so on.

The arrangement window will also contain an area that gives a visual representation of each recorded Track. Along the top is a numeric bar divided into seconds. Each recorded Part can be measured along this bar to see how long it lasts. When you have more than one Track recorded, you will be able to see how each stops and starts in relation to the others.

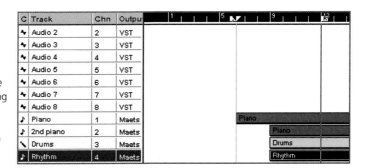

Close-up
*If you make mistakes with your recordings don't worry. Just stop playing and click the yellow **Stop** button on the transport bar. Then click on the Part you have recorded and press the **Delete** key.*

Key word
Round *This describes a tune or song that is made up of the same parts that follow each other at equal intervals and at the same pitch.*

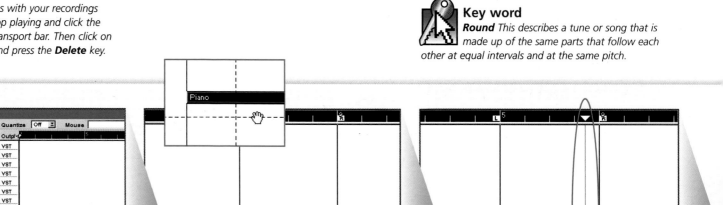

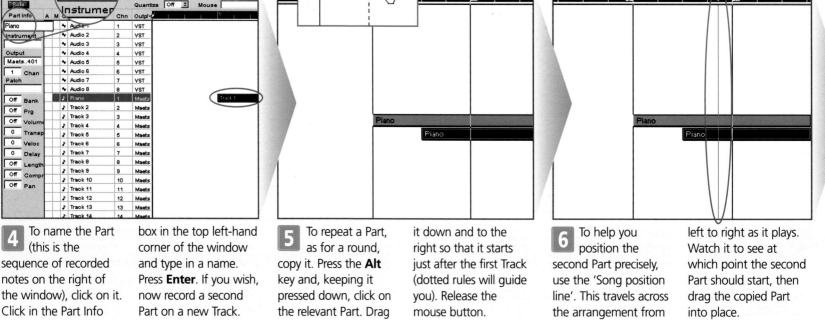

4 To name the Part (this is the sequence of recorded notes on the right of the window), click on it. Click in the Part Info box in the top left-hand corner of the window and type in a name. Press **Enter**. If you wish, now record a second Part on a new Track.

5 To repeat a Part, as for a round, copy it. Press the **Alt** key and, keeping it pressed down, click on the relevant Part. Drag it down and to the right so that it starts just after the first Track (dotted rules will guide you). Release the mouse button.

6 To help you position the second Part precisely, use the 'Song position line'. This travels across the arrangement from left to right as it plays. Watch it to see at which point the second Part should start, then drag the copied Part into place.

Program controls

Whatever program you use, you will almost certainly have a set of controls to help you in your compositions. In Cubase, this set of controls is called the transport bar. You can make it appear, and disappear, by pressing the **F12** key at the top of your keyboard.

The transport bar is the control panel for playing and recording single tracks, and for setting their tempo and other features.

Parts do not always need to be recorded. You can draw Drum Parts, for example, in the pane on the right of the arrangement window, then fill in the notes, tempo, etc, afterwards.

DRAWING PARTS

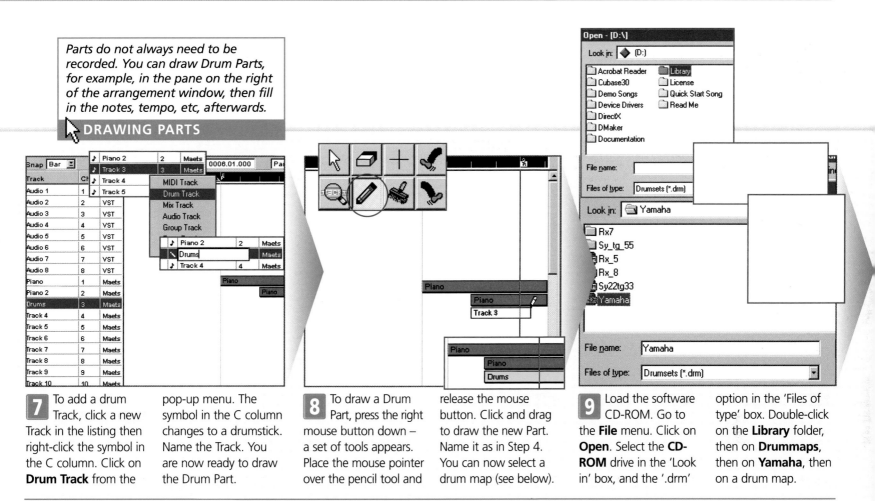

7 To add a drum Track, click a new Track in the listing then right-click the symbol in the C column. Click on **Drum Track** from the pop-up menu. The symbol in the C column changes to a drumstick. Name the Track. You are now ready to draw the Drum Part.

8 To draw a Drum Part, press the right mouse button down – a set of tools appears. Place the mouse pointer over the pencil tool and release the mouse button. Click and drag to draw the new Part. Name it as in Step 4. You can now select a drum map (see below).

9 Load the software CD-ROM. Go to the **File** menu. Click on **Open**. Select the **CD-ROM** drive in the 'Look in' box, and the '.drm' option in the 'Files of type' box. Double-click on the **Library** folder, then on **Drummaps**, then on **Yamaha**, then on a drum map.

Choosing a drum map

Your music software will provide a range of drum 'maps'. Each comprises up to 64 sounds (for example, cymbals, maracas and tambourine) which you use to create a drum Part.

If possible, select the drum map specifically for your make of keyboard (or sound card). This means that the sounds listed will exactly match those your instrument can produce. If your keyboard is not listed in the Drummaps folder, select the **Roland** folder, then the **Gs_stand** map. This is a general MIDI drum set that will work with most MIDI keyboards.

To create the drum rhythm, click on the grid to add beats for the appropriate sounds. Use the numeric bar at the top of the grid to help you position them accurately. If you make a mistake, simply click on a beat to delete it.

*To listen to any single Track among the many that you have recorded, first click on the Track then click the **Solo** button on the main screen and the **Play** button on the transport bar.*

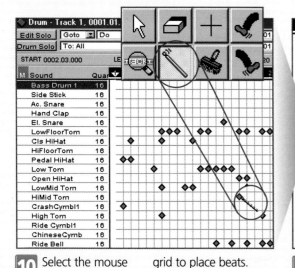

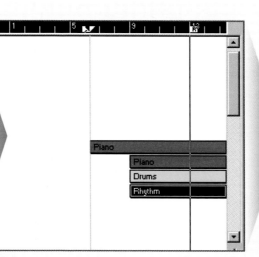

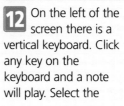

10 Select the mouse pointer (see Step 8). To enter Edit Mode double-click on the drum Part. Select the drum tool. Click on the grid to place beats. Click **Play** on the transport bar to hear the Part. When you're happy, go to the **File** menu and click **Close**.

11 It is also possible to compose a Part entirely in Edit Mode. Click on a new Track in the listing. Select the pencil tool (see Step 8) and click and drag to draw a new Part in the arrangement window. Name the Track and the Part. Double-click the Part to enter Edit Mode.

12 On the left of the screen there is a vertical keyboard. Click any key on the keyboard and a note will play. Select the pencil tool and draw the notes where you want them on the grid. You can make notes any length. To hear your work, click **Play**.

Special effects

Some music software comes with its own range of special effects, and you can buy extra effect software from shops or through Internet sites. Effects include: Choirus, which adds depth and animation to sounds using 'delay', 'feedback' and extra 'width'; Auto Panner, which alternates the sound being played between the left and right speakers; and Espacial, which has a 'reverb' effect that adds ambience. All these effects are available in Cubase.

Choirus

This is a chorus and flanger effect which adds "depth" and "ani...
It basically works as follows: The original signal is delayed and...
lay is continuously varied by an "LFO". This delayed signal is...
with the original.

Parameter	Explanation
Delay	This is the basic amount of delay applied to the sign...

Bright idea
Reorganise Tracks by creating a Group for them (intro, chorus, and so on). Go to the **Structure** *menu and click on* **Build Group***. Select and add the Parts you want to include. You can then move or repeat the Group in the arrangement, which makes remodelling the song easy.*

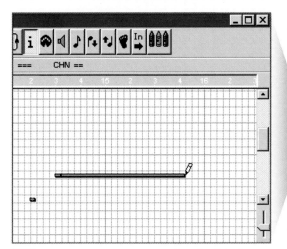

13 To create a neat finish to your song, with all the Tracks ending at the same time, click on each Part in turn and select the pencil tool. Click the last note and drag it to the point where the song ends. Check this using the 'Song Position line' during a playback.

14 You can alter the way the parts of your arrangement work together through the Inspector (see below). To change the volume of a Track, for example, click the Track then type a new value in the **Volume** box.

15 To save your arrangement, go to the **File** menu and click on **Save Arrangement**. Select a folder to store your arrangement in, type in a file name, then click on the **Save** button.

The Inspector

Within the arrangement window is the 'Inspector', a panel on the left of the Track list. Through it you can experiment with the properties of Parts. For example, you can change the Transpose setting so that all notes in the Part are played higher or lower on the keyboard. This is useful for experimenting with changes of key. If you prefer the changes, you can make them permanent by using the Freeze Play Parameters facility in the Functions menu.

To turn the Inspector on and off, click the small button in the bottom left-hand corner of the arrangement window.

Learning to read music

Let your computer teach you the principles of musical notation

You don't have to be able to read music to compose it on your computer, and it is not necessary to know the names of individual notes to be able to play them or compose a tune. But as you become more confident and proficient at composition you may want to learn to read music. If so, a range of specialist software is available to help.

This project uses a program called Music Ace. Aimed at the complete novice, it teaches you notation through easy-to-follow lessons and related games. You will also be given the opportunity to test your knowledge by composing simple tunes. Much of the other educational music software available will follow these basic principles.

Check that your computer meets the minimum system requirements of the program before you install the software onto your hard disk.

► **BEFORE YOU START**

1 Go to the **Start** menu, select **Programs** then click on your music software. The opening screen of Music Ace contains musical notes playing a tune. Adjust the volume using the slide bar on the left of the screen. To begin, click on the **Start** button.

A range of music education programs, including Music Ace, can be sampled and downloaded from the Internet. A good starting point is the Shareware Music Machine Web site (http://www.hitsquad.com/smm/Win95/Music_Skills).

► **OTHER PROGRAMS**

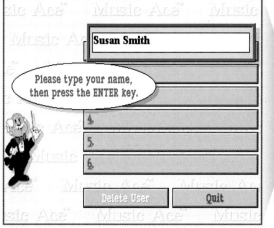

2 A music maestro will guide you through each stage of the program. Click in the first box, type your name then press the **Enter** key. Music Ace can accommodate several users, and it uses the names to keep track of each user's progress.

3 You are now presented with the Main Screen through which you choose whether to use the Doodle Pad (a music creation tool), follow a lesson or play a music game related to the lesson. To start a lesson click on the **Lesson** button.

4 Lesson 1 deals with basic music notation. An animated tutorial teaches you about the positioning of notes. After the tutorial you will be asked questions – click on the appropriate button to respond. Continue the exercises to the end of the lesson.

Set your preferences

The screen in which you elect to start a lesson or play a game also contains a Preferences button. Click on this to customise the way Music Ace works.

One set of choices, the Maestro Options, allows you to set the way in which on-screen help is delivered by the cartoon character, Maestro Max. If you wish, turn his voice or speech balloons off.

Use the Control Bar

Every lesson has a Control Bar running across the top of the screen. This provides access to basic options and settings.

To terminate the current lesson and return to the Main Screen click on the **Menu** button. The button to its right shows the name of the current lesson. To change the volume click on the **Vol** button. To move forwards or backwards in each lesson click on the relevant **Skip** buttons. Click on the **Pause** button to stop the lesson at the current point (the button changes to **Resume** – click on it to continue). To go straight to the game that relates to the lesson, click on the **Game** button.

Watch out

*Be aware that if you click on the **Skip** buttons to move forwards or backwards within a game your score will be set to zero.*

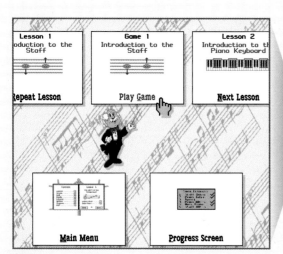

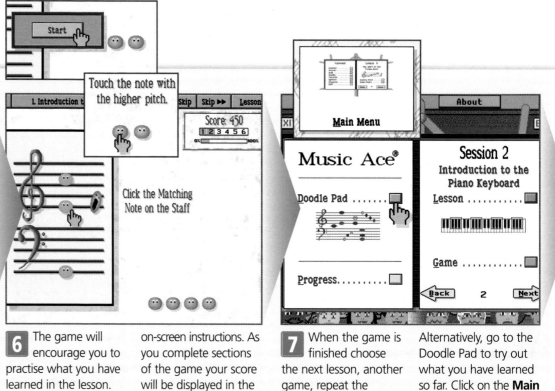

5 When a lesson ends you will be offered several options: to repeat the lesson, go to the main menu, check your progress, try the next lesson, or play the related game. To play the game click the **Play Game** button.

6 The game will encourage you to practise what you have learned in the lesson. To begin, click the **Start** button and follow the on-screen instructions. As you complete sections of the game your score will be displayed in the top right-hand corner of the screen.

7 When the game is finished choose the next lesson, another game, repeat the previous lesson or game, or view your progress.

Alternatively, go to the Doodle Pad to try out what you have learned so far. Click on the **Main Menu**, then on the **Doodle Pad** button.

Assessing your progress

The lessons in Music Ace are broken down into sections. An indicator in the top right-hand corner of the screen shows you how far you have progressed through your current lesson. Completed sections are shown in green; the one you are working on in red.

Choosing lessons

You may not want to complete lessons or games in sequence – you may want to select specific ones to work on particular areas. You can do this from the Main Menu. Click on the **Next** arrow on the lesson page to leaf through the range of lessons available. When you find the one you want, click the **Lesson** or **Game** button to access it.

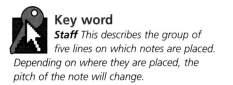

Key word
Staff This describes the group of five lines on which notes are placed. Depending on where they are placed, the pitch of the note will change.

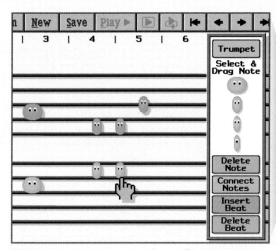

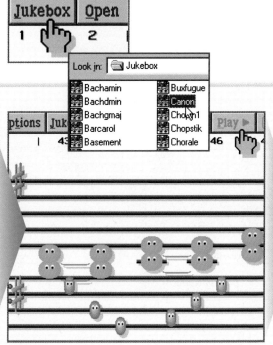

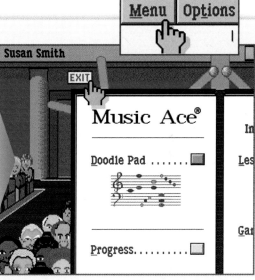

8 To move a note onto the 'staff' ready for playing, select and drag it from the box on the right of the screen. Move notes on the staff by dragging them. Each note plays as you move it. To hear your tune, click the **Play** button on the Control Bar.

9 Music Ace has a library of songs for you to listen to and edit. To open one in the Doodle Pad click on the Control Bar's **Jukebox** button, then double-click on a song. Click **Play** to hear it. Edit it by moving its notes on the staff and adding new notes.

10 To end your session, click on the **Menu** button on the Control Bar, then on one of the **Exit** buttons in the Main Menu. The next time you run Music Ace, click on your name from the user list – Music Ace will remind you of your progress.

Using the Doodle Pad

To change the instrument you are composing with, click on the instrument name at the top of the box on the right of the screen. Each time you click, a different instrument name will appear – Oboe, Marimba, Trumpet, Jazz Guitar, Clarinet and Grand Piano. When the instrument you want appears, all notes you create thereafter will sound like that instrument, and will appear in a different colour.

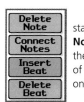

To adjust the length of a note on the staff, first delete the note (click on **Delete Note** in the box on the right of the screen then click on the note). Next, click on one of the four different note sizes and drag it onto the staff.

To change the tempo (speed) and loudness of your composition, drag the markers along the slide bar in the bottom left-hand corner of the screen.

Profit from your

Make the most of your money by using your

Investment circles have taken off around the globe, and the most successful have been known to outperform those of professional fund managers. These circles contain up to 15 people who enjoy making the most of their finances by selecting, purchasing and monitoring their own stocks and shares. They also save money by avoiding management charges.

All this has become possible in recent years because of the computerisation of the world's stock exchanges. People outside the world's financial citadels can act as their own fund managers, using their computers to access and act upon a wealth of up-to-date financial information: stock prices are updated on the Internet as soon as they change.

So if you are thinking of playing the markets, make the Internet your first stop. There are many sites where you can gather data on companies your group is thinking of investing in. It's easy to find out how your stock has performed, current earnings-to-share ratios, liabilities, assets and profit forecasts. In fact, you can find virtually everything you need to make an informed assessment.

There are many financial news sites listing on-line share price

---

Investment circle

Create a folder called 'Investment circle'. Add sub-folders for each mini-project.

Investment circle
- Investors
- Research
- Accounts
- Communications
- Investments
- Contacts

investment circle

PC as a window on the financial markets

data, enabling you to track shares you may be interested in or have already purchased. You can then paste downloaded data into your portfolio spreadsheet – and even use it to calculate projections for your share dividends.

Once you have decided on your investments, you have to choose an on-line broker and open an account. You can then trade shares on the world markets without getting up from your computer.

If you set up an on-line bank account for your group you can also access your current financial status in a matter of seconds.

With your portfolio in place you can use your PC to administer your investment circle. You could set up

an investors' database to hold relevant information. For example, some members may prefer not to invest in certain industries or countries on ethical grounds.

Create more spreadsheets to monitor members' individual holdings and produce a newsletter to keep everyone informed.

If your group wants to diversify into other areas such as antiques trading, the Internet holds a great deal of useful data. Sites that carry price guides, tips on authenticity, where to buy and what to look for, are easily accessible and will help you make informed choices. You could also try some on-line bidding at some of the world's leading auction houses.

Prepare to invest

- Recruit members and agree aims, level of investment and club rules
- Appoint club officers and outline their responsibilities
- Research and select an on-line broker
- Open a club bank account and agree the signatories
- Set up on-line banking facilities
- Produce copies of initial research material for members

Ideas and inspirations

Adapt the following projects and exercises then apply them to setting up your own investment circle. You may find that you don't need all of them to get things up and running, so include only the documents you need for your own requirements.

96 Searching the Internet
Use search engines to locate on-line brokers, share price and stock performance information.

268 Build a shares portfolio
Set up a spreadsheet for your investment circle to keep track of your portfolio's performance.

	A	B	
1	Budget summary - summer pro		
2	Item	Estimated costs	Actu
3	Costumes	107.99	
4	Refreshments	144.24	
5	Props	98.00	
6	Printing/publicity	50.00	
7	Total	400.23	
8			
9			
10	Item	Estimated revenue	Actu
11	Refreshments	330.00	
12	Tickets	2,200.00	
13	Total	2,530.00	
14			
15	Balance		

272 Keep your accounts
Use separate worksheets in a spreadsheet to keep track of individual and group holdings.

164 Create a newsletter
Produce performance updates for your group. If other members are on-line, e-mail it to them.

150 Write a formal letter
Keep it professional if you need to send a formal letter to, say, request a prospectus.

Also worth considering...

316 Membership database
Create a record of members' details and notes on any investment or non-investment preferences.

Family budget planner

Take control of your household's incomings and outgoings

Keeping track of your household budget makes good financial sense. You can keep an eye on day-to-day outgoings and also see when major expenses, such as a family holiday, lie ahead, and so make provision for them in good time.

The best way to take care of your home accounts is with a spreadsheet program. A spreadsheet allows you to set up professional looking accounts that are easy to use because all the calculations are done for you. Once you have set up your household accounts document, you simply type in your income and expenses, and the spreadsheet updates your balances automatically.

This project is geared towards household accounts, but its structure can be used for a business accounts spreadsheet, too.

Collect all the information you are going to need to create your spreadsheet. Keep details of all your income and expenditures to hand.

BEFORE YOU START

1 Go to the **Start** menu, select **Programs** and click on **Microsoft Excel**. Save your new document by going to the **File** menu and selecting **Save As**. In the 'Save in' box select a suitable folder for it to be stored in. Type in a file name, then click on **Save.**

*You can create similar spreadsheets in Microsoft Works. Open Microsoft Works then, in the Works Task Launcher, click on the **Works Tool** tab then on the **Spreadsheet** button.*

OTHER PROGRAMS

Templates on CD-ROM

You can type in text in capital letters using the Caps Lock key. Press it down before you start typing, then press it again when you have finished.

Balance carried over

Add a 'Balance carried over' row to transfer credits or debits from the previous month.

Short cut
*To style all your section headings in the same way at the same time, hold down the **Ctrl** key and click on each of the headings in turn. Now style as usual.*

Household Accounts

	A	B	C	D	E	F
1					Household Accounts 1999	
2						
3						
4	INCOME					
5	Primary Income					
6	Second Income					
7	Interest Accrued					
8	Balance carried over					
9						
10	Total					
11						
12						
13						
14						
15						
16						
17						
18						

4	INCOME
5	Primary income
6	Second income
7	Interest accrued
8	Balance carried over
9	
10	Total
	EXPENDITURE
	Mortgage/Rent
	Car loan
	Car insurance
6	Petrol/Repairs
7	Other loans
18	Credit cards
19	Telephone
20	Cable TV etc
21	Gas
22	Electric
23	Water

23	Water
24	Food
25	Council Tax
26	Childcare
27	House insurance
28	Contents insurance
29	
30	Total Household Expenditure
31	
32	ADDITIONAL EXPENDITURE
33	Entertainment
34	Clothes
35	Holidays
36	Savings & Investment
37	
38	Total Additional Expenditure
39	
40	OUTSTANDING BALANCE

Microsoft Excel

File Edit View Insert Format Tools Data W

Arial 10 **B** *I* U

D1 Household Accounts 1999

Household Acco

	A	B	C	D	E
1				Household Accounts 19	
2					
3					
4	INCOME				
5	Primary Incom				
6	Second Income				
7	Interest Accrued				
8	Balance carried over				
9					
10	Total				
11					
12					

Font size dropdown: 8, 9, 10, 11, 12, 14, 16, 18, 20, 22, 24, 26

Household A
Bold

---

2 Click on cell **D1** and type in the heading of your spreadsheet. Click on cell **A4** and type in 'Income'. Click on the cells below 'Income' in column A and type in your sources. When you have finished, click on the cell two rows below your last entry and type in 'Total'.

3 Click on the cell two rows below 'Total' and type in 'Expenditure'. Type in your areas of expense in the cells below. Where appropriate, type in 'Total Household Expenditure'. Include a section on 'Additional Expenditure'. Finish with 'Outstanding Balance'.

4 To style your heading, click on cell **D1** then click on the **Bold** toolbar button. Click on the arrow beside the font size box on the toolbar, scroll through and select a font size. Continue to style the rest of your text in the same way.

Changing format
When you enter text into a spreadsheet its style is determined by the format of the cell you are typing it into. Formats can be altered by clicking on the cell, going to the **Format** menu and selecting **Cells**. Click on the **Font** tab, then select a font, font size, style and colour from the lists displayed.

Format Cells

Number | Alignment | Font | Border | Patterns | Protectio

Font:
Arial
- Abadi MT Condensed Lic
- Algerian
- American Uncial
- Arial

Font style:
Regular
- Regular
- Italic
- Bold
- Bold Italic

Size:
10
- 8
- 9
- 10
- 11

Underline:
None

Color:
Automatic

☑ Normal fo

Effects
☐ Strikethrough

Preview

Inserting new data
To insert a new row of expenses or income, click on the grey numbered box of the row where you'd like your new one to be placed. Go to the **Insert** menu and click on **Rows**. A new row will appear above the row you clicked on.

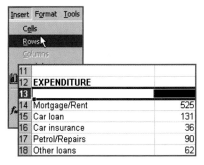

Insert Format Tools
- Cells
- Rows
- Columns

11		
12	EXPENDITURE	
13		
14	Mortgage/Rent	525
15	Car loan	131
16	Car insurance	36
17	Petrol/Repairs	90
18	Other loans	62

To adjust the width of a column, place the mouse pointer over the right-hand edge of the grey column header. When it becomes a double-headed arrow, press the left mouse button and, keeping it pressed down, drag the column edge to the desired width.

If the range of cells that AutoSum selects is incorrect, use the mouse to highlight the correct group of cells and press the **Enter** key.

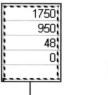

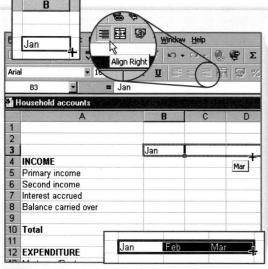

5 Adjust column widths (see above) then type 'Jan' in cell B3. Place the mouse pointer in the lower right-hand corner of B3. When it becomes a cross, click and drag to the right. The months appear in these cells. Select the row then the **Bold** and **Align Right** buttons.

6 Starting in cell B5, and continuing in the cells below, enter the figures for all your income and expenditure for the month of January. In cells where there is no amount to enter, type in a zero.

7 To calculate Jan's Total income (then total expenditure and additional expenditure), click on the relevant cell in column B, then click the **AutoSum** toolbar button. A formula appears, indicating the range of cells to add up. If the range is correct, press the **Enter** key.

Split the screen

Windows allows you to split the screen to make viewing figures across different columns and rows easy.

Go to the **Windows** menu and click on **Split**. Place your mouse pointer over the 'split' line. When it changes appearance, hold down the left mouse button and drag the line to the desired position. You can scroll through each part of the split screen separately.

Add a splash of colour

Adding background colour to your spreadsheet may help you identify sections more easily.

To add coloured shading, click on the cells in question, then click on the arrow next to the toolbar's Fill Color button. Now click on your choice of colour from the panel that appears.

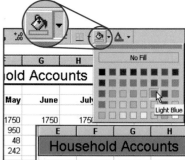

Calculating spreadsheet data can be complicated. Using Works' in-built calculation tools makes it much easier. For further help, see page 30.

▶ CALCULATING YOUR DATA

Short cut
To save yourself typing in cell references to the formula in the Entry Bar, click on the relevant cell at the appropriate point in the calculation. Excel and Works automatically enter the cell reference into the formula.

	A	B	C
1			
2			
3		Jan	Feb
4	**INCOME**		
5	Primary income	1750	1750
6	Second income	950	950
7	Interest accrued	48	48
8	Balance carried over	0	-60
9			
10	**Total**	2748	
11			

Microsoft Excel
File Edit View Insert Format Tools Data Window Help

Arial ▼ 10 ▼ **B** *I* U

SUM ▼ ✗ ✓ = =B10-B30-B38

Household accounts

	A	B	C	D
33	Entertainment	400		
34	Clothes	150		
35	Holidays	200		
36	Savings & Investments	270		
37				
38	**Total Additional Expenditure**	1020		
39				
40	**OUTSTANDING BALANCE**	=B10-B30-B38		
41				
42				
43			-60	

Microsoft Excel
File Edit View Insert Format Tools Data Window Help

Arial ▼ 10 ▼ **B** *I* U

SUM ▼ ✗ ✓ = =B40

Household accounts

	A	B	C	D
2				
3		Jan	Feb	Mar
4	**INCOME**			
5	Primary income	1750	1750	
6	Second income	950	950	
7	Interest accrued	48	48	
8	Balance carried over	0	=B40	
9				
10	**Total**	2748	-60	

		Jan	Feb	Mar
	INCOME			
	Primary income	1750	1750	1750
	Second income	950	950	950
	Interest accrued	48	48	48
	Balance carried over	0	-60	96
	Total	2748	2688	2844
	EXPENDITURE			
	Mortgage/Rent	525	525	525
	Car loan	131	131	131
	Car insurance	36	36	36
	Petrol/Repairs	90	74	101
	Other loans	62	62	62
	Credit cards	20	20	20

Househo...

8 To calculate Jan's Outstanding Balance, click on the relevant cell, then enter the following formula in the Entry Bar to subtract Expenditure from your Total income: type an '=' sign, then use cell references to subtract expenses from income. Press **Enter**.

9 Type in figures for February. To carry over January's balance, click in the relevant cell (here, cell C8) then type an '=' sign, followed by the cell reference for January's Outstanding Balance. Press **Enter**. Now you are ready to calculate totals for the year.

10 Place the mouse pointer over the lower right-hand corner of the cell that holds January's Total income (here, B10). When it becomes a cross, click and drag to the right. The formula is copied to all the other months. Repeat for other totals.

Using your budget planner

Once you have created your spreadsheet, update it every week or so. Where possible, type in expenses you know are due well in advance. That way, you will have a better idea of how much disposable income you will have at the end of every month.

Household accounts

	A	B	C	D	E
1					
2					
3		Jan	Feb	Mar	Apr
4	**INCOME**				
5	Primary income	1750	1750	1750	1750
6	Second income	950	950	1050	950
7	Interest accrued	48	48	52	48
8	Balance carried over	0	-95	-236	68
9					
10	**Total**	2748	2653	2616	2816

Fixtures & Fittings			
Item Type	Description	Value	Where Stored
Electrical	Sharp Microwave 700w	£300.00	Kitchen
Electrical	Panasonic 26" Television	£300.00	Lounge
Electrical	Technics Music System	£900.00	Lounge
Electrical	BT Answerphone	£175.00	Hall
Electrical	Zeus Aquarium	£800.00	Bedroom
Electrical	Bose Clock Radio	£27.00	Lounge
Electrical	Sony Video Recorder	£300.00	Kitchen
Electrical	Fridge	£200.00	Kitchen
Electrical	Freezer	£375.00	Kitchen
Electrical	Kenwood Food Processor	£129.00	Kitchen
Electrical	Siebart Cooker	£400.00	
		SUM: £3,906.00	
Furniture	Two-seat Sofa	£400.00	Lounge
Furniture	Two Armchairs	£400.00	Lounge
Furniture	Oak Table & Six Chairs	£600.00	Dining Room
Furniture	Painting - Dali Sketch	£5,000.00	Lounge
Furniture	Grandfather Clock	£6,000.00	Hall
Furniture	Vase	£900.00	Hall
Furniture	Persian Rug	£750.00	Hall
Furniture	Sleepeze Double Bed	£500.00	Bedroom
Furniture	Silent Night Single Bed	£300.00	Bedroom
Furniture	Silent Night Double Bed	£350.00	Bedroom
Furniture	Ikea Dressing Table	£275.00	Bedroom
Furniture	Ikea Coffee Table	£120.00	Lounge
		SUM: £15,595.00	
		SUM: £19,501.00	

Catalogue and value your home contents

Save time and money by keeping a record of your possessions

If you have ever had to look for a receipt or guarantee in order to make a claim on a faulty product, you'll know how frustrating that search can be. Calculating the value of your household possessions when your contents' insurance needs renewing is just as time-consuming. So don't waste your energy sorting through endless old bills, invoices and receipts every time. Instead, create a database to catalogue your home contents. With it you can record, sort, retrieve and update vital information quickly and easily.

Gather together all the information you have about your home contents, such as dates of purchase, values, guarantees, and so on.

BEFORE YOU START

Works Task Launcher

TaskWizards	Existing Documents	Wo

Click one of the Works tools

Word Processor
·Create letters, memos, form letters, and mailing labe

Spreadsheet
·Do budgeting and calculations, create charts and

To create a new database

Database
·Create address books, lists and reports

1 Go to the **Start** menu, select **Programs** and click on **Microsoft Works**. In the Works Task Launcher click on the **Works Tools** tab. Click on the **Database** button then, in the next dialogue box, click on the button beside 'To create a new database'.

You can also create a database using Microsoft Excel. Use the spreadsheet to type in your headings, and the Filter feature to create your reports.

OTHER PROGRAMS

Templates on CD-ROM

Short cut
When recording items, include a serialised reference field. Your PC will automatically assign a number to each item that you enter, so you won't need to type in the numbers yourself.

Watch out
Don't lose information from your database – save and name it as soon as you have created it. Save it regularly as you work, and immediately after you make any updates.

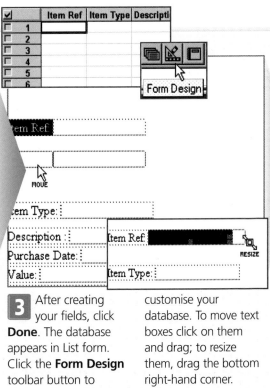

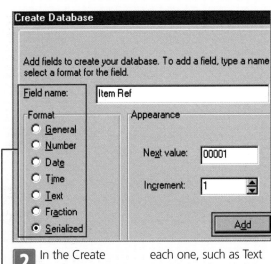

2 In the Create Database dialogue box, input your fields – which are categories of information – and specify a format for each one, such as Text or Number (enter the fields and formats listed below). When you have typed in each field, click on the **Add** button.

3 After creating your fields, click **Done**. The database appears in List form. Click the **Form Design** toolbar button to customise your database. To move text boxes click on them and drag; to resize them, drag the bottom right-hand corner.

4 To add a heading click at the top of the page and type it in. To style your title, field names or text boxes, click on them, go to the **Format** menu and click on **Font and Style**. Select fonts, sizes, styles and colours. Click on the **Alignment** tab and select the Left option.

Fields and Formats

Field	Format
Item Ref	Serialized
Item Type	Text
Description	Text
Purchase Date	Date
Value	Number
Product Ref	Text
Guarantee	Text
Where Stored	Text
Purchased	Text

Format style
When you select Number, Date, Time or Fraction as a format, you are given a list of options in the Appearance section. Click on your preferred style.

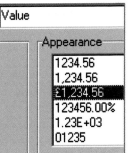

Different views
There are three ways to view your database:

 List View is best for quick reference as it allows you to view lots of entries at the same time.

Form View displays one entry at a time and is the best for entering data.

Form Design doesn't let you enter information; instead it lets you add, delete, move and resize fields, alter font styles and add colours.

Short cut
*To style several text boxes in the same way at once, select them all by holding down the **Ctrl** key and clicking on each box in turn. Any style change will be applied to all boxes.*

It's possible to extract data for specific reasons. An inventory of fixtures and fittings will be useful should you rent out your property.

MAKING A REPORT

Key Word
Report *This is a printed summary of information stored in a database. From your Home Contents database you could make a report on uninsured and insured household items.*

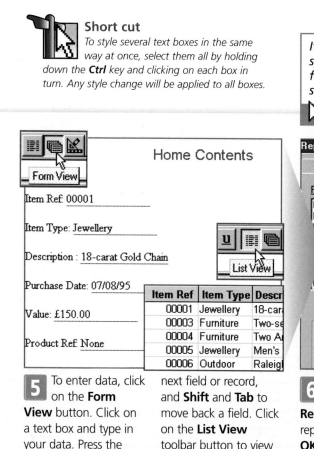

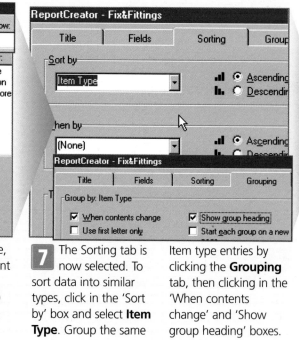

5 To enter data, click on the **Form View** button. Click on a text box and type in your data. Press the **Tab** key to move to the next field or record, and **Shift** and **Tab** to move back a field. Click on the **List View** toolbar button to view your list.

6 Go to the **Tools** menu and click on **ReportCreator**. Enter a report name and click **OK**. In the next box click the **Fields** tab. In the 'Fields available' pane, click the fields you want in your report (in the order you want them) then click **Add**. Click **Next** when done.

7 The Sorting tab is now selected. To sort data into similar types, click in the 'Sort by' box and select **Item Type**. Group the same Item type entries by clicking the **Grouping** tab, then clicking in the 'When contents change' and 'Show group heading' boxes.

Finding information

To search for specific data, go to the **Edit** menu and click on **Find**. Type in a key word or words for what you want to search for, select the 'All records' option, then click on **OK**. The database view changes to show only those records that match your search. To return to the full database view, go to the **Record** menu, select **Show** and then click on **All Records**.

In Form View you can move through entries fast by clicking on the arrows on either side of the Record counter at the foot of the window.

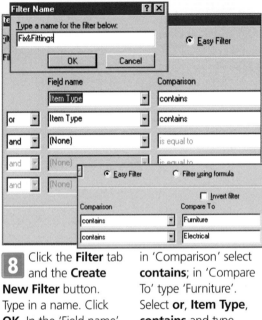

*Microsoft Works automatically saves any report that you create. To print or update an old report, go to the **View** menu and click on **Report**. A list of your reports appears. Click on the relevant one then click on **Preview** or **Modify** as appropriate.*

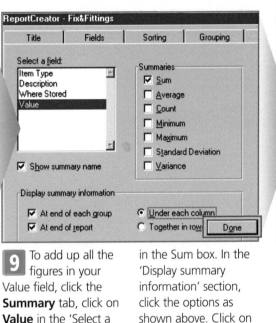

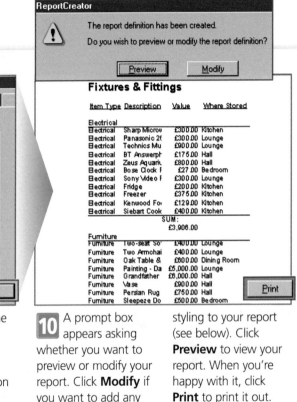

8 Click the **Filter** tab and the **Create New Filter** button. Type in a name. Click **OK**. In the 'Field name' box select **Item Type**; in 'Comparison' select **contains**; in 'Compare To' type 'Furniture'. Select **or**, **Item Type**, **contains** and type 'Electrical'. Press **Enter**.

9 To add up all the figures in your Value field, click the **Summary** tab, click on **Value** in the 'Select a field' window and click in the Sum box. In the 'Display summary information' section, click the options as shown above. Click on the **Done** button.

10 A prompt box appears asking whether you want to preview or modify your report. Click **Modify** if you want to add any styling to your report (see below). Click **Preview** to view your report. When you're happy with it, click **Print** to print it out.

Reporting in style

To add a professional touch to your reports, adjust the fonts, font sizes and add colour.

Click the **Report View** toolbar button. Click the cell or row you want to style and go to the **Format** menu and click on **Font and Style**. In the Format dialogue box click the various

tabs, selecting your fonts, sizes, styles, colours and background patterns as you do so.

If your columns are too close together, adjust their widths. Place the cursor on the right-hand edge of the column heading, hold down the mouse button and drag to the desired width.

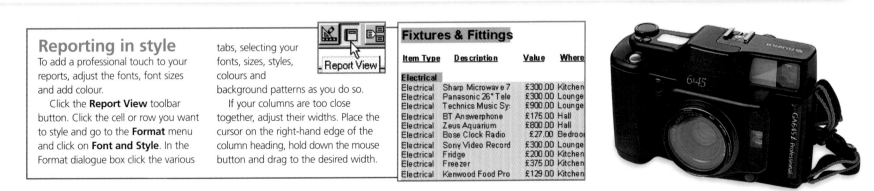

Calculate your bills

Keep a track of your spending to help predict future bills

A spreadsheet is ideal for keeping track of the amount you spend on household bills and it can help you estimate and plan for future bills. Not only can you enter details about utilities, such as gas and electricity, but you can enter expenses that crop up once a year, such as the television licence and club subscriptions. These are often the bills that get overlooked.

With the spreadsheet program in Excel you can also create a pie chart to analyse your expenses. This gives a useful visual guide to your spending and can help you spot financial 'black holes' that are eating up your money.

Collect your most recent bills, and make a note of any regular household expenses for which you don't have documentation.

▶ **BEFORE YOU START**

1 Go to the **Start** menu, select **Programs** and click on **Microsoft Excel**. Save and name the new spreadsheet by clicking on the **Save** toolbar button. Select a folder to save it in through the 'Save in' box, and type in a name in the 'File name' box. Click on **Save**.

*You can create similar spreadsheets in Microsoft Works. Open Microsoft Works then, in the Works Task Launcher, click on the **Works Tool** tab then on the **Spreadsheet** button.*

▶ **OTHER PROGRAMS**

Templates on CD-ROM

Short cut
To style several cells in the same way at the same time, press the **Ctrl** *key and, keeping it pressed down, click on each cell in turn. Style as usual.*

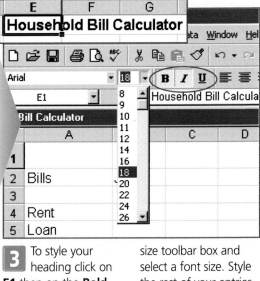

2 Click in cell **E1** and type in your heading. In cell **A2** type in 'Bills'; in cell **A4** type in your first type of bill. Continue to enter the types of bill in the cells below. When you have typed in your last bill click in the cell two rows below and type in 'Total'.

3 To style your heading click on **E1** then on the **Bold** and **Italic** toolbar buttons. Click on the arrow beside the font size toolbar box and select a font size. Style the rest of your entries then adjust the width of column A to fit your text (see below).

4 Type 'Jan' in cell **B2**. Place the cursor in the lower right-hand corner of the cell. When it changes to a black cross, click and drag along row 2 to reveal the other months until you reach 'Dec'. Release the button. Click on the **Bold** toolbar button.

Inserting new data

To add a new bill, click on the grey numbered box of the row above where the new one is to be placed. Go to the **Insert** menu and click on **Rows**. A blank row will appear in place. Type in your text as in Step 2.

To adjust the width of a column, place the cursor over the right-hand edge of the grey column header. When it becomes a double-headed arrow click and drag the edge to the desired width.

Close-up

When you enter figures into a spreadsheet, they automatically align on the right-hand side of the column. This way, the decimal points align neatly above each other.

	A	B	C	D
1				
2	**Bills**	**Jan**	**Feb**	**Mar**
3				
4	Rent	350.00		
5	Loan	121.00		
6	Phone	34.27		
7	TV	28.99		
8	Council Tax	36.00		
9	Water	19.65		
10	Gas	0.00		
11	Electricity	0.00		
12	Credit Card	45.00		
13	Car Insurance	37.50		

Bill Calculator

Σ *fx* A↓Z
+.0 .00
AutoSum

	A		C	D	E	F
1						Household
2	**Bills**	**Jan**	**Feb**	**Mar**	**Apr**	**May**
3						
4	Rent	350.00				
	Loan	121.00				
	Phone	34.27				
	TV	28.99				
	Council Tax	36.00				
	Water	19.65				
10	Gas	0.00				
11	Electricity	0.00				
12	Credit Card	45.00				
13	Car Insurance	37.50				
14						
15	Total	=SUM(B4:B14)				
16						

672.41

14			
15	Total:	672.41	
16			

14			
15	Total:	672.41	

Household Bill Calculator

Mar	**Apr**	**May**	**Jun**	**Jul**	**Aug**	S
350.00	350.00	350.00	350.00	350.00	350.00	
121.00	121.00	121.00	121.00	121.00	121.00	
34.27	34.27	34.27	34.27	34.27	34.27	
28.99	28.99	28.99	28.99	28.99	28.99	
36.00	36.00	36.00	36.00	36.00	36.00	
19.65	19.65	19.65	19.65	19.65	19.65	
86.29	0.00	0.00	0.00	0.00	0.00	
74.59	0.00	0.00	0.00	0.00	0.00	
45.00	45.00	45.00	45.00	45.00	45.00	
37.50	37.50	37.50	37.50	37.50	37.50	
833.29	672.41	672.41	672.41	672.41	672.41	

5 Starting in cell **B4**, and continuing in the cells immediately below, enter the amounts paid out in January for each type of expenditure. If you did not pay anything for a particular bill, type '0' into the relevant cell.

6 To calculate January's total expenditure on bills, click in the cell to the right of 'Total', then click on the **AutoSum** toolbar button. The cells to be calculated are outlined with a dotted line, and a formula appears in the Total cell. Press **Enter**.

7 To copy the formula for the other months of the year, first place the cursor in the lower right-hand corner of the cell. When it becomes a cross, click and drag until you reach column O. Microsoft Excel will automatically update all cell references.

Decimal places

For financial spreadsheets you need to format your figures so they display two figures after the decimal point. Select the relevant cells, go to the **Format** menu and click on **Cells**. In the Format Cells dialogue box the Number tab is selected. Click on **Number** in the category pane, and set the number of decimal places to '2'. Click **OK**.

Format Cells

| Number | Alignment | Font | Border | Patterns |

Category:
General
Number
Currency
Accounting
Date
Time
Percentage
Fraction

Sample
0.56

Decimal places: 2

☐ Use 1000 Separator (,)

Negative numbers:

To copy and paste a formula, click on the formula cell then click on the **Copy** *toolbar button. Highlight all the cells you want the formula to appear in, then click on the* **Paste** *toolbar button. The cell references automatically update themselves.*

To add a background colour, select the cells then click on the arrow next to the **Fill Color** *toolbar button. Click on the colour from the menu.*

Household Bill Calculator

	Aug	Sep	Oct	Nov	Dec	Totals
	50.00	350.00	350.00	350.00	350.00	=SUM(B4:M4)
	21.00	121.00	121.00	121.00	121.00	
	34.27	34.27	34.27	34.27	34.27	
	28.99	28.99	28.99	28.99	28.99	
	36.00	36.00	36.00	36.00	36.00	
	19.65	19.65	19.65	19.65	19.65	
	0.00	0.00	0.00	0.00	0.00	**Totals**
	0.00	0.00	0.00	0.00	0.00	
	45.00	45.00	45.00	45.00	45.00	4,200.00
	37.50	37.50	37.50	37.50	37.50	
	672.41	672.41	672.41	672.41	672.41	

Aug	Sep	Oct	Nov	Dec	Totals
350.00	350.00	350.00	350.00	350.00	4,200.00
121.00	121.00	121.00	121.00	121.00	1,452.00
34.27	34.27	34.27	34.27	34.27	411.24
28.99	28.99	28.99	28.99	28.99	347.88
36.00	36.00	36.00	36.00	36.00	432.00
19.65	19.65	19.65	19.65	19.65	235.80
0.00	0.00	0.00	0.00	0.00	86.29
0.00	0.00	0.00	0.00	0.00	74.59
45.00	45.00	45.00	45.00	45.00	540.00
37.50	37.50	37.50	37.50	37.50	450.00
41	672.41	672.41	672.41	41	=SUM(B15:M15)

8229.80

Household Bill Calculator

Feb	Mar	Apr	May	Jun	Jul	Aug	Sep	Oct	Nov
350.00	350.00	350.00	350.00	350.00	350.00	350.00	350.00	350.00	350.00
121.00	121.00	121.00	121.00	121.00	121.00	121.00	121.00	121.00	121.00
34.27	34.27	34.27	34.27	34.27	34.27	34.27	34.27	34.27	34.27
28.99	28.99	28.99	28.99	28.99	28.99	28.99	28.99	28.99	28.99
36.00	36.00	36.00	36.00	36.00	36.00	36.00	36.00	36.00	36.00
19.65	19.65	19.65	19.65	19.65	19.65	19.65	19.65	19.65	19.65
0.00	86.29	0.00	0.00	0.00	0.00	0.00	0.00	0.00	0.00
0.00	74.59	0.00	0.00	0.00	0.00	0.00	0.00	0.00	0.00
45.00	45.00	45.00	45.00	45.00	45.00	45.00	45.00	45.00	45.00
37.50	37.50	37.50	37.50	37.50	37.50	37.50	37.50	37.50	37.50
672.41	833.29	672.41	672.41	672.41	672.41	672.41	672.41	672.41	672.41

Rent
Loan
Phone
TV
Council Tax
Water
Gas
Electricity
Credit Card
Car Insurance

8 Type 'Totals' in the cell to the right of 'Dec'. Click on the cell two rows below 'Totals', then double-click on **AutoSum**. The yearly total for your first type of bill will appear. Copy and paste this formula into the cells below to calculate the totals for your other bills.

9 Paste the same formula into the cell two rows below the final figure in the 'Totals' column. Press **Enter**. The total amount you have spent on bills in the course of the previous year will appear. This completes the calculation sheet.

10 To add a pie chart, see below. When you are happy with your spreadsheet go to the **File** menu and click on **Page** **Setup**. Check your print options then click on **Print**.

Make a pie chart

To make a pie chart, press the **Ctrl** key and select the cells containing your types of bill in column A, and their respective yearly totals in the Totals column (here, column N). Click the **Chart Wizard** toolbar button. In the Chart Wizard dialogue box select **Pie** from the 'Chart type' window, then a style from the 'Chart sub-type' pane. Click **Finish**. Your chart will appear in your spreadsheet. Click on it and drag it into position. To resize it, click and drag one of the corner tabs.

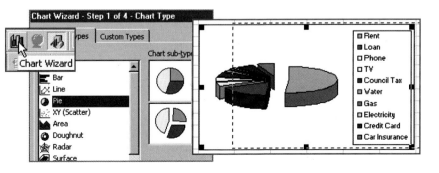

Chart Wizard - Step 1 of 4 - Chart Type

Chart Wizard

Types | Custom Types

Chart sub-type

- Bar
- Line
- Pie
- XY (Scatter)
- Area
- Doughnut
- Radar
- Surface

Rent
Loan
Phone
TV
Council Tax
Water
Gas
Electricity
Credit Card
Car Insurance

Calculate your car costs

Use your PC to help you get the best mileage for your money

A spreadsheet is ideal for monitoring all sorts of expenditure. As well as creating a budget planner for all your household expenses (see page 252), it's also possible to keep close track of large, individual expenses, such as buying and running a car or building an extension to your house.

By recording all your motoring expenses you can work out your annual costs and build up a comprehensive analysis of your car's value for money. You can also anticipate motoring bills, and so plan a budget to accommodate them. Perhaps you could put away a fixed amount of money every month. Then, if a major expense such as emergency repairs crops up, you will be better prepared.

Once you have set up the car running costs spreadsheet here, all the calculation work will be done for you. All you have to do is enter your monthly figures.

Write down all the costs your car incurs. Include repayments, road tax, insurance, spare parts and servicing, as well as oil and fuel.

BEFORE YOU START

1 Go to the **Start** menu, select **Programs** then **Microsoft Excel**. A blank spreadsheet will open. Go to the **File** menu and select **Save As**. Select a suitable folder in which to save your spreadsheet, type in a file name and then click on **Save**.

*You can use Microsoft Works to create a spreadsheet. Open Works, then, in the Works Task Launcher, click on the **Works Tool** tab then on the **Spreadsheet** button.*

OTHER PROGRAMS

Templates on CD-ROM

Short cut

If your columns are not wide enough to accommodate your text, place the cursor over the border between the column headings. When it changes to a double-headed arrow, double-click. The column will automatically resize itself to fit the text.

	A
25	Mileage
26	Month start
27	Month end
28	Monthly Total
29	
30	Cost per mile

Below the cell in which you type 'Mileage' (here, cell A25), type in 'Month start', 'Month end' and 'Monthly Total'. Two cells below that, type in 'Cost per mile'.

Car Costs

	A	B	C	D	E
1	Car Running Costs				
2					
3					
4	Vehicle Information				
5	Make:	Volkswagen			
6	Model:	Golf GTI			
7	Year:	1997			
8	Reg No:	P714 LYJ			
9	Price:	9,700			
10					
11					
12					
13					
14					
15					

Jan

Jan ... Jun

	A	B	C	D	E
1					
2					
3					
4	Vehicle Information				
5	Make:	Volkswagen			
6	Model:	Golf GTI			
7	Year:	1997			
8	Reg No:	P714 LYJ			
9	Price:	9,700			
10					
11			Jan	Feb	Mar
12	Expenses				
13					
14					
15					
16					
17					
18					

6	Model:	Golf GTI			
7	Year:	1997			
8	Reg No:	P714 LYJ			
9	Price:	9,700			
10					
11			Jan	Feb	Mar
12	Expenses				
13	Repayments				
14	Insurance				
15	Road tax				
16	MoT test				
17	Service				
18	Spare parts				
19	Oil				
20	Car valet				
21	Fuel				
22					
23	Total Costs				
24					
25	Mileage				

2 In cell **A1** type in a heading. In cell **A4** type 'Vehicle Information'. Continuing in the cells below, type in the headings as shown above, then fill in your car's relevant details in the adjoining cells in column B starting in cell **B5**.

3 Click on cell **C11** and type in 'Jan'. Place the cursor in the bottom right-hand corner of the cell. When it becomes a cross, click and drag until you reach column N. Excel will automatically enter the months of the year. Click on cell **A12** and type in 'Expenses'.

4 Starting in cell **A13**, and continuing in the cells below, type in your different types of car cost. Two cells below the final entry (here, **A23**) type in 'Total Costs'. Two cells below that, type in 'Mileage' (see above).

Merge and centre headings

It is possible to merge a number of cells together, then centre the contents within that 'larger' cell. This is particularly useful for headings – use it for your 'Car Running Costs' and 'Vehicle Information'.

To select the cells you wish to merge, click on the first one, then drag the cursor over the others. Now click the **Merge and Center** toolbar button.

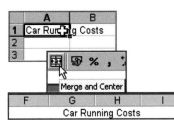

Bright idea

You can use your spreadsheet to calculate your fuel consumption. Enter a row for the amount of fuel bought in gallons/litres every month. Then divide the number of gallons/litres by the Total Monthly Mileage to work out how many gallons/litres your car uses per mile.

Total Costs | 0

Copy the formula for the other months of the year. Place the cursor in the lower right-hand corner of a cell. When it becomes a cross, click and drag until you reach column N. Excel will automatically update the cell references.

Bright idea

To account for annual bills, such as insurance, on a monthly basis, click on the relevant cell in January's column, type '=', the total annual amount, then '/12'. Eg (=515/12). Copy the formula to every month using the technique described left.

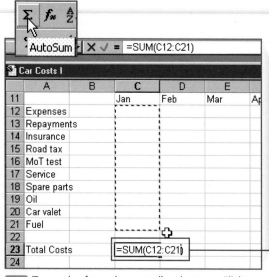

5 To set the formula for working out monthly costs, click the Total Costs cell for January (here, **C23**), then the **AutoSum** toolbar button. Click and drag over the cells to be added together then press **Enter**. Copy the formula for other months (see above).

6 To enter a formula for the total monthly mileage for January, click the relevant cell (here, **C28**) and type '='. Click the 'Month end' for January cell (**C27**), type '-', then click the 'Month start' for January cell (**C26**). Press **Enter**. Copy the formula to the other months.

7 To enter a formula for the total cost per mile for January, click the relevant cell (here, **C30**) and type '='. Then click the 'Total Costs' for January cell (**C23**), then '/', then the cell for January's mileage total (**C28**). Press **Enter**. Copy the formula to the other months.

Styling your work

To style the text in your spreadsheet and add some colour, first select the relevant cell or cells. (To style several cells in the same way at the same time, click and drag the cursor over them, or click on the first cell, hold down the **Shift** key, and click on the other cells in turn.)

Now go to the **Format** menu and click on **Cells**. Click on the various tabs and select a suitable font, size, style, effect and background colour. Click **OK**.

To create a border, select the cells then click on the **Border** tab in the Format Cells dialogue box. Select a style and colour, click **Outline** and then **OK**.

To align text to the left, right or centre, click on the relevant cells then on the appropriate alignment toolbar button.

Watch out

Don't be alarmed if you see '#DIV/0!' in any of your cells. It means that Excel is trying to divide a number by zero. This will change when you enter figures for your spreadsheet and AutoSum has something to work with.

99	0.74	
66	19055	
67	489	6499
56	0.69	=SUM(O23/O28)

*To calculate your annual cost per mile, click on the cell to the right of December's Cost Per Mile (here, **O30**), type '=', then click on the cell for the Total Annual Costs (**O23**), then type '/' (division sign on the numeric keypad). Now click on the cell for the Total Annual Mileage (**O28**). Press **Enter**.*

C	D	E	F	G	H
Jan	Feb	Mar	Apr	May	Jun
175.25	175.25	175.25	175.25	175.25	175
42.76	42.76	42.76	42.76	42.76	42
0	0	150	0	0	
0	0	22	0	0	
0	0	254.26	0	0	
25.45	0	12.96	23.55	0	
5.99	5.99	5.99	5.99	5.99	5
35	35	35	35	35	
97.56	79.98	85.87	75.3	89.03	98
382.01	338.98	784.09	357.85	348.03	355

M	N	O
	Dec	Annual Costs
175.25	175.25	=SUM(C13:N13)
42.76	42.76	

K				O
Sep			Dec	Annual Costs
175.25	175.25	175.25	175.25	Annual Costs
42.76	42.76	42.76	42.76	2103
0	0	0	0	
0	0	0	0	
0	0	0	0	
0	17.69	12.51	0	
5.99	5.99	5.99	5.99	
35	35	35	35	
88.90	91.76	99.67	78.67	
347.9	368.45	371.18	337.67	

J	K	L	M	N	O
	Sep	Oct	Nov	Dec	Annual Costs
175.25	175.25	175.25	175.25	175.25	2103
42.76	42.76	42.76	42.76	42.76	513.12
0	0	0	0	0	150
0	0	0	0	0	22
.55	0	0	0	0	389.81
.44	0	17.69	12.51	0	107.6
.99	5.99	5.99	5.99	5.99	71.88
35	35	35	35	35	420
.42	88.90	91.76	99.67	78.67	1049.57
496.41	347.9	368.45	371.18	337.67	4826.98
16618	17110	17566	17899	18566	
17110	17566	17899	18566	19055	
492	456	333	667	489	=SUM(O28:N28)

6499

8 Your spreadsheet is now ready for you to enter values. Click on the cells and type in the relevant amounts (enter '0' if you do not have a value). For payments that remain the same every month, type the figure in once then copy it to the other months.

9 Click on cell **O11** and type in 'Annual Costs'. To calculate the total annual costs for your first expense, click on cell **O13** then on **AutoSum**. Press **Enter**. Copy the formula into the cells below, stopping at the Total Costs row.

10 To calculate your annual mileage, click on the cell to the right of December's mileage Monthly Total (here, **O28**), then **AutoSum**. Press **Enter**. (To calculate your annual cost per mile, see above.) To print, go to the **File** menu and click on **Print**.

Calculating second car costs

You can create a spreadsheet for a second car. Go to the **Edit** menu and select **Move or Copy Sheet**. In the dialogue box, make sure your spreadsheet is selected in the 'To book' box. Click on **Sheet 2** in the 'Before sheet' box, ensure the 'Create a copy' box is ticked, then click **OK**.

Rename the sheet tab by double-clicking on it and typing the new name. All you need do then is highlight any text or figures that need changing.

Move or Copy

Move selected sheets

To book:

Car Costs.xls

Before sheet:

Sheet1
Sheet2
Sheet3
(move to e

☑ Create a cop

Styling numbers

To give your values a uniform format, select all the cells in which you are to enter currency figures (not mileage). Go to the **Format** menu and click on **Cells**. In the Category window click on **Number**, and select **2** in the 'Decimal places' box. Click **OK**.

Format Cells

Number | Alignment | Font | Border | P

Category:
General
Number
Currency
Accounting

Sample
175.25

Decimal places: 2

Build a shares portfolio

Follow the stock market with your own monthly guide

A spreadsheet is an excellent tool for taking care of financial calculations, and there's nothing quite as confusing as fluctuating share prices. Because share prices change continually, it's a good idea to assess their performance every month. Your financial adviser or stockbroker will be able to give you detailed advice about the best strategy for buying and selling shares, but using a spreadsheet means you can keep a close watch on the overall trends of all your shareholdings.

Save As		
Save in:	Stocks and shares portfolio	
		Save
File name:	Share Table	
Save as type:	Microsoft Excel Workbook	

1 Go to the **Start** menu, select **Programs** then click on **Microsoft Excel**. Save and name your new document by clicking on the **Save** toolbar button. Type in a file name then select a folder in which to save it in the 'Look in' box. Click on **Save**.

Templates on CD-ROM

To adjust the width of a column to accommodate your text, double-click on the right-hand edge of the grey column heading. The column will adjust to fit the widest piece of text in that column.

To style your text, highlight it then select a font, size and style from the toolbar.

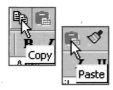

To copy and paste your formula, highlight it then click on the **Copy** toolbar button. Highlight all the cells you want the formula to appear in, then click on the **Paste** toolbar button.

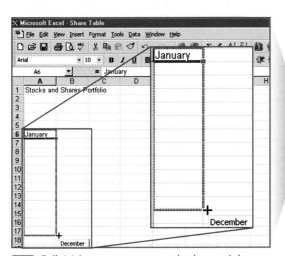

B	C	D	E	F	G	H
Cable & Wireless		**General Motors**		**Coca-Cola**		**Total portfolio value (£)**
Share price	No. of shares	Share price	No. of shares	Share price	No. of shares	=(B6*C6+D6*E6+F6*G6)/100

2 Cell A1 is automatically selected. Type in your heading. Click on cell **A6** and type in 'January'. Place the mouse pointer over the lower right-hand corner of the cell. When it becomes a cross, click and drag down the column until 'December' appears.

3 Click in cell **B4** and type in the first company name. Select **B4** and **C4** then click the **Merge and Center** toolbar button. In cell **B5** type in 'Share price' and in **C5** type in 'No. of shares'. Continue to enter company names along row 4 as shown.

4 Click in cell **H4** and type 'Total portfolio value (£)'. In cell **H6** (this is the row of your first month) type in '=' then your formula (see below). Press the **Enter** key. Enter the formula into the cells below for subsequent months by copying and pasting it.

You don't need to start your Shares Portfolio with January. Type in whichever month you want, then click and drag the cursor as described in Step 2. The program will fill in the other months automatically.

Calculating your shares
The formula for calculating the total share portfolio needs to multiply the current share price by the number of shares for each company and then add them together (place this part of the formula in brackets).

To convert the value into pounds sterling, you must then divide by 100 (share prices are given in pence). Here, the formula is: '(B6*C6+D6*E6+F6*G6)/100'.

You don't need to type cell references into the formula – simply click on the cells themselves at the appropriate point to enter them.

B	C	D	E	F	G	H
Cable & Wireless		**General Motors**		**Coca-Cola**		**Total portfolio value (£)**
Share price	No. of shares	Share price	No. of shares	Share price	No. of shares	=(B6*C6+D6*E6+F6*G6

Cells that contain formulas will display '0' until you enter figures in the relevant share price and share number cells. The calculation cells will update themselves automatically as you enter these figures.

Watch out
Remember that the cell references here are correct for those who hold shares in three companies. For those who hold shares with fewer or more companies, you must adjust the references.

H	I
Total portfolio value (£)	Monthly change in value (£)
0	
0	=H7-H6
0	
0	
0	
0	
0	
0	
0	
0	
0	
0	

Format menu items shown:
Format Tools Data Windo
- Cells...   Ctrl+1
- Row
- Column
- Sheet
- AutoFormat...
- Conditional Formatting...

H	I
Initial portfolio value (£)	
22286.50	
Total portfolio value (£)	**Monthly change in value (£)**
22276.50	-10.00
22247.00	-29.50
22221.50	-25.50
22206.00	-15.50
22186.00	-20.00
22896.90	710.90
22908.20	11.30
22933.90	25.70
22387.60	-546.30
22732.00	344.40
22732.50	0.50
22726.70	-5.80
Yearly change in value(£)	440.20

H21 =

	A	B	C	D	Share price
1	Stocks and Shares Portfolio				3632
2					3628
3	Sell now	3632			3622
4		**Cable & Wireless**		G	3624
		Share price	No. of shares	Share	3603
	January	3632	100		3597
	February	3628	100		3626
	March	3622	100		3637
	April	3624	100		3644
10	May	3603	100		3648
11	June	3597	120		3653
12	July	3626	120		
13	August	3637	120		
14	September	3644	120		
15	October	3648	130		
16	November	3653	130		

5 Click in cell **I4** and type 'Monthly change in value (£)'. In cell **I7** (the row for your second month) enter a formula that subtracts the Total portfolio value in February (H7) from the Total value in January (H6). Press **Enter**. Copy and paste the formula into the cells below.

6 In **H2** type 'Initial portfolio value (£)'. In **H3** enter the total value of the shares when you bought them. To calculate the change in value for January, click in cell **I6** and type in '=H6-H3'. Type in your share price data and the formulas will update.

7 Now create a warning for when your share value falls below your selling price. In **A3** type in 'Sell now'. In **B3** enter the selling price for the first company. Highlight column B, go to the **Format** menu and click on **Conditional Formatting** (see below).

Yearly change in value(£)	
	440.20

*Click in cell **H19** and type 'Yearly change in value (£)'. In cell **I19** type in the formula '=H17-H3'.*

Set up a warning
In the Conditional Formatting dialogue box click on the arrow beside the second box and select **less than or equal to**. Click in the third box, then on the cell **B3**.
Click the **Format** button and select a font colour, then click **OK**. Share prices that are less than or equal to your selling price will appear in this colour. Repeat for all your share price columns.

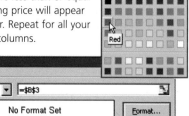

Conditional Formatting
Condition 1
Cell Value Is | less than or equal to | =B3
Preview of format to use when condition is true: | No Format Set | Format...

To highlight more than one column at a time, press the **Ctrl** key and click on each grey column heading in turn.

Stocks and Shares Portfolio

To style the heading, highlight it, go to the **Format** menu and click on **Cells**. Click on the **Font** tab and select a font, size, style and colour. Click **OK**.

To centre your heading, select cells **A1** to **I1** and click on the **Merge and Center** button. To add a background colour, click on the arrow beside the Fill Color toolbar button and select a colour from the drop-down palette.

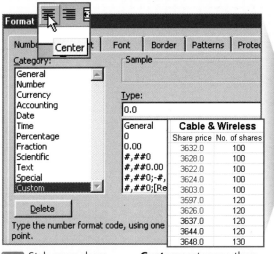

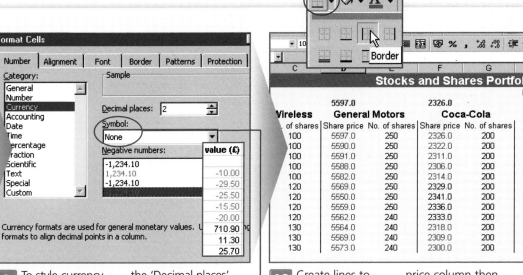

8 Style your share price columns by highlighting them, going to the **Format** menu and clicking on **Cells**. Click on the **Custom** category, then type in '0.0' in the Type box. Click **OK**. To centre columns, highlight them and click on the **Center** toolbar button.

9 To style currency, select columns H and I, go to the **Format** menu and click on **Cells**. Click on the **Currency** category. In the 'Decimal places' box type in '2'. In the 'Negative numbers' box click on your choice of style for negative amounts. Click on **OK**.

10 Create lines to separate your columns so that you can read your data more easily. Select the cells in each share price column then click on the arrow beside the Border toolbar button. Click on the button that adds a left border.

In the 'Symbol' box you can choose whether or not to display a currency symbol, such as '£' or '$'.

Printing your table

Your spreadsheet will probably be quite wide, so to make it fit on a sheet of A4 go to the **File** menu and select **Print Preview**. Click on the **Setup** button. The Page tab is selected. Click the Landscape option then, in the Scaling section, select the 'Fit to' option. Click **OK**.

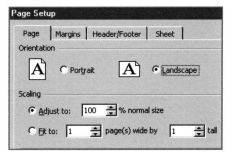

Manage a special event

Learn how to keep track of the budget, and raise money

Managing a budget for, say, a school play or a benefit dinner can be a complex business. Not only must you keep track of a range of expenses, but you also have to weigh up outgoings against projected income to ensure you make a profit. If that profit is earmarked for a particular use – a new computer lab, for instance – you will have a better idea of how much you need to raise, and so be able to budget accordingly.

Using a spreadsheet program on your PC will make light work of budget calculations and projections. Microsoft Excel also allows you to create accounts for specific aspects of a project such as ticket sales, and incorporate these within the accounts for the whole project.

Note each area in which you will have to spend money, and all sources of income. Ask colleagues to provide figures for their projects.

BEFORE YOU START

Save As

Save in: New Productions

File name: Summer show

Save as type: Microsoft Excel Workbook

Save

1 Go to the **Start** menu, select **Programs** and click on **Microsoft Excel**. Save your document by going to the **File** menu and selecting **Save As**. In the 'Save in' box select a suitable folder for it to be stored in, type in a file name, then click on **Save**.

You can create a similar spreadsheet in Microsoft Works. However, Works does not have multiple worksheets within the same document, so you must create separate documents for each area of budgeting.

OTHER PROGRAMS

Key word

Format *This refers to the process of setting the appearance of text (font, style, size and colour), and figures in cells (number, currency, date, etc).*

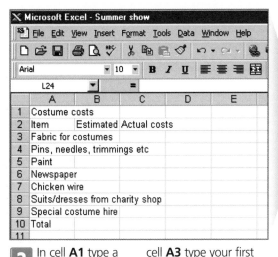

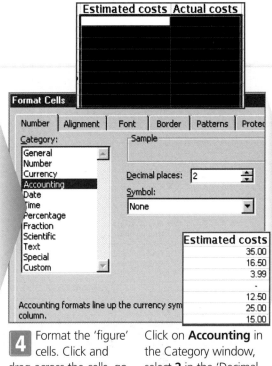

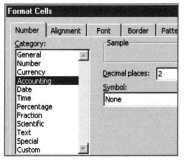

2 In cell **A1** type a heading for your first sheet; in cell **A2** type 'Item'; in cell **B2** 'Estimated costs'; and in cell **C2** 'Actual costs'. In cell **A3** type your first expense, continuing to enter expenses in the cells below. In the cell below your final expense type 'Total'.

3 To style your text, click on the cell, go to the **Format** menu and click on **Cells**. Click on the **Font** tab in the dialogue box. Select a font, style, size and colour, then click **OK**. To style several adjacent cells in the same way at once, click and then drag over the cells.

4 Format the 'figure' cells. Click and drag across the cells, go to the **Format** menu and click on **Cells**. Click on the **Number** tab. Click on **Accounting** in the Category window, select **2** in the 'Decimal places' box and **None** in the Symbol box. Click **OK**. Enter the estimates.

To adjust the width of a column to accommodate your text, double-click on the right-hand edge of the grey column heading. The column will automatically adjust to fit the widest piece of text in that column.

The Accounting format

When you select the Accounting format for cells, the decimal points and currency symbols (if you use them) are aligned directly above each other, making your account-keeping easier.

You should also be aware that when you type '0' into a cell to indicate that there is no cost, it will be expressed as '-' as soon as you click out of that cell.

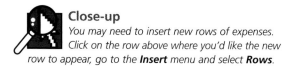

Close-up
*You may need to insert new rows of expenses. Click on the row above where you'd like the new row to appear, go to the **Insert** menu and select **Rows**.*

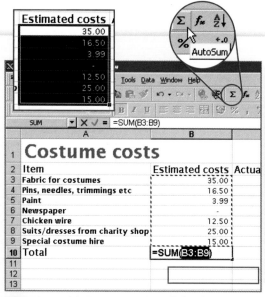

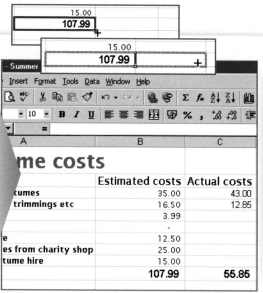

Costume costs

	A	B
1	Costume costs	
2	Item	Estimated costs Actual
3	Fabric for costumes	35.00
4	Pins, needles, trimmings etc	16.50
5	Paint	3.99
6	Newspaper	-
7	Chicken wire	12.50
8	Suits/dresses from charity shop	25.00
9	Special costume hire	15.00
10	Total	=SUM(B3:B9)
11		
12		
13		

SUM = =SUM(B3:B9)

me costs

	A	B	C
		Estimated costs	Actual costs
	tumes	35.00	43.00
	trimmings etc	16.50	12.85
		3.99	
		-	
	e	12.50	
	es from charity shop	25.00	
	tume hire	15.00	
		107.99	55.85

You can keep accounts for various aspects of the same project within one Excel document. Simply create a separate worksheet for each one (see below left).

ADD MORE WORKSHEETS

Sheet1 \ Sheet2 \ Sheet3

	A	B	C	D
1	Ticket sales (estimated)			
2	No.	Item	Ticket price	Estimated revenue
3	500	Standard seats	3.00	
4	100	Privilege seats	4.00	
5	200	Children's seats	1.50	
6			Total	
7				
8				
9	Ticket sales (actual)			
10	No.	Item	Ticket price	Actual revenue
11	389	Standard seats	3.00	
12	79	Privilege seats	4.00	
13	184	Children's seats	1.50	
14			Total	
15				

5 Now add up your figures in the Estimated costs column. Click in the Total cell for column B (here, **B10**), then click the **AutoSum** button on the toolbar. Press the **Enter** key and the total will appear.

6 Copy the formula for Actual costs. Click the Total cell for Estimated costs (here, **B10**) then place the cursor in its lower right-hand corner. When it turns into a cross, click and drag across to the Actual costs column. The sum will adjust as you enter each cost.

7 To create a second worksheet for, say, income from tickets, click on the **Sheet2** tab at the bottom of the screen. The spreadsheet above has sections for estimated and actual revenue from sales of differently priced seats.

Naming and adding worksheets

To make it easier to navigate between worksheets, rename them. To rename Sheet1 double-click on the **Sheet1** tab at the bottom of the screen and type in a title (here, Costumes), then click away.

To add more worksheets, go to the **Insert** menu and click on **Worksheet**. A new one will appear. To re-order the sequence of worksheets, click on its tab at the bottom of the screen and drag it to its new position.

Adding grids

To enclose your worksheet details in a grid, select the relevant cells, go to the **Format** menu and click on **Cells**. In the dialogue box click on the **Border** tab. First, select a Line Style and colour, then, in the Presets section, click on the **Outline** and **Inside** buttons, then click **OK**.

To add a background colour, select the cells, go to the **Format** menu and click on **Cells**. Click on the **Patterns** tab. In the 'Cell shading' section click on your choice of colour, then click **OK**.

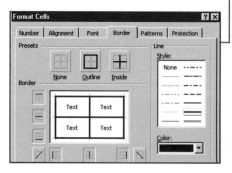

Watch out
If you name your worksheets you must use the new names, rather than Sheet1, 2, etc, when referring to them in cell references. So, you might type 'Costumes!B10' rather than 'Sheet1!B10'.

Ticket price	Estimated revenue
3.00	=A3*C3
4.00	

Lucida Sans ▼ 12 ▼ B I U
SUM ▼ X ✓ = =SUM(D3:D5)

	A	B	C	D
1	**Ticket sales (estimated)**			
2	No.	Item	Ticket price	Estimated reven
3	500	Standard seats	3.00	1,500
4	100	Privilege seats	4.00	400
5	200	Children's seats	1.50	300
6			Total	=SUM(D3:D5)
7				
8				
9	**Ticket sales (actual)**			
10	No.	Item	Ticket price	Actual revenue
11		Standard seats	3.00	
12		Privilege seats	4.00	
13		Children's seats	1.50	

	A	B	C
1	**Budget summary - summer production**		
2	Item	Estimated costs	Actual costs
3	Costumes	=Sheet1!B10	
4	Refreshments		
5	Props		
6	Printing/publicity		
7	Total		
	Item	Estimated revenue	Actual revenue
	Refreshments		
12	Tickets		
13	Total		
14			
15	**Balance**		
16			
17			
18			

107.99

	A	B	C
1	**Budget summary - summer production**		
2	Item	Estimated costs	Actual costs
3	Costumes	107.99	
4	Refreshments	144.24	
5	Props	98.00	
6	Printing/publicity	50.00	
7	Total	400.23	
	Item	Estimated revenue	Actual revenue
	Refreshments	330.00	
12	Tickets	2,200.00	
13	Total	2,530.00	
14			
15	**Balance**		
16			
17			

8 To estimate income from standard seat sales, click in the relevant cell (here, **D3**), type '=' then a formula for the total seats multiplied by the price (A3*C3). Repeat for other seats. Click in the Total cell (**D6**), click **AutoSum** and press **Enter**. Repeat for actual sales.

9 Open a worksheet to add up costs and revenue of the individual parts of the project. Create columns as shown. In the costs and revenue columns enter the sheet and cell references of your totals for other worksheets. Eg: '= Sheet1!B10' (total for the Costumes Sheet).

10 Now calculate total costs and revenue. Click in the Total cell for Estimated costs (here, **B7**) click the **AutoSum** button and press **Enter**. Copy the formula into the Actual costs cell (see Step 6). Repeat for revenue. If you wish to work out balances, see below.

Calculating balances

To calculate Estimated and Actual balances, click in the Estimated Balance cell (here, **B15**), type '=', then a formula that subtracts the total estimated costs from the total estimated revenue (B13-B7). Press **Enter**. Copy and paste the formula into the Actual Balance cell (see Step 6).

5	Props	98.00
6	Printing/publicity	50.00
7	Total	400.23
8		
9		
10	Item	Estimated revenue
11	Refreshments	330.00
12	Tickets	2,200.00
13	Total	2,530.00
14	2,129.77	
15	Balance	=B13-B7

Printing out worksheets

To print a worksheet, first go to the **File** menu and click on **Print Preview** to see how it looks. To make adjustments press the **Esc** key and edit accordingly. When you're happy with how it looks, click **Print**, specify the pages you require then click **OK**.

275

Form a Neighbourhood

Your PC can make it easier for friends and neighbours

Project planner

Create a folder called 'Neighbourhood Watch'. Add sub-folders for mini-projects.

- Neighbourhood Watch
  - Membership
  - Contacts
  - Crime database
  - Holiday diary
  - Communications
  - Meetings & events

Any community-based project benefits from sound organisation, good communication and a high local profile. Your PC can help make each of these objectives achievable.

Neighbourhood Watch schemes rely on volunteer members keeping an eye on each other's properties, particularly during working hours and holiday periods. Knowing who is available to patrol the area, and which houses are unoccupied, will make your Neighbourhood Watch scheme more efficient.

The ideal starting point is to create a tailored membership form using a database program. Distribute this to prospective members then, when you receive the completed forms, enter the details into a members' database.

Your database will then help in identifying who is at home and who is out, and at what times. By including work and holiday schedules, and using the program's 'sort' facility, you can compile a day-to-day list of unoccupied properties, the ones most at risk. Then, using the information

Watch group
to guard against local crime

on members' availability, you can produce a rota of neighbours who can keep an eye out for suspicious behaviour.

Once you have set up your scheme, your computer can help you to log incidents of crime. Use your database's Form Design feature to create an incident report form on which members can record the date, time, place and type of any incident.

If you set up a separate crime database you will soon be able to build up a profile of the types of crime that occur in your area and when crime is most likely to take place. You can then review your activities and patrols accordingly.

To raise the profile of your scheme, use your PC's graphics capabilities to design a poster for members to display in their windows. You could also design a letterhead for correspondence, and produce a newsletter to keep members informed of any special events and new members, as well as raise awareness of crime trends and home security.

And if you're connected to the Internet, you can take a look at the wide range of Neighbourhood Watch information on the World Wide Web. You'll find messaging forums, details on training, useful contact numbers, home insurance information and lists of the type of items that most appeal to thieves. You can even join a weekly e-mailing list, giving tips on, among other things, home security.

Starting your watch

- Search the Internet for information on setting up a Neighbourhood Watch scheme
- Canvas interest and arrange first meeting
- Appoint a group chairperson and other officials.
- Invite the local police to make a presentation
- Organise press coverage of launch and use it to recruit new members
- Arrange affiliation to a national/regional organisation
- Compile a patrol schedule and holiday diary, and set up a crime database

Ideas and inspirations

Below are project ideas to help you set up an effective Neighbourhood Watch group that the local community – and criminals – will take seriously. The projects can be adapted to your own requirements. And using the PC will cut down on paperwork.

168 **Membership database**
Record members' details, including contact phone numbers and car registration numbers.

164 **Create a newsletter**
Design an eye-catching publication to keep your neighbours informed of developments.

216 **Design a poster**
Attract attention to a forthcoming meeting or publicise your scheme.

182 **Create a diary**
Use this handy feature to keep track of members' travel plans, absences and availability.

146 **Design a letterhead**
Give your scheme's correspondence an official and businesslike appearance.

Also worth considering...

No matter how successful your group is, you may benefit from the experience of others.

96 **Search the Internet**
Find out more about established Neighbourhood Watch schemes, and correspond by e-mail.

Get Mail

Record a family history

Explore your past with a database of relatives and ancestors

Compiling a family history can be a hugely rewarding exercise. It's amazing how soon knowledge about a family's past is lost if no-one writes it down, but it is equally astonishing how much fascinating detail you can quickly and easily find out about your ancestors, once you start.

The database program in Microsoft Works is ideal for making systematic records of your family's history. Dates of birth, occupations, marriages and so on can all be noted – or left blank until your research bears fruit. You can also make space to record interesting facts about your forebears: the homes where they lived, the medals they won, famous people they met, the traces they left behind. Use your PC to explore your roots – your grandchildren will thank you for it one day.

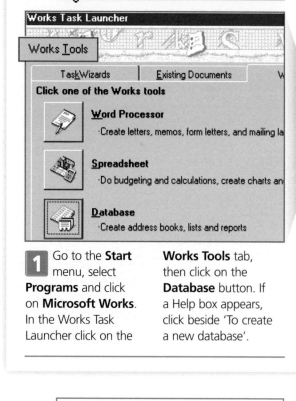

It's quicker to input all your information in one go. But don't worry if you need to do more research as it is easy to amend or add information at any time.

BEFORE YOU START

1 Go to the **Start** menu, select **Programs** and click on **Microsoft Works**. In the Works Task Launcher click on the **Works Tools** tab, then click on the **Database** button. If a Help box appears, click beside 'To create a new database'.

You can also create a family database in Microsoft Excel. This will let you input and view your data in table form, ready for sorting and styling according to your needs.

OTHER PROGRAMS

Templates on CD-ROM

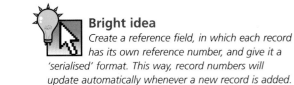

Bright idea
Create a reference field, in which each record has its own reference number, and give it a 'serialised' format. This way, record numbers will update automatically whenever a new record is added.

*To select more than one field at a time, press the **Ctrl** key and, keeping it pressed down, click on all the boxes you want to alter.*

✓		Record No	Surname
☐	1		
☐	2		
☐	3		
☐	4		
☐	5		
☐	6		
☐	7		
☐	8		
☐	9		
☐	10		

Form Design

Create Database

Add fields to create your database. To add a field, type a name and select a format for the field.

Field name: `Record No`

Format
- ○ General
- ○ Number
- ○ Date
- ○ Time
- ○ Text
- ○ Fraction
- ● Serialized

Appearance

Next value: `00001`

Increment: `1`

[Add]
[Done]

Record No:

MOUE

Surname:
Date of birth:
Mother:

First na
Place o
Father

Family History

Format

| Alignment | Font | Border |

Font: `es New Roman Special G1`
Size: `44`
Color: ▣ Dark Green

- Symbol
- Tahoma
- Tempus Sans ITC
- Times New Roman
- Times New Roman Spe
- Times New Roman Spe

| 24 |
| 30 |
| 32 |
| 36 |
| 40 |
| 48 |

Style
- ☑ Bold
- ☑ Italic
- ☐ Underline
- ☐ Strikethrough

Sample:

Family History

2 Now create fields, or categories, for your database. Type the name of your first field in the 'Field name' box and select a format for it. When you have named and formatted a field, click on **Add**. When you have entered all your fields click on the **Done** button.

3 Your database appears in List form. Now name and save it. Then customise the look of it by clicking on the **Form Design** toolbar button. To move a text box click on it and drag it. (To resize it, see below.) Leave space at the top of the page for a heading.

4 Click at the top of the page and type in your heading. To style it, highlight it then go to the **Format** menu and click on **Font and Style**. Select a font, size, colour and style for it, then click **OK**. Style your field names using the same method.

Fields and formats

Consider using the following fields and formats. For an added sense of history, include a field for biographical facts.

Field	Format	Field	Format
Record No.	Serialized	Married to	Text
Surname	Text	Marriage date	Date
First names	Text	Children	Text
Date of birth	Date	Occupation	Text
Place of birth	Text	Date of death	Date
Mother	Text	Burial place	Text
Father	Text	Notes	Text

Resizing text boxes

To increase the size of a text box, click on it then place the mouse pointer over the bottom right-hand corner. When the pointer changes to a double-headed arrow, click the mouse and, keeping the button pressed down, drag it across the screen.

Notes:

RESIZE

Different views

There are four ways to view your address list:

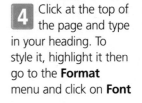

List View is best for quick reference. It lets you view several entries at the same time.

Form View displays one entry at a time and is clearer for entering data.

Form Design lets you add and delete fields and alter their layout.

Report View allows you to compile selective reports from your database.

*To move to the next field or record, press the **Tab** key. To move back, press the **Shift** and **Tab** keys.*

Key word
Report *A report extracts designated information from a database. For example, from your family database you could make a report on relatives who emigrated, or who fought in wars.*

Form View

Family His

Record No: 00020

Surname: Bromley

Date of birth: 06/02/1880

Mother: Not yet known

First names:

Place of birth:

Father:

Married to: Mary Bromley

Marriage date

List View

ormat Tools Window Help

10

"Grimley Moor Cemetery, Leeds

	Date of death	Burial place	
	/A	N/A	
	/A	N/A	
	03/54	Eversham Park Ce	Served in Dorset Regin
	2/71	Eversham Park Ce	
	06/62	Grimley Moor Cem	Arrested murderer Davi
	/01/62	Grimley Moor Cem	
	30/02/43	Banbury Cemetery	Drove "The Flying Scot
	14/07/40	Du Pont Cemetery	Worked as domestic s
	23/05/39	Leeds Municipal C	Served under Kitchene
	17/01/57	Highgate Cemetery	

Find

Find what: Bertram

Match
○ Next record   ● All records

dow Help

	Surname	First names	Date of birth
11	Bertram	Jim Bruce	29/11/59
12	Bertram	Sandra Kim	25/02/60
14	Bertram	Jamie Stuart	13/08/85
15	Bertram	Hayley Sonia	13/08/85
26			
27			
28			
29			
30			
31			
32			

5 To enter information, first click on the **Form View** toolbar button. Click on the text boxes adjoining the field names and type in the relevant data. To move to the next field or record, press the **Tab** key. To move back, press the **Shift** and **Tab** keys.

6 When you have entered all your data click on the **List View** toolbar button to view your database. To see all the data in a particular cell, click on it. Its contents appear in the Entry bar at the top of the form.

7 To find a specific record or piece of information, such as everyone who has the same surname, go to the **Edit** menu and click on **Find**. Type a key word in the 'Find what' box, select the 'All records' option, then click **OK**. Works will display all relevant records.

Adding ClipArt

To decorate your 'Family Tree' database, go into 'Form Design' and click in the form. Go to the **Insert** menu and select **ClipArt**. Type 'Tree' into the 'Search for clips' box then press **Return**. Click on your choice of image, then on the **Insert clip** button on the pop-up toolbar. For details on resizing and repositioning your image, see page 188.

Scrolling

You can scroll through your records quickly by clicking the arrows either side of the Record counter at the foot of the Form View window.

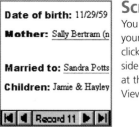

Date of birth: 11/29/59

Mother: Sally Bertram (n

Married to: Sandra Potts

Children: Jamie & Hayley

Record 11

You may want to create a report – in other words, print out all or parts of your database – for the family to see or to help you in your research.

CREATING A REPORT

*If the report's contents are too close together, click on **Modify** and adjust the column widths. Place the mouse pointer on the right-hand edge of the column heading, then click and drag to the right.*

To print all records, select the 'All records' option.

What to Print
- ○ All records
- ● Current record only

[OK]

Report Name [?][X]

Type a name for the report below:

[Family History]

| Grouping |

Fields available:

| Date of birth |
| Place of birth |
| Father |
| Mother |
| Married to |
| Marriage date |
| Children |
| Occupation |

[Add >]
[< Remove]
[Add All >>]
[<< Remove All]

Field order:

| Surname |
| First names |
| Date of birth |
| Father |
| Mother |
| Children |

Display options
- ☑ Show field names at top of each page
- ☐ Show summary information only

Family History

Surname	First names	Date of birth	Father
Potts	James Brian	11/10/57	Jeffrey P
Potts	Gillian	05/09/60	William V
West	Walter	25/09/08	Ernest W
West	Janice	01/01/11	Harold N
tts	Robert Alfred	06/03/14	Jacob P
tts	Alice	17/07/14	Henry B
otts	Jeffrey Francis	17/06/36	Robert P
Potts	Jane	15/10/36	William V
West			
West			
Bertram			
Bertram			
West			
Bertram			

ReportCreator

⚠ The report definition has been created.

Do you wish to preview or modify the report defin

[Preview] [Modify]

Family Histo

Record No: 00001

Surname: Potts

Date of birth: 11/10/57

Mother: Jane Potts (nee West)

Married to: Gillian West

Children: Robert & Emily

First names: James B

Place of birth: Putney

Father: Jeffrey Potts

Marriage date:

8 To create a printed record, go to the **Tools** menu and click on **ReportCreator**. Type in a name for your report and click **OK**.

Click the **Fields** tab. Click each field you want to print in turn, clicking on **Add** as you do so. When you have finished click on **Done**.

9 A prompt box appears. Press the **Preview** button to see how your report looks. If you are satisfied with the appearance,

click on **Print**. To make changes, press **Esc**, click on a section of text, go to the **Format** menu and click on **Font and Style**.

10 To print out a record in Form View, click on the **Print Preview** toolbar button. If you are happy with how it

looks, click **Cancel**, go to the **File** menu and select **Print**. Under 'What to Print' select the 'Current record only' option. Click **OK**.

Sorting your records

You can 'sort' or prioritise information within your database. For example, you may want to rank family members from the oldest to the youngest.

In the ReportCreator dialogue box click on the **Sorting** tab. Click on the arrow beside the first 'Sort by' box, scroll through and select the field you want – in this case, 'Date of birth'. Select the Ascending option, then click **Done**.

ReportCreator - Family History

| Title | Fields | Sorting | Grouping |

Sort by

[Date of birth ▼]

- ● Ascending
- ○ Descending

Then by

[(None) ▼]

- ● Ascending
- ○ Descending

Create a recipe collection

Keep all your family's favourites together in a database

Most people keep recipes in different places – in books, written down on bits of paper, or cut out from magazines. Tracking them all down can take time.

Save yourself the trouble by creating a recipe database. This allows you to keep all your recipes together, and lets you sort them to find the right recipe for the occasion. When you've found the recipe you want, you can print it out to use or make copies for friends. Once you've created your database, you can add new recipes as you discover them.

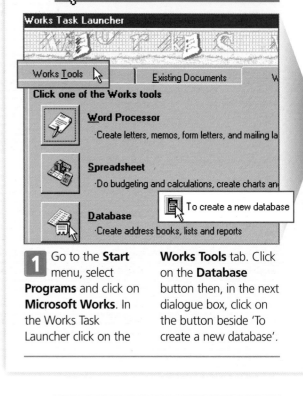

Give some thought to the type of information you want stored in your database. Don't worry if you can't find all your recipes when you start – add them at a later date.

BEFORE YOU START

Works Task Launcher

Works Tools | Existing Documents

Click one of the Works tools

Word Processor
·Create letters, memos, form letters, and mailing la

Spreadsheet
·Do budgeting and calculations, create charts an

To create a new database

Database
·Create address books, lists and reports

1 Go to the **Start** menu, select **Programs** and click on **Microsoft Works**. In the Works Task Launcher click on the **Works Tools** tab. Click on the **Database** button then, in the next dialogue box, click on the button beside 'To create a new database'.

You can also create a recipe collection in Microsoft Excel. This will let you input and view your recipes in table form, ready for sorting according to your needs.

OTHER PROGRAMS

Templates on CD-ROM

Bright idea
*Always include a serialised reference
number field in your database so that
each record will have a unique reference number.
Works automatically updates the number.*

*Once you have selected a
format, select a style for it
in the Appearance section.*

Create Database

Add fields to create your database. To add a field, type a name, select a format for the field.

Field name: | Recipe ref:

Format
- General
- Number
- Date
- Time
- Text
- Fraction
- ● Serialized

Appearance

Next value: | 00001

Increment: | 1

Recipe1

✔		Recipe ref	Recipe type	Recipe name	Date of entr
☐	1				
☐	2				
☐	3				
☐	4				
☐	5				
☐	6				
☐	7				
☐	8				
☐	9				
☐	10				
☐	11				
☐	12				
☐	13				
☐	14				
☐	15				
☐	16				
☐	17				
☐	18				

View Record Format Tools Win
- ✔ List   Shift+F9
- Form   F9
- Form Design   Ctrl+F9
- Report...
- ✔ Toolbar
- ✔ Gridlines
- Headers and Footers...

Recipe ref:
Recipe Type:
Recipe name:
Date of entry:
Calories:
Number served:
…o time:
…king time:
Ingredients:

Garnishes:

2 In the Create Database dialogue box input your field names. You can specify a format for each field. When you have typed in your field name click on **Add**. When you have entered all your fields click on **Done**. Save your document by clicking on the **Save** toolbar button.

3 Your database appears in List form with the field names appearing at the top of columns. To structure your database go to the **View** menu and select **Form Design**. You can now adjust the position and size of text boxes to make sure your recipe details are visible.

4 Click on the text box adjoining each field name. Keeping the mouse button pressed down, drag it into position. When positioning text boxes leave about 8 cm at the top of the page for your heading.

Format the fields like this:

Field	Format
Recipe ref	Serialized
Recipe type	Text
Recipe name	Text
Date of entry	Date
Ingredients	Text
Instructions	Text
Number served	Number
Calories	Number
Cooking time	Text

Field name:

Format
- General
- Number
- Date
- Time
- Text
- Fraction
- ● Serialized

Sizing field boxes

To increase the size of fields, click on the field box to highlight it then move the mouse pointer over the bottom right-hand corner. When the cursor changes to a double-headed arrow, click the mouse and, keeping the button pressed down, drag the box to the size you require.

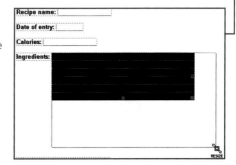

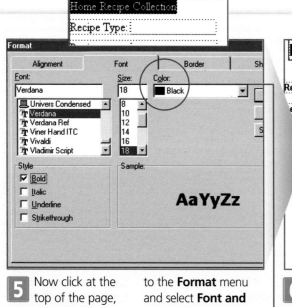

Close-up
When you type words into each field they will appear in the Entry Bar above your form. It is here that you correct typing mistakes and edit your text.

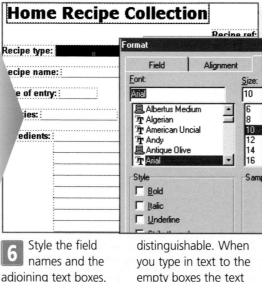

5 Now click at the top of the page, above your first field name, and type your heading. With your heading highlighted go to the **Format** menu and select **Font and Style**. In the dialogue box select a font, font size, colour and style. Click **OK**.

6 Style the field names and the adjoining text boxes, using different fonts for each to make them distinguishable. When you type in text to the empty boxes the text will appear in the style you have set.

7 To input recipes, go to the **View** menu and select **Form**. Type the information into the fields you have made. Press the **Tab** key to go to the next field or record, **Shift** and **Tab** to move back. When you have typed in all your recipes, click on the **List View** toolbar.

*If you have a colour printer, why not add colour to your recipes? In the Format dialogue box select white as your font colour then click on the **Shading** tab. Now select a foreground colour and pattern. Click **OK**.*

Short cut
*To style several field names or text boxes in the same way, click on the first box, press the **Ctrl** key and, keeping the Ctrl key pressed down, click on all the boxes you want to style. Go to the **Format** menu and select **Font and Style**. Now style as you wish.*

Bright idea
You can view your database at different levels of magnification by using the Zoom tool at the bottom of the screen. Simply click on the '+' and '-' buttons.

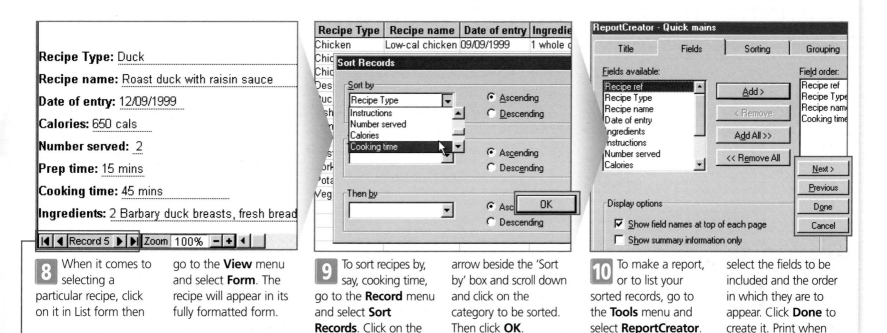

Recipe Type: Duck

Recipe name: Roast duck with raisin sauce

Date of entry: 12/09/1999

Calories: 650 cals

Number served: 2

Prep time: 15 mins

Cooking time: 45 mins

Ingredients: 2 Barbary duck breasts, fresh bread

| Record 5 | Zoom 100% |

8 When it comes to selecting a particular recipe, click on it in List form then go to the **View** menu and select **Form**. The recipe will appear in its fully formatted form.

9 To sort recipes by, say, cooking time, go to the **Record** menu and select **Sort Records**. Click on the arrow beside the 'Sort by' box and scroll down and click on the category to be sorted. Then click **OK**.

10 To make a report, or to list your sorted records, go to the **Tools** menu and select **ReportCreator**. Name your report then select the fields to be included and the order in which they are to appear. Click **Done** to create it. Print when you are satisfied.

Scrolling recipes

You can scroll through all the records on your database by clicking on the arrows in the record counter at the foot of the Form View window. This moves you through each formatted recipe.

Amending a report

To amend a report go to the **View** menu and select **Report**. Click on the report to be changed then click on **Modify**. To increase space between columns, adjust their width. Click on the right-hand edge of the column header and drag to the right.

Design a baby book

Keep a special book of memories for all the family to enjoy

Watching children grow up is one of the greatest pleasures in life, and creating a record of their early years allows you to relive the experience time and time again. By designing a baby book on your PC you can use as many photographs as you like, and print copies of the book for your relatives, without needing to make expensive photographic reprints.

Add a few personal design touches, and your baby book will delight your family for generations to come.

Work out which photographs you want to include in your book, and scan them in. For more information on scanning, see page 202.

BEFORE YOU START

1 Go to the **Start** menu, select **Programs** then click on **Microsoft Word**. A document will open. Go to the **File** menu and select **Page Setup**. Click on the **Paper Size** tab. Select your paper size and orientation. Click **OK**. Now save and name your document.

You can create a baby book using Microsoft Works. You can style your text as normal, but you need to import scanned photographs through Paint (see page 211 for details).

OTHER PROGRAMS

Templates on CD-ROM

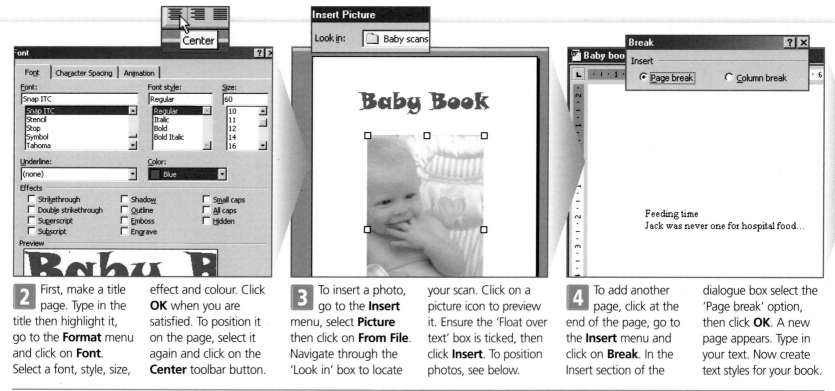

2 First, make a title page. Type in the title then highlight it, go to the **Format** menu and click on **Font**. Select a font, style, size, effect and colour. Click **OK** when you are satisfied. To position it on the page, select it again and click on the **Center** toolbar button.

3 To insert a photo, go to the **Insert** menu, select **Picture** then click on **From File**. Navigate through the 'Look in' box to locate your scan. Click on a picture icon to preview it. Ensure the 'Float over text' box is ticked, then click **Insert**. To position photos, see below.

4 To add another page, click at the end of the page, go to the **Insert** menu and click on **Break**. In the Insert section of the dialogue box select the 'Page break' option, then click **OK**. A new page appears. Type in your text. Now create text styles for your book.

Placing your pictures

To ensure you can move and resize pictures with ease, go to the **Insert** menu, select **Picture**, then click on **From File**. When the dialogue box appears, click in the box marked 'Float over text' so that it has a tick in it. You must do this before inserting any pictures.

Move a picture into position by clicking on it and dragging it. Resize a picture by clicking on a corner handle and dragging it diagonally.

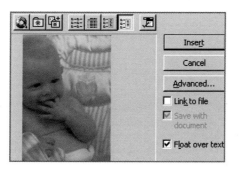

Page and picture borders

To add a border around a page, go to the **Format** menu and click on **Borders and Shading**. Click on the **Page Border** tab and choose the type of border you want. Click on the arrow beside the 'Apply to' box and scroll down to 'This section – First page only'. Then click **OK**.

To put a frame around a photo, click on the photo, go to the **Format** menu and click on **Borders and Shading** again. In the Line section of the dialogue box, select a colour, style and thickness. Then click **OK**.

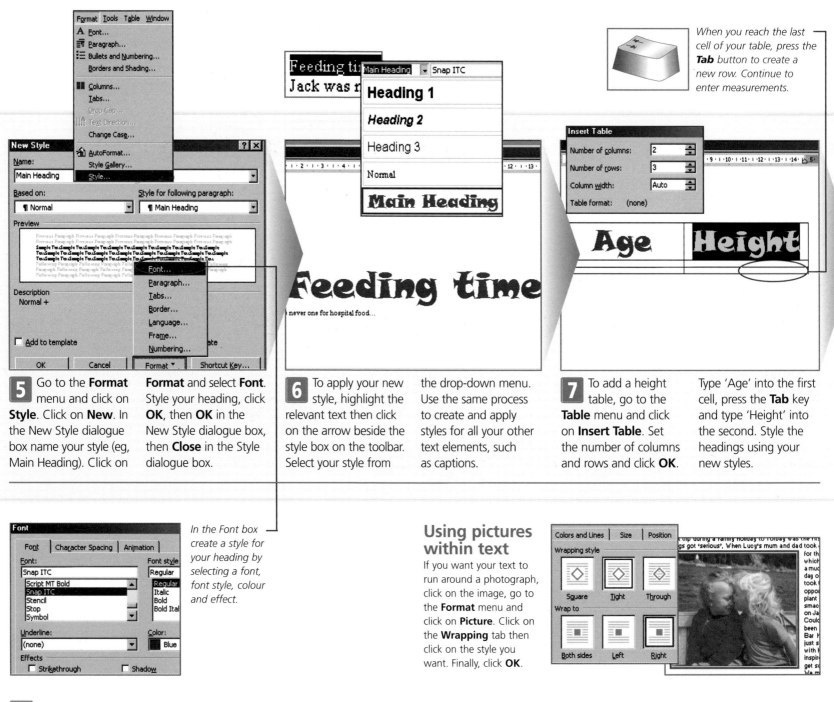

*When you reach the last cell of your table, press the **Tab** button to create a new row. Continue to enter measurements.*

5 Go to the **Format** menu and click on **Style**. Click on **New**. In the New Style dialogue box name your style (eg, Main Heading). Click on

Format and select **Font**. Style your heading, click **OK**, then **OK** in the New Style dialogue box, then **Close** in the Style dialogue box.

6 To apply your new style, highlight the relevant text then click on the arrow beside the style box on the toolbar. Select your style from

the drop-down menu. Use the same process to create and apply styles for all your other text elements, such as captions.

7 To add a height table, go to the **Table** menu and click on **Insert Table**. Set the number of columns and rows and click **OK**.

Type 'Age' into the first cell, press the **Tab** key and type 'Height' into the second. Style the headings using your new styles.

In the Font box create a style for your heading by selecting a font, font style, colour and effect.

Using pictures within text

If you want your text to run around a photograph, click on the image, go to the **Format** menu and click on **Picture**. Click on the **Wrapping** tab then click on the style you want. Finally, click **OK**.

Bright idea
You could also create a table of developmental milestones, in which you note down when your baby started smiling, crawling, talking, and so on.

*If you don't want your WordArt to appear on the title page, click on the **Page Setup** button on the Header and Footer toolbar. With the Layout tab selected, click in the 'Different first page' box, then click **OK**.*

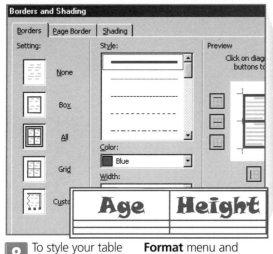

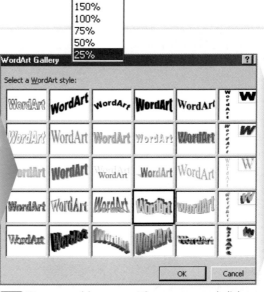

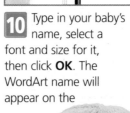

8 To style your table with coloured borders, etc, click in the table, go to the **Table** menu and click on **Select Table**. Go to the **Format** menu and click on **Borders and Shading**. Select a setting, line style, colour and width, then click **OK**.

9 You can add your baby's name to each page. Using the Zoom facility on the toolbar, view your page at 25%. Go to the **View** menu and click on **Header and Footer**. Go to the **Insert** menu and select **Picture** then **WordArt**. Click on a style then on **OK**.

10 Type in your baby's name, select a font and size for it, then click **OK**. The WordArt name will appear on the page. Click on it and drag it into position. The name will appear in the same position on every page of your baby book.

Print Preview

Once you have added all the elements to your book, go to the **File** menu and click on **Print Preview** to see how they look on the page. If you are happy, click on the **Print** toolbar button. If you need to make adjustments to the page, press the **Esc** key to return to your page layout.

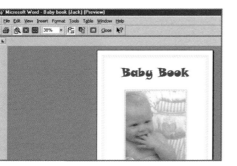

Watch your health

Keep a detailed record of your family's medical history

Everyone values their health, and that of their family, above all things. Yet few people keep accurate records of their own illnesses and treatments.

This information is useful in establishing patterns of illness, in providing up-to-date records for healthcare workers, and in keeping an account of medical and dental expenses.

With your PC, you can create a database that keeps detailed records of your family's health: what medications have been prescribed; dates of inoculations, check-ups and operations; allergies suffered. You can extract specific data when someone gets ill (for example, the name of a medicine that helped last time), and you can print out lists of future appointments.

Gather all the information you have about your family's health records, such as dates of check-ups, details of consultations, and so on.

► **BEFORE YOU START**

1 Go to the **Start** menu, select **Programs** and click on **Microsoft Works**. In the Works Task Launcher click on the **Works Tools** tab. Click on the **Database** button. If a First-time Help box appears, click on the button beside 'To create a new database'.

*You can create a family health database in Microsoft Excel. Go to the **Start** button, select **Programs** and click on **Microsoft Excel**. Enter your data into the grid that appears.*

► **OTHER PROGRAMS**

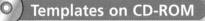
Templates on CD-ROM

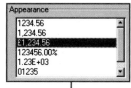

Some formats, such as Number and Date, give a choice of appearance. Click on your choice from the list displayed.

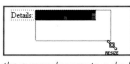

To resize a text box, click on it then place the mouse pointer over the bottom right-hand corner. When the cursor changes to a double-headed arrow, click the mouse and drag the corner until the box is the right size.

Bright idea
When styling your fields and text boxes, use different fonts for each one to make them stand out.

2 In the Create Database dialogue box input your field names. Type the name of your first field in the box, click a format for the field then click the **Add** button. Continue to add all the fields you want, then click **Done**. Your document appears in List form.

3 Name and save your document. To ensure your details are visible and appear as you wish, adjust the design of your file. Click on the **Form Design** toolbar button. Click on the text boxes and drag them to move them. To adjust the size of text boxes, see above.

4 To add a heading to each record, click at the top of the form and type it in. Highlight it, go to the **Format** menu and select **Font and Style**. Select a font, size, colour and style. Click **OK**. In the same way, style the field boxes and adjoining text boxes.

Fields and formats

For a family health database, you might want to create these fields together with these formats.

Field	Format
Record ref	Serialized
Name	Text
Date of birth	Date
Consult type	Text
Consult date	Date
Appoint time	Time
Appoint type	Text
Details	Text
Comments	Text
Treatment cost	Number

Let the Wizard help

The Microsoft Works Wizard has five health databases already set up – Medication Record, Hospital & Illness Record, Family Medical History, Dental Record and Personal Medical History.

Go to the **Start** menu, select **Programs** then click on **Microsoft Works**. In the Works Task Launcher click on **User Defined Templates** in the pane, then scroll down to the health templates. Click on one to open it.

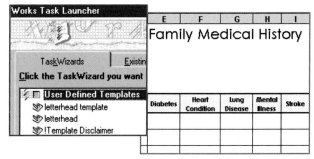

In Form View you can move through entries quickly by clicking on the arrows either side of the Record counter at the foot of the window. To change the magnification of the screen, click on the '+' or '-' signs beside the Zoom tool.

| ◄◄ | ◄ | Record 16 | ► | ►► | Zoom | 100% | – | + |

You can extract and print data from your database. It's a good idea, for example, to print out a list of future appointments to put on display.

SORTING AND PRINTING

Form View

Family Health Reco

Name: John

Consult type: Optician   Record ref : 000

Consult date: 01/03/00   Appoint type: Ch

Appoint time: Treatment cost:

Details:

Comments:

List View

"Rosie unable to go to playschool to

Family Health Records

	Record ref	Name	Consult type	Consult date
1	00001	Rosie	GP	23/02/99
2	00002	John	GP	01/03/99
3	00003	John	Dentist	03/02/99
4	00004	Robert	Dentist	11/01/99
5	00005	Robert	Dentist	15/01/99
6	00006	Robert	Dentist	22/01/99
7	00007	John	Optician	05/03/99
8	00008	Gill	Dentsit	01/07/99
9	00009	John	GP	01/10/99
10	00010	Gill	GP	01/10/99
11	00011	Robert	GP	01/10/99

lame	Consult type	Consult date	Appoint time	Appoint type
	GP	23/02/99	11:00 AM	Runny nose
	GP	01/03/99	08:30 AM	Vaccinations
	Dentist	03/02/99	03:00 PM	Checkup
	Dentist	11/01/99	08:00 AM	Painful tooth

Find

Find what: John   OK   Cancel

Match: ○ Next record   ● All records

Record ref	Name	Consult type	Consult date
00002	John	GP	01/03/99
00003	John	Dentist	03/02/99
00007	John	Optician	05/03/99
00009	John	GP	01/10/99
00014	John	Dentist	01/02/00

5 To enter your first record, click on the **Form View** toolbar button. Click on the text boxes and type in the relevant data. Press the **Tab** key to move to the next field, and **Shift** and **Tab** to move back. When you finish a record, press **Tab** to take you to the next.

6 To see all your records at a glance, click on the **List View** toolbar button. If you cannot see all the information in a particular cell, click on it then view the contents in the Entry bar at the top of the screen.

7 To search for specific data in List View, go to the **Edit** menu and click on **Find**. Type in a key word for what you want to search for (here, records involving John), select the 'All records' option, then click **OK**. All records concerning John will appear in a list.

Background colour

You can give the background of your form a colour and pattern. In Form Design click on an area of white space, outside a field or text box, go to the **Format** menu and click on **Shading**. Select a pattern and background colour from the choices available, then click **OK**.

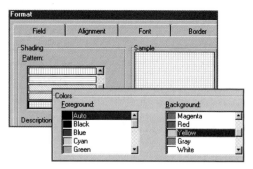

Showing all

To see all your records after you've done a Find search or created a Report, go to the **Record** menu, select **Show** then click on **All Records**.

Bright idea
To make an appointments list you probably won't need all your fields. Choose Consult date, Name, Consult type, Appoint time and Appoint type in that order.

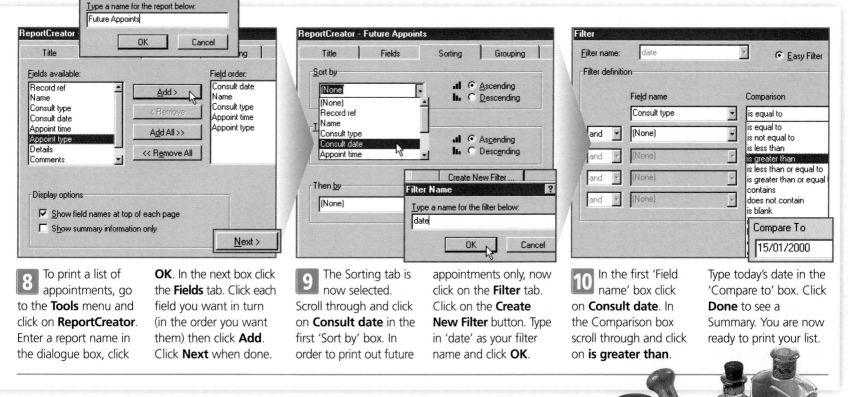

8 To print a list of appointments, go to the **Tools** menu and click on **ReportCreator**. Enter a report name in the dialogue box, click

OK. In the next box click the **Fields** tab. Click each field you want in turn (in the order you want them) then click **Add**. Click **Next** when done.

9 The Sorting tab is now selected. Scroll through and click on **Consult date** in the first 'Sort by' box. In order to print out future

appointments only, now click on the **Filter** tab. Click on the **Create New Filter** button. Type in 'date' as your filter name and click **OK**.

10 In the first 'Field name' box click on **Consult date**. In the Comparison box scroll through and click on **is greater than**.

Type today's date in the 'Compare to' box. Click **Done** to see a Summary. You are now ready to print your list.

Printing your list

Once you have sorted your fields and set up a filter system you can print out your document.

Click on **Preview** to see your new report, then click on the **Print** button.

Family Health Records - Future Appoints				
Consult date	**Name**	**Consult type**	**Appoint time**	**Appoint type**
01/02/00	John	Dentist	09:45 AM	Check-up
14/02/00	Robert	Dentist	10:00 AM	Check-up
21/02/00	John	Optician	11:30 AM	Check-up
23/02/00	Gill	Dentist	02:00 PM	Check-up
24/02/00	Robert	GP	03:45 PM	Blood test

Plan a new kitchen

Try out a variety of room designs to find the one that suits you

Drawing up a plan for your new kitchen helps you decide how best to arrange it for ease of use and optimum storage. You can create a two-dimensional plan on your PC using Microsoft Word. The plan can be easily adjusted as you make new additions, and you can create several alternative versions for comparison.

When you are planning your kitchen think about how you will use it. If you do a lot of cooking, make sure you have plenty of work surfaces and that the three key elements (cooker, fridge and sink) are close to each other and easily accessible.

Measure the dimensions of your kitchen, including all doors, windows and appliances. Also note the position of electrical sockets and plumbing outlets.

► BEFORE YOU START

1 Go to the **Start** menu, select **Programs** then click on **Microsoft Word**. A document opens. Go to the **Insert** menu and select **Text Box**. Click in the top left of the page and drag down to the bottom right of the page to create an outline for your kitchen.

It isn't possible to create a detailed plan to scale in Microsoft Works or Windows accessory program, Paint. However, you can buy specialised interior design programs.

► OTHER PROGRAMS

Templates on CD-ROM

In the Line section select a colour, style and width for your kitchen border.

 *As soon as you have opened your new document, save and name it. Click on the **Save** toolbar button and save the document into a suitable folder.*

Format Text Box

| Colors and Lines | Size | Position | Wrapping | Picture |

Size and rotate

Height: `25 cm` Width: `17.5 cm`

Rotation: `0°`

Scale

Height: `104 %`

☐ Lock aspect ratio
☐ Relative to original picture

Original size

Height:

Format Text Box

| Colors and Lines | Size | Position |

Fill

Color:

Line

Color:

Dashed:

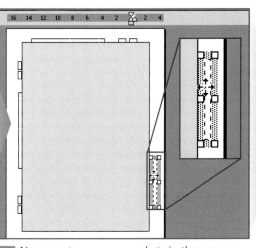

Format Text Box

| Colors and Lines | Size | Position | Wrapping | Picture |

Fill

Color: ☐ Semitransparent

Line

Color: Style:

Dashed: Weight:

Arrows

Begin style: End style:

Begin size: End size:

2 To make sure your text box is to scale, go to the **Format** menu and select **Text Box**. Click on the **Size** tab. Specify the height and width of your box. Click on the **Colors and Lines** tab and select a colour for your box in the Fill section. Click **OK**.

3 Now create individual text boxes for all your fixed features, such as doors, windows and electrical sockets in the same way. To move them, click on the edge of the box and drag to the required position.

4 It's a good idea to colour the fixed features in the same way. To select all the boxes at once, press the **Shift** key and click on each of them. Go to the **Format** menu and click on **Text Box**. Click on the **Colors and Lines** tab, select a colour and click **OK**.

Drawing to scale

Measure your kitchen in centimetres, then choose a scale so that it fits onto an A4 page. For example, if your kitchen measures 650 cm by 450 cm, divide each figure by 25 to create a box of 26 cm by 18 cm. Scale all your elements in the same way.

Avoid clashes

To indicate the space needed to open a door, draw an arc. Go to the **Insert** menu, select **Picture**, then click on **AutoShapes**.

Click on the **Basic Shapes** button on the AutoShapes toolbar. Click on the **Arc** icon, then click on your document and draw. Add a straight line to form a complete segment. Adjust the arc's shape and size by clicking on a handle and dragging it.

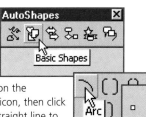

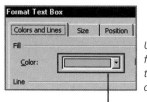

Use different colours for each appliance to make them distinguishable.

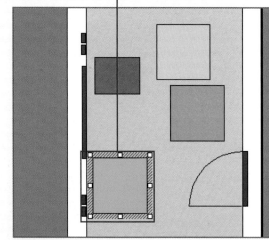

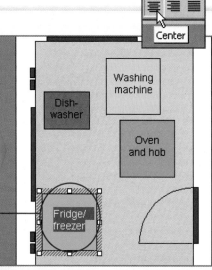

5 You now have the basic structure of your kitchen in place. Create more text boxes to represent your floor-standing

appliances, such as a washing machine and cooker. Remember to scale them the same way you scaled your kitchen dimensions.

6 To name an appliance, click in the box and type the name. To move the text down, click at the start of the word

and press the **Return** key. To position it centrally within the text box, highlight it then click on the **Center** toolbar button.

7 Move your appliances into position by clicking on the edge of the boxes and dragging them.

Remember to allow for the space needed to open appliance doors. If you wish, draw arcs to indicate them.

Style changes
To change the size and font of your text, highlight it, go to **Format** menu and click on **Font**. Select a font and size then click **OK**. To rotate text, go to the **Format** menu and click on **Text Direction**. Select an option in the Orientation section then click **OK**.

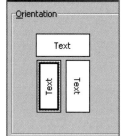

*You may find it easier to position the items on your plan by increasing the magnification of your page. Click on the arrow beside the Zoom tool on the toolbar and click on **Whole Page**.*

Watch out
If you create a multi-levelled plan, you must create the text boxes on the lowest level first, then proceed upwards. Otherwise, some elements will be hidden.

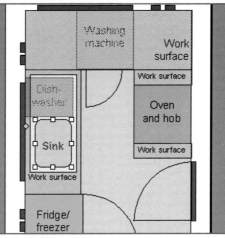

8 Create a semi-transparent text box for your work surface. This will allow you to see the floor-standing items below.

Go to the **Format** menu and select **Text Box**. In the Fill section select a colour and click in the Semitransparent box. Click **OK**.

9 Continue to add and position as many elements as you need. Take into account door spacing and the floor space needed to move around comfortably. Experiment with repositioning items to see the effect. You can save different versions for comparison.

10 Finally, add smaller items such as the microwave and toaster. They need not be exactly to scale as this is merely to show you whether your design is feasible in terms of your electric sockets. To print out a copy of your plan, click on the **Print** toolbar button.

Creating different plans

You don't need to start from scratch to create different versions of your plan – you just save them as you go along.

Whenever you want to save a version of what you have done, go to the **File** menu and click on **Save As**. Give the plan a different name to the original (eg, Kitchen plan 2) then click on **Save**.

Bright idea
Add wall units to your plan by creating semitransparent boxes as described in Step 8.

Take the effort and stress out

Finding, buying and moving to a new property is hard work – make sure

Project planner

Create a folder called 'Moving House.' Add folders to cover each part of the process.

- Moving House
  - Mortgage
  - Solicitor
  - House details
  - Correspondence
  - New house
  - Moving out letters

Moving house can be one of the most exciting events of your life, but also one of the most stressful. Big decisions and large amounts of money are involved, and you will need all the help you can get to make the process go smoothly.

You can get your PC involved as soon as you start looking for a new home. Use the Internet to look for property, gather information about mortgages, find a solicitor, and investigate the local amenities in the place you want to move to.

Before deciding which is the best mortgage for you, you could input the details of different packages into a spreadsheet program and compare the costs. All the various and confusing factors such as cashback offers, varying interest rates, compulsory

# of moving house

your computer is the last thing you pack

life cover and indemnity guarantee premiums can be built into the equation, so you can see the best deal at a glance. Keep another spreadsheet for outgoings such as search fees, deposit and estate agent's fees.

When you find the house you want, you can create folders for all the correspondence with solicitors, lenders, estate agents and surveyors. There is no need even to print off a copy for yourself: the file on the PC is your record.

And once the deal is complete, you have the whole matter of moving to deal with. The key to a successful move is sound budgeting and effective planning, and here too you should make the most of your PC. Make a spreadsheet to track the cost of a removal van and other moving expenses. You might also make a checklist of appointments – have you cancelled the milk, transferred the TV licence, arranged to have the utility meters read?

Before moving day you can print off labels for packing boxes. Then, once you are safely installed in your new home, remember to send a card (which you have designed yourself) or an e-mail to all your friends, to let them know your new address.

Countdown to moving

- Book time off work for the move
- Inform friends, bank, work and schools of your move
- Re-catalogue and value home contents
- Set up a budget document for the move
- Source removal firms and insurance (request quotes)
- Purchase or hire packing boxes and materials
- Plan packing schedule
- Arrange final readings and closing accounts for utilities: gas, electricity, telephone and water
- Arrange house clearance for unwanted items
- Design invitations for new house-warming party

Ideas and inspirations

Below are some suggestions to get your house move started. The projects can be adapted to your particular circumstances. You may want to give various tasks to different family members. Plan early to avoid the last-minute rush that plagues most home-moves.

260 Calculate your bills
Use a spreadsheet to budget for your move (don't forget to include any house sale profit).

256 Catalogue home contents
Create a database to keep a record of how much each of your possessions is worth.

310 Create a 'moving' planner
Use the principles of a travel planner to set out all aspects of the move and allot various tasks.

196 Change-of-address slips
Produce eye-catching cards to inform friends and colleagues of your new contact details.

172 Packing labels
If your boxes are clearly marked you'll be able to unpack items at your own pace, as you need them.

Also worth considering…

Once you've moved into your new house, put your own stamp on it by designing your dream garden.

300 Design your new garden
Try out a variety of designs and planting schemes to find out which suits you and your family best.

Design your ideal garden

Transform the world outside your back door

Whether you are landscaping your entire garden, or just want to add a patio, you will find specialist, garden design programs extremely helpful. You can use them to experiment with layout, materials and planting before you spend any money at the DIY store or garden centre.

This project uses a program called 3D Landscape, but there are others available. All garden design software comes with a help guide to point out aspects of design you need to think about. Considering soil type, drainage and steepness of slopes well in advance, for example, can save costly mistakes.

Draw a rough sketch of your house, garden and other existing features, but note measurements (in metres) accurately. You will use these in the scale plan you produce on your PC.

BEFORE YOU START

1 When the program opens you will see the 3D Landscape welcome page. Click on the **Designer** leaf icon to begin laying out your garden design, or click on the **How-To Guide** book icon for advice and tips on all aspects of using the program.

There are other garden design programs available, including Geoff Hamilton's Garden Designer, Expert Landscape Design 3D, and Imagine Home and Landscape.

OTHER PROGRAMS

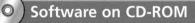
Software on CD-ROM

*If necessary, click the **Zoom In** button to enlarge your view of the plot. Then drag the scroll bars to adjust your position. To demagnify, click the **Zoom Out** button.*

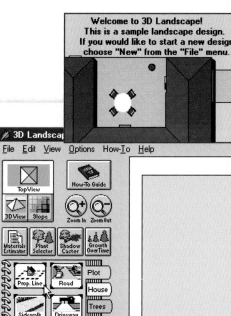

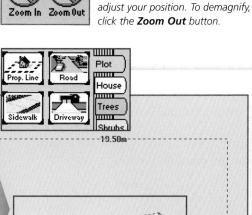

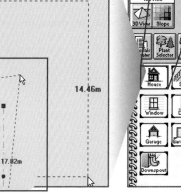

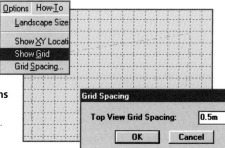

2 When you click on **Designer** a sample design appears. Go to the **File** menu and click on **New**. You will see an overhead view of an empty plot of land, with design buttons (split into sections by tabs on a spiral binder) on the left-hand side.

3 Now draw your garden. Click the **Plot** tab, then the **Prop. Line** button. Click and drag to draw a rectangle. Drag the corner or middle handles to adjust the shape. If you drag a middle handle, two new ones appear, to allow further changes.

4 Now add a house to the plot. Click the **House** tab in the spiral binder, then the **House** button. Click and drag within the plot to draw your house. Adjust the shape and size as you did with the plot. Then click on the house and drag it into position.

*To ensure the area you are given to work in is a suitable size, go to the **Options** menu and click on **Landscape Size**. Now set your dimensions in proportion to the size of your garden. Make the area slightly larger than your actual garden to include adjacent roads and buildings.*

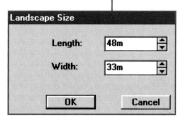

Working in detail
To help you position your objects correctly within your plot, display the grid. Go to the **Options** menu and click on **Show Grid**. To adjust the size of the squares on your grid, go back to the **Options** menu, click on **Grid Spacing**, and alter the setting in the dialogue box.

Most objects in 3D Landscape have an Inspector, which allows you to make detailed adjustments and view relevant tips. To open an Inspector, double-click on the object.

Short cut
To remove an object you have created, click on it and press the **Delete** key. Or, click on it, go to the **Edit** menu and click on **Cut.**

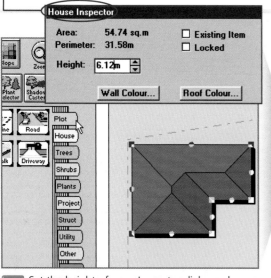

5 Set the height of your house by double-clicking on it (this will affect the kind of shadow it will cast over your plot). In the House

Inspector dialogue box type in the correct measurement. Change the colour of the roof and walls by clicking on the relevant buttons.

6 Now add other fixed, man-made features. These can be found as buttons under the various toolbar tabs. Some items, such as a

driveway, need to be drawn in the same way as the house. Others, such as windows, are a fixed shape and are just dropped into place.

7 You can now add ground cover – a lawn or a patio for example. Click through the toolbar tabs to see menus of available

items then click and drag to draw them. You can draw the lawn over man-made features as it will disappear under them.

Dealing with slopes

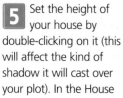

If your garden slopes or undulates – or if you wish to experiment with such landscaping – click on the Slope button in 3D Landscape. To learn how to use it, go to the **Help** menu and click on **Tutorial**. Click on the **Search** button, type in 'Slope View' and press the **Enter** key.

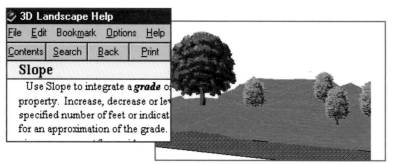

Now place existing trees and plants, and choose new ones suited to your conditions. 3D Landscape can predict their growth over the years and the shadows they will cast.

ADDING THE RIGHT PLANTS

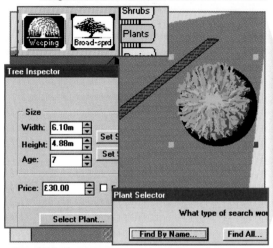

Shrubs

Plants

Weeping · **Broad-sprd**

Tree Inspector

Size
Width: 6.10m
Height: 4.88m
Age: 7

Price: £30.00

Set S...
Set S...

Select Plant...

Plant Selector

What type of search wo...

Find By Name... · Find All...

Plant Selector

What type of search would you like?

Find By Name... · Find All... · Find By Attributes...

Options
☒ Limit Search To Selected Shape
☒ Limit Search to Local Conditions · Local Conditions...

Set Local Conditions for Plant Searches

Hardiness Zone
Zone: Any
Zone Map...

Soil pH
☐ Acid
☒ Neutral
☐ Alkaline

Soil Type
☐ Clay
☒ Loam
☐ Sand

OK · Cancel

Zone: 8 / 8 / 9 · Minimum annual temperature: -12 to -6 °C

OK · Cancel

Plant Library Results

2 Plants Found
Salix alba 'Tristis' (Golden Weeping Willow)
Salix babylonica (Babylon Weeping Willow)

Salix babylonica (Babylon Weeping Willow)

Soil: Acid, Neutral, Alkaline, Clay, Loam, Sand, Moist
Maintenance: Medium

Mature
Sunlig
Hardin
Water
Flower

Babylon Weeping Willow is a graceful weeping tree w
olive-green foliage. Weeping Willows need to be stak
develop a high 'height of head' so that people can w
mature trees. Several cultivars are available. Native

Use: A

OK · Search Again... · Cancel

8 Click the **Trees** tab, select a type and click on your plot to add one. Double-click on the tree to bring up the Tree Inspector. Click

the **Select Plant** button. In the Plant Selector click **Find By Name** if you know the name, or **Find All** to see a menu.

9 When you open Plant Selector you can limit your search to local conditions. Click the relevant box then the **Local Conditions**

button. Click the relevant boxes then click **Zone Map**. Select a zone (7, 8 or 9 for the UK) and click **OK**. Then click **Find All**.

10 A list of options appears in the Plant Library Results dialogue box. When you click on one, its details are displayed.

Compare your options to see which would be suitable for you. After reviewing them, click on the one you prefer. Then click **OK**.

Select the right tree

When you select a tree, check its predicted height in the Tree Inspector box (double-click on the tree). Click on the arrows beside the Age box and the width and the height of the tree change accordingly. The size of the tree will affect shading conditions as it grows, and may grow so tall as to block out light.

Tree Inspector

Weeping
G

Size
Width: 6.10m
Height: 4.88m
Age: 7

Set Size to Defa
Set Size from A

Price: £30.00 · ☐ Existing Plant

Refine your search

You can choose a plant according to a detailed range of attributes, including flower colour and the level of maintenance it requires. Click the **Find By Attributes** button in Plant Selector and select your specifications from the drop-down menus. Click on **Search**.

Plant Selector

What type of search would you like?

Find By Name... · Find All... · Find By Attributes...

Find Plants By Attributes

Type	Tree		Sunlight
Shape	Weeping		Water Prefs
Deciduous	Deciduous		Flower Colour
Usage	Any		Flower Season

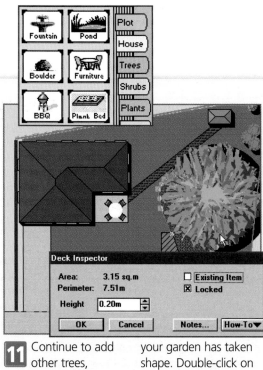

To add, remove or change items in your garden, you need to use the overhead view. However, to see how your plans look from different aspects, you can use the 3D View.

▶ SEE HOW IT REALLY LOOKS

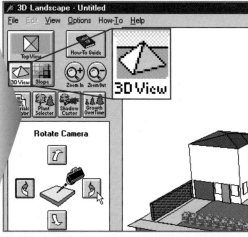

11 Continue to add other trees, shrubs, plants and man-made structures, such as patio furniture and a barbecue, until your garden has taken shape. Double-click on each item and use the Inspector to specify appropriate details, particularly heights.

12 To switch from an overhead view, click the **3D View** button, then click on the arrows that appear to rotate the camera. The arrows above and below move the eye level up or down; those to the left and right move the eye level around your plot.

13 If a fence, wall or hedge obstructs your 3D view, switch on the **Top View** button, click on the item, go to the **Edit** menu and click on **Cut**. After viewing in 3D View, return to **Top View**, go to the **Edit** menu and click **Paste**. You'll need to drag the object back into place.

Saving and printing your design

When you are happy with your design, go to the **File** menu and select **Save**. Give your design a name and save it into a suitable folder. Then click **OK**.

To print your design, set up which view you want to use (Top View or 3D), go to the **File** menu and select **Print Setup**. Check that the right printer, size of paper and orientation is selected, and click **OK**. Go to the **File** menu again and select **Print**. Choose the 'Scale To Fit Page' option to print your landscape on one sheet of paper, then click **OK**.

Print

Printer: HP LaserJet 4MV,\\'LaserWriter\31[047]Soc
LaserJet 4V

Scale
● **Scale To Fit Page**
○ **Print To Scale:** 5mm = 1 Metre (1x1 pag

OK   Cancel   Setup...

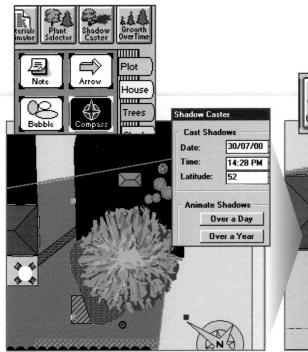

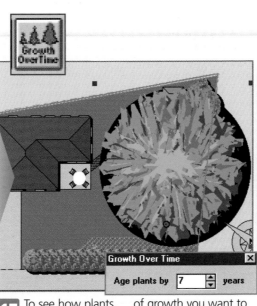

If your plan includes items that you already own, double-click on these objects and click in the Existing Item box in the Inspector. This will exclude them from the costings made in the Materials Estimator.

Shadow Caster

Cast Shadows

Date: 30/07/00
Time: 14:28 PM
Latitude: 52

Animate Shadows

Over a Day
Over a Year

Materials Estimator

☒ Show Detail ☐ Show Existing ☒ OK 2   OK

Description	#	Units
7.52 sq.m Concrete Patio		
Note: Consider using hand-mixed concrete if delivery of ready-mix is difficult.		
Note: The materials used for forms may vary depending on layout.		
Note: Footings may be need to be deeper in some conditions.		
Note: Use form release compound if removing edging.		
ready-mix concrete, 3000 psi	0.82	cu.metre
ready-mix concrete delivery charge	1.00	load
shed gravel (base - 5cm layer)	0.46	cu.metre
0 6x6 Welded wire mesh	7.52	sq.metre
cm Doby wire mesh spacers	20.20	each
000guage Polyethylene (cure slab)	7.52	sq.metre
5cmx10cmx3.6m Pressure-treated	3.61	each
5cmx10cmx4.8m (screed board)	1.00	each
8d Hot-dipped galvanized nails	0.41	kilo
16d Hot-dipped galvanized nails	0.41	kilo
#3 Rebar, 10mmx6m	1.81	each
Form stakes, 60cm	21.68	
23.62 sq.m Pond	1.00	

Print...

Growth Over Time

Age plants by 7 ▲▼ years

14 To show shade, click the **Tools** tab then the **Compass** button. Drag the pointer to match the direction of north in your garden. Click the **Shadow Caster** button and specify a date, time and latitude. You can also animate the shade over a day or year.

15 To see how plants will grow over time, click the **Growth Over Time** button, type in how many years of growth you want to see, then click **Update Plant Ages**. Look at the shade plants will create at that time, too.

16 Finally, estimate the cost of new additions to the plot. Click the **Materials Estimator** button and check the Show Detail box for extra detail. Ensure the Show Existing box is not ticked to remove existing objects. To print, click the **Print** button.

All the help you could need ...

You've produced and printed the blueprint for your ideal garden. Now put your plans into action. The How-To Guide contains plenty of information and tips, including:

● How to design on sloping plots.
● Which professionals to call in and when.
● How to estimate and buy materials.
● Price estimates for a range of materials and plants.
● How to choose lawn seed and improve your soil.
● The right rental tool for the job.
● Useful telephone numbers.

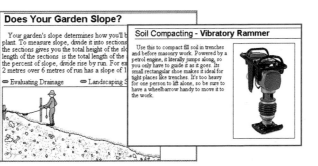

Does Your Garden Slope?

Your garden's slope determines how you'll b plant. To measure slope, divide it into sections the sections gives you the total height of the slo length of the sections is the total length of the of slope, divide rise by run. For ex 2 metres over 6 metres of run has a slope of 1

⇨ Evaluating Drainage   ⇨ Landscaping S

Soil Compacting - Vibratory Rammer

Use this to compact fill soil in trenches and before masonry work. Powered by a petrol engine, it literally jumps along, so you only have to guide it as it goes. Its small rectangular shoe makes it ideal for tight places like trenches. It's too heavy for one person to lift alone, so be sure to have a wheelbarrow handy to move it to the work.

It's important that the schedule you devise is appropriate for your level of fitness. If you do not exercise regularly, consult your doctor first.

BEFORE YOU START

Save As

Save in: ☐ Family folder

☐ Anne

File name: Beginner's Running Log

Save as type: Works SS

☐ Create Backup Copy

1 Go to the **Start** menu, select **Programs** and click on **Microsoft Works**. In the Works Task Launcher click on the **Works Tool** tab then on the **Spreadsheet** button. Click on the **Save** toolbar button. Save the document into an appropriate folder.

Devise a fitness plan

A simple spreadsheet can help you schedule regular exercise

Along with your training shoes, stop watch and sheer determination, your computer can play an integral part in devising and maintaining an effective fitness plan. Using a spreadsheet program, such as the one in Microsoft Works, you can create a fitness log to keep track of your progress, using both figures and written comments.

Getting in shape can involve many forms of exercise. These pages show you how to put together a jogging schedule, but you can adapt the project to suit any fitness plan.

Keeping a log of your progress can help you to see how well you are doing, or how far you have to go to achieve your goals, and allows you to make changes if you've overestimated or underestimated your time and abilities. It also allows for breaks for illness or injury.

You can create a similar fitness schedule using Microsoft Excel and Lotus 1-2-3.

OTHER PROGRAMS

Templates on CD-ROM

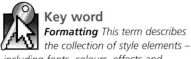

Key word
Formatting This term describes
the collection of style elements –
including fonts, colours, effects and
alignment – that determine how a cell looks.

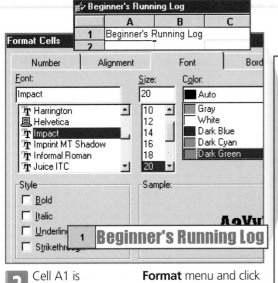

2 Cell A1 is automatically selected in your spreadsheet. In it, type in a title for your plan. Highlight it, go to the **Format** menu and click on **Font and Style**. Select a font, size and colour. The row height will automatically adjust to include your text.

3 Starting in cell **A2**, and continuing in the cells along the same row, type in headings as shown. In cell **A3** type in 'Monday'. Drag the bottom right-hand corner of the cell down so that the rest of the days of the week appear in the cells below. In cell **A10** type in 'Total'.

4 To change the position of text within cells, select a cell or block of cells with the mouse, then click on your choice of alignment toolbar button. Click **OK**.

Adjusting column widths

Some of the text that you enter into cells may not be visible. To adjust the width of cells in a single column, to accommodate your text, place the mouse pointer on the right-hand edge of the grey lettered box at the top of the column. When the mouse pointer changes to a double-headed arrow, hold down the left mouse button and drag the column edge to the required width.

Your jogging schedule

When you start your schedule, concentrate on running continuously for a certain time, rather than covering a certain distance. Don't push yourself too hard. In the early sessions, alternate between brisk walking and running.

Before each jogging session warm up by walking briskly for 10 minutes. Cool down afterwards by walking for 5 minutes then stretching. Hamstring stretches are especially helpful.

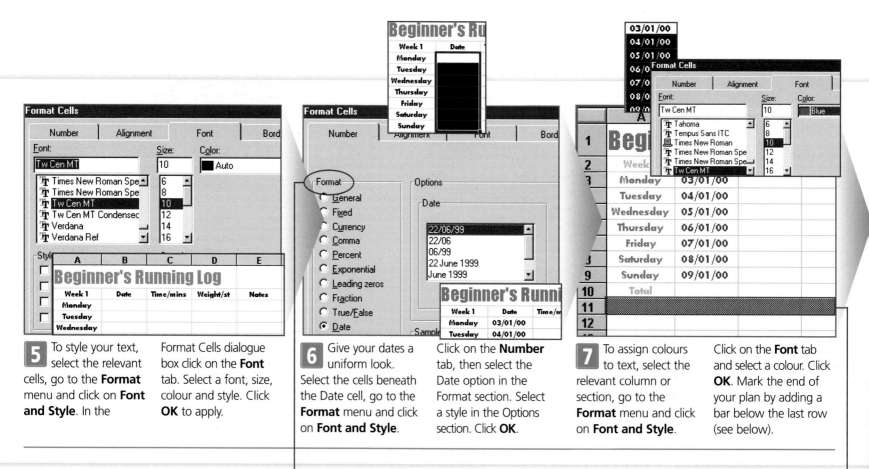

5 To style your text, select the relevant cells, go to the **Format** menu and click on **Font and Style**. In the Format Cells dialogue box click on the **Font** tab. Select a font, size, colour and style. Click **OK** to apply.

6 Give your dates a uniform look. Select the cells beneath the Date cell, go to the **Format** menu and click on **Font and Style**. Click on the **Number** tab, then select the Date option in the Format section. Select a style in the Options section. Click **OK**.

7 To assign colours to text, select the relevant column or section, go to the **Format** menu and click on **Font and Style**. Click on the **Font** tab and select a colour. Click **OK**. Mark the end of your plan by adding a bar below the last row (see below).

Number formats

You need to select a format for the 'Time/mins' column. Go to the **Format** menu and click on **Font and Style**. Click on the **Number** tab and select the Fixed option in the Format section. Select a style from the Options section – here, we select two decimal places. Click **OK**.

Adding rules

To add a rule beneath your weekly schedule, click on a grey numbered box on the left of your spreadsheet below the Total row. This will highlight the row. Go to the **Format** menu and click on **Font and Style**. Click on the **Shading** tab then, in the Shading section, click on your choice of pattern. Click **OK**.

Key word

Template *A template is created to use as the basis for further documents which share the same basic features. A template is opened, edited, then saved under a different file name.*

When you paste your plan in this way, the current week of your schedule appears at the top of the document, so you don't have to scroll down.

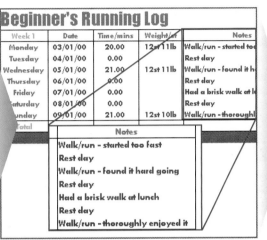

8 To place lines between sections, select a section, go to the **Format** menu and click on **Font and Style**. Click the **Border** tab. Select where you want the border and a line style. Click **OK**. To remove gridlines, go to the **View** menu and click on **Gridlines**.

9 Your fitness schedule is finished – now the hard work really starts. Fill in the relevant data every day and monitor your progress. Remember to build in rest days.

10 Use your plan as a template for Week 2, etc. Starting in row 2, select the cells in the plan then click on the **Copy** toolbar button.

Go to the **Insert** menu and click on **Insert Row**, then click on the **Paste** toolbar button. Amend the week number and dates.

Adding up totals

To calculate, say, the total number of minutes you have run in a single week, use the Works AutoSum facility.

Click in the cell below the cells containing your times, then click on the **AutoSum** toolbar button. Press the **Enter** key. For AutoSum to work, you must enter times into all the cells in the week, even if that time is zero.

Make a holiday planner

Keep all your family's travel details up to date and in order

Holidays are a time to relax and forget the stresses and strains of everyday life. But even relaxation has to be planned if you are to get the most out of it.

There are some things you need to plan in advance, especially if you are going abroad. Do you have the right visas? Is your passport still valid? Have you had the immunisations you need? Are there important articles you must remember to pack?

Your computer can help here. Spreadsheets are ideal for preparing lists of things that need to be done, and checking them off as they are completed. You may find that several separate spreadsheets are helpful when planning your annual holiday.

Ensure that all the information you are putting into your spreadsheet is correct. This is especially important when using formulas.

BEFORE YOU START

	A	B	C
1	HOLIDAY PLANNER		
2			
3	Destination: Orlando, Florida, USA		
4			
5	Departure date:		
6	Time:		
7	Check-in:		
8	Airport:		
9	Terminal:		
10	Flight no:		
11	Local arrival time:		
12			
13	Return date:		
14	Time:		
15	Check-in		
16	Airport:		
17	Terminal		
18	Flight no:		
19	Local arrival time:		

1 Go to the **Start** menu, select **Programs** then click on **Microsoft Excel**. A new spreadsheet opens. Click on the **Save** toolbar button and save and name your document. Cell A1 is automatically selected. Type your checklist into column A as above.

*You can also make a holiday planner in Microsoft Works. Open Works then, in the Works Task Launcher, click on the **Works Tools** tab, then the **Spreadsheet** button.*

OTHER PROGRAMS

Templates on CD-ROM

To adjust the width of a column, place the mouse pointer over the right-hand edge of the grey column header. When it becomes a double-headed arrow drag the edge to the desired width.

$ Holiday checklist		Width: 15.43
	A	B
1	HOLIDAY PLANNER	
2		

Watch out

The currency converter does not take into account the commission you will be charged when you exchange cash or buy travellers' cheques.

=E9*E10

To enter a multiplication sign, press the **Shift** key and '**8**' simultaneously.

	A	B	C	D
1	HOLIDAY PLANNER			
2				
3	Destination: Orlando, Florida, USA			
4				
5	Departure date:	01-Apr		
6	Time:	9.15am GMT		
7	Check-in:	7.15am GMT		
8	Airport:	Heathrow		
9	Terminal:	Terminal 4		
10	Flight no:	BA 507		
11	Local arrival time:	12.15pm EST		
12				
13	Return date:	15-Apr		
14	Time:	6.15pm EST		
15	Check-in	4.15pm EST		
16	Airport:	Orlando International		
17	Terminal	Main		
18	Flight no:	BA 607		
19	Local arrival time:	7.15am GMT		

$ Holiday checklist				
	A	B	C	D
1	HOLIDAY PLANNER			
2				
3	Destination: Orlando, Florida, USA			
4				
5	Departure date:	01-Apr		
6	Time:	9.15am GMT		
	Check-in:	7.15am GMT		Currency converter
	Airport:	Heathrow		
	Terminal:	Terminal 4		Sterling:
	Flight no:	BA 507		Exchange rate:
	Local arrival time:	12.15pm EST		Foreign currency =
2				
13	Return date:	15-Apr		Foreign currency:
14	Time:	6.15pm EST		Exchange rate:
15	Check-in	4.15pm EST		Sterling value =
16	Airport:	Orlando International		
17	Terminal	Main		
18	Flight no:	BA 607		
19	Local arrival time:	7.15am GMT		
20				

	B	C	D	E
	orida, USA			
	GMT		Currency converter	
	GMT			
	4		Sterling:	1000.00
			Exchange rate:	1.57
	m EST		Foreign currency =	=E9*E10
			Foreign currency:	
	m EST		Exchange rate:	
	m EST		Sterling value =	
	ndo International			
	07			

2 Adjust the width of column A so that your text, except for your title and subtitle, fits neatly within the column (see above). Type your travel details into the relevant cells in column B. If necessary, adjust the width of this column, too.

3 You can now create a currency converter. This will automatically work out how much foreign currency your sterling buys, and vice versa. Type the text shown above into column D, starting in cell D7 and continuing in the cells immediately below.

4 To calculate the foreign currency you can buy, click in **E11** then type in '=E9*E10'. Press **Enter**. To convert into sterling, click in **E15** and type in '=E13/E14'. Press **Enter**.

Formatting your cells

You will be entering different types of data into column B, including dates and times. You can select a style for each by clicking on the cell in question then going to the **Format** menu and selecting **Cells**. The **Number** tab is selected.

In the Category pane click on the type of information to be entered. Then, in the Type pane, click on your preferred style. Click **OK**.

Format Cells			
Number	Alignment	Font	Border

Category:
- General
- Number
- Currency
- Accounting
- Date
- Time
- Percentage
- Fraction
- Scientific
- Text
- Special

Sample

Type:
- 3/4
- 3/4/97
- 03/04/97
- 4-Mar
- 4-Mar-97
- 04-Mar-97
- Mar-97

Let the Wizard help

Microsoft Works has a Wizard that can help you plan your holiday. When you open Works the Works Task Launcher appears. Scroll through the options in the pane and click on **User Defined Templates**. The folder will open. Scroll through the contents and double-click on one of the Travel Planner options to open it.

Works Task Launcher

TaskWizards   Existing Documents

Click the TaskWizard you want to begin
- Home Budget, Personal
- Graph Paper, 10x10
- Graph Paper, plain sm
- Graph Paper, plain lg
- Graph Paper, plain
- Graph Paper, 5x5 sm
- Graph Paper, 5x5
- Sizes & Favourites
- Gift List
- Greeting Card Register
- Travel Planner, Budget
- Travel Planner, Checklist

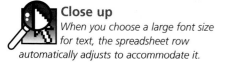

Close up
When you choose a large font size for text, the spreadsheet row automatically adjusts to accommodate it.

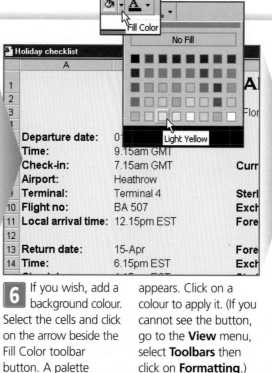

5 To style your heading, highlight it, go to the **Format** menu and select **Cells**. Choose a font, style, size and effect, then click **OK**. Style the rest of your text in the same way. To select adjacent cells in one go, click on the top cell then drag over the others.

6 If you wish, add a background colour. Select the cells and click on the arrow beside the Fill Color toolbar button. A palette appears. Click on a colour to apply it. (If you cannot see the button, go to the **View** menu, select **Toolbars** then click on **Formatting**.)

7 To colour all your text with the same colour, select the relevant cells and click on the arrow beside the Font Color toolbar button. As before, a colour palette appears. Click on a colour to apply it.

Centre your heading

To position the heading in the centre of your page, click on cell **A1** and drag your cursor along the top row of cells until the full width of your form is covered (here, to column F). Then click the **Merge and Center** toolbar button.

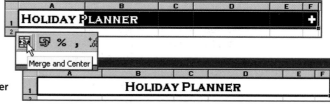

Bright idea
*If you want to add another page to your spreadsheet, go to the **Insert** menu and click on **Worksheet**. Another sheet tab will appear at the bottom of your screen.*

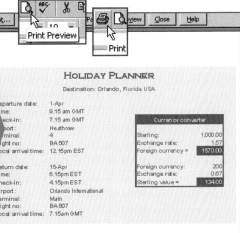

8 To separate your currency converter from the rest of your travel details, place a border around it. Select the relevant cells, go to the **Format** menu and click on **Cells**. Click on the **Border** tab. Select a line style, colour and outline for your border, then click **OK**.

9 Before printing your planner, see how your page looks by clicking on the **Print Preview** toolbar button. If it needs adjusting, press the **Esc** key and edit the layout accordingly. When you are happy with it, click on the **Print** toolbar button to print it.

10 Using the same process, it is possible to create a packing list and a list of tasks to complete before going on holiday.

At the bottom of the page you will see a series of tabs. Click on the **Sheet 2** tab. A blank spreadsheet page appears for you to use.

Currency converter

To make your headings really stand out, reverse your 'fill' and 'font' colours. In this case, the background has been coloured red, and the text light yellow.

Setting up your page

You may need to adjust the page settings of your document prior to printing if, for example, it is wider than 210 mm.

Go to the **File** menu and click on **Page Setup**. Click on the **Page** tab, then select the Landscape option in the Orientation section. Ensure **A4** is selected in the 'Paper size' box. Now click the **Margins** tab and centre your printout either **Horizontally** or **Vertically**. Click **OK**.

Plan a holiday you'll

Don't leave your holiday enjoyment to chance –

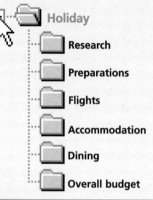

Project planner

Create a folder for the entire project, called 'Holiday'. Add sub-folders for each element.

- Holiday
  - Research
  - Preparations
  - Flights
  - Accommodation
  - Dining
  - Overall budget

Everyone dreams of escaping from their day-to-day routine. For some, the ideal escape is a beach and a book on a desert island; for others it is a hectic round of entertainment and shopping in a big, cosmopolitan city. Your computer can help you achieve your dream.

With your PC you can access Web sites on the Internet to check out national, regional and resort destinations. You can look up weather forecasts to help you decide which clothes to pack. You can even find out about wider weather patterns to ensure your visit doesn't coincide with monsoons or hurricanes. You may also be able to read about local

remember forever

your PC can help it go smoothly

events listings such as carnivals or exhibitions, scheduled for when you will be at your destination.

Through the Internet you can purchase travel guides, order brochures, check which inoculations or other health precautions, if any, are needed, and book flights, hire cars and organise excursions and accommodation. You may even be able to check train timetables, ferry services and bus routes for destinations on the other side of the world, and pick up tips from fellow travellers.

In short, every aspect of your holiday arrangements can be researched, sourced and paid for via your computer.

Your computer is the ideal tool for precision planning. You can create a database to organise all the essential tasks that need completing before your departure, and set up a spreadsheet to project costs and a budget for your holiday. You can then create a diary to organise your trip day by day and take it away with you in printed form.

On your return you'll be able to scan in pictures from your trip and produce your own photo album to send to all your friends, either on paper or by e-mail. Or you could send a holiday newsletter to friends and family, with anecdotes and pictures from your trip!

The adventure starts here

- 6 months: book time off work
- 5 months: check whether inoculations are required
- 4 months: budget for holiday
- 3 months: confirm booking/itinerary
- 1 month: organise travel insurance
- 2 weeks: buy currency/travellers' cheques

Ideas and inspirations

Below are project ideas to make your holiday run as smoothly, and be as memorable, as possible. All the projects can be adapted to your own circumstances and will give you further ideas of your own. Just alter the wording, layout or search details of each exercise as you work.

96 **Find information on the Net**
Research destinations and weather conditions, and book accommodation and tickets on-line.

252 **Travel budget planner**
Spreadsheet software on your PC helps you plan the finances for any purchase or project.

310 **Make a holiday planner**
Produce a document containing all the practical details of your trip, from time zones to car hire.

84 **Use your PC as a fax**
Confirm bookings and itineraries with hotels and tour operators by fax.

220 **Create a photo album**
Make sure your trip is one you'll remember for the rest of your life with a pictorial souvenir.

Also worth considering…

Once you've finished, don't let your research go to waste. You can use information again and again.

168 **Create a contact database**
You can produce address and contact lists specific to transport, accommodation and new friends.

A collector's database

Keep a detailed record on every addition to your collection

Whatever you collect, whether it's stamps, coins or wine, or music albums or CDs, it is useful to keep a log of each item you own. As your collection grows, it becomes necessary to keep a check on its contents, its value and even the whereabouts of each item. You can use a database program on your PC to keep such records.

Creating a database is straightforward, and once you have entered all your details you can find any information you need quickly and simply. Not only do you have all the information about your collection in one place, but a database is also a way of spotting 'gaps' in your collection and can help you to plan future purchases.

Classical CDs

CD ref: 00003

Composer: Bach

Title: Preludes and Fugues

Musician(s): Academy of St. Martin-in-the-Fields

Venue: St Paul's Cathedral, London

Conductor: Marriner

Date: 05/96

Label: Philips

Catalogue No: 7458929722

Purchased: 02/97

Price: 14.45

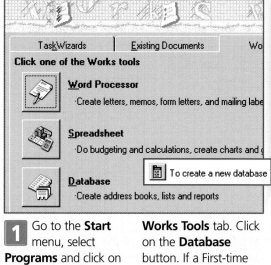

For a music database, gather together all your CDs, records and cassettes. If you have kept receipts for them, have these to hand, too.

► BEFORE YOU START

1 Go to the **Start** menu, select **Programs** and click on **Microsoft Works**. In the Works Task Launcher click on the **Works Tools** tab. Click on the **Database** button. If a First-time Help box appears, click the button beside 'To create a new database'.

You can also make a record of your collection using Microsoft Excel. Use the spreadsheet to type in your headings and data, then the Filter feature to create your reports

► OTHER PROGRAMS

Templates on CD-ROM

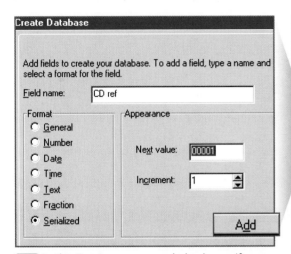

Key word

Fields *A field is a category of information. Fields appear as columns of data in a database. The combination of several fields about a single subject make up a record.*

Create Database

Add fields to create your database. To add a field, type a name and select a format for the field.

Field name: CD ref

Format
- General
- Number
- Date
- Time
- Text
- Fraction
- ● Serialized

Appearance

Next value: 00001

Increment: 1

[Add]

Unsaved Database 1

✓		CD ref	Composer
	24		
	25		
	26		
	27		
	28		

Classical CDs

✓		CD ref	C		nductor
	1				
	2				
	3				
	4				
	5				
	6				
	7				
	8				
	9				
	10				
	11				
	12				
	13				
	14				
	15				
	16				
	17				
	18				
	19				
	20				

Classical CDs — Form Design

Composer: CD
Title:
Musician(s):
Conductor:
MOVE
nue: Date
abel:
Catalogue No.:
Purchased:
Price:
RESIZE

2 In the Create Database dialogue box add your field names. Type in the first field name (make this your reference field – see below), specify a format for it, then click on **Add**. Continue to add the rest of your fields. When you have finished, click on **Done**.

3 Your database first appears in List View. Name and save it immediately by clicking on the **Save** toolbar button. Name your document, locate a suitable folder in which to store it, then click on the **Save** button.

4 To customise your database, click the **Form Design** toolbar button. To move a text box, click on it and drag it. To resize a text box, click on it, then click on the bottom right-hand corner of the box and drag it across the screen to the required size.

Fields and formats

For a music database consider entering these fields and formats. It is a good idea to include a serialised reference number as Works will automatically update each record with a new number.

Field	Format
CD ref	Serialized
Composer	Text
Title	Text
Musician(s)	Text
Conductor	Text
Venue	Text
Date	Date
Label	Text
Catalogue No	Number
Purchased	Date
Price	Number

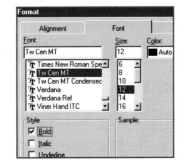

Format

Alignment	Font

Font: Tw Cen MT

- Times New Roman Spe
- Tw Cen MT
- Tw Cen MT Condensec
- Verdana
- Verdana Ref
- Viner Hand ITC

Size: 12 — 6, 8, 10, 12, 14, 16

Color: Auto

Style
- ✓ Bold
- Italic
- Underline

Sample:

Styling fields

You can assign fonts, colours, effects and styles to your fields and their adjoining text boxes. Click on the **Form Design** toolbar button (see Step 4), then on a field name or adjoining text box.

Go to the **Format** menu and click on **Font and Style**. Select a font, size, style and colour, then click **OK**. Click on the alignment toolbar buttons to position the text within the text boxes. To style several text boxes in the same way at once, press the **Ctrl** key and, keeping it pressed down, click on the boxes in turn, then style them.

Fields that have been formatted as 'serialized' will automatically update themselves as you enter new records.

CD ref: 00007

*To move to the next field or record, press the **Tab** key. To move back, press the **Shift** and **Tab** keys.*

To extract and display specific information from your database – for an insurance valuation, perhaps – you need to create a report.

CREATE A REPORT

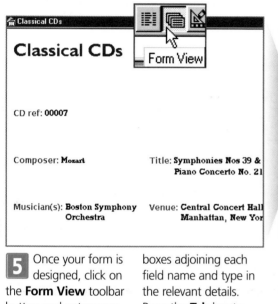

Classical CDs

Form View

CD ref: **00007**

Composer: **Mozart**   Title: **Symphonies Nos 39 & Piano Concerto No. 21**

Musician(s): **Boston Symphony Orchestra**   Venue: **Central Concert Hall Manhattan, New Yor**

List View

"Preludes and Fugues - Warsaw

		Composer	Title	Mus
1	00003	Bach	Preludes an	Acad
2	00001	Beethoven	Piano Conce	Berlin
3	00002	Beethoven	Symphony N	Vienn
4	00013	Beethoven	5th Sympho	Englis
5	00008	Chopin	Miniatures	L.A.
6	00004	Corbetta	Guitar Music	Jakol
7	00006	Mozart	Cosi Fan Tu	New
8	00007	Mozart	Symphonies	Bosto
9	00015	Schulti	American Sy	Englis
10	00005	Tchaikovsky	Symphony N	Ljublj
11	00009	Tchaikovsky	Swan Lake	Israe
12	00010	Verdi	Rigoletto	Englis

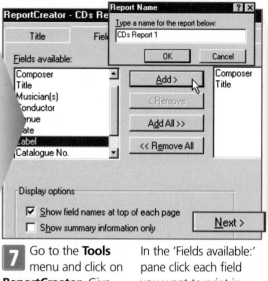

ReportCreator - CDs Re

Title   Field

Report Name   ? X

Type a name for the report below:

CDs Report 1

OK   Cancel

Fields available:

Composer
Title
Musician(s)
Conductor
Venue
Date
Label
Catalogue No.

Add >
< Remove
Add All >>
<< Remove All

Composer
Title

Display options

☑ Show field names at top of each page
☐ Show summary information only

Next >

5 Once your form is designed, click on the **Form View** toolbar button and enter your data. Click on the text boxes adjoining each field name and type in the relevant details. Press the **Tab** key to move to another record.

6 When you have finished entering all your records, click on the **List View** toolbar button. Not all your data will be visible. To see all the data in a particular cell, click on the cell and the contents will appear in the Entry Bar at the top of the window.

7 Go to the **Tools** menu and click on **ReportCreator**. Give your report a title then click **OK**. In the next box click on the **Fields** tab. In the 'Fields available:' pane click each field you want to print in turn, clicking on **Add** as you do so. Click **Next** when you finish.

You can move through your records quickly in Form View by clicking on the arrows on either side of the Record counter at the bottom of the window.

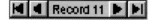

Searching for information

To search for specific data – say, all the music you have by a particular composer – go to the **Edit** menu and click on **Find**. Type in a key word, or words, for what you want to search for, select the 'All records' option, then click on **OK**.

The database changes to show only those records that match your search. To return to the full database view, go to the **Record** menu, select **Show** and then click on **All Records**.

Find

Find what: English National Orchestra

Match

○ Next record   ◉ All records

Classical CDs

☑		CD ref	Composer	Title	Musician(s)	Co
☑	4	00013	Beethoven	5th Sympho	English Nation	Ber

*Works automatically saves all reports. To print or update an old report, go to the **View** menu and click on **Report**. A list of reports appears. Click on the relevant one then click on **Preview** to view it (then go to the **File** menu and select **Print** to print it), or **Modify** to update it.*

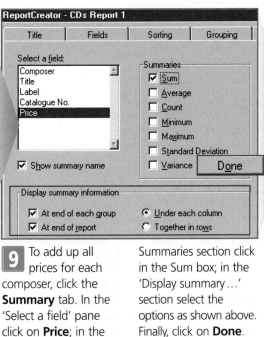

8 The Sorting tab is selected. To organise your data in order of, say, composer, click in the 'Sort by' box and select **Composer**. Click the **Grouping** tab, then click in the 'When contents change' and 'Show group heading' boxes.

9 To add up all prices for each composer, click the **Summary** tab. In the 'Select a field' pane click on **Price**; in the Summaries section click in the Sum box; in the 'Display summary…' section select the options as shown above. Finally, click on **Done**.

10 A prompt box appears asking whether you want to preview or modify your report. Click **Modify** if you want to add any styling to your report (see below). Click **Preview** to view your report. When you're happy with it, click **Print** to print it out.

Styling a report

In the same way that it's possible to style documents, you can also adjust the fonts and sizes, and add colour and effects, in your reports.

Click the **Report View** toolbar button. Select the cell or row you want to style and go to the **Format** menu and click on **Font and Style**. In the Format dialogue box click the various tabs, selecting your fonts, sizes, styles, colours and background patterns as you do so.

To adjust column widths, place your cursor on the right-hand edge of the column heading. When the cursor changes appearance, click and drag to the desired width.

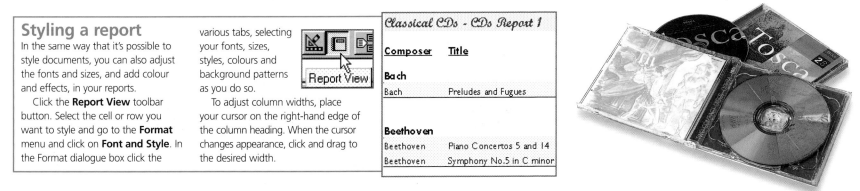

Record your golf scores

Keep track of your rounds and calculate your handicap

A spreadsheet is a great way of keeping records of your sporting achievements. Here, we create a golf scorecard but you could design a spreadsheet for any sport. With it, you can record every course and round played. Each time you input a score-card, your playing handicap will be updated.

There are two handicap calculators: one is an overall handicap, based on every scorecard entered into the system; the second calculates your current handicap by taking an average of your last three rounds.

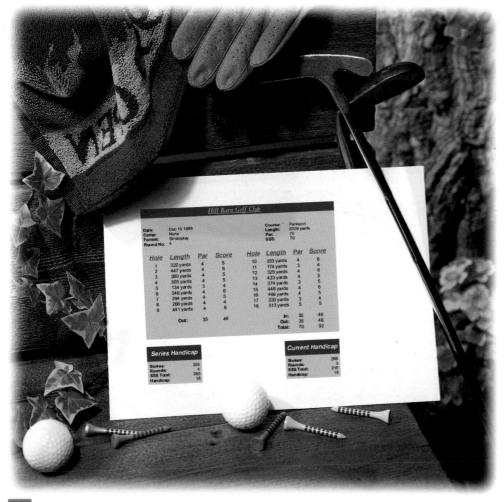

Collect at least three of your recent scorecards to provide scores and the course data you need to complete your spreadsheet.

BEFORE YOU START

1 Go to the **Start** menu, select **Programs** and click on **Microsoft Excel**. To name and save your document, click on the **Save** toolbar button. Select a suitable folder in which to save it in the 'Save in' box, type in a file name then click on **Save**.

*You can also record your golf scores in Microsoft Works. Open Works then, in the Works Task Launcher, click on the **Works Tools** tab then on the **Spreadsheet** button.*

OTHER PROGRAMS

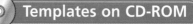
Templates on CD-ROM

Watch out
Make sure that you enter the headings and data into exactly the same cells as used below. If you do not, the cell references used in the handicap calculation formulas will not be correct.

Close-up
Unless directed otherwise, AutoSum adds figures immediately above the selected AutoSum cell. To adjust the formula, include new cell references (simply click on the cells themselves to do this) and appropriate calculation symbols, such as '+', '-', '/' and ''.*

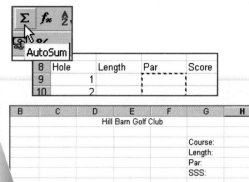

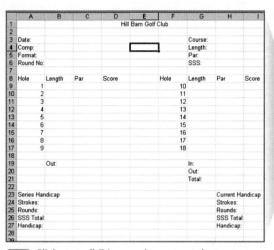

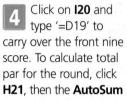

2 Click on cell **E1** and type in the course name. Type in the text for the rest of the spreadsheet as shown above. It is important that you use the same cells as here, otherwise your formulas won't work. Now you are ready to add your Score and Par totals.

3 Click on cell **C19**, then on the **AutoSum** button. Select cells **C9** to **C17** and press **Enter**. When course data is entered, AutoSum will add it up. Repeat for all Par and Score columns. Then click **H20** and type '=C19' to carry over par from the front nine.

4 Click on **I20** and type '=D19' to carry over the front nine score. To calculate total par for the round, click **H21**, then the **AutoSum** button. Highlight cells **H19** and **H20**. Press **Enter**. For total score, click **I21**, then **AutoSum**. Select cells **I19** and **I20**. Press **Enter**.

Working out handicaps

A handicap is the number of strokes a golfer takes, on average, to play a course, over and above Standard Scratch Score (SSS). SSS is the score a scratch golfer, with a handicap of '0', should take to play the course.

SSS can differ from par for the course as it takes account of the difficulty of the course, while par for each hole is dictated by length. The handicap calculators in this project are 'Series' and 'Current'.

Series is calculated by subtracting SSS total for all rounds from the total number of strokes, and then dividing the remainder by the number of rounds played.

The Current Handicap is calculated by subtracting the SSS total for the last three rounds from the strokes played in the last three rounds, and then dividing the remainder by three.

Series Handicap = (B24 [total number of strokes played] minus B26 [SSS total for all rounds] divided by B25 [number of rounds played])

$$=(B24-B26)/B25$$

Format the cell to ensure your handicap is rounded to a whole number. Click on the cells showing your Current and Series handicaps, go to the **Format** menu and click on **Cells**. The Number tab is selected. Click on **Number** in the Category pane, and set 'Decimal places' to '0'. Click **OK**.

Hole	Length	Par	Score
1	322 yards	4	5
2	447 yards	4	5
3	380 yards	4	6
4	305 yards	4	5
5	134 yards	3	4
6	346 yards	4	5
7	294 yards	4	4
8	266 yards	4	4
9	441 yards	4	6

5 To set up the Series Handicap calculator, click on cell **B24** and type in '=I21'. Click on **B25** and type '=B6'. Click on **B26** and type '=H6'. Then click **B27** and type in the formula '=(B24-B26)/B25'. For the Current Handicap, click in **I25** and type 'Last 3'.

6 To centre your heading, select cells **A1** to **I1**. Click the **Merge and Center** button. Style your document (see below). To widen a column to fit all the text, place the mouse pointer on the right edge of the column heading and double-click.

7 To centre the hole numbers and other data at the same time, drag the cursor over the relevant cells. Click on the **Center** toolbar button. Now enter all the course, length, par and score data. Excel will automatically calculate your formulas.

Using the toolbar to add style

You can style text and colour through the toolbar. To change cells, select them then use the toolbar's drop-down lists for font and font size. Click on the **Bold**, **Underline** and **Italicise** toolbar buttons to further enhance the text. To alter text colour, click the arrow beside the Font Color toolbar button and select from the colour palette. To add a background colour click the arrow beside the Fill Color toolbar button and choose a colour.

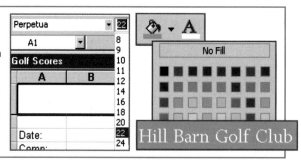

Adding worksheets

When you open an Excel document, you are given three sheets to work with (tabs for each sheet appear at the bottom of each page). To add more sheets for new rounds, click on the **Insert** menu and select **Worksheet**.

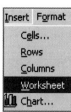

To update your Series Handicap, apply the same formulas each time, but use the sheet number from the previous sheet.

Current Handicap = (I24 [total number of strokes played in last three rounds] minus I26 [SSS total for last three rounds]) divided by 3 [number of rounds played]

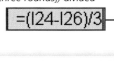

=(I24-I26)/3

Sheet1 / Sheet2 / Sheet3 /

Golf Scores

	A	B	C	Sc
4	Comp:	N		
5	Format:	Strok	Copy	
6	Round No:	1	Paste	
7				
8	*Hole*	*Length*	*Par*	*Sc*
9	1	322 yards	4	
10	2	447 yards	4	
11	3	380 yards	4	
12	4	305 yards	4	
13	5	134 yards	3	
14	6	346 yards	4	

Series Handicap

23	Series Handicap	
24		=I21+Sheet1!B24
25	Rounds	
26	SSS Tot	

11	5	1
12	6	3
13	7	2
14	8	266 yards
15	9	441 yards	4	4

Series Handicap

23		
24	**Strokes:**	353
25	**Rounds:**	4
26		=H6+Sheet1!B26

Out: 35 40

Series Handicap

23	Series Handicap	
24	Strokes:	172
25	Rounds:	2
26	SSS Total:	140
27	Handicap:	16

16	400 yards	4	5
17	220 yards	3	4
18	513 yards	5	5
	In:	35	46
	Out:	35	40
	Total:	70	86

Current Handicap

Strokes:	259
Rounds:	3
SSS Total:	210
Handicap:	=(I24-I26)/3

8 To create a second scorecard, copy and paste the document. Highlight cells **A1** to **I27** and click on the **Copy** toolbar button.

Click the **Sheet 2** tab and then the **Paste** button. Adjust column widths and fill in the scorecard, overwriting data where different.

9 For each new scorecard, carry over total strokes and SSS from the previous card. On Sheet 2, click **B24** then type '121+Sheet1!B24'. Click **B26** and type 'H6+Sheet1!B26'. After three rounds set the Current Handicap calculator.

10 Click on cell **I24** and type '121+Sheet1!!I21+Sheet2!I21'. Click **I26** and type 'H6+Sheet1!H6 +Sheet2!H6'. To work out the Current Handicap, click on **I27**, then type in '(I24-I26)/3'. To print, click on the **Print** button.

Current Handicap

For the Current Handicap calculation you must total up the strokes and SSS for the last three rounds:
- *Strokes:* to add the last two rounds to the current score, click **I24** and type '=I21+Sheet1!I21+Sheet2!I21'.
- *SSS:* to add SSS for the last two rounds to current SSS, click **I26** and type '=H6+Sheet1!H6+Sheet2!IH6'.
After, say, 50 rounds, the formulas remain the same, but the sheet references change: SSS for the last three rounds would be '=SUM(H6+Sheet48!H6+Sheet49!H6)'.

= =(I21+Sheet1!I21+Sheet2!I21)

Current sheet total score

Sheet 1 total score

Sheet 2 total score

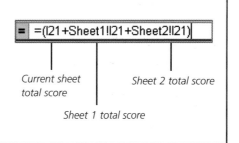

Design your own cross-stitch pattern

Use your computer to create your own embroidery projects

You can use your computer to enhance your enjoyment of any hobby or interest. Designing patterns for cross-stitch on your PC is just one example. Not only can you use your imagination to the full, but any errors can be corrected and amendments made in a matter of seconds.

By using the Windows' accessory program Paint, you can design the most intricate of patterns. The program allows you to construct your design stitch by stitch and experiment with colours. Our design fits on an A4 sheet and is for a 38 cm (15 in) square cushion, with each square representing a cross-stitch.

Make a rough sketch of your design on squared paper, experimenting with colour and ensuring you get the scale of the objects correct.

BEFORE YOU START

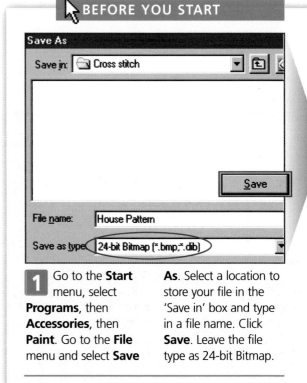

1 Go to the **Start** menu, select **Programs**, then **Accessories**, then **Paint**. Go to the **File** menu and select **Save As**. Select a location to store your file in the 'Save in' box and type in a file name. Click **Save**. Leave the file type as 24-bit Bitmap.

You can also design a cross-stitch pattern using other, more advanced graphics packages such as Adobe Illustrator and CorelDraw for PCs. Ask at your local PC store for details.

OTHER PROGRAMS

Templates on CD-ROM

Close-up
It's a good idea to start your design at the centre of the grid and work your way out. This way, you can copy and paste items and keep your design well balanced. Use the scroll bars to find your way to the centre.

*To colour in half the house, click on the **Brush** tool, select a style option for it, then a colour, then click on the part of the house you wish to colour.*

*To draw straight lines with the Pencil tool, click on the grid, press the **Shift** key then, keeping it pressed down, drag the cursor. This eliminates any shaky hand movement.*

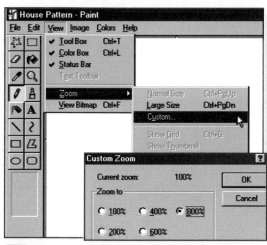

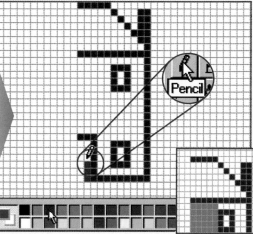

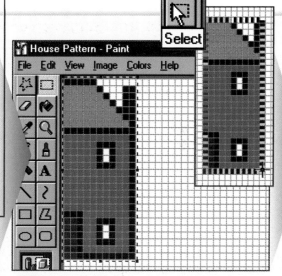

2 Now set up your canvas. Go to the **View** menu, select **Zoom** then **Custom**. In the dialogue box click the **800%** option then OK. Go to the **View** menu again, select **Zoom** then **Show Grid**. This brings up a square-by-square grid to represent your fabric.

3 For the outline of your first item (here, a house), click on a colour from the Color box at the bottom of the screen. Click the **Pencil** tool then click on the canvas and drag to draw the outline of one half of the house.

4 Now copy and paste your 'half house'. Click the **Select** tool then click and drag over the house. Go to the **Edit** menu and select **Copy**. Go to the **Edit** menu again and select **Paste**. The copied house appears in the top left corner of your screen.

Using the Tool box

Some tools, such as the brush and eraser tools, have a variety of styles which appear below the tool panel. Click on a style before using the tool.

The functions of the most popular tools are described here (to find out what other tools do, place your mouse pointer over the relevant tool button – a description will pop up):

 Free-Form Select Selects an irregular-shaped area. Click and drag the pointer to select.

 Select Selects a rectangular area. Click on the canvas and drag diagonally.

Eraser/Color Eraser Acts just like a rubber. Click and drag the pointer over the area to erase it.

Fill With Color Colour in a specific area with the colour of your choice. Click on the relevant area.

Pick Color Picks up a colour from the canvas. Apply the colour elsewhere by selecting another tool.

Magnifier Shows an area in close-up. Just click on the area. Also demagnifies magnified areas.

 Pencil Draws a thin freehand line. Click and drag the pointer to draw.

 Brush Used to draw a brushstroke style line. Select a brush then click and drag the pointer.

 Airbrush Gives a textured paint effect. Choose a spray radius then click and drag the pointer.

 Line Draws a straight line. Select a thickness then click and drag the pointer.

Curve Used to draw a curve. You draw a line first then click on the line and drag it to make a curve.

To make your border corners, click on the **Pencil** tool, then on the appropriate colour from the Color box, and do it manually.

To ensure your side borders are mirror images of each other, it may be necessary to rotate the top border by 270° for the second side border.

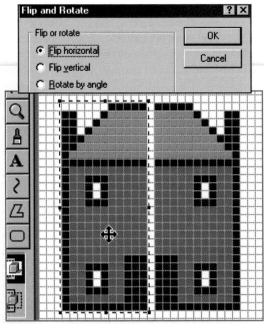

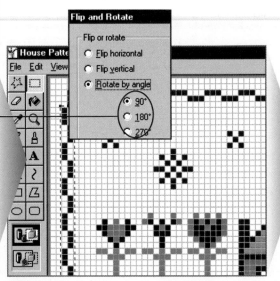

5 Go to the **Image** menu and click on **Flip/Rotate**. In the dialogue box click the 'Flip horizontal' option, then **OK**. Click on the image and drag it into position. Draw one each of the other items in your design, and copy and paste them into position in the same way.

6 To add a uniform border around your design, draw just a small section of it at the top of your design. Then select, copy, paste and reposition it to complete the top and bottom borders.

7 To add the side borders, select, copy and paste the top border. Go to the **Image** menu and click on **Flip/Rotate**. Select the 'Rotate by angle' option, then 90°. Click **OK**. Move the side border into position.

Customise colours

To create a new shade, customise an existing colour. Double-click on the colour in the Color box. In the Edit Colors dialogue box click on the **Define Custom Colors** button. To create your colour, move the slider on the right up or down until you get the right tone in the Color/Solid window. To save your new colour, click on the **Add to Custom Colors** button, then **OK**.

When you want to use it again, double-click on the Color box colour you customised. In the Edit Colors dialogue box your new shade appears in the 'Custom colors' section. Click on it to select it.

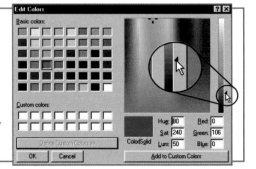

You need to print your design with the grid in place. Paint does not allow this, but it can be done using other built-in features of your PC.

When you press the Alt and the Print Screen keys a snapshot of the current window is taken and stored. The Print Screen key is to the right of the F12 key.

Watch out

When you paste an item, click on it immediately to move it. If you click on something else, the pasted item becomes de-selected, and you will need to select it again by dragging the cursor over it.

PRINTING YOUR DESIGN

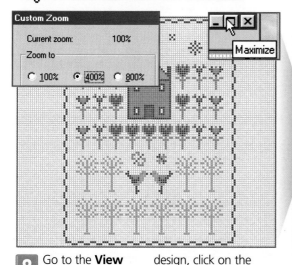

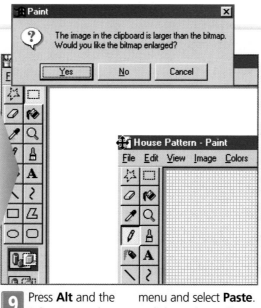

8 Go to the **View** menu, select **Zoom** then **Custom**. In the dialogue box select the 400% option. (If you can't see all your design, click on the **Maximize** button.) If the grid isn't visible go to the **View** menu, select **Zoom** and then **Show Grid**.

9 Press **Alt** and the **Print Screen** keys (see above). Now save your file then go to the **File** menu and click on **New**. Go to the **Edit** menu and select **Paste**. A dialogue box will appear and ask whether you want to enlarge the bitmap. Click on **Yes**.

10 A snapshot of your Paint window appears. Select the areas you don't need – the Paint window's Tool box, for example – and press the **Delete** key. Go to the **File** menu and click on **Save As**. Name and save your file. Go to the **File** menu and select **Print**.

Correcting mistakes

 If you make a mistake when drawing, go to the Color box and click on the colour white. Then click on the affected squares to make them white again.

 To correct larger mistakes, click on the **Eraser** tool, select a size of eraser then drag it across the affected area.

Now that you are familiar with Paint, use it to edit photographs and other images, or to paint an original picture. See pages 212 and 224 for more ideas.

OTHER IDEAS TO TRY

Organise a reunion and relive

Whether bringing distant family members together, or catching up with

Project planner

Create a folder called 'Reunion'. Then add sub-folders for each area of the project.

- 📁 **Reunion**
  - 📁 People
  - 📁 Communications
  - 📁 Event logistics
  - 📁 Finance
  - 📁 Suppliers
  - 📁 Design & logos

It is all too easy to lose touch with the people who used to be part of our lives. All of us have friends we would like to see more often. That is what makes a reunion such a special occasion – and your PC can make it easier to bring together people separated by the years and the continents.

Start by setting up an event planner database. Record what tasks need to be taken care of, by when and by whom. Add guest information such as address, e-mail address and phone or fax numbers, as well as contact information for caterers and any other professionals you need to recruit to make the reunion a success.

The rapid spread of the Internet means that there are now worldwide e-mail directories of people who are on-line. Once you have compiled your initial guest list, try searching on-line for those you haven't been able to trace through other means. Some people might be easier to contact using your PC as a fax. Use any of these methods to receive information

the good old days

old schoolfriends, your PC can help you

from your old school, college, workplace or anyone else helping in the search for 'missing' friends or colleagues. For letters, fax transmissions and e-mails, you could create an attention-grabbing 'reunion' letterhead, then adapt it for subsequent gatherings.

Using your word processing program, produce a newsletter to keep everyone updated on the arrangements. This could also take the form of a 'missing persons bulletin', to encourage other guests to help you trace 'lost' invitees and supply you with most recent known contact details.

When you have a rough idea of how many people will be attending the event, book the venue and arrange catering and entertainment, if required, at the same time as keeping track of expenses through a spreadsheet.

One item you won't have to pay for is the invitations. Just design and print them on your PC – you can personalise the design and create a stir from the start.

Tasks to do

- Contact your old company or college for a list of previous employees or students
- Conduct research over the Internet
- Draw up a guest list
- Mail, fax or e-mail a proposal to potential guests
- Start to compile a reunion database
- Design and send final invitations
- Scan in and e-mail photos of the event

Ideas and inspirations

Co-ordinating guests, possibly from all over the world, requires military-style planning. Make sure you dip into your armoury of PC-based skills to reduce as much of the hard work as possible. Adapt the following projects as desired, then prepare for a truly memorable occasion.

96 **Searching the Internet**
Locate people anywhere in the world via e-mail address databases and make contact with them.

310 **Event planner database**
Set up a document to handle the logistics of your reunion and delegate jobs to others.

168 **Compile a guest list**
Make a database to incorporate people's address, phone, fax and e-mail details.

164 **Create a newsletter**
If the timescale for planning your event is long, you may wish to update guests on your progress.

200 **Create an invitation**
It may be the first or the last task you carry out, but it's sure to be distinctive with your PC's help.

Also worth considering…

You can adapt virtually any communications skill you have learned to help you plan the reunion.

84 **Use your PC as a fax**
Make sure overseas guests receive updates if they don't have e-mail.

Troubleshooting

Frozen screens, printing errors, corrupt programs and malevolent computer viruses can befall any PC user. But in most cases these and many other problems are easy to solve. Wherever the fault lies – in Windows, in an application or in the computer hardware – this section will help you identify the symptoms, diagnose the problem and come up with a remedy.

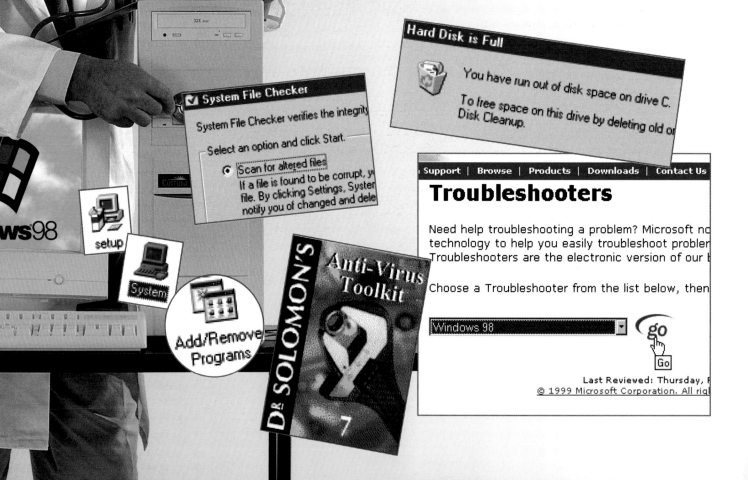

Microsoft Windows 98

setup

System

Add/Remove Programs

Hard Disk is Full

You have run out of disk space on drive C.

To free space on this drive by deleting old or Disk Cleanup.

System File Checker

System File Checker verifies the integrity

Select an option and click Start.

- Scan for altered files

If a file is found to be corrupt, y file. By clicking Settings, System notify you of changed and dele

Dr SOLOMON'S Anti-Virus Toolkit 7

Support | Browse | Products | Downloads | Contact Us

Troubleshooters

Need help troubleshooting a problem? Microsoft no technology to help you easily troubleshoot problem Troubleshooters are the electronic version of our b

Choose a Troubleshooter from the list below, then

Windows 98

go

Go

Last Reviewed: Thursday, F
© 1999 Microsoft Corporation. All rig

In this section

Hardware Hiccups

Problems sometimes occur with the physical machinery of your computer, its cables, components and 'moving parts'. The advice on these pages will help you to fix most common hardware difficulties.

Win with Windows

Windows is the element of your system which allows communication between your hardware and your programs. Without it, your PC is useless. So deal with any problems as soon as they arise to be sure that your computer stays in peak condition.

Software Solutions

When a program behaves in an unexpected way, you may be inclined to think that you have done something wrong. But programs do malfunction. Software Solutions can help you understand and overcome the most common program faults.

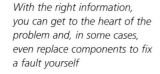

With the right information, you can get to the heart of the problem and, in some cases, even replace components to fix a fault yourself

Error Deleting File

Cannot delete example1: Ac[...]

Make sure the disk is not full or write [...] and that the file is not currently in use.

O[...]

Keyboard Properties ? ×

| Speed | Language |

Installed keyboard languages and layouts

Language: Layout:

Af Afrikaans   United States 101

```
COUNTRY   SYS     17069  09/04/91    5:00
EGA       SYS      4885  09/04/91    5:00
FORMAT    COM     32911  09/04/91    5:00
KEYB      COM     14986  09/04/91    5:00
KEYBOARD  SYS     34697  09/04/91    5:00
NLSFUNC   EXE      7052  09/04/91    5:00
DISPLAY   SYS     15792  09/04/91    5:00
EGA       CPI     58873  09/04/91    5:00
HIMEM     SYS     11552  09/04/91    5:00
                   8169  09/04/91    5:00
                   5873  09/04/91    5:00
                   0912  09/04/91    5:00
                   8335  09/04/91    5:00
                2058566  bytes
               11087872  bytes free
```

My computer won't start up

There are steps you can take when you can't get your PC to start working

Start-up problems are the most serious of hardware hiccups. It is hard to cure the sickness when the patient cannot tell you what is wrong. But there are things you can do to diagnose the problem when your computer will not start at all. Then, if you cannot solve the problem yourself, you can at least give some useful leads to a specialist PC repairer.

Usually, when your computer won't start, it is due to problems with the hard disk. This vital component stores Windows Files and all your documents. If the Windows files get damaged, your PC may not be able to load Windows.

The hard disk consists of a 'read/write' head which hovers over magnetised disks. The distance between the head and the disks is less than the thickness of a human hair. If the read/write head touches the disk the result is a 'head crash' – a damaging collision between the head and the fast spinning platters. A head crash can destroy large amounts of data on the hard disk, including the data needed to get the computer working again. Solving this problem is complicated, and should only be attempted once all other possible causes have been addressed.

Are you connected?

If your monitor shows nothing at all when you turn the computer on, check that the power lights are lit on the system unit and monitor. If not, check that both elements are plugged in, that the socket switches are on and that the fuses in the plugs haven't blown.

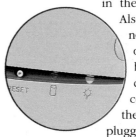

Also check that the brightness and contrast controls on the monitor have not been turned down. Then check that the cable that connects the monitor to the PC's graphics card is plugged in.

Try resetting

If none of this helps, turn your computer off, leave it for a minute, then switch it on again. If the screen is still blank, note down the number of bleeps given during the start-up routine. This may be helpful to a PC specialist when diagnosing the problem.

Key word
POST *The POST (Power On Self Test) routine checks that your most vital hardware components are working correctly. If the POST messages move up the screen too fast for you to read them, press the **Pause** key in the top right of your keyboard. Press **Enter** to continue.*

What does your computer think is wrong?
Make a note of any error messages given by the Power On Self Test (POST) routine after you turn on your PC. Common messages are displayed below; others may be explained in your PC's manual. At the very least, this data may be of use to a repairer or the staff at the other end of a service line.

`201 Memory error` These messages denote a faulty memory chip. For your computer to function normally again, a small memory circuit board must be replaced. You need to get the right type, so contact your PC's maker or get a local PC dealer to fit it for you.

`Parity error`

`Starting Windows 98` If this appears before your system 'freezes', you probably have a Windows configuration problem. See page 352 for further assistance.

`Operating system not found` If you get either of these, you have a problem with your hard disk. Start the PC from your rescue disk.

`Boot disk failure`

`This is not a bootable floppy` Both these messages mean there is a floppy disk in the [A:] drive and that your PC is trying to use it to start up. You may get the supplementary message 'Replace and press any key when ready', in which case eject the floppy disk and press any key. Otherwise, eject the disk, turn off the PC, then switch it on again. Always eject CDs and floppy disks before you shut down your PC.

`Non-system disk`

`CMOS checksum failure` This indicates that your CMOS (Complimentary Metal Oxide Semiconductor) battery has run down and needs replacing by a repairer. Your PC will then work as before, with no data loss. The CMOS stores data about your system set-up, including your type of hard disk and the date and time. It is powered by a small battery that recharges itself whenever the PC is switched on, so make sure you turn it on at least once a month for an hour or so.

Using a start-up or rescue disk
If all else fails you may need to use a rescue disk to get in to your computer.

If you've checked the connections and power supply and Windows still won't start up, switch your PC off then locate your rescue disk. You should have made one when you first bought your PC (see page 60). If you did not make one, or you have mislaid it, take your PC to a repair shop where they should still be able to help.

If you do have a rescue disk, insert it in your floppy drive and switch on your PC and monitor again. The

 PC should start up, using the files on the floppy disk. At the prompt 'A:\>', type 'c:' then press the **Return** key.

Your computer will attempt to access the hard disk, or C: drive. If you get a 'C:\>' prompt, the hard disk is working, but to a limited extent. A specialist should be able to save your files. (If you know how to use DOS commands you may even be able to do this yourself.)

If you get a message such as 'Drive C: not found' then you have a serious hard-disk fault. A specialist might be able to save some of the data on the hard disk, but you may have lost all your work.

Watch out
Don't move your system unit, which houses the hard disk, when it is switched on. This can cause the hard disk's read/write head to touch the disk platters, in turn causing a head crash and destroying a great deal of data. When the computer is turned off, the head moves away from the platters and you can move your PC in safety.

My printer isn't working

Check your hardware and software to solve printing problems

Nothing is more frustrating than to put the finishing touches to a document, only to find that you can't print it out. But don't worry. While printing problems are the most common of hardware hiccups, they are also amongst the easiest to solve.

Sometimes it is a simple question of maintenance: is there paper in the tray? Has the ink (or the toner) run out? Otherwise, there is a limited number of things that can go wrong: paper jams, loose connections, and mistaken set-up commands cover most difficulties. The steps on this page should lead you to the root of any problem. After a while, you will develop a feel for what has gone wrong with your own printer – and while you are gaining that experience, you can always use the Help files in Windows 98.

In the hardware

If you send a document to print, and it fails to do so, the first thing you should check is that the printer is switched on – is the power light on? Check that it is switched on at the mains socket too.

Next, make sure there is paper in the printer paper tray, and that none of it has become jammed as it has been fed through. If the printer runs out of paper you should get an error message on your computer screen. If your printer is quite old, it may start to jam up more often – getting the rollers replaced may help. Otherwise, you may need to buy a new printer.

When your computer recognises that you have a printing problem, Windows will alert you by bringing up an error message suggesting certain action that you can take.

Printers Folder

? There was an error writing to LPT1: for the printer (HP LaserJe
There was a problem sending your document to the printer.
Make sure the printer cable is connected and that the printer i
To continue printing, click retry.
Windows will automatically retry after 5 seconds.

[Retry]   [Cancel]

Is the printer connected?

The printer has its own connection port at the rear of the system unit. You need to make sure that all the visible connections are correctly fitted. Check that the cable is securely plugged in and that the screws are screwed in firmly. Also make sure that the cable is connected properly to the printer, and that the clips are secured.

Start again

One way of quickly solving a printer problem is to try resetting the printer. To do this, just turn it off, wait a few seconds, then turn it on again.

Getting ready to print

The first step to successful printing is making sure you have made the correct settings.

Page Setup

Occasionally, a page will fail to print, or will print out wrongly, if your page isn't 'set up' correctly. Get into the habit of checking your Page Setup before you print. To do this, go to the **File** menu and click on **Page Setup.**

In the Page Setup dialogue box you set the parameters for the way the document will print – its physical size and orientation. If you want A4 size, click on the **Paper Size** tab and select **A4** in the 'Paper size' box. Check you have the correct orientation, too. With Portrait the page's width is the shorter dimension. With Landscape, the page's length is the shorter.

Print Preview

In many programs you can look at how the page appears before printing by going to the **File** menu and clicking on **Print Preview**. You will be able to see any set-up problems, such as if text runs over to other pages because the orientation is wrong.

Paper source

Your printer may have more than one feeder tray for paper, such as a manual feed tray needed to print envelopes. If so, make sure that you have selected the right tray to print from. In the **Page Setup** dialogue box click on the **Paper Source** tab and select the appropriate tray. Then check that the tray you want to print from has the right size paper in it.

Troubleshooters

If none of the above solutions works, you may have a software problem. Windows includes a series of troubleshooters that explain how to rectify software problems with your printer.

Go to the **Start** menu and click on **Help**. With the Contents tab selected, click on **Troubleshooting**, then on **Windows 98 Troubleshooters** then on **Print**. The Wizard will then help you diagnose and solve the problem by asking you to complete a course of action for each possible cause of printer failure.

Printer tools

Many printers come with a set of tools on a disk or CD-ROM that check for common printer faults and may even try to fix them. Load the disk and follow the on-screen instructions.

Reinstalling your printer

If all else fails, you could try reinstalling your printer. Go to the **Start** menu, select **Settings** then **Printers**. Click on your printer's icon and press the **Delete** key to uninstall the printer. Then double-click on the **Add Printer** icon. Follow the on-screen instructions to identify the type of printer you are installing.

Locate and load the CD-ROM or floppy disk that came with your printer then click on **Have Disk**. The disk will run its automatic installation procedure.

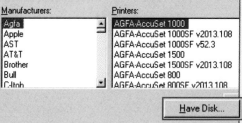

Checking ink levels

If the printer is printing your work but the printed text is faint or invisible, check that the ink or toner has not run out. Most printers will have a light on the front that will indicate if either is running out. Sometimes with colour inkjet printers, the cartridge for one colour gets blocked or runs out sooner than the others. This can lead to strange colours being printed. It may be possible to clear a temporary blockage – check the printer's manual for details. If this doesn't work out, you'll have to replace the cartridge.

Remember to refer to the printer handbook for details of buying and replacing toner or ink cartridges.

My keyboard isn't working

Hardware or software may be at fault if your keyboard is playing up

Your keyboard is perhaps the most vulnerable part of your computer. It gets the heaviest wear and tear; it is more likely to be moved and dropped; it takes a physical pounding every time you type a letter; and it is also exposed to dust, dirt and the occasional spillage. Fortunately, most modern keyboards are hardwearing and can take a lot of punishment before they start malfunctioning.

The best way to avoid problems in the first place is to look after your keyboard (see page 64). But even if you take good care of your equipment, you may find keys start to stick or fail to respond when you press them. The problem may be due to a faulty connection or (more rarely) to a software error. You need to check every possibility before you rush out and buy a new keyboard: the remedy could be as simple as giving the keys a quick clean.

If the whole keyboard fails

If none of the keys on your keyboard is responding, you should first check whether your PC has crashed. Try using your mouse to move the mouse pointer on screen. If it moves as usual, the problem must lie with your keyboard.

First check the connections. Make sure it is plugged in properly and into the right socket in the system unit (it is possible to plug the keyboard into the mouse port by mistake). It is also possible that the lead itself has been damaged in some way – check for signs of damage.

If all else fails, borrow a keyboard from a friend and see whether it works with your PC. If it does, you may need to buy a new keyboard.

If a key won't respond

If one of the keys on your keyboard isn't working properly check whether dirt has built up between the keys. Use a dust spray, or work cleaning cards dipped in cleaning solution between the keys, to solve the problem. As a final measure, gently lever off the offending key and check for debris trapped underneath.

If this doesn't work, and you know the software isn't to blame (see opposite), it is less expensive to buy a new keyboard than to have the current one repaired.

Dealing with a spillage

If you spill a drink on your keyboard, unplug the keyboard, wash it using a clean sponge and a bowl of soapy water and leave for a day or two to dry thoroughly. Modern keyboards can be washed without suffering ill-effects.

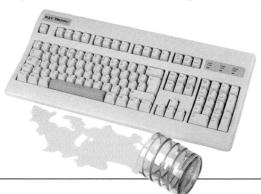

Solving keyboard software problems

Windows has several settings that can affect the use of your keyboard. Check these if you are having problems with the keyboard or if the settings don't suit your special needs.

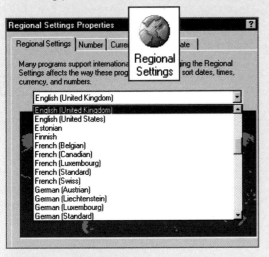

If this doesn't solve the problem, return to the **Control Panel** and double-click on the **Keyboard** icon. In the dialogue box click on the **Language** tab. If the correct language is not displayed in the pane – English (British) for the UK; English (United States) for the US – click on the **Add** button. Click the arrow to the right of the Language box, scroll down and click on the correct language, then click **OK**. (To remove the wrong language, click on it then click on the **Remove** button.)

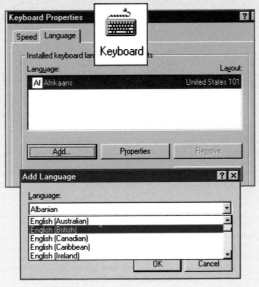

Select the correct language

If you press a key and a different letter or symbol appears on your screen, you probably have a problem with your software settings. Sometimes, a new PC will be set up for a different country, and this can affect the way it displays certain characters such as currency signs.

To check this, go to the **Start** menu, select **Settings** then click on **Control Panel**. Now double-click on the **Regional Settings** icon. Ensure the correct country is selected then click **OK**. If you select a different country you will need to restart your computer before the settings take effect.

Make your keyboard easier to use

If you have difficulty using your keyboard because of a disability, Windows 98 has a special Accessibility function that will make it easier. You can set up your PC so that you don't have to press more than one key at a time (StickyKeys). You can also set it up to ignore multiple presses of the same key (BounceKeys), or to warn you when you have pressed an important key, such as the Caps Lock (ToggleKeys).

To arrange this, go to the **Start** menu and select **Programs**, then **Accessories**, then **Accessibility** and finally **Accessibility Wizard**. Click **Next**, then **Next** again. Click in the 'I have difficulty using the keyboard or mouse' box, then click **Next** to view your options.

Watch out

If you press a key and an unexpected character appears, it may not necessarily mean the language your PC is using is incorrect. You may simply be using the wrong font. Some fonts, such as Zapf Dingbats and Wingdings, are entirely composed of unusual characters. Highlight the character then look at the font box on the toolbar to view the font used.

My mouse isn't working

If your mouse stops responding, it isn't necessarily broken

Don't be alarmed if something seems to go wrong with your mouse. As with most hardware difficulties, there are ways of working out where the problem lies.

If your cursor starts to move in a jerky way, or stops moving altogether, there are four likely causes. The two most common reasons are that the inside of your mouse needs to be cleaned (see page 64) or that your mouse is not properly connected (see opposite). When you open up your mouse to clean it, you can also check for a third possible problem – that one or other of the mouse rollers has worn out. If this is the case, buying a new mouse is the best remedy.

The final, and least likely, reason for a fault is a software conflict. This means that your computer does not recognise the mouse. A software conflict is only likely to occur with an older style PC that uses a serial mouse. This problem can usually be resolved by plugging the mouse into a different serial port (see opposite).

Different types of mouse

Most computers use a conventional mouse connected directly to the system unit. However, other styles of mouse are available.

● Pen mice and trackballs work in a similar way to conventional mice, and all of the troubleshooting tips above and opposite apply to them.

● Touchpads and tiny joysticks, used mainly with laptop computers, do not plug into the computer and so cannot be cleaned easily. If you experience problems with these, and your computer is still under guarantee, take it back to the shop where you bought it. If it is not under guarantee, take your computer to a specialist repair shop.

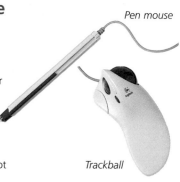

Pen mouse

Trackball

Touchpad

Bright idea
*If you want to shut down your computer but your mouse isn't working, press the **Windows** key on your keyboard (near the bottom left-hand corner). This will bring up the Start menu. Now press the **U** key to shut down, and **Return** for OK.*

Watch out
If your mouse isn't plugged in properly when you turn on your computer, Windows will give you a warning message and you will find that the mouse will not respond to your hand movements.

Pointing you in the right direction
If you are having problems with your mouse, first check that the hardware is connected and in working order, then check for software trouble.

Check your connection
If your mouse stops responding while you are working, first check that the cable is plugged in properly to the system unit, and that it's in the correct port. Most modern mice have their own port and connector, but it's possible to plug a 'PS/2' mouse into the keyboard port by mistake. If you have to plug the cable back in, re-start the computer to get the mouse working again.

The mouse port
Not all computers have PS/2 ports for the mouse and keyboard. You may find that your mouse has a larger plug that fits into a different socket – the serial port (also called the communications port). Switch off the PC then disconnect and reconnect the mouse in its serial port. Then switch the PC back on.

Choosing a serial port
If you use a mouse that connects to a serial port, and you've checked that its plug is firmly connected but you are still experiencing a problem, switch your computer off and plug the mouse into the second serial port. Switch the PC back on. If your mouse works properly in its new port, there may be a problem with the first serial port. Contact your PC manufacturer for advice.

Cleaning your mouse
If your mouse isn't responding as it should, you may need to clean it. For instructions on cleaning your mouse, see page 64.

If all else fails...
If none of the above works, try borrowing a mouse that definitely works from another computer. Make sure the mouse has the same connector as yours. If the borrowed mouse works on your computer, there must be something wrong with the mechanics of your mouse. If you are sure your mouse is broken and it is not under guarantee, then you will have to buy a new one.

Adapting to a serial port
If you have a PC with serial ports and no PS/2 mouse ports, you need a serial mouse. It is possible to use a mouse with a newer PS/2-style plug, but you will need an extra adaptor that converts it to fit a serial port.

My speakers don't work

What to do if the only sound coming from your PC is silence

Computer speakers will generally give many years of use without any need for maintenance, apart from regular cleaning. Over time – years, in fact – the sound computer speakers generate may become increasingly crackly. This is merely a sign of wear and tear, and the most economical solution is to replace them.

So seldom do computer speakers malfunction that, if you're using your computer and no sound comes out of them, the likelihood is that the problem lies not with the speakers but with the way they have been connected to the PC or with the software you are using.

A little knowledge of how speakers connect to your computer and interact with your software should help you get to the bottom of the problem fast.

Some sound advice

It may seem obvious, but first check that the volume control is turned up. Next, check that the speakers are switched on – is there a power light? If your speakers need to be plugged into a mains socket, check that they are. Also check that they're plugged into your computer properly. Speakers are

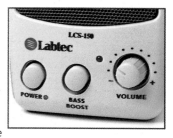

plugged into a sound card in the system unit. The sound card usually has a number of connectors, for microphones as well as speakers. Swap the speaker plug around until you hear the speakers. If you have stereo speakers, you need to make sure they are connected to each other.

Software options

Another user may have disabled the sound facility on the piece of software you are using. Many games allow you to turn off the sound, out of consideration to those who share your space. If you can find no reference to sound in the program, check that sound is actually supposed to come from the software you are using (look in the manual).

Watch out

Your speakers contain magnets. If you place them on your desk and then place floppy disks near to them, the data on the floppy disks may be lost or become corrupted. The same applies to built-in speakers or ones that have been mounted to the sides of your computer's monitor.

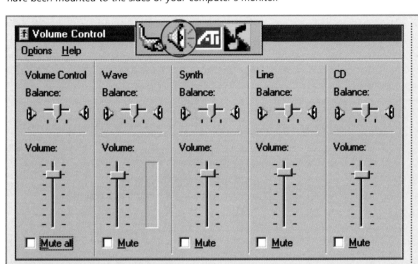

Checking your volume control

If none of the checks to your connections and external controls reveals the fault, then you probably have a software problem. First check that the speaker volumes are not turned off.

Locate the small speaker that appears on the right-hand side of the Windows Taskbar and double-click on it. In the Volume Control dialogue box check that none of the Mute boxes are ticked (if they are, click in them), and that the volume sliders are near the top of their respective scales.

If you have stereo speakers check that the Balance options are even before closing the dialogue box.

Extra help

Remember that Windows has its own built-in Help menus which explain how it works. Go to the **Start** menu and click on **Help**. In Windows Help, click on the **Contents** tab and then click on **Troubleshooting** in the window. A list of contents appears. Click on **Windows 98 Troubleshooters** then **Sound**. You will be given a list of possible problems in the right-hand pane. Click on the relevant box, then scroll to the base of the list and click **Next** for step-by-step instructions from Windows Help.

Types of speakers

Most PCs emit sound through their own separate, free-standing speakers. However, it's possible that your PC's speakers are built into the monitor, one on either side of the screen. These speakers also connect by cables to the main system unit.

Ensure your speakers are part of your regular cleaning routine (see page 64), and that their cables are kept clear of any obstruction.

If all else fails...

Borrow a pair of speakers from a friend and connect them to your PC. If these work (keep the volume low to avoid damage), then you need to get your own speakers repaired or replaced.

Bright idea

If you can't borrow a pair of speakers, you may be able to use your Hi-Fi speakers. Use a cable to connect between the speakers port on your system unit and the auxiliary jack socket of your amplifier. (You may need to get a special cable.) Do not place your Hi-Fi speakers too close to your PC as they are magnetic and may corrupt your hard disk.

My modem isn't working

How to solve problems linking to the Internet or sending e-mail

Sometimes, a piece of software or hardware that's been functioning well for months can suddenly go wrong or stop working altogether. If something like that happens with your modem, don't panic. There are a number of reasons why your modem might not be working, and most of the problems are easily resolved.

Problems with your ISP

You should first check whether the problem is at your end. Try to connect to your Internet Service Provider (ISP) to see if the modem starts to dial. If you hear a series of loud, high-pitched tones (the sort you hear when you connect to a fax machine) then you know your modem is trying to make a connection. If such a connection does not complete, the cause could well be with the service provider's equipment rather than yours. In this case, call your ISP to find out if other customers are having problems and, if so, when the fault will be fixed.

Modem checks

If, when you try to make a connection, your modem does not emit the usual high-pitched tones, the problem may be with the modem set-up on your computer – the modem might not be properly installed, for example. Sometimes, if you add a new piece of hardware or software to your computer,

it can affect the way your modem is set up. Run through the set-up procedure in the modem manual to check that everything is arranged correctly. Alternatively, run the modem troubleshooter (see opposite).

Plugs and switches

Although it may seem obvious, check that the modem is properly connected. If you have an internal modem, check that the cable which connects it to the phone socket is plugged in at both ends. If you have an external modem, check that all its cables are firmly plugged in, and that the right cables are plugged into both the PC and the mains supply. Check that the modem and the mains power are switched on.

If you are sure that your modem is set up correctly, that your phone line is working and that all your cables are correctly fitted, but you still can't make a connection, it's possible that the head of the modem cable that connects the modem to the phone line is damaged. This head is made up of a series of delicate copper wires that are covered by a clear plastic adaptor which slots into the back of the modem. Buy a new cable from a computer shop and reconnect your modem (see opposite).

Key word
Troubleshooter *This is a special facility in Windows that diagnoses and helps you fix problems. The modem troubleshooter takes you through possible problems step by step until you find out what is causing the breakdown. It then shows you how to make the necessary repairs.*

The Modem Troubleshooter

If your ISP and your connections seem to be OK, try using the help available in Windows.

Before troubleshooting

Go to the **Start** menu and select **Settings** then **Control Panel**. (Alternatively, double-click on **My Computer**, then on **Control Panel**.) Double-click on the **Modems** icon and check that your modem is listed (this means your computer recognises it as installed).

If your modem is not listed, it may have been accidentally removed by another installation. Reinstall it using the software and instructions that came with it. If the modem is listed, click **OK** to close the box and run the Modem Troubleshooter.

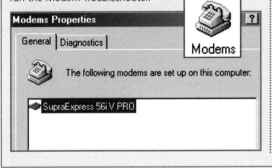

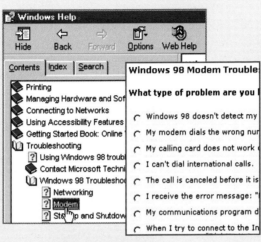

Windows 98 Troubleshooter

In Windows 98 go to the **Start** menu and click on **Help**. In the Windows Help dialogue box, with the Contents tab selected, click on **Troubleshooting** then **Windows 98 Troubleshooters**, then **Modem**.

A list of symptoms appears in the right-hand pane of the window. Click on a symptom that's relevant to your problem, then click the **Next** button. Now follow the on-screen instructions to try to solve your problem.

Windows 95 Troubleshooter

In Windows 95 go to the **Start** menu and click on **Help**. In the Windows Help dialogue box, with the Contents tab selected, click on **Troubleshooting**, then on **If You Have Trouble Using Your Modem**. A box will appear asking what the problem is. Click on a relevant option. Further boxes will appear asking you more specific questions, then you will be given possible solutions. Follow the instructions that appear on screen. They may require you to check some original settings, and you may need to check details with your ISP.

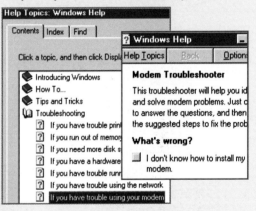

Reinstalling your modem

First make sure that your modem is correctly attached to your computer. Then go to the **Start** menu, select **Settings**, then **Control Panel**. Click on the **Modems** icon. An Install New Modem dialogue box appears. Follow the instructions to let your computer know that you want to install a modem. When prompted to choose a driver file, insert the floppy disk or CD-ROM that came with the modem, and click the **Have Disk** button. The disk will run an automatic installation procedure for the modem.

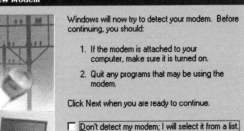

Upgrading your hardware

Improve the capabilities of your PC by adding or replacing a component

As your computer gets older, or if you add new software to an elderly machine, you may find that it does not run as quickly as it did when you first started using it. The best way to resolve this problem – short of uninstalling the new programs – is to install more RAM (Random Access Memory).

RAM is the place where your PC stores the program you have open and the data you are currently working on. Installing more RAM will help your computer to function better, but it will not improve the output of your new programs. If, for example, you load the latest computer game on an old machine, you may find it is incapable of producing the quality of image or sound effects that you would like. It is possible to upgrade individual hardware and software components to improve your PC's performance, but if you find there are several elements you want to upgrade, you may decide that it would be more cost-effective to invest in a completely new system.

Before installing new components, be sure to back up important data from your hard disk – in case anything goes wrong (see page 359 for advice on backing up).

Watch out
As with all mains-powered devices, treat your PC with caution. Before removing the cover from the system unit make sure the power is off. Take no risks with electricity: switch the power off at the wall then unplug the power cable from the rear of the system unit.

Bright idea
Innovations in PC hardware take place all the time, which means it's hard to know whether this month's hot new item will be next month's white elephant. Wait to see if the latest products establish themselves, and let the premium prices drop a little before you buy.

The basics of upgrading
Upgrading your PC will often involve opening up the system unit. Here we show you how to fit a graphics card – use it as a guide to fitting a sound card or internal modem.

Fitting a new graphics card

A graphics card generates the picture signal and sends it to the computer monitor. Newer graphics cards display 3D graphics more smoothly than older cards. The cards are designed to fit into either a PCI or AGP slot at the rear of your system unit (older PCs are likely to have only PCI slots). To make sure you buy the appropriate card for your PC, consult your PC's manual or contact the manufacturer.

Switch off your PC, remove the power cables from the back of the system unit, then take its cover off (consult your PC's manual to find out how to do this). Locate your existing graphics card – the monitor cable will be attached to it from the rear. Unplug the monitor cable then remove the screw that holds the card in place and put it to one side. Carefully pull out the card, then gently insert the new card in its place, making sure the socket on its backing plate is facing outwards from the back of the system unit. Secure the card by replacing the screw, then replace the system unit's cover.

Replace all the cables and turn on your PC. Windows should automatically run the Add New Hardware Wizard (see below), displaying the message: 'Windows has found new hardware and is installing new drivers for it'.

Insert the floppy disk or CD-ROM that came with the new graphics card. Windows 98 will look on the disk for the new driver (the software that interacts between Windows and the hardware itself). Windows 95 users need to specify the location of the driver by clicking on the button marked **Have disk** and typing in the letter of the disk drive you are using ('a' for floppy; 'd' for CD-ROM). Follow the on-screen instructions, then restart your PC to see the effects of your new graphics card.

Remove the existing graphics card to make space for the new one

Gently insert the new card, pushing it firmly if necessary to make sure it is in place

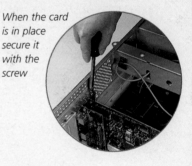

When the card is in place secure it with the screw

Locating the hardware for the Wizard
When you add new items of hardware, Windows will usually detect them and automatically run the Add New Hardware Wizard when you restart your PC. This function takes you through the process of setting up your PC to use the new hardware.

If Windows does not detect the new piece of hardware, you will need to start the Add New Hardware Wizard yourself. To do this,

go to the **Start** menu and select **Settings** then **Control Panel**. Double-click on the **Add New Hardware** icon.

The Wizard will begin by looking for any new hardware. If it finds the relevant hardware it will prompt you to insert the disk that holds the driver for it (see *The basics of upgrading*, above). If the Wizard does not detect the hardware, tell it to do so by clicking on the relevant option from a list. You will then be prompted to insert the disk.

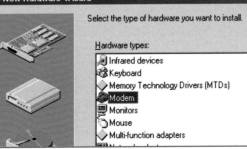

Watch out
Make sure you get the right type of memory. Modern PCs use DIMMs (dual inline memory modules), older ones use SIMMs (single inline memory modules). SIMMs are a different size and need to be fitted in pairs of the same capacity.

What to get and why
Think carefully before you upgrade. Be sure the new hardware will make a real difference.

Upgrading memory
Installing extra RAM in your PC is one of the most cost-effective upgrades you can make. Windows 95 and 98 need at least 32 Mb of RAM, but they will perform much better with 64 Mb. If you find that your PC operates very slowly, or that the hard disk light flickers constantly as you use your PC, you are almost certainly short of RAM.

Fitting memory is easy. Remove the cover from the system unit and 'clip' the chip into the appropriate slot (your PC's manual will show you the exact location). Make sure you fit the correct type of memory for your machine (DIMMs or SIMMs – see above). If in doubt, take your PC to a dealer to have RAM installed.

Sound cards
Although new PCs come with sound facilities, a specialist sound card will give you better sound quality and allow you to appreciate innovations such as 3D sound that appear in the latest computer games.

New sound cards will also give you more realistic instrument sounds and 'acoustic environments' that make it seem as though sound is coming from a distance or even around corners. Innovations such as DVD videos might also mean that you need a new sound card for the best audio reproduction.

Fitting a sound card is straightforward. It is almost the

same procedure as replacing your graphics card (see page 345). The sound card is easy to identify – the speakers cable will be attached to it from the rear.

Graphics cards
Most computers are sold with a graphics card that will handle most programs with ease. But if you use intensive graphics software such as Photoshop, or if you want to run the most recent 3D games at top speed, you might find that you need to upgrade to a faster graphics card.

Some graphics cards will help your computer to create better images when viewing video, television programmes or DVD movies on your computer screen (see below).

Shaping up for DVD
Digital Versatile Discs (DVDs) are a fairly new format for storing video as well as audio and computer data. They are, essentially, an updated version of CD-ROM discs, and can store as much as eight hours of video footage. (Attempts to record movies on CD-ROM discs failed because image quality suffered even when squeezing just an hour of footage on to a single disc.) It is not possible to save information on to DVD-ROM discs, but you can play games and watch videos supplied on them.

If you buy a DVD-ROM drive, you will receive an MPEG 2 video decoder board and a Dolby Digital decoder to install along with your drive to get the most from DVD movies. But to get maximum benefit it may be worth upgrading other aspects of your PC. MPEG decoder boards can be connected to your television, which may produce better-quality images.

To take full advantage of the audio output of DVD, you could upgrade your speakers, too. And if your graphics card has less than 8 Mb of RAM, you will need to upgrade it to get the most out of the DVD format.

Bright idea
Software manufacturers have a vested interest in encouraging you to buy products that might mean having to upgrade hardware. So, if in doubt, read product reviews in computer magazines for impartial advice on whether such an item is worth buying.

Floppy disk drives

The standard 1.44 Mb floppy disk drive that comes with most PCs is gradually being superseded by other devices such as Zip drives which store far more on a disk (see page 44 for details of storage drives). But beware: no standard format has yet emerged, so the disk drive you upgrade to may become outdated within a year or so. If you wish to fit a new floppy drive, get a dealer to do this.

Monitors

Buying a bigger and better-quality monitor won't make your PC run any faster, but it will improve the quality of the images you see on-screen. They will be sharper and will flicker less. Most PCs are sold with a 15-inch monitor. (Monitors are measured diagonally across the screen, from one corner to another.) Buying a 17 or 21-inch monitor will make using your PC more pleasurable, especially if you use a lot of games or a DVD. However, new monitors can be expensive: the larger it is, the more expensive it will be.

Your new monitor plugs into the same socket on the graphics card as your old one. Check before you buy a monitor whether you also need a new graphics card.

Hard disks

Modern programs take up a lot of hard disk space, especially if they use graphics, sound or videos. If your hard disk is nearly full your PC will run more slowly (for guidance on how to check its capacity and available space, see page 54). Buying a new hard disk and using your current one for extra storage is one solution. Installing a new hard disk and making the necessary adjustments to the old hard disk is a job for a PC dealer.

New processors

You can even upgrade the central processing unit (CPU) of your PC. This is the main chip on the motherboard, through which signals between all the other circuit boards are routed.

The latest Pentium III processor chips work at speeds of up to 500 MHz, which means they 'think' up to 500 million times a second. Faster processors yield a range of benefits, including a vastly improved ability to run computer games and handle video editing.

Buying a new processor can be one of the most expensive upgrades you can do, and you should leave the installation of it to a PC dealer. There are many different processors to choose from, and you may also need a new motherboard. Your dealer will advise you as to which is the best processor for your PC and needs. If your CPU is old or slow, you may well be better off buying a whole new computer.

Speakers

The standard speakers supplied with a PC are adequate for normal use. However, if you want the loudest, Hi-Fi quality sounds, and you have a new sound card, you may want to upgrade your speakers. Upgrading speakers is very easy – you simply plug the new speakers into the sound card in your computer's system unit.

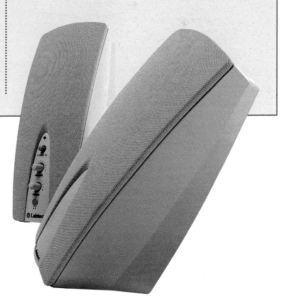

Problems after upgrading

Here's how to solve hitches encountered with new hardware

Upgrading your system with new hardware will rarely present you with a problem. Usually, after you connect additional hardware to your computer, Windows automatically detects it and installs the relevant software files for operating it. The process is designed to be straightforward and you should be able to complete it yourself. However, if you are concerned, you can ask a dealer to carry out the upgrade for you.

If problems do arise, they are most likely to have been caused by a faulty connection or an incorrectly fitted card. Other problems, such as hardware conflicts and using the wrong driver, can also arise, but these can be resolved with very little fuss.

Troubleshooting new hardware

Take some precautions to help things run smoothly when you tackle problems with new hardware.

Before you begin

Make a note of the relevant settings on your PC before you start. This will remind you of the original, correct settings for the device you are upgrading, and let you retrace your steps if something goes wrong. You don't have to write down the details of every screen that appears – Windows lets you save a screen as a file (see below) to keep as a record.

If, for example, you are upgrading your CD-ROM drive, save the CD-ROM device Properties screen. Go to the **Start** menu, select **Settings** then **Control Panel**. Double-click on **System**. Click on the **Device Manager** tab. Double-click on **CD-ROM** to display the attached devices. Right-click the appropriate device and select **Properties** from the menu. Save this screen. Click on the other two tabs and save these screens, too.

LG CD-ROM CRD-8322B Properties
General | Settings | Driver
LG CD-ROM CRD-8322B
Device type: CDROM
Manufacturer: (Standard CD-ROM device)
Hardware version: Not available
Device status
This device is working properly.

Saving a screen as a file

To save a screen as a file, do the following:
1 Press the **Print Screen** key on your keyboard.
2 Open your Paint program (go to the **Start** menu and select **Programs**, then **Accessories**, then **Paint**).
3 Go to the **Edit** menu and click on **Paste**. You will be asked whether you want the canvas enlarged. Click on **Yes**. This will paste in the snap shot of the screen as a picture.
4 Go to the **File** menu and click on **Save As** to save the file. You can view this file later in Paint to compare settings.

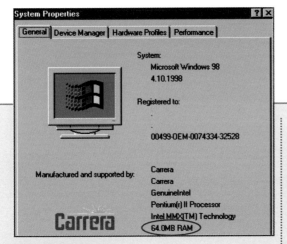

System Properties

General | Device Manager | Hardware Profiles | Performance |

System:
Microsoft Windows 98
4.10.1998

Registered to:

00499-OEM-0074334-32528

Manufactured and supported by:
Carrera
Carrera
GenuineIntel
Pentium(r) II Processor
Intel MMX(TM) Technology
64.0MB RAM

Carrera

Key word
Expansion card *This is a circuit board that adds certain functions to a computer. Expansion cards can be added for improved or additional features. For example, a sound card gives a PC the ability to record and play sound.*

Memory problems

If your computer is unable to locate a new memory chip (for extra RAM), it may be because it is not plugged in properly. To check the memory, right-click the **My Computer** Desktop icon and click on **Properties** in the pop-up menu. With the General tab selected, the dialogue box will tell you how much memory your PC thinks it has. If your RAM memory has increased, your memory card is fitted correctly.

If a series of error messages mentioning memory problems and 'parity errors' are displayed (often on a blue screen), your memory may be of the wrong type. In that case, return your PC to the dealer for the correct replacement chips.

Hard drives

Your PC may not recognise a new hard drive. If so, take the computer back to your dealer. There are several possible solutions, but they require specialist knowledge.

External drives

If a new external drive is not recognised by your PC, first check that the card is properly connected. Then ensure that any new card fitted at the same time as the drive, such as a SCSI card, is correctly seated in its slot. If the problem persists, you may be using the wrong driver or have a hardware conflict (see page 351).

Sound cards

If you're not hearing any sounds from your PC after fitting a new sound card, first check that the card has been fitted properly, that your speakers are plugged in, and that all the connections have been made, including the cable from the CD-ROM to the sound card. If this doesn't solve the problem, or the sound from the speakers is very poor, you may have a driver problem.

Monitor problems

If your new monitor does not work, first check that it is properly plugged into the power supply and the graphics card. Check the settings by turning up the brightness and contrast controls. If it still doesn't work, connect another monitor that you know works (this may be your old one). If this one works, then the new monitor is faulty and should be taken back to your dealer. If the other monitor doesn't work either, the fault lies with the graphics card.

Graphics cards

If the graphics card is not working at all, you won't see anything on your screen. But you should still hear your hard disk 'whirring' when you turn on your PC and the 'start' sound that indicates that Windows has loaded. The most likely explanation is that the card is not connected properly. Switch the PC off at the mains, open the system unit and make sure the card is seated along its full length.

If your screen is 'snowy' or your Windows display looks strange, you have a graphic driver problem. Make sure you use the latest driver – you can visit the card manufacturer's Web site to obtain the latest drivers.

This may also be the case if the only screen resolution available is the standard 640 by 480 with 16 colours. To view the resolution settings, double-click on the **Display** icon in your **Control Panel**. Click the **Settings** tab – the resolution is shown under 'Screen area'.

Colors
16 Colors

Screen area
Less ——□———— More
640 by 480 pixels

☑ Extend my Windows desktop onto this monitor.   Advanced...

OK   Cancel   Apply

Cables and cards

If you are carrying out the upgrade yourself, never pull out a cable or change a setting without noting down how it looked originally.

Cables inside the system unit can often be re-inserted the wrong way round, or accidentally pulled out. Make notes of the colour of each

cable, and which side of the plug each cable fits into.

Cards need to be seated firmly in their slots, with the whole length of the card properly seated along its entire length. You need to apply firm, but not excessive pressure to your connections, making sure you support each part as they are plugged together.

Watch out
Even if your monitor's power is switched off, do not open it and poke about inside to repair a fault. Monitors can retain electricity when switched off, and you may receive a nasty shock.

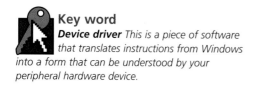

Key word
Device driver *This is a piece of software that translates instructions from Windows into a form that can be understood by your peripheral hardware device.*

Watch out
*When you click on the **Device Manager** tab in the System Properties dialogue box, devices should appear just once in the list (unless you have more than one installed). If any appear twice, remove them, then reinstall the relevant device by running the Add New Hardware Wizard.*

Troubleshooting drivers

The first step in solving problems is checking that your device drivers are working as they should be.

Device driver problems

To check whether your device drivers are working properly, go to the **Start** menu and select **Settings** then **Control Panel**. Double-click on the **System** icon. Click on the **Device Manager** tab, then scroll down the list of device types.

If a device has a driver problem, a yellow icon will be next to it. This may indicate a problem with the hardware, such as a poor connection, so check this first. If the connection is secure, you either have a hardware conflict (see opposite) or your driver needs updating.

Click on the '+' sign beside individual device types to view the drivers installed for the device you are upgrading. To hide the drivers, click the '-' sign.

Updating device drivers

Windows 98 will automatically update device drivers for you, using Windows Update. Alternatively, you can find and install the drivers yourself.

To use Windows Update you need to have access to the Internet. Go to the **Start** menu and select **Settings** then **Windows Update**. This will initiate a connection to the Internet, and you will be taken to the Windows Update Web site. Click on the link to **Product Updates** then follow the instructions on screen. If you are prompted to install and run downloadable components, click on **Yes**.

If you are using Windows 95, or you want to update device drivers manually, you will have to find and install

Upgrade in stages

It's a good idea to upgrade a number of items of equipment in stages. Add each part as a separate exercise, checking that each has been installed properly before installing the next. If a problem arises, it is then easier to tell which part is responsible.

the drivers yourself. If you want the latest driver for your upgraded hardware, look on the manufacturer's Web site and download the new driver file. If you do not have Internet access, request a driver on a floppy disk or CD-ROM by calling the manufacturer's technical support line.

If you have the CD-ROM version of Windows, you can obtain some drivers from the Drivers folder. If the driver you need is in the folder, go to the **Start** menu and select **Settings** then **Control Panel**. Double-click on the **Add New Hardware** icon and follow the instructions. When you are asked 'Do you want Windows to search for your new hardware?' click on **No**. Click on the hardware type for the driver you are installing, then click **Have Disk**. Enter the location of the driver file and follow the instructions.

You can also install specific device drivers. Go to the **Start** menu and select **Settings** then **Control Panel**. Double-click on the **System** icon. In the System

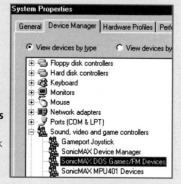

Key word

Hardware conflict *This occurs when your PC is unable to recognise a piece of hardware. This can happen when the hardware is set up incorrectly, or because it is incompatible with your particular PC or the software you are attempting to use it with.*

SonicMAX DOS Games/FM Devices Proper

General | Driver | Resources

SonicMAX DOS Games/FM Devices

Provider: VideoLogic
Date: 9-18-1998

To view details about the driver files loaded for t
Driver File Details. To up...
Update Driver.

Update Driver...

Properties dialogue box click on the **Device Manager** tab then double-click on the device in question. A dialogue box appears. Click the **Driver** tab. Click **Update Driver** and follow the on-screen instructions.

Update Device Driver Wizard

What do you want Windows to do?

○ Search for a better driver than the one your device is using now. (Recommended)

○ Display a list of all the drivers in a specific location, so you can select the driver you want.

Update Device Driver Wizard

Windows will search for updated drivers in its driver database on your hard drive, and in any of the followi selected locations. Click Next to start the search.

☑ Floppy disk drives

☐ CD-ROM drive

☐ Microsoft Windows Update

☑ Specify a location:

D:\SONSTPRO\WIN9X

Solving hardware conflicts

If an icon indicating a problem with the device appears in the System Properties dialogue box (see opposite), and you do not have an updated driver, try to install an old driver from your Windows CD-ROM.

Open up the System Properties dialogue box and click on the **Device Manager** tab. Click on the problem device, then click on the **Remove** button. Place your Windows CD-ROM in the CD-ROM drive. Go to the **Start** menu and select **Settings** then **Control Panel**. Double-click on the **Add New Hardware** icon. Follow the Wizard's instructions to reinstall the device you uninstalled, then restart your PC. Go back to the System Properties dialogue box (found in Control Panel) and click on the **Device Manager** tab. Scroll through the list of devices to check whether the problem remains with

Add New Hardware

Add New Hardware Wizard

This wizard installs the software for a new hardware device.

Before continuing, close any open programs.

To begin installing the software for your new device, Next.

your device. In most cases you will have solved the problem.

If the yellow symbol is still there, you have to take further action. Windows Help includes detailed instructions on solving hardware conflicts. Go to the **Start** menu and select **Help**. With the Contents tab selected, click on **Troubleshooting**, then on **Windows 98 troubleshooters** (in Windows 95 select **Hardware conflicts**, then **Hardware conflict troubleshooter**). Scroll down the list and click on **Hardware Conflict**. Now follow the detailed on-screen instructions.

Windows Help

Hide | Back | Forward | Options

Contents | Index | Search

📁 Troubleshooting
  ❓ Using Windows 98 troublesh
  ❓ Contact Microsoft Technical :
  📁 Windows 98 Troubleshooters
  ❓ Networking
  ❓ Modem
  ❓ Startup and Shutdown
  ❓ Print
  ❓ DriveSpace 3
  ❓ Memory
  ❓ MS-DOS Programs
  ❓ Display
  ❓ DirectX
  ❓ Sound
  ❓ The Microsoft Network
  ❓ Hardware Conflict
  ❓ Dial-Up Networking
  ❓ Direct Cable Connection
  ❓ PC Card

Is there a box with resource settings on the Resources tab?

To determine whether a device appears on the Device Manager tab twice

1. Click **Start**, point to **Settings**, click **Control Panel**, and then double-click **System**.

2. On the **Device Manager** tab, look for duplicate devices.

Windows won't start up

If your operating system refuses to load, here's what to do

Windows 95 and 98 can work well under a variety of conditions and with a wide range of hardware devices. But there are still times when Windows can let you down.

The good news is that both versions of Windows, especially 98, have a wide range of repair programs and on-line help facilities, including extensive troubleshooter Wizards. But if you can't get your PC to start up in Windows, how are you supposed to access these trouble-shooting functions? The answer is to use a special starting-up procedure known as 'Safe mode'.

Starting in Safe mode

If Windows won't start up normally, the chances are that when you turn your PC on, it will, by default, open up in Safe mode. This is a basic level of operation that gives you a limited version of Windows to work with. It allows you the chance to discover – and hopefully put right – whatever it is that is giving Windows problems.

If your PC does not automatically go into Safe mode, you can make sure it does so by intervening during the start-up process. After the computer comes on, but before the Windows start-up screen appears (this comes up whether Windows will load or not), hold down the **Ctrl** key (or **F8** with Windows 95) until the text-only Windows Startup menu appears – this offers you a list of start-up options. Select Safe mode by pressing **3**, then press the **Enter** key.

Sources of help in Windows

If you are experiencing problems with Windows, there are a number of troubleshooting facilities on your PC to help you. All of them can be accessed and used in Safe mode as well as in normal mode.

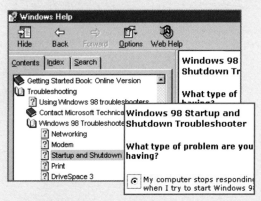

Windows 98 Troubleshooter

This troubleshooting facility is part of the help system that uses a Windows Wizard (a step-by-step guide) to analyse the problem you're having and come up with a solution. To access the Wizard, go to the **Start** menu and click on **Help**.

In the dialogue box click on the **Contents** tab. Click on **Troubleshooting**. The folder opens to reveal three sub-folders. Click on **Windows 98 Troubleshooter**. A detailed list of topics appears. Click on **Startup and Shutdown**. In the right pane select the 'My computer stops responding when I try to start…' option, then click on **Next**. Further questions are then asked, to which you must respond. Potential solutions are then offered.

System Information

If Windows 98 is causing problems, a new diagnostic program called System Information has a range of software tools designed to give you (or a technical support engineer) a helping hand. To access this, go to the **Start** menu and select **Programs**, **Accessories**, **System Tools** and then **System Information**.

One of the most useful System Information tools is the System File Checker (go to the **Tools** menu and click on **System File Checker**). This looks for corruption of system files and allows you to copy clean versions from the Windows 98 CD-ROM.

README Files

Located in the main Windows folder (on drive C), README files contain helpful information that typically describe problems with specific pieces of hardware, such as a printer or modem. To list all the README files, go to the **Start** menu, select **Find** then click on **Files or Folders**. Type '*.TXT' in the Named box and select 'C:\Windows' in the 'Look in' box. Click **Find Now**. You'll be presented with a number of files.

One of these files – 'Faq' (Frequently Asked Questions) – lists answers to a number of common questions. Double-click on any of these README documents to open them. It's a good idea to print out a README file as it can be difficult to read the file on your screen while trying to sort out problems at the same time.

Troubleshooting on-line

Although Windows 95 and 98 have their own in-built range of troubleshooting Wizards, even more are to be found at Microsoft's Web site:

http://support.microsoft.com/support/tshoot/

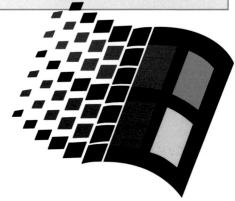

Windows won't close down

This is what to do when your operating system freezes

Occasionally, Windows 95 or 98 will appear to freeze on screen – a condition known as 'hanging'. You'll realise this has happened when the cursor doesn't respond to your mouse movements, and you can't issue any keyboard commands.

If your computer has these symptoms but you're still not sure whether Windows has hung, press the **Num Lock** key (found above the numeric keypad on the right of the keyboard) on your keyboard a few times. If the Num Lock light above the key doesn't go on and off, then you know the system is definitely hung.

Whereas the remedy for a hung program is fairly straightforward because you can still access help facilities, having Windows hang on you can be a bit more tricky. This is because Windows governs everything you do, including accessing help facilities, and once it seizes up you can't carry out any of your normal actions.

First steps to closing Windows

When Windows hangs, you won't be able to restart by going to the Start menu as usual. Instead, press the **Ctrl + Alt + Del** keys together. You then have two choices – either click **Shut Down** or, if you had programs running when Windows hung, shut them down and save any changes you made by selecting each in turn then clicking **End Task**. A dialogue box will appear asking if you want to save changes. Click **Save**. If you had Internet Explorer open, close this last as it doesn't have active documents.

Sometimes, closing programs in this manner can unfreeze Windows. If it doesn't, then restarting Windows usually does the trick. But if the problem persists, run the Windows Troubleshooter to diagnose and solve your problem.

Bright idea
If you cannot solve the problem using Windows troubleshooters you should consider reinstalling Windows. This is not as daunting a process as it sounds. See page 356 for more details.

Close up
Where possible, make sure you restart or shut down your computer through the Start menu. This will mean that all current information is saved and that each program closes before Windows.

Using the Troubleshooter to diagnose problems

If you often experience problems when you try to close Windows down, its own step-by-step Help facility will be able to give you guidance.

Working through solutions

The Help facility that comes with Windows 98 is a good place to start when attempting to find out why Windows has trouble closing down and

how to solve the problem. (Windows 95, however, does not have a Shutdown troubleshooting option.)

To access the Windows Help facility, go to the **Start** menu and click on **Help**. The Windows Help dialogue box appears. With the Contents tab selected, you will be presented with a list of options to explore. Click on **Troubleshooting**. The folder opens to reveal three sub-folders.

If you haven't already done so, click on **Using Windows 98 Troubleshooters** to familiarise yourself with the way the Troubleshooter operates.

If you'd prefer to solve the problem immediately, click on **Windows 98 Troubleshooter**. A detailed list of topics appears. Click on **Startup and Shutdown**. In the right-hand pane select the 'My computer stops responding when I try to shut down …' option, then click on **Next**.

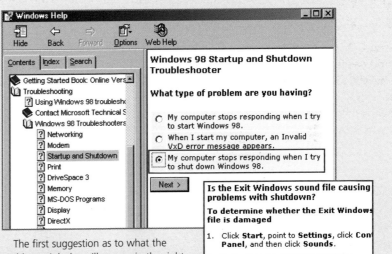

The first suggestion as to what the problem might be will appear in the right pane, and a course of action to remedy it will be offered. You will be asked whether the action solved the problem. If not, further suggestions will be given.

This can be a laborious process. But, although time-consuming, the Wizard will take you through a host of problems and their solutions in a succinct and clear way.

*If you cannot shut down Windows by pressing the **Ctrl + Alt + Del** keys, use the Reset button on your system unit. If your PC has no Reset button, switch the PC off and on again.*

Reinstalling Windows

If you can't repair a fault with the operating system, reload it

Reinstallation is the way to solve otherwise unsolvable problems. The process leaves all your work and your programs unaffected, and returns Windows to its original, problem-free state.

Complete reinstallation may be necessary if, for example, you keep experiencing serious crashes. All you need to begin reinstallation is your Windows CD-ROM (unless Windows isn't starting up, in which case you also need a rescue disk – see page 60). You must back up your work before you start (see page 359).

Reinstalling Windows does have its risks and should be tackled only after you have tried all other remedies. On some PCs it can create additional problems. Settings may be lost or the screen may run at a much lower resolution. Expert advice can help (see below).

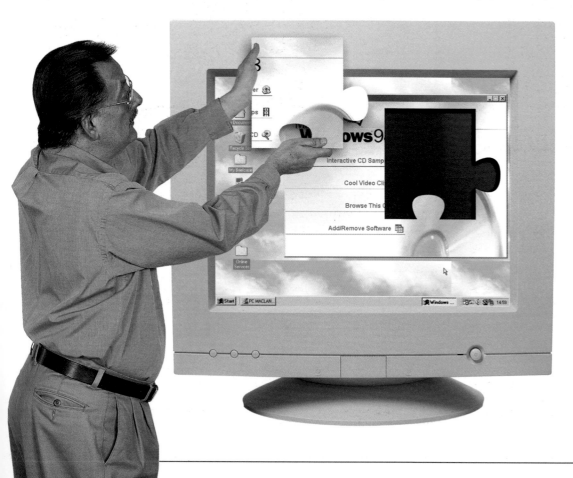

More often than not you will be able to reinstall from within Windows as shown here. However, if Windows won't start up, you must use a rescue disk (see overleaf).

NORMAL REINSTALLATION

1 Put your Windows CD-ROM into the CD drive and close all your programs (including anti-virus software). Double-click on **My Computer**, the **CD-ROM** drive icon, then **setup**. The Windows installation Wizard will guide you through the process.

Getting expert help

If you are worried about the reinstallation process, consider getting expert guidance. For extra help during reinstallation, call the Microsoft technical support line or, if Windows came preinstalled, your PC's manufacturer.

Bright idea
Copy the Windows 95 or 98 folder from the Windows CD-ROM to your [C:] drive. This means that, if you misplace your CD-ROM, you can run the Setup program from that folder and so install Windows straight from your hard disk.

Watch out
During the set-up procedure you will be asked to enter your Windows 95 or 98 product key or serial number (you'll find this on your Windows CD sleeve or manual cover). Be careful to input the number correctly and not to lose it.

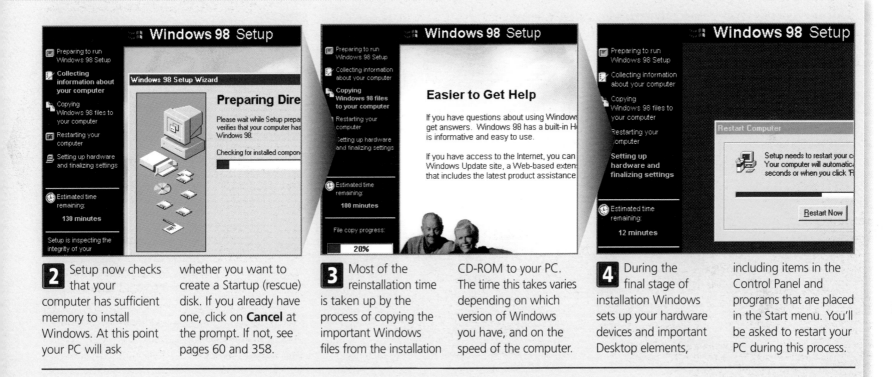

2 Setup now checks that your computer has sufficient memory to install Windows. At this point your PC will ask whether you want to create a Startup (rescue) disk. If you already have one, click on **Cancel** at the prompt. If not, see pages 60 and 358.

3 Most of the reinstallation time is taken up by the process of copying the important Windows files from the installation CD-ROM to your PC. The time this takes varies depending on which version of Windows you have, and on the speed of the computer.

4 During the final stage of installation Windows sets up your hardware devices and important Desktop elements, including items in the Control Panel and programs that are placed in the Start menu. You'll be asked to restart your PC during this process.

Where are you?

Because Windows 98 has been designed to work seamlessly with the Internet, part of the reinstallation procedure requires that you establish where in the world your computer is located.

This is because, should you become connected to the Internet, Windows can deliver news and services to your Desktop that are tailored to your country.

During the second stage of Windows installation – 'Collecting information about your computer' – you will be presented with a list of countries in the Establishing Your Location dialogue box. Click on the relevant one, then on the **Next** button.

Establishing Your Location

Windows 98 makes it easy to get region-specific news and other information through media such as channels, which are Web sites designed to deliver content from the Internet to your computer.

Selecting the correct location establishes the basic settings for receiving this information.

Select your country or region from the list below.

Turkey
Turkmenistan
Uganda
Ukraine
United Arab Emirates
United Kingdom
United States

Watch out
*If, after following the procedure below,
Windows still won't load, it may be that
your hard disk isn't working properly. For more
information on how to diagnose and deal with hard
disk problems see page 332.*

How to reinstall when Windows won't load

If Windows won't start up, you need to use a rescue disk before you can access
your Windows CD-ROM and follow the procedure outlined on page 356.

Make a rescue disk

If Windows doesn't start normally when you switch
on your PC you'll need a rescue disk before you can
begin reinstallation. This is a floppy disk that contains
vital Windows files and several special utility programs
that might come in handy in an emergency.

Usually, Windows 95 and 98 will ask you to create
a rescue disk during your initial installation. However,

if you bought your PC with Windows preinstalled, you
will not have been prompted to make one.

Creating a rescue disk is extremely straightforward –
all you need is a blank 1.44 Mb floppy disk. For full
instructions on what to do, see page 60. When the
process is completed, label the disk, slide the write-
protect tab open and store it in a safe place.

It's a good idea to test the disk before you use it to
make sure it works properly. Shut down your computer,
place the rescue disk in the floppy drive, then switch on
your computer. With Windows 98 a short text menu
appears on the screen after the disk loads. You can use
this to reinstall Windows from the CD-ROM. With
Windows 95, an A: prompt appears immediately,
without a menu.

Using the rescue disk in Windows 98

To use your rescue disk during reinstallation, place it in
the floppy drive and turn on your computer. When the
simple DOS menu appears, insert your Windows 98 CD,
then press the appropriate number for 'Start computer
with CD-ROM support'.

 When the A: prompt appears on screen
(left), type in '?: SETUP.EXE' (? is the letter
of the alphabet which follows the letter of
your normal CD-ROM drive in the alphabet). In the
example shown, the CD-ROM drive is normally drive D,
so the command begins with E.

```
A:\>E:SETUP.EXE
```

The drive name of your CD-ROM changes because
the contents of the rescue disk are copied onto a
temporary new drive. After the reinstallation, your drive
names will revert to normal.

After typing in this Setup command, press **Enter**.
Your PC should then access your Windows CD-ROM
and begin the reinstallation procedure. You can then
follow the steps outlined on the previous page until
Windows has been reinstalled. If your computer fails to
access the CD-ROM you may have more serious
problems and should seek expert advice.

Otherwise, follow the steps through, then turn your
computer off, take out both the rescue disk and the
CD-ROM and start up your computer again. Your
computer and Windows should start up as normal and
you can carry on working as before.

Give your hard disk a check-up

Before reinstalling Windows, run ScanDisk to make
sure your hard disk does not have a problem. Go to
the **Start** menu and select **Accessories**, then
System Tools then **ScanDisk**. In the dialogue box,
select the Thorough option, then click on **Start**. This
will check for problems with the disk itself and the
files stored on it. If you click in the 'Automatically fix
errors' box, it can be left to run unattended, and
will fix any problems it comes across.

Close-up
*If Windows Backup isn't installed, go to the **Start** menu and select **Settings** then **Control Panel**. Double-click on **Add/Remove Programs**. Click on the **Windows Setup** tab, scroll down and double-click on the **System Tools** folder (**Disk Tools** in Windows 95). Click in the **Backup** box, then click **OK**.*

Backing up your work
Before reinstalling Windows it's a good idea to make a back-up, or copy, of your files. This will guarantee that reinstallation won't erase your work.

Making a back-up
By copying your word processor documents, spreadsheets and databases onto a separate disk, you can be sure your work is safe should anything serious occur during reinstallation. If your files become damaged (this is highly unlikely), you can simply copy them back onto your computer from the storage disk.

The number of files you have to copy – and the amount of memory they use – will dictate which type of storage disk you choose. See page 44 for advice.

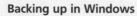

Backing up in Windows
To back up data in either Windows 95 or 98, you simply need to copy the relevant files onto the removable storage disk (see page 52 for details of how to do this).

If you have only a few files or folders to back up, this won't be too much of a chore (about 60 one-page letters should fit on a single 1.44 Mb floppy disk). However, if you have a lot of valuable data, this type of backing up can take some time. Fortunately, you can take advantage of the special Windows Backup program. This collects together all the data to be backed up then translates it into a special compressed archive format, which means it can be copied more quickly and uses less storage space than through the conventional method.

To access Windows Backup, go to the **Start** menu and select **Programs**, then **Accessories**, then **System Tools** and

finally **Backup**. A Wizard takes you through the process. You can choose either to back up all the contents of My Computer or selected files and folders.

To copy files back onto your computer, insert the storage disk, open Windows Backup and click on the **Restore** tab. The program decompresses and translates your data into its usual format, then copies it back onto your hard disk.

Update Windows 98
Once Windows 98 has been reinstalled you might want to update it to make sure that it is running at its full potential. Windows 98 users connected to the Internet can use the Windows Update Web site to download the latest drivers or troubleshoot certain problems.

To access Windows Update you need to connect to the Internet. Then go to the **Start** button and select **Settings**, then **Windows Update**. When the page loads you can browse the selection of software 'add-ons' to be downloaded, and select which ones you want.

My program has crashed

If an application stops responding to your commands, here's what to do

When a program crashes, your mouse pointer will appear as an hourglass and you will not be able to type or to access menus. It may seem that your PC has stopped working – but if the hourglass pointer changes back to an arrow when you move it onto your Desktop, this means Windows is still working. Windows runs each program in its own protected memory space, so problems with one active program do not usually affect the others.

It is possible to exit the crashed program using keyboard commands, and then to open it again. If you have not saved changes in the document you were working on before the crash, you will lose some of your work when you exit the program. This is why it is vital to make a habit of saving your work regularly, and why it's also worth remembering to save work in other programs that are running.

Closing a crashed program

When a program crashes you won't be able to close it in the usual way – for example, by going to the **File** menu and clicking on **Close**. The best way to proceed is to press the **Ctrl + Alt + Del** keys simultaneously.

This brings up the Close Program dialogue box which lists all the programs currently running on your PC, including those that are running invisibly in the background. Scroll down the list until you see the name of the program that's crashed – it will be labelled 'Not Responding' – then click the **End Task** button.

The crashed program window should then close. If it doesn't, another dialogue window will open, giving you the option of either waiting for the program to close by itself or terminating it immediately by clicking the **End Task** button. You should then restart Windows; this ensures that any of the left-over chunks of program code are flushed out of the PC's memory.

Occasionally, more than one program may have crashed and so it may be necessary to revisit the Task List for other programs that are 'Not Responding'.

Close-up
*If you cannot exit from the crashed program by pressing the **Ctrl** + **Alt** + **Del** keys, you must press the **Reset** button on your system unit.*

Bright idea
*Some programs allow you to save data automatically at set intervals. In Word, for example, go to the **Tools** menu and click on **Options**. Click on the **Save** tab and select an interval time – say, 15 minutes – from the 'Save AutoRecover info every' box. Click **OK**.*

What to do after your computer crashes

Once you have exited from a crashed program, you should check your PC for any resultant problems, and maybe even reinstall the program.

Clearing up after a crash

Many programs, including Word and Excel, create one or more temporary files when you're working on a document. These files are automatically deleted when you quit the program normally, but are stored if that program crashes. Every now and then these files should be deleted, especially if you're experiencing a lot of crashes.

The best way to find and delete the files is to first close all running programs, then go to the **Start** button, select **Find** and then click on **Files or Folders**. Select the **Name & Location** tab. Type '*.TMP' in the Named box, then highlight the contents of the 'Look in' box and type in 'C:\WINDOWS\TEMP'. Click **Find Now**.

Look for files with the '.TMP' suffix, plus those that start with the '~', or tilde, character. Either drag them onto your Recycle Bin, or right-click and select **Delete** from the pop-up menu.

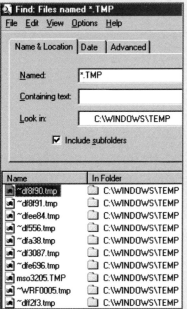

Reinstalling a problem program

If a program persistently crashes, the easiest remedy is to reinstall it. To do this, load the program's installation CD-ROM, double-click on **My Computer**, then on the CD-ROM drive icon. Click on the **Setup** icon. Most programs will install over an older version of themselves without losing any alterations.

If this doesn't solve the problem, uninstall the program first. Go to the **Start** menu, select **Settings** then **Control Panel**. Click on the **Add/Remove Programs** icon, then on the relevant program, and follow the on-screen instructions. Restart your PC and install the program from scratch.

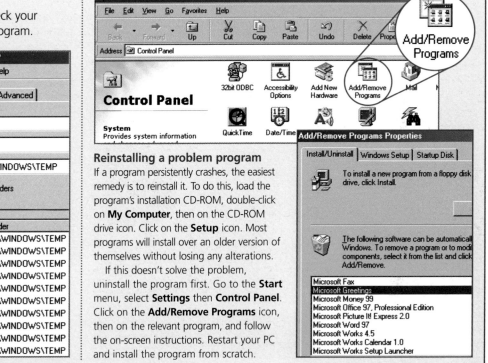

Automatic clean-up

Windows 98 comes with a utility called Disk Cleanup that is designed to remove unwanted temporary (TMP) files. To access it, go to the **Start** menu and select **Programs**, **Accessories**, **System Tools** then **Disk Cleanup**. A dialogue box selects [C:] drive to search through – click **OK**. In the next dialogue box, with the Disk Cleanup tab selected, select **Temporary files** from the window then click **OK**.

Disk Cleanup is also part of the Windows 98 Maintenance Wizard, and so will perform automatic clean-ups at set intervals. To find out how to set up your Wizard, see page 62.

I can't read a document

Find out how to open and read seemingly impenetrable files

As a rule, if you receive a file from another source, such as the Internet, and you do not have the program in which it was created, then you will not be able to open the file.

But there are ways around this problem. Your software may recognise the type of document and be able to convert it. If not, you can ask the sender to supply it in a 'neutral format'. So, for example, a text document saved as 'Text Only' should be readable in any word-processing program (though you cannot retain text styling in this 'no-frills' format). Here are some other ways you can access 'unreadable' documents.

Find out what type of file it is (word processor, spreadsheet, etc), which program created it, and if it can be sent to you in a different format.

► BEFORE YOU START

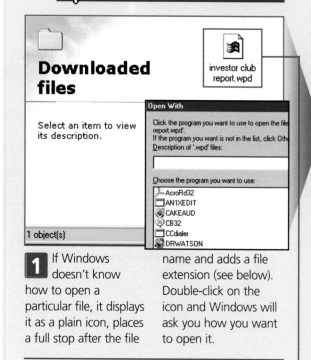

1 If Windows doesn't know how to open a particular file, it displays it as a plain icon, places a full stop after the file name and adds a file extension (see below). Double-click on the icon and Windows will ask you how you want to open it.

A quick guide to file extensions

Most files on your PC have a short suffix, called a file extension. For example, Word adds '.doc' to its documents, so 'Letter1' becomes 'Letter1.doc'. This helps identify the type of file you have received and so the type of program which will open it:

● **Text file** .asc .doc .htm .html .msg .txt .wpd
● **Image file** .bmp .eps .gif .jpg .pict .png .tif
● **Sound file** .au .mid .ra .snd .wav
● **Video file** .avi .mov .mpg .qt
● **Compressed file** .arc .arj .gz .hqx .sit .tar .z .zip

Clicking in this box (to remove the tick) means that you can choose a different program to open the problem file if your first choice fails. Otherwise, the same program will be used each time – and will fail each time.

☐ Always use this program to open this file

Open With ? ✕

Click the program you want to use to open the file 'investor club report.wpd'.
If the program you want is not in the list, click Other.
Description of '.wpd' files:

[   ]

Choose the program you want to use:

- WB32
- Winamp
- winhlp32
- **Winword**
- winzip32
- WORDPAD
- WScript

☐ Always use this program to open this file

2 Windows lists all the programs you have on your PC and asks you which one you want to open the file with. Using the file extension as a clue, click on a program. Click in the 'Always use this program to open this file' box (see above), then click **OK**.

3 If the file won't open with the program you have selected, try another one. If the file opens but is unreadable (above), close it without saving it and try using another program to open it.

East Esher & Ewell

Investor Club

File name: [Investor club report]

Save as type: [Word Document]

Draft report by John Arnold

4 If the file opens and it is readable, save it in that program's format. Go to the **File** menu and click on **Save**. Type in a file name, select a suitable format in the 'Save as type' box, then click on **Save**. This new version of the file will open without any problems.

Opening compressed documents

Winzip32

To reduce the amount of space a file takes up on a hard disk or as an e-mail document, many people 'compress' them. If you receive a compressed file (with the file extensions shown left)

you will need the same compression program in order to decompress it and then open it. WinZip is a common compression program. You can download it from the Internet (www.winzip.com) free of charge.

If you don't have the relevant program to decompress a file, ask the sender to mail it again in an uncompressed version.

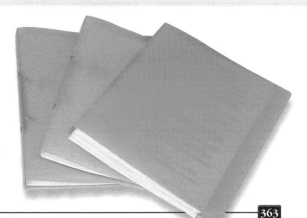

I'm getting error messages

What to do when your computer warns you there's a problem

When your PC has difficulty carrying out one of your commands it will display an error message. Generally, error messages include a description of the error, a possible reason for it and, if appropriate, a way to resolve the problem. Some error messages are easier to understand than others.

Do not ignore error messages. If you do, you may lose your work or, at worse, make your computer unusable. Follow the on-screen advice, which may mean exiting from the program you are using or restarting your computer. There are many error messages – the ones described here are the most common.

Storage problems

One of the most common error messages appears when Windows detects that your hard disk is getting full and storage space is becoming limited. This can seriously affect the performance of your PC, and may prevent you saving files. (Windows 95 users will notice that their PC becomes increasingly slow prior to the appearance of an error message.)

If the 'Hard Disk is Full' message appears, click on the **Disk Cleanup** button to delete unnecessary files and create more space.

Understanding error messages

The wording of the messages you get on your screen may differ slightly from those given here. Do not be alarmed by their technical tone.

Error messages caused by hardware

● Hardware conflict

Many error messages arise from a hardware 'conflict'. This is when two devices, for example a scanner and printer, try to use the same part of your PC at the same time. (For possible solutions see page 351.)

If your hardware seems to be working properly but you still get error messages, a software driver (the software that interacts between Windows and the hardware itself) may be the cause. Contact your hardware manufacturer to request the latest version of its driver. You may be able to download this free of charge from the company's Web site.

If your computer freezes – or 'hangs' – when you try to use a particular device, or if a device refuses to work, this, too, can be the result of a hardware conflict.

● Parity Error, Fatal Exception, or Illegal Operation
These messages are usually accompanied by a blue

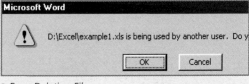

screen. They can be caused by a software error or, especially if you see a Parity Error message, may indicate problems with your PC's memory. If you get one of these messages, make a note of what the message says and of what you did immediately before it appeared on screen, then contact your PC dealer for advice.

Error messages caused by software

● This file is being used by another user
This occurs when you try to open the same document in different programs at the same time. Close down the document before opening it in a second program.

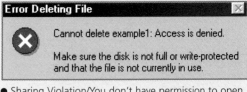

● Error Deleting File
This happens when you try to delete a file that is open on your Desktop or Taskbar.

● Sharing Violation/You don't have permission to open this file.
This can be caused by having a file open in two programs at the same time. It may also be caused by a program trying to open a file that is either corrupted or missing.

● File Corruption
Sometimes, a file gets 'mangled' by Windows. The best way to avoid this happening is to use the Maintenance Wizard with ScanDisk (see page 62). If this doesn't work you must reinstall the affected files, which may mean reinstalling the program that is causing the problem.

● Missing or Out-of-Date Files
This message appears if somebody deletes a file by mistake, or if a program overwrites, deletes or renames a file as it is installed or uninstalled. If the problem is with a program, you need to reinstall it.

Special Windows files – DLLs (Dynamic Link Libraries) – are shared by many programs to provide special functions. These files are susceptible to deletion and overwriting by other programs. If the error message tells you that a particular Windows file is causing the problem, replace it from the Windows CD-ROM. To add DLLs, reinstall the software that is producing the error message.

What to do if you cannot understand messages

If you do not understand an error message, follow these steps to help prevent the problem from reoccurring:
● Save any opened files. Shut down the program that prompted the message, then restart it.
● If the message reappears, shut down the program (and any others running) and restart your computer (go to the **Start** button, select **Shut Down** then **Restart**).
● If the message occurs again, make a note of what it says (ignore all those numbers) and seek expert advice. If the error is prompted by Windows rather than a program, contact your PC dealer. If a program is causing the problem, contact the software manufacturer.

ScanDisk messages

ScanDisk is run as part of the Windows Maintenance Wizard. It will scan your hard disk, looking for problems and fixing them before they are able to cause serious errors.

If ScanDisk finds any errors it will display a message and, in most cases, fix them itself. If ScanDisk has detected errors that it cannot fix, contact your PC dealer.

If it doesn't find any problems, you will see a message like the one shown, right. The important line is the one at the top – 'ScanDisk did not find any errors on this drive'. Everything else is just a list of statistics and you can ignore it.

Using anti-virus software

Run specialist packages to preserve or restore your PC's health

Although the spread of computer viruses is often reported in the media, the problem is not as widespread or difficult to deal with as most people think. Simple preventative steps (see page 58), will help you reduce the risk of getting a virus and put you in a better position to eradicate any that you do get.

Anti-virus software

There are many packages available. In general, they detect viruses on storage disks, such as floppies, and files that have been downloaded from the Internet. Such programs stop viruses infecting your PC in the first place.

Most anti-virus packages can be set up to scan your system regularly, but you should also get into the good habit of running the program every time you want to use a disk or download a file.

If a virus does make its way onto your computer, the software will alert you by bringing up a warning on screen. At this point you must use the disinfecting function in the anti-virus program. This is normally a straightforward process, performed by following the on-screen instructions given by the program. Sometimes, the infected item cannot be repaired. In this case you should delete the file or, in the case of a program, uninstall, then replace it.

Keeping up to date

Because more than 400 new viruses appear every month, it is vital to keep your software defences up to date. This doesn't necessarily mean having to buy new software. The best anti-virus packages can be updated by downloading new information from their related Web sites. Check your software for details on how to do this.

> *A good, anti-virus package such as Dr Solomon's Anti-Virus Toolkit is essential. Ask at a local computer store for advice on which package is best for your needs.*
>
> ▶ **BEFORE YOU START**

Bright idea
There are several useful Web sites that offer information about viruses. Some also provide software updates to help you defend your PC from infection. It is well worth exploring the Internet for such sites.

Key word
Virus *A virus is a computer program whose sole purpose is to get into your PC and cause unwanted and unexpected behaviour, such as erase files, display messages and attack your PC's set-up.*

Make the software do the work

Without the right software you might never know your PC is infected until it's too late.

The main types of viruses that are likely to infect your computer are 'file viruses', 'macro viruses' and 'boot and partition sector viruses'. Each one attacks different parts of your computer, including your hard disk, programs and document files. Because viruses can attack both program files and document files, anti-virus programs are designed to check both types at once.

Stopping viruses at source

Dr Solomon's Anti-Virus Toolkit is typical of the effective anti-virus programs now available. It features two automatic virus-scanning programs – Win Guard and

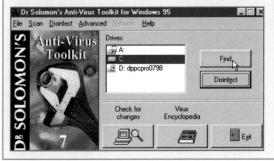

Virus Guard – that continually check for known viruses. Win Guard works through Windows, while Virus Guard works through DOS, thus checking for viruses all the time your computer is working. If a virus is detected then an alarm sounds and a warning message is displayed on your computer screen.

Both programs will also stop infected files being downloaded from the Internet. You should also use the software to scan any floppy disks you intend to use.

```
KEYB      COM      14986  09/04/91    5:00
KEYBOARD  SYS      34697  09/04/91    5:00
NLSFUNC   EXE       7052  09/04/91    5:00
DISPLAY   SYS      15792  09/04/91    5:00
EGA       CPI      58873  09/04/91    5:00
HIMEM     SYS      11552  09/04/91    5:00
                    8169  09/04/91    5:00
                    5873  09/04/91    5:00
                    0912  09/04/91    5:00
                    8335  09/04/91    5:00
                        2058566 bytes
                       11087872 bytes free
```

Disinfecting your system once a virus is found

If your software detects a virus you should use the disinfecting or cleaning function in the software to remove it. In the case of Dr Solomon's, this means selecting the affected drive and clicking on **Disinfect**.

If an infected file cannot be repaired then it will generally be renamed to prevent it being used again. You will then have the option of deleting it. Files that you delete may need to be replaced. If these are system files

(the files that make up Windows) then you will definitely need to do so. To reinstall program software, see page 361; to reinstall Windows, see page 356.

Worst-case scenario

With proper use of an anti-virus program, you should be able to detect and remove any viruses before they cause really serious damage. The worst situation you could find yourself in is that a virus has destroyed the contents of your hard disk.

In such a case you will have to restore the hard disk from your original system disks. This is like restoring your computer to its original state, as it was on the day you bought it. The original settings for it will be restored, but you will probably have lost all your documents and data files.

Viruses affect computers in different ways. Some contain messages that appear automatically on screen

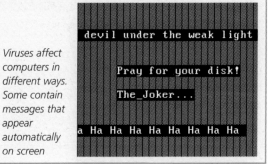

Minimise the risk of losing work

Since one of the effects of a virus is the loss of data, it is vital that you have adequate back-up files. This will help you to replace any files or data destroyed by a virus. If you only back-up infrequently, you will lose any data changes that you have subsequently made. It therefore pays to ensure that your PC is backed up on a weekly basis and, if you use your PC daily, even more frequently. See page 359 for details.

My text doesn't look right

If your fonts look odd on screen or when printed, the solution is easy

Font problems are one of the easiest things to solve. Fonts are automatically loaded on your PC when you install Windows, and others may be installed whenever you load new programs. Every time you type you are using one of these fonts.

The most likely reason that a font looks strange on screen (perhaps jagged or fuzzy) is if you have opened a file that uses a font not installed on your system. This might happen if you open a file sent to you by someone else. To fix this you must install the font or allocate a different font to the affected text.

If a font prints out differently to how it looks on screen, you have probably selected a printer-only font (see opposite).

Is it a font problem?

If a font looks strange on screen or when printed, first check whether there really is a problem. Some fonts, for example, are specifically designed to look unusual. Wingdings and Zapf Dingbats are made up entirely of unusual characters.

To check how a font should look, go to the **Start** menu and select **Settings**, then **Control Panel**. Double-click on the **Fonts** icon. All the fonts installed on your PC will be listed in the Fonts folder. Double-click on the font in question to bring up a sample of what it should look like. If the sample text shown looks the same as the text in your document, you have simply chosen an unusual-looking font.

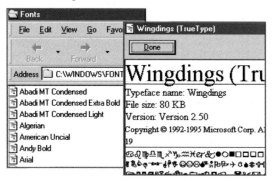

If a font prints out strangely, the problem may be with your printer, not with the font itself. If a document contains a lot of photographs and diagrams, your printer will have to use a lot of its memory to process it. If your printer has insufficient memory, some of the images will fail to print out and the appearance of the font may also be affected.

Watch out
*To reinstall a font, first make sure you delete the problem font. Go to the **Start** menu and select **Settings** then **Control Panel**. Double-click on the **Fonts** icon. Right-click on the font and select **Delete** from the pop-up menu. Then install the font as outlined below.*

Close-up
If the problem font came with a software package such as Windows, it should be on the relevant installation disk. However, it may be difficult to reinstall the font without reinstalling the entire software package. An easier solution is to use a different font instead.

Solving font software problems

If you're sure it is the font that is causing you problems, you need to check which type of font it is, and whether it is installed on your system.

Types of font
The type of font you are using may affect the way it appears on screen or when printed. TrueType fonts are designed to print the same way as they look on-screen, whereas printer-only fonts can look slightly different on screen to how they appear when printed.

To check which type of font you are using, first highlight some of the affected text. Click on the arrow beside the font box on the toolbar. If the font has a 'TT' symbol next to it in the drop-down menu, it is a TrueType font; if it has a printer symbol next to it, it is a printer-only font.

If you don't like the way a printer-only font looks, change to a TrueType font. If a TrueType font is causing problems, you may need to reinstall it (see above).

Is the font installed?
Check the name of the font in the font box on the toolbar. Then click onto a section of text that doesn't use the font in question, return to the font box and check whether the name of the problem font appears in the list. If it doesn't, then the font is not installed.

Either install the font on your system (see right) or change the text to another font. To do this, highlight the text and select a new font from the font box. The document may 'reflow', becoming longer or shorter, as different fonts take up different amounts of space.

Adding new fonts to your collection

Installing TrueType fonts
You can buy more TrueType fonts for your PC from computer stores, or obtain them for free from the Internet or CDs mounted on PC magazine covers. To install a new font first place the disk or CD-ROM containing it into the relevant drive. Go to the **Start** menu and select **Settings** then **Control Panel**. Double-click on the **Fonts** icon.

Now go the **File** menu and click on **Install New Font**. In the Add Fonts dialogue box click on the arrow beside the Drives box and select the drive containing the loaded floppy disk or CD-ROM (**a:** for floppy; **d:** for CD-ROM). In the Folders section, scroll through and double-click on the folder that contains the font. The contents of that folder will be displayed in the 'List of fonts' pane. Click on the relevant font then on **OK**. The font will be installed into your Fonts folder.

Installing printer-only fonts
Printer-only fonts are not stored on your PC but on your printer and it is sometimes possible to install extra ones. Go to the **Start** menu and select **Settings** and then **Printers**. Right-click on your printer icon and select **Properties**. In the Printer Properties dialogue box, click on the **Fonts** tab and look for a button marked 'Install Printer Fonts'. If this or a similar button is available, click on it and follow the instructions. If a similar tab or button does not appear, you cannot install fonts on your printer.

Multilanguage support

If you open a document written in a language that uses a different alphabet – say, Greek – your PC will fail to read the foreign characters and the document will look like gibberish.

To avoid this you need Multilanguage Support. Insert your Windows CD-ROM in the CD-ROM drive. Go to the **Start** menu and select **Settings**, then **Control Panel**. Click on the **Add/Remove Programs** icon. Click the **Windows Setup** tab, scroll down and

double-click on **Multilanguage Support**. Click in the box beside the language you want your PC to recognise. Click **OK**, then **OK** again. Windows will now install the language. But before opening the document again you will need to restart your PC and change the keyboard layout for different languages (see page 337).

If the document is in a language such as Hebrew, that does not read from left to right, you will need a special version of Windows.

Problems with passwords

You can unlock your computer even if you forget your password

If several family members or colleagues use the same computer, it may help you to have passwords for each user. This simple security measure not only ensures screensavers protect work from prying eyes during absences from the screen, but also allows each user to have their own customised Desktop and Windows settings. You can set up your PC to ask you for a password every time you turn it on, and whenever a screensaver needs deactivating.

Although passwords are a handy feature of Windows, you may be alarmed when you forget your password or when another user alters your password setting accidentally. Fortunately, the Windows password set-up is not sophisticated, and any problem can quickly be solved.

Types of password

Two types of password can protect work, and keep your Desktop arrangement as you like it:

Windows passwords

When you set a Windows password (to find out how, see page 70), a prompt box appears during the Windows start-up procedure asking you for that password. This password has two uses. Firstly, it gives you and your PC an identity on a network (this is where two or more computers are connected either physically or over the Internet). Entering the password confirms your identity, and gives you access to all the files you are entitled to use on the network. Secondly, a password allows each user to access their own Windows and Desktop set-up.

Screensaver passwords

The second type of password is for your screensaver. This operates when your screen has been left idle for a set period (to set up a screensaver, see page 70). However, screensavers disappear as soon as you, or anyone, moves your mouse or makes a keyboard command.

To ensure the screensaver remains operative until you decide to deactivate it, set a password for it. Right-click on the Desktop and select **Properties** from the pop-up menu. Click on the **Screen Saver** tab, click in the 'Password protected' box then click **Change**. Type in your password. Type it in again to confirm it then click **OK**.

To deactivate it, simply type your password into the on-screen dialogue box and click **OK**.

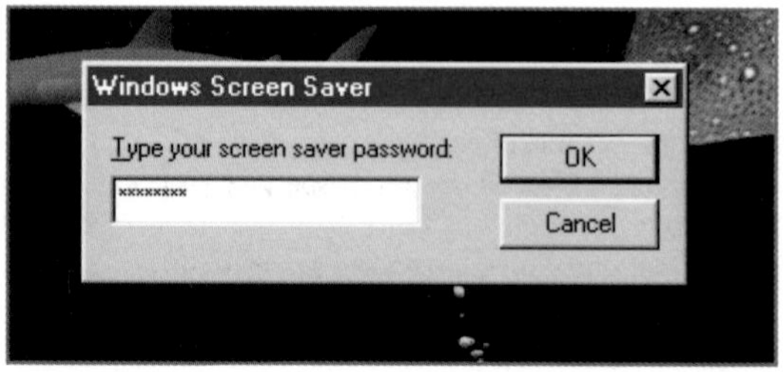

Windows Screen Saver

Type your screen saver password:

****

OK

Cancel

Bright idea
When you enter a new password, Windows shows it as a series of asterisks. This is to stop anyone noting it down. Because you can't read what you have typed, Windows asks you to re-enter the password to make sure you haven't made a mistake first time around.

Watch out
*If you forget your screensaver password and need to press the **Reset** button to solve the problem, remember that you will lose any unsaved documents that you were working on at the time.*

What to do if you forget your password
There is no need to panic if you forget your password. You can easily bypass the security and get into your computer.

Screensaver passwords
Once activated, a screensaver will cover your Desktop until you enter a password to deactivate it. If you forget your password you will be unable to deactivate it and shut down your PC in the normal way. The only thing you can do is push the **Reset** button on your hard disk, something that should only be done as a last resort.

The PC will restart and Windows will load (if you have used the same password for Windows and for your screensaver, click on **Cancel** when the password prompt box appears).

Right-click on the Desktop and select **Properties** from the menu. Click the **Screen Saver** tab. You can then either disable password protection by clicking in the 'Password protected' box, or set a new password. Fortunately, Windows doesn't insist that you supply the old password first – just enter the new one, enter it again to confirm it then click **OK**.

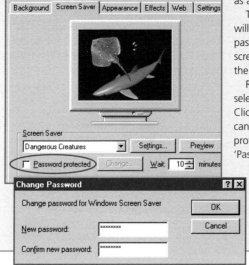

Windows passwords
If you forget your Windows password, click the **Cancel** button in the prompt dialogue box that appears before Windows loads. You will then gain access to Windows, but not to any of the customised preferences you set up.

You now need to change or delete your password. Windows stores passwords in a Password List File (PWL), which takes the form: username.pwl. So, Kathryn's passwords, for example, would be kept in a file called 'Kathryn.pwl'. If you are having problems remembering your passwords, delete this file.

To find it, go to the **Start** menu, select **Find** then click on **Files or Folders**. The Find dialogue box appears. In the Named box type '*.PWL', in the 'Look in' box select drive **[C:]**, then click on **Find Now**. All PWL files will appear in the pane below the dialogue box. Right-click on the file containing your user name and click on **Delete** from the pop-up menu. Windows will then create a new PWL file to store any new passwords you create.

You needn't use passwords at all if you don't want to. Click on the **Cancel** button when the prompt box appears on start-up.

Tips for secure passwords
A secure password is one that cannot be easily guessed. For this reason make sure your password adheres to several of the following:
● It is at least six characters long.
● It contains a mix of capital letters and lowercase letters.
● It contains at least one digit or special character such as a punctuation mark.
● It cannot easily be guessed (for example, do not use your child's, spouse's or pet's name).
● It is changed frequently.

A

A: The floppy disk drive on a PC. In speech it is referred to as the 'A drive'. See *Floppy disk*.

Accessories Mini-programs, such as Calculator or Notepad, built into Windows to perform simple tasks.

Active window The window you are working in. To activate a window, click on it and it will jump to the front of your screen, in front of any other open windows. See *Window*.

Alt key A key on the keyboard which gives commands when pressed in combination with other keys.

Application program A piece of software that performs specific kinds of tasks. For example, Microsoft Word is a word processing application program that is used to create text-based documents such as letters.

Archive To transfer files to a separate storage system, such as a Zip disk.

Arrow keys The four keys at the bottom of the keyboard that move the cursor up, down, left and right.

Attachment A file such as a picture or spreadsheet that is sent with an e-mail message.

Audio file A file containing a digital recording of sound. In Windows, audio files usually have '.wav' after their file name. See *Digital*.

B

Back-up A duplicate copy of a file, made in case of accidental loss or damage to the original.

Benchmark software Standard, most widely used program packages. This book uses Microsoft Office 97 (Standard Edition) and Microsoft Works Suite 99 as its benchmark software. One or other of the two packages comes preinstalled on many PCs.

BIOS Basic Input/Output System. Instructions that control the computer's hardware at the most basic level. The BIOS tells the operating system which hardware to expect to come into operation and how it is arranged.

Bit The smallest unit of computer memory, Bit is a contraction of 'binary digit'. Its value can be only 0 or 1. All computers use the binary system to process data.

Bitmap An on-screen image made up of tiny dots, or pixels. See *Pixel*.

Bits per second (bps) A measurement for the speed with which data can be sent to or from a computer via a modem.

Boot or boot up To switch on the computer.

Bug An accidental error or fault in a computer program. Bugs may cause programs to crash, which can lead to data loss.

Button An on-screen image that can be clicked on using the mouse. Clicking on a button performs a function, such as opening a dialogue box or confirming an action.

Byte A unit of computer memory, made up of eight bits. It takes one byte of memory to store a single character, such as a letter of the alphabet.

C

C: The hard drive of a PC, on which all programs and documents are stored. In speech it is referred to as the 'C drive'.

Cache A section of high-speed memory that stores data recently used by the PC's processor, thereby increasing the speed at which that data can be accessed again.

CD-ROM Compact Disc Read Only Memory. A storage device, identical in appearance to a normal CD, containing up to 650 Mb of data. Most software programs come on CD-ROM. CD-ROMs are usually inserted into and accessed from the 'D drive' on the PC.

Cell A small rectangular section of a spreadsheet or database, into which text or figures are entered. Click on a cell to make it active, ready for entering data.

Chip A device that processes information at the most basic level within a computer. A processor chip carries out calculations and a memory chip stores data.

Click To press and release the left mouse button once. Used to select menu and dialogue box options and toolbar buttons.

ClipArt Graphic images that can be inserted into text-based documents and then resized and manipulated.

Clipboard When text is cut or copied from a document it is stored on the Clipboard. The Clipboard stores only one piece of data at a time, regardless of its size. At any moment it can contain a single full stop or many pages of text, but each new cut or copy automatically overwrites the previous material on the Clipboard. You can put the current cut or copied material back into as many documents as you like using the paste command. See *Copy*, *Cut*, and *Paste*.

Close A menu option, usually found under the File menu, that shuts the active document, but not the program. A document can also be closed by clicking the close button in its top right-hand corner.

CMOS Complementary Metal Oxide Semiconductor. A type of memory chip that stores the computer's configuration settings and the date and time. To protect its data, this memory is maintained by battery. See *Configuration*.

Compressed files Files that have been temporarily condensed so they use less memory and can be copied or downloaded in a fraction of the time it would otherwise take.

Configuration The settings used to ensure hardware or software runs as the user requires.

Control Panel Any adjustments made to your system or its settings are made via the Control Panel. In the Control Panel you change the way your Desktop looks, add new hardware or alter your PC's sound output.

Control Panel

Copy To make a duplicate of a file, image or section of text.

CPU Central Processing Unit. The brain of your PC which carries out millions of arithmetic and control functions every second. The power of a CPU is usually defined by its speed in MegaHertz (MHz), which is the number of times it 'thinks' a second. For example, a 400MHz CPU carries out 400 million calculations a second.

Crash Your PC has crashed if it has stopped working, the screen has 'frozen' and there is no response to keyboard or mouse commands. A crash usually requires you to restart the computer.

Cursor A marker, usually a flashing vertical line, that indicates where the next letter or digit typed in will appear in the document.

Cut To remove selected text and/or images to the Clipboard, where they are stored for later use.

D

D: The CD-ROM drive on a PC. In speech it is referred to as the 'D drive'. See *CD-ROM*.

Data Any information processed by, or stored on, a computer.

Database A program used for storing, organising and sorting information. Each entry is called a record and each category of information held in a record is called a field.

Default Settings and preferences automatically adopted by your PC for any program when none are specified by the user.

Defragmenter A program which 'tidies' files on the hard disk. When a file is saved to the hard disk, Windows may not be able to save all parts of it in the same place, so its elements become fragmented. This makes the retrieval of the file much slower. The 'defrag' program solves this problem by regrouping all related data in the same place.

Delete To remove a file, folder, image or piece of text completely. If you delete text or other item from a document by accident, you can immediately undelete it using the Edit/Undo function or the Undo toolbar button.

Desktop When Windows has finished starting up, it presents you with a set of icons on screen. The icons represent the items you would find in an office, such as files, a wastebin and a briefcase. These icons, together with the Taskbar and Start button are known collectively as the Desktop. See *Icon* and *Taskbar*.

Dialogue box A window that appears on screen displaying a message from the program currently in use. This usually asks for preferences or information to be input by the user.

Dial-up connection The process of accessing another computer via a telephone line.

Digital Data that exists in binary number form as '0's and '1's. Computers process digital data.

Digital image An image stored in number format, that can be transferred to hard disks or removable storage disks, displayed on screen or printed.

Disk A device for storing digital data. A hard disk is composed of a stack of rigid disks; a floppy disk has just one flexible plastic disk.

Disk tools Programs that manage and maintain the hard disk, ensuring data is stored efficiently and that the hard disk runs at optimum speed.

Document A single piece of work created in a program. Also referred to as a file. See *File*.

DOS Disk Operating System. The standard operating system for PCs before the advent of *Windows*.

Dots per inch (dpi) The number of dots that a printer can print on one square inch of paper. The more dots, the greater the detail and the better quality the printout.

Double-click To press and release the left mouse button twice in quick succession.

Download To copy a file or program from another computer to your own. For example, when you collect e-mail from an Internet Service Provider, you are downloading it.

Drag A mouse action used to highlight text, reshape objects or move an object or file. To move an object with the mouse pointer, for instance, click on it and keep the left mouse button held down. Move the mouse pointer and the object moves with it.

Drive A device that holds a disk. The drive has a motor that spins the disk, and a head that reads it – like the stylus on a record player.

Driver Software that translates instructions from Windows into a form that can be understood by a hardware device such as a printer.

DVD Digital Versatile Disc. A CD-like disc that can store 4.7Gb or more of information – several times more data than a CD-ROM.

E

E-mail Electronic Mail. Messages sent from one computer to another through the Internet.

Error message A small window that appears on screen warning the user that a fault has occurred and, where appropriate, suggesting action to remedy it.

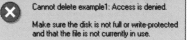

Expansion card An add-on piece of hardware that fits into the system unit and expands the functions of the PC – for example, a sound card.

External hardware Additional computer equipment, such as a printer or scanner, attached by cable to the system unit.

F

Field A category of information in a database, such as Name, Address or Telephone Number.

File Any item stored on a computer, for example, a program, a document or an image.

File extension A three-letter code that appears at the end of a file name to indicate its format (what type of file it is).

File format The way in which files created by different programs are ▶

saved. This differs from program to program, so that one program may have difficulty reading files created by another. Common file formats are listed below:

Text	.asc .doc .htm .html .msg .txt .wpd
Image	.bmp .eps .gif .jpg .pict .png .tif
Sound	.au .mid .ra .snd .wav
Video	.avi .mov .mpg .qt
Compressed	.arc .arj .gz .hqx .sit .tar .z .zip
Program	.bat .com .exe

File Manager A program that enables users to organise all the items stored on a hard disk. Users can copy, rename or delete files, move them from one folder to another, and create new folders.

Find A program that searches a PC for a file, if given information such as the file name or creation date.

Floppy disk A portable data storage device. Each 3.5 inch disk can hold up to 1.44 Mb of information. Often used to back up data from the hard disk. See *Hard disk*.

Folder An electronic storage compartment used to keep related files and relevant documents in the same place on the hard disk.

Font A particular style of type, such as Helvetica or Times New Roman. Most fonts can be displayed and printed in different sizes.

Format To alter the appearance of a document – for example, its typography, layout, and so on.

Freeware Programs, usually produced by hobby programmers,

for which users do not pay a fee. Freeware can often be downloaded from the Internet.

Function keys The 12 keys (labelled F1, F2, and so on) at the top of the keyboard. Their function depends on which program is in use. So, for instance, Shift + F7 in Word will call up the Thesaurus.

G

.GIF file Graphics Interchange Format. This is a commonly used format for storing images and bitmapped colour graphics, especially on the Internet.

Gigabyte (Gb) A unit of memory capacity. A single gigabyte is 1000 megabytes which is equivalent to about 200 copies of the Bible.

Graphics Pictures, photographs, illustrations, ClipArt and any other type of image.

H

Hard disk A computer's high-speed storage device. It contains the operating system, the programs and all created files. The hard disk is referred to as the 'C drive'.

Hardware The physical parts of a computer, including the system unit, monitor, keyboard and mouse.

Header The area at the top of a page in a document. Text entered in the header (such as a title) appears on every page of the document.

Help key Usually the F1 key. Pressed to access advice and information on how to perform the task the user is currently engaged in.

Highlight To select a word, a section of text or a group of cells, by clicking and dragging over them using the mouse.

I

Icon A graphic representation of a file or a function, which is designed to be easily recognisable as the item it represents. For example the printer icon on the toolbar accesses the print function.

Import To bring an element from another file, such as a photograph, illustration or ClipArt image, into the active document.

Inkjet printer A printer that works by squirting tiny drops of ink onto the surface of the paper.

Install To copy a program on to the hard disk and then set it up so it is ready for use. Programs are usually installed from a CD-ROM.

Internet Millions of computers throughout the world linked together via telephone and cable lines. Computer users can communicate with each other and exchange information over the Internet for the price of a local telephone call.

ISP Internet Service Provider. A company that provides connection to the Internet (compare *OSP*).

J

Jaz disk A portable storage device that is capable of storing up to 2 Gb of data. See also *Floppy disk, Zip disk*.

JPEG Joint Photographics Experts Group. A compressed format for storing images so that they take up less space on a computer.

K

Keyboard shortcut A method of issuing a command using a combination of keystrokes. To the practised user, this is quicker than manipulating the mouse.

Kilobyte (Kb) A unit of memory capacity. A single kilobyte is equivalent to 1000 bytes. A short letter created in Word uses about 20 Kb. See *Gigabyte, Megabyte*.

L

Landscape See *Orientation*.

Laptop A portable computer.

Laser printer A printer that uses a laser beam to etch images onto a drum and then transfers the image to paper. The reproduction quality is usually higher than with an inkjet printer. See *Inkjet printer*.

Launcher A window in some software suites, such as Microsoft Works, through which the suite's various components are opened.

Logging on The process of accessing computers or files using a password or other instructions. Some Web sites also require users to log on.

M

Maximise To increase the size of a window so that it fills the entire screen. The Maximise button is the middle button in the set of three in the top right-hand corner of a window. Once used, this button becomes a Restore button. Click on it to restore the window to its original size.

Megabyte (Mb) A unit of memory capacity. A single megabyte is 1000 kilobytes, which is equivalent to a 400 page novel.

Memory A computer's capacity for storing information. See also *RAM* and *ROM*.

Menu bar The line of menu options that runs along the top of a window. When a menu is selected, its entire list of options (a drop-down menu) will be displayed.

MIDI Musical Instrument Digital Interface. A universal standard language by which specially adapted musical instruments communicate with computers. MIDI cable leads are required to connect the instrument to the computer.

Minimise To reduce a window to a button on the Taskbar. The Minimise button is the left button in the set of three in the top right-hand corner of a window. To restore the window to the screen, click on its button on the Taskbar.

Modem A device that converts electronic signals from a computer into sound signals that can be transmitted by phone then reconverted by another modem into the original electronic data.

Monitor The viewing screen on which you see your computer's files. Images are made up of thousands of tiny dots.

Motherboard The circuit board which houses a PC's central

processing unit (see *CPU*), some memory and slots into which expansion cards can be fitted. See *Chip, Expansion card* and *Memory*.

Mouse pointer A small arrow on screen that moves when the mouse is moved. Other representations of the pointer, depending on the program being used and the type of action being carried out, include a pointing hand, a pen and a cross. When you click in a text document, the cursor will appear. See *Cursor*.

Multimedia Sound, images, animated graphics, text and video are all different types of media – means of communicating. A single document using more than one of these is said to be a multimedia document. A computer able to provide and display different media simultaneously is referred to as a multimedia computer.

My Briefcase An icon found on the Desktop of any PC running Windows. Duplicate versions of documents placed in the briefcase can be transferred to a laptop or other computer to be worked on. When you wish to return the documents to your PC, My Briefcase allows you to update the original files on your PC that have been worked on while travelling in the Briefcase.

My Computer An icon found on any PC Desktop running Windows. Click on the icon to access all the computer hardware present in the system, such as the hard drive [C:], floppy drive [A:],

CD-ROM drive [D:], printer and tools for monitoring and adjusting the system set-up. See *Icon*.

My Documents A folder icon found on the Desktop. The folder stores the files and documents that have been created by users. See *Icon*.

N

Network The connection of several computers and printers so that they can share files and messages.

O

On-line The status of a computer that is actively connected via a modem to the Internet. Also used as a general term for people who are able to connect to the Internet. See *Internet*.

Open To look inside a file or folder to view its contents. To open a file or folder, either double-click on it, right-click on it and select Open from the pop-up menu, or select it, go to the File menu and click Open.

Operating system The software that controls the running of a computer, allowing, for example, programs to communicate with hardware devices such as printers. Windows is now the most popular operating system for PCs.

Orientation An option available when creating a document. Users can choose to set up a page as either Landscape (of greater width than height) or Portrait (of greater height than width), depending on how they want the final version of the document to appear.

OSP Online Service Provider. A company that provides not only Internet access (compare *ISP*), but also additional content, such as shopping, entertainment and leisure channels, chat rooms and newsgroups. OSPs include AOL, Compuserve and MSN.

P

Page break The point at which one page ends and another begins. To insert a page break in Microsoft Word, press the Ctrl key and, keeping it pressed down, press the Enter key.

Parallel port A socket at the rear of a system unit that allows you to connect a printer.

Paste The insertion into a document of text or other data that has previously been cut or copied.

PC-compatible Software or hardware that will work on a standard PC.

PCI slot A spare space inside a PC for extra expansion cards, such as a sound or graphics card.

Peripheral A device such as a scanner that can be connected to a PC, but is not vital to its function.

Pixel An individual dot on a computer screen. The number of pixels horizontally and vertically on the screen determines the level of detail and quality of image that can be displayed. This can be set and altered by the user.

Plug-ins Programs that are needed to open and run certain files, such as video clips or sound files. Web sites often provide plug-ins for visitors to download, so that they are able to view the entire site. See *Download*. ▶

Point size Measurement used to describe the size of fonts. For example, this page is in 9 point; newspaper headlines are usually between 36 and 72 point.

Port A socket at the rear of the system unit that allows users to connect a peripheral device, such as a modem, to the PC.

Portrait See *Orientation*.

Printer driver A piece of software that helps Windows to communicate with the printer. See *Driver*.

Print Preview On-screen display that shows users exactly how the active document will look when printed.

Processor The central processing unit (CPU) of a PC. See *Chip, CPU*.

Program A product that allows the user to interact with the computer's hardware to perform a specific type of task. For instance, a word processing program allows the user to direct the computer in all aspects of handling and presenting text.

Prompt A window that appears on screen to remind users that additional information is required before an action can proceed.

Properties The attributes of a file or folder, such as its creation date and format. Some Properties, such as the author's name, can be altered. To access the Properties window, right-click on an item and select Properties from the pop-up menu.

R

RAM Random Access Memory. The memory used for the temporary storage of information on active documents and programs.

Record An individual entry in a database comprising several categories of information. For example, an address book database comprises entries – or records – each of which has a name, address and telephone number.

Recycle Bin A Desktop feature that allows you to delete files. To delete a file completely, drag it onto the Recycle Bin, right-click and select Empty Recycle Bin from the menu.

Reset button A button on the system unit that allows users to restart a PC if it 'freezes' and refuses to respond to any commands. The Reset button should only be used as a last resort.

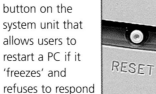

Resolution The degree of detail on a screen or a printed document. It is measured in dots per inch (dpi). The more dots per square inch, the greater the detail.

ROM Read Only Memory. Memory chips used by the computer for storing basic details about the PC, such as *BIOS*.

Run command A Windows feature that allows you to type in the name of the program you wish to use, or the DOS command you wish to execute. To enter a command, go to the Start menu and click on Run.

S

Save To commit a document to the computer's memory. To do so, press the Ctrl + 'S' keys, or click

on the Save toolbar button or go to the File menu and click on Save.

Save As A way of saving a file under a different name or format. If the file was previously saved under a different name or format, that version will remain unchanged. This is useful for saving an edited file, while still keeping the original.

Scanner A device for converting images on paper into electronic images that can then be manipulated and reproduced by a PC. See *Digital, Digital image*.

Screensaver A picture that appears on-screen when the PC is left idle for a specified time.

Scroll To move through the contents of a window or menu vertically or horizontally.

Search engines Huge databases on the World Wide Web that are used to locate information on the Internet. They can look for either key words or phrases, or for categories, then sub-categories.

Select To choose a file, folder, image, piece of text or any other item, by clicking on it or highlighting it, before manipulating it in some way. For example, selecting some text before styling it.

Serial port A socket at the rear of the system unit where peripheral devices, such as a modem, are connected. Most PCs have two serial ports, identified as COM1 and COM2. Compare *Parallel port*.

Shareware Programs, or reduced versions of programs, that can be sampled for free for a limited period. Users must then purchase the program to continue to use it.

Shortcut An icon on the Desktop that links to a file, folder or program stored on the hard disk. It is created to provide quicker access to the file, and looks identical to the icon of the linked item, except that it has a small arrow in the bottom left-hand corner.

Software Programs that allow users to perform specific functions, such as to draw up accounts. Microsoft Excel and Microsoft Outlook are examples of software.

Software suite A collection of programs that come in a single package, often supplied when a PC is bought. For example, Microsoft Works is a software suite that includes word processing, database and spreadsheet programs.

Sound card A device that lets users record, play and edit sound files. Fits into an expansion slot within the system unit. See *Sound file*.

Sound file A file containing audio data. To hear the sound, double-click on the file (you will need speakers and a sound card).

Spreadsheet A document for storing and calculating numerical data. Spreadsheets are used mainly for financial planning and accounting.

Start button The button on the left of the Taskbar through which users can access the Start menu and its options, which include Programs or Help. It is sometimes referred to as the Windows button.

Status bar A bar that appears along the bottom of program windows, giving users information about the document being worked on.

Styling Altering the appearance of the content of a file. For example, by making text bold (heavier-looking and more distinct) or italic (slanting to the right), or by changing its colour and size. See *Format*.

Super disk A portable storage device similar in appearance to a floppy disk. Each disk can store up to 200Mb of data. A super-disk drive can also read floppy disks. See also *Floppy disk, Jaz disk, Zip disk*.

System software The software that operates the PC, managing its hardware and programs. Windows is the system software for PCs.

System unit The rectangular box-shaped part of the PC that contains the hard disk, the CPU, memory and sockets for connections to peripheral devices.

T

Tab A function used for setting and pre-setting the position of text.

Tab key A key on the keyboard used to tabulate text, to move between cells in spreadsheets, or to move from one database field to the next.

Taskbar A bar usually situated along the bottom of the screen in Windows that displays the Start button and buttons for all the programs and documents that are currently open. The Taskbar can be moved to any of the four sides of the screen by clicking on it and dragging it to a new location.

Task Wizard See *Wizard*.

Template A format for saving a document, such as a letterhead, the basic elements of which you regularly want to use. When you open a template, a copy of it appears for you to work on, while the template itself remains unaltered for further use.

Tile To reduce in size a group of open windows and then arrange them so that they can all be seen on screen at once.

Toolbar A bar or window containing clickable buttons used to issue commands or access functions. For example, spreadsheet programs have a toolbar that contains buttons that are clicked on to perform calculations or add decimal places. Other toolbars include ones for dealing with pictures or drawing. See *Taskbar*.

U

Undo A function in some programs that allows you to reverse the task (or last three tasks) most recently carried out. Go to the Edit menu and click on Undo.

Uninstall To remove programs from the PC's hard disk. Software is available for uninstalling programs that do not contain an inbuilt uninstall option.

Upgrade To improve the performance or specification of a PC by adding new hardware components such as a higher capacity disk drive. See *Hardware*.

URL Uniform Resource Locator. A standard style used for all Internet addresses on the World Wide Web.

The first part of the URL, such as www.yahoo.com, indicates the location of a computer on the Internet. Anything that follows, such as /myhome/mypage.htm, gives a location of a particular file on that computer.

USB Universal Serial Bus. A hardware connector that allows users to add devices such as mouse, modems and keyboards to a computer without having to restart. See *Hardware*.

Utilities Software that assists in certain computer functions, such as uninstalling and virus-scanning.

V

View A menu in many programs through which users can change the way a file is displayed on screen. For example, in a Works database users can choose to see a document in List, Form or Form Design View.

Virus A program designed to damage a computer system. Viruses can be 'caught' through floppy disks or through programs downloaded from the Internet.

W

Wallpaper In Windows an image or pattern used as the background on the Desktop.

Window Each program or file on your PC can be viewed and worked on in its own self-contained area of screen called a Window. All windows have their own menu bar, through which users can issue

commands. Several windows can be open at once on the Desktop.

Windows The most popular operating system for PCs, which allows users to run many programs at once and open files on screen in windows. See *Operating system*.

Windows Explorer A program that allows users to view the contents of a PC's hard disk in a single window. See *Hard disk*.

Wizard A tool within a program which guides users through the process of customising a pre-designed document.

WordArt A graphic text image that can be customised and imported into a document for decorative effect.

Word processing Text-based operations on the PC, such as writing letters.

World Wide Web The part of the Internet, composed of millions of linked Web pages, that can be viewed using Web browsing software. Other functions of the Internet such as e-mail do not count as part of the World Wide Web. See *Internet*.

Z

Zip disk A portable storage device that is capable of storing up to 100Mb of information. Zip disks require a separate drive.

Zip file A file that has been compressed with the WinZip compression program. The term is not related to Zip drives or disks. ■

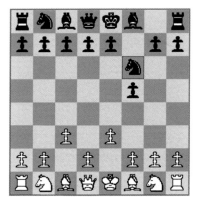

▶

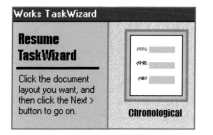
■

Acknowledgments

We would like to thank the following individuals
and organisations for their assistance in producing this book.

Photography: Steve Tanner and Karl Adamson. Styling: Mary Wadsworth. Picture
agencies: Popperfoto, Hulton Getty, Colorsport, Comstock, Tony Stone, Pictor, The
Stock Market. Equipment: Fujifilm, Carrera Technology Ltd, Logitech, Iomega, Yamaha
Kemble Music Ltd, Bite, KYE Systems UK Ltd, PMC Electronics Ltd.
Software: Guildsoft Ltd, Arbiter Group PLC, Focus.

Music Ace Offer

Guildsoft Ltd is delighted to offer readers of *How To Do Just About Anything On A
Computer* 20 per cent off the award-winning Music Ace range - including MusicAce 2.
To claim this offer call Guildsoft on 01752 895100 and quote the following code:
001GURDG01. Alternatively, you can send an e-mail to sales@guildsoft.co.uk, or visit
Guildsoft Online at www.guildsoft.co.uk

400-002-1